KIDNAPPING *THE* ENEMY

KIDNAPPING

THE ENEMY

The Special Operations to Capture Generals Charles Lee & Richard Prescott

Christian M. McBurney

WESTHOLME
Yardley

This book is dedicated to my father,
Dr. Alexander A. McBurney,
who spurred my interest in early American and
Revolutionary War history.

Copyright © 2014 Christian M. McBurney
Maps by Tracy Dungan
Maps copyright © 2014 Westholme Publishing

All rights reserved under International and Pan-American Copyright Conventions. No part of this book may be reproduced in any form or by any electronic or mechanical means, including information storage and retrieval systems, without permission in writing from the publisher, except by a reviewer who may quote brief passages in a review.

ISBN: 978-1-59416-183-4

Book Club Edition

Printed in the United States of America.

CONTENTS

Preface vii

1. The Ambitious Charles Lee   1

2. Widow White's Tavern   27

3. A Severe Blow to the Cause   52

4. A Prisoner of High Value   79

5. Richard Prescott Commands   105

6. The Overing House Raid   124

7. An Officer of Equal Rank   140

8. The Generals Are Exchanged   160

9. The Ordeal of William Barton   189

Appendix: Some Minor Participants in the Special Operations and What Became of Them   209

Notes   220

Bibliography   305

Acknowledgments   326

Index   327

PREFACE

This book focuses on two outstanding special operations of the Revolutionary War. The first is the stunning capture of Major General Charles Lee, second-in-command in the Continental army, behind only George Washington, by Lieutenant Colonel William Harcourt and a party of British dragoons in December 1776. While leading a reconnaissance mission in northern New Jersey, Harcourt learned from Loyalist informers that Lee was staying at a tavern in nearby Basking Ridge, three miles from his troops. The cavalry commander seized the moment: changing his mission to nabbing Lee, he and his men set out for the village. Cornet Banastre Tarleton's advance party gained valuable information along the way by threatening captured American soldiers with death. Reaching Basking Ridge, Harcourt's force surrounded the tavern in which Lee was staying. And after a short but violent struggle with the American general's guards, they captured Lee, along with a French officer. Then, with American militia hunting for them, Harcourt's quick-moving raiders raced down back roads to safety in British-held Pennington.

The book also explores the capture of Major General Richard Prescott, the commander of British troops in Newport, Rhode Island, by state troops led by Lieutenant Colonel William Barton. Barton seized Prescott so the Americans would have a British officer of the same rank to exchange for Lee. Barton meticulously planned his raid on Aquidneck Island, on which stood the important commercial town of Newport, then occupied by more than 3,000 British and German soldiers. During the night of July 10, 1777, Barton's hand-picked detachment crossed Narragansett Bay in whaleboats, sneaking past British navy ships along the way. After landing, Barton carefully led his men along a hidden path to the farm house in which General Prescott spent his nights. The raiders forced open its doors and seized the sleepy British general in his bed. They then hurried to their boats and slipped back across the bay to Warwick, avoiding a flurry of British artillery and rocket fire. Not only had Barton captured an officer who could be traded for Lee, he had removed from action a man who was infamous for his harsh treatment of American patriots.

Barton's feat was even more incredible than Harcourt's. It required careful advance planning, and Prescott was taken from an island filled with British troops and surrounded by British warships. An elated Washington called it "among the finest partisan exploits that has taken place in the course of the war on either side." Barton's raid was the outstanding special operation of the Revolutionary War, and still ranks as one of the greatest in American military history.

Both missions were acclaimed and celebrated by their respective sides and produced gloom in opposing camps. British military and civilian leaders considered Charles Lee the Americans' best general. And they believed that his capture, in conjunction with numerous serious setbacks dealt the Americans in New York and New Jersey, portended the end of the war. Instead, American patriots, stunned though they were by Lee's loss, responded with renewed vigor in their struggle for independence. In fact, Lee's capture ultimately made possible the momentum-changing American victories at Trenton and Princeton.

Barton's spectacular feat thrilled American patriots, who expected the captured Prescott to yield Lee in a prisoner exchange. It eventually did, in April 1778. In London, Britain's newspapers had a field day embarrassing Prescott, reporting in humorous epigrams that the general had been caught in bed with a harlot and carried away without his pants. Characteristically turning to racial mockery, Americans recounting Barton's achievement lampooned the role of an African-American who reportedly had used his own head to crash through Prescott's door.

The following pages also explore the evolution of British treatment of American captive officers. In the war's early stages, it was unclear whether American officers of the Continental army would be treated as gentlemen and allowed certain privileges, or be treated as rebels and criminals, denied any privileges, and perhaps even hanged. The Continental Congress ensured that the British would follow the former course by threatening retaliation against British army officers held captive by the Americans if Lee were mistreated.

This story also traces the tragic decline of two of its central figures, Charles Lee and William Barton, due to their misplaced pride and honor. A transplanted Englishman and the most colorful commander in either army, Lee was brilliant but spiteful, filled with valuable military experience but arrogant, and amusing but bitingly sarcastic. At the time of his capture, Lee seemed just a step away from replacing George Washington as commander of the Continental army. After his shocking capture put an end to this prospect, Lee narrowly escaped death at the hands of the British for having deserted the army in which he had formerly served as an officer. He also committed treason while a British prisoner. Following his exchange and his subsequent command of the main American force in the Battle of Monmouth Court House, Lee in short order found himself subject to a court-martial and suspended from service in the Continental army. He never saw command again.

William Barton's life turned out much differently than he had hoped. Late in his life, he found himself imprisoned in Vermont for more than thirteen years. It will be seen that the pride and honor he gained as the captor of General Prescott played a crucial role leading to his lengthy incarceration. Only the intercession of a more famous Revolutionary War hero led to Barton's freedom, and allowed him to spend his last years with his wife, family, and friends in Rhode Island. While there were other attempts to kidnap high-ranking military officers and government officials during the Revolutionary War, including ones against British commander-in-chief Henry Clinton, George Washington, Thomas Jefferson, the traitor Benedict Arnold, and even a future king of Great Britain, the low success rates of these special operations make the raids that snared Lee and Prescott all the more impressive.

Charles Lee in England about 1770. This caricature was "allowed by all who knew General Lee to be the only successful delineation either of his countenance or his person." The dog could be Spada, Lee's Pomeranian. Engraving by A. H. Ritchie from a drawing by Barham Rushbrooke. (*Society of the Cincinnati*)

I

The Ambitious Charles Lee

As the sun rose on November 22, 1776, Major General Charles Lee, the second-ranking general in the Continental army of the newly formed United States, realized that he had a good opportunity to replace his superior, George Washington, as commander-in-chief. What is more, he thought he deserved the job. At the time, his reputation was on the rise and Washington's was on the decline. Further, Washington's division of 3,000 soldiers was on the run in New Jersey, while Lee's quasi-independent force of 7,000 was resting at North Castle, New York.

During the second half of 1776, Washington had led the Continental army to a string of disastrous defeats in the New York City area. In the Battle of Brooklyn on August 27, the British army under General Sir William Howe crushed Washington's army, which barely escaped intact from Brooklyn Heights across the East River to Manhattan Island. Washington then fought the Battles of White Plains and Harlem Heights, resulting in the loss of New York City and virtually all of Manhattan to Howe.

Most devastatingly, the commander-in-chief, at Major General Nathanael Greene's urging, left 2,875 American soldiers at Fort Washington, the American army's last outpost on Manhattan. On

November 17, Howe's British regulars and German (or Hessian) allies overran the beleaguered defenders, killing fifty-three and capturing the rest. Three days later, Howe sent across the Hudson River a 5,000-man force that easily captured Fort Lee (named for Charles Lee), opposite Fort Washington. While the 2,000 troops garrisoning the fort managed to escape, heaps of valuable military stores were lost. Howe then began to chase Washington's main army out of northern New Jersey.[1]

These debacles brought into question the very existence of the Continental army as a fighting force. Only Howe's incompetence in following up his victories had allowed Washington's army to escape destruction. The period after the fall of Fort Washington was the darkest the patriot cause had yet experienced, and some military men began to look for scapegoats. Even several of Washington's own staff members began to question his leadership, and to see Charles Lee as his successor.

Charles Lee was the most remarkable personality on either side of the American Revolution. He was, as his friend, physician-patriot Benjamin Rush, stated, "a medley of opposite contradictory qualities."[2] Lee possessed many admirable qualities, but had at least an equal number of negative ones. An Englishman by birth, he was well educated, widely read, and spoke five European languages. He could be witty and charming in conversation, had the most military experience of any American army officer, and was often brilliant in his military analysis. Further, he had shown his courage on a number of occasions, and was unafraid to write stirring patriotic letters promoting independence from England at a time when many others hesitated. On the other hand, he was frequently vain, arrogant, overly ambitious, petulant, argumentative, short-tempered, unrestrained in his writings, and devastatingly sarcastic and critical of others, particularly his superiors. In an age when gentlemen were expected to show that their manners were above those of the common crowd, Lee often went unwashed, wore dirty clothes, and used coarse speech. His sole close, long-term relationship with a woman was with his sister, Sydney. Indeed, he seemed closer to his omnipresent dogs than to any humans.

Lee was born in Dernhall, Cheshire County, in the northwest of England at the end of 1731, or in early January 1732. His parents possessed some wealth, but more importantly at that time in the socially stratified world of England, they had good lineage. His mother, Isabella Bunbury Lee, was from the genteel Bunbury and Hanmer families. His father, John Lee, had by 1743 assumed the colonelcy of the 55th (later renamed the 44th) Regiment of Foot. Charles and his sister, Sydney, were the only survivors of seven children. While it appears that he was fond of his father, Charles did not get along with his mother, who may have suffered from mental illness.

Charles Lee received an excellent education for the times, attending private schools in Switzerland and England. John Lee raised his son to master the military arts, and Charles happily and diligently studied to that end. In 1746, at the age of fourteen, he received an ensign's commission in his father's regiment, and upon completing his schoolwork two years later, he began his service. In 1751, after his father unexpectedly died of illness, Lee used some of his inheritance to purchase a lieutenancy in the same regiment.[3]

Lee, as described by a fellow British officer, "was five feet eight inches high, slender in his make, but able to endure the greatest hardships, little caring what he ate or drank, or on what he slept."[4] A relative portrayed him as "extremely thin" with an "ugly" face capped by "an aquiline nose of enormous proportion."[5] A German officer, after meeting Lee in 1777, described him as "a man of medium height, very thin; his nose is so large that its shadow darkens the other half of his face."[6] Lee's prominent nose led one American officer to nickname him "Naso."[7] Women did not find him attractive.

Lee started his military career in earnest when he travelled with his regiment to North America in 1755 to participate in the Seven Years' War (called the French and Indian War in North America).[8] He had an active role in the war, if not a brilliant one. In mid-1756, Lee purchased a captain's commission in the 44th Regiment and a year later served in the failed expedition against the French fortress of Louisbourg, on Cape Breton Island. In the unsuccessful "grand assault" on Fort Ticonderoga on July 8, 1758, ordered by Major General James Abercrombie, Lee, leading his company, suffered a grievous wound from a musket shot that shattered two of his ribs and passed through his body. After recovering, he served in the 1759 expedition to capture Fort Niagara, where in the final assault two musket shots creased the top of his head. He then led fourteen men into the wilderness, arriving at Fort Pitt (now Pittsburgh) after a 240-mile trek, not accomplishing much, but not losing a man under his care either.[9]

The most prominent characteristic of Lee's military service was his penchant for recklessly criticizing his superiors and getting into trouble. While convalescing from his Ticonderoga wounds, for example, he sent to England a blistering written attack on General Abercrombie, whom he called a "stupid blunderer," a "damn'd beastly poltroon," and "our booby-in-chief."[10] New York judge and historian Thomas Jones wrote that compared to other British officers in the French and Indian War, the "quarrelsome, satirical, and abusive" Lee "was under more arrests, had more court martials held upon him, and more courts of inquiry into his conduct, than all the officers of the army put together. He was thought by many to be insane, and was known by the name of 'Mad Lee.'"[11] If Jones was not always a reliable observer, there seems to be much truth in these remarks.

When Lee returned to England in 1761 he was promoted to major of the 103rd Regiment. The next year he accompanied a British expeditionary force sent to Portugal to fight an invading Spanish army, and served under Colonel John Burgoyne. There he had his greatest military success prior to the Revolutionary War when he led a raiding party of 250 grenadiers and 50 light horsemen in a surprise attack on a larger Spanish force outside the town of Vila Velha and destroyed large quantities of Spanish military stores.[12]

With his regiment disbanding at the end of the Seven Years' War, Lee sought to continue his military career by becoming a soldier of fortune. In 1765, he joined the Polish army in Warsaw as an aide to King Stanislaus Poniatowski; a year later he went to Turkey with the Polish ambassador. After returning to England and failing to obtain a promotion, Lee returned to Poland in 1769 as a major general and served as an observer during a Russian army campaign against the Turks.[13]

In 1766, Lee's letters from Europe to his friends in England revealed his sympathy with the Whigs, who emphasized individual liberty and were deeply concerned with abuses of royal power. He enthusiastically supported opposition to the Stamp Act, writing to his sister from Constantinople, "May God prosper the Americans in their resolutions, that there may be one asylum at least on the earth for men, who prefer their natural rights to the fantastical prerogative of a foolish perverted head because it wears a crown."[14] With his caustic criticisms of King George III and the king's ministers becoming widely known, it is little wonder that Lee began making enemies in the English establishment, and that the king ignored lobbying efforts to promote him. When he was finally appointed in 1772 to the rank of lieutenant colonel, on half-pay, the promotion did not alter his political leanings.[15]

In 1773, Charles Lee, angry and frustrated, lacking options in England, and excited about the ideas of liberty being espoused in America, decided to leave Britain and seek a new life across the Atlantic.[16] "Liberty I adore," he explained, and "where she lives, that is my country."[17] Lee arrived in New York on November 10 and immediately joined the political agitation. During the next ten months, he travelled as far south as Virginia and as far north as Massachusetts, impressing patriot leaders, especially radicals such as Richard Henry Lee of Virginia (no relation) and Samuel Adams of Massachusetts. One of Lee's first, and most important, contributions to the patriot cause was publishing a pamphlet in 1774 that sought to dispel the common belief that, if it came to an armed rebellion, American citizen soldiers would be no match for British regulars.[18]

In August 1774, Lee arrived in tense Boston, which was occupied by British troops, to be feted by Samuel Adams and other patriot leaders. A Boston newspaper described him as one "of the greatest military characters of the present age."[19] One of Lee's acquaintances, John Bernard, said of him, "His celebrity at this period, both as a soldier and a politician, may be gathered from the enthusiasm with which all classes hailed his advent."[20] After Lee departed Boston, he saw a prospect for advancement and demonstrated his dedication to the patriot cause by purchasing a farm in Berkeley County, Virginia (now Jefferson County, West Virginia), near the home of his friend, Horatio Gates, another former British officer sympathetic to republican principles.

Following the outbreak of hostilities at Lexington and Concord in April 1775, and the subsequent start of the siege of Boston by newly formed patriot forces, the second Continental Congress began selecting generals to lead the new Continental army. Though he believed himself to be the most experienced and best officer available, Lee probably did not expect to be named commander-in-chief, given his English background and recent arrival. Still, after Washington's selection for that post, some in Congress favored Lee for the second spot. But John Adams successfully argued that with a force of 16,000 New England men the only Continental force in the field, fellow Massachusetts native Artemas Ward should be selected.

Lee settled for appointment as the army's second major general, in part due to the influence of Washington, who wanted an experienced officer.[21]

A disappointed Lee nevertheless griped about out his third-place finish, describing the Harvard-educated Ward as "a fat old gentleman who had been a popular church warden, but had no acquaintance whatever with military affairs."[22] His opinion of Ward, like so many of his opinions, was harsh but accurate. Within a year, Ward would resign, leaving Lee as Washington's senior subordinate. It was remarkable that this Englishman, who had been in North America for less than two years, had so rapidly climbed to such a high position.

After accepting his appointment, Lee on June 22, 1775, wrote to the British Secretary of War, Lord William Barrington, whom Lee detested, resigning his commission as lieutenant colonel. On August 3, Lee's name, along with those of two other British officers assisting in the "unnatural rebellion," was stricken from the British army's half-pay list.[23]

Thus began Lee's complicated relationship with his superior officer, George Washington. From the first, Lee saw himself as the military brains of the Continental army and Washington as a mere political appointee. Washington, in turn, felt self-conscious about his own shortcomings, considering Lee's wide military experience, worldly travels, ability to quote Greek and Latin, and incisive criticisms. Due to this inferiority complex, the Virginia planter showed Lee more deference than he ought to have during the 1776 New Jersey campaign. Washington, though, quickly recognized contradictory qualities in Lee, calling him "the first officer in military knowledge and experience we have in the whole army" and adding that "he is zealously attached to the cause, honest and well-meaning," but warning that he was also "rather fickle and violent I fear in his temper."[24]

Given command of the left wing of the American army outside Boston, Lee did effective work training raw soldiers and preparing fortifications. This time gave influential Boston patriots a chance to take stock of their new military leaders. While George Washington garnered praise for his command style, demeanor, and conduct, Lee came across as an eccentric, with his then-uncommon love of dogs becoming a particular object of comment. During a visit with John Adams's wife Abigail, Lee shocked her by insisting that she shake the paw of his Pomeranian, Mr. Spada.²⁵ When Abigail informed her husband of the incident, the stout Massachusetts patriot conceded that Lee was "a queer creature," but that "you must love his dogs if you love him," and added that he was willing to "forgive a thousand whims for the sake of the soldier and the scholar."²⁶

General George Washington admired General Lee's military background and intelligence, but was worried about his fickle temper. An engraving from 1776. (*Library of Congress*)

At a time when many Americans hesitated to sever ties with Great Britain and King George III, Lee was one of the first leaders of the patriot cause to call for independence. In a January 3, 1776, letter to key Continental Congress delegate Robert Morris, Lee stated that he had lost "all hope of reunion" and had concluded that "we must be independent or slaves."²⁷ On April 5 he wrote to Richard Henry Lee, one of Congress's most important delegates, complaining, "For God's sake, why do you dawdle in the Congress so strangely? Why do you not at once declare yourself a separate independent state?"²⁸

At the beginning of February 1776, Washington ordered Lee to take command of American forces in New York City, and bolster area defenses. Recognizing that Manhattan could not be held indefinitely due to the British navy's ability to dominate the waters around the island, Lee resolved to make the British pay a high price for it. "I am much pleased with your plans for the defense and security of New York," Washington informed Lee.²⁹

On March 1, 1776, Congress appointed Lee to head the new Southern Military District, and the general promptly headed south to establish his headquarters at Williamsburg, Virginia. When he received word on May 8 that a large invasion fleet under the command of Lieutenant General Henry Clinton and Commodore Sir Peter Parker was on the move, Lee correctly surmised that it was headed for Charleston, South Carolina. With 1,900 Virginia and North Carolina Continentals, Lee immediately departed Williamsburg for the bustling port, arriving on June 8. There he showed surprising and admirable restraint. With most of its defenders proud South Carolinians under the command of Governor John Rutledge, Colonel William Moultrie, and other local leaders, Lee realized that he could not simply insist on having his way, even though Rutledge formally gave him command of all troops. Lee correctly pointed out that Moultrie's palmetto fort on Sullivan's Island, while "impregnable" from a frontal assault, could be pounded by warships along the fort's unfinished west side. This left the fort's defenders susceptible to being cut off by a sea force. But when Rutledge rebuffed his request to abandon the fort, Lee, rather than rant and rave, made the best of the situation, building and improving defensive works around the city as best he could.

Fortunately for the American defenders, on June 28, Commodore Parker's attempt to flank the fort by sea stalled when several of his ships ran onto hidden sand bars. Clinton's attempt to attack Sullivan's Island by land, meanwhile, failed when an unexpectedly deep channel blocked his troops. After a furious exchange of artillery fire with Parker's warships off the island's coast, the British withdrew.[30]

In his written reports to Congress, Washington, and others, Lee rightly credited Moultrie and the officers and men under his command. But as the titular commander of the defenders, Lee benefited from the reflected glory. He received the thanks of Congress on July 20, and his friend in Philadelphia, congressional delegate Benjamin Rush, wrote to him, "It would take a volume to tell you how many clever things were said of you and the brave troops under your command after hearing of your late victory."[31]

With Lee's services in great demand, the Continental Congress ordered the general back to New York, where, wrote John Adams, "Some officer of his spirit and experience seems to be wanted."[32] On October 14, just weeks after the debacle that was the Battle of Brooklyn, Lee arrived at Washington's headquarters.[33] The Continental army was now concentrated in northern Manhattan, but word had arrived of General Howe's landing on Throgs' Neck, in the Bronx, two days earlier. Meanwhile, Vice-Admiral Viscount Richard Howe, General Howe's older brother, had sent ships up the Hudson River in an attempt to prevent the Americans from crossing into New Jersey. Some in Washington's army were now looking to Lee as a potential savior.[34]

On October 16, Washington called a council of war to discuss a potential retreat off the island. Disagreeing with other senior officers who argued that the army was safe where it was, Lee "strongly urged the absolute necessity" of retreat. He emphasized that the enemy controlled all surrounding waters and had armies in the Americans' front and rear, and that there was only one escape route open, via the bridge at Kingsbridge.[35] "For my part," Lee reportedly said, "I would have nothing to do with the islands [Long Island and Manhattan] to which you have been clinging so perniciously."[36] Washington agreed and, except for the detachment left at Fort Washington, he ordered his army to cross from Harlem Heights over to the Bronx, with the goal of reaching White Plains in Westchester County, New York.

General Howe, with his powerful force of 20,000 men, intercepted the American army on October 28 at White Plains. The two sides fought to a draw, and the next day Washington and his army slipped away to safety.[37] Lee's outspoken advice for Washington to retreat off Manhattan Island immediately had helped prevent Howe from trapping and destroying the main Continental army.

Now, Washington was in a quandary, wondering what General Howe would do next. Hoping to cover as much of the countryside around New York City as possible, Washington decided to disperse his 14,000 troops in contingents at North Castle in Westchester County, New York; Peekskill, New York, in the Hudson Highlands; Hackensack and Haverstraw, New Jersey; Fort Washington on Manhattan Island; and Fort Lee, on the opposite shore of the Hudson River, in New Jersey. Washington personally took command of 2,500 troops in New Jersey, which he dubbed his "flying" army, one that would not remain static. Crossing the Hudson River on November 12, he left Major General Nathanael Greene, his most trusted senior officer, to command Forts Washington and Lee. With his and Greene's troops, Washington hoped to forestall any effort by Howe to advance on Philadelphia, the new country's capital and most populous city.[38]

On November 10, at North Castle, Lee assumed command of Washington's largest contingent—7,000 men—to protect the approach to New England in the event Howe's army turned in that direction. Having divided his army in the face of a concentrated, mobile, and powerful enemy, Washington needed a plan to recombine them once Howe's goal became clear. He provided Lee with the following instructions: "If the enemy should remove the whole, or the greatest part of their force, to the west side of the Hudson River, I have no doubt of your following with all possible dispatch."[39] Out of deference to Lee's seniority and military skill, the commander-in-chief did not give Lee an outright order. But his implication that Lee should quickly link up with his own command if Howe invaded New Jersey in force was unambiguous.[40]

Unknown to Washington, Lee, at North Castle, saw things differently. In a letter to James Bowdoin, the president of the Massachusetts Council, he explained why he thought he had an independent command. "[T]he idea of detaching and reinforcing from one side to the other [of the Hudson River], on every motion of the enemy, was chimerical." His division, and Washington's, Lee wrote, "must rest each on its own bottom."[41]

In making decisions at this stage in the war, Washington usually consulted with his top commanders and deferred to generals in the field who were closest to the action. Thus, he allowed Nathanael Greene to keep the 2,850 soldiers at Fort Washington, despite his personal belief that it should be abandoned.[42]

In a November 16 letter to his friend, Joseph Reed, the adjutant general and a trusted member of Washington's staff, Lee wrote: "I confess I cannot conceive what circumstances give to Fort Washington so great a degree of value and importance as to counterbalance the probability or almost certainty of losing 1,400 of our best troops. In this persuasion, I cannot help expressing my concern that General Greene has reinforced it."[43] Lee may have hoped that Reed would show the letter to Washington, but it was too late. Fort Washington, the last American outpost on Manhattan Island, was overrun that same day.

Word of the fort's fall infuriated Lee. "I was at General Lee's just after the news came," wrote Continental artillery officer Captain Samuel Shaw of Massachusetts. According to Shaw, Lee "was in a towering passion, and said that it was a splendid affair for Mr. Howe, who was returning chagrined and disgraced at being able to make no further progress this campaign."[44] Benjamin Rush heard that "in the first transports of his rage and grief," Lee "cried out, 'Had it been called Fort Lee, it would have been evacuated long ago.'"[45] To Washington, on November 19, Lee wrote more tactfully, but still in exasperation, "Oh General, why would you be over-persuaded by men of inferior judgment [Greene's] to your own? It was a cursed affair."[46]

With each successive defeat in the New York campaign, increasing numbers of American officers and soldiers alike quietly questioned Washington's ability to lead the army, while wondering if Lee

"The Landing of the British Troops in the Jerseys." Cornwallis's force lands on the morning of November 20, 1776, ready to seize Fort Lee. Watercolor by Captain Thomas Davies, 1776. (*National Archives*)

would do better. Following the calamitous Battle of Brooklyn, and before Lee had joined the main army, the commander of one of the best Continental regiments, Colonel John Haslet of Delaware, complained about the situation on Washington's staff: "We have alarm upon alarm. Orders now issue, and the next moment reversed. Would to Heaven General Lee were here, is the language of officers and men."[47] Now, with Lee spreading word that he had opposed the decision to retain Fort Washington, Major James Wilkinson, an aide to General Horatio Gates, felt that the "fall of that place enhanced [Lee's] reputation."[48]

If the loss of Fort Washington was a turning point for Lee, news of the capture of Fort Lee, situated on the opposite river bank in New Jersey, to General Charles Cornwallis's 5,000-man invasion force on November 20, was a watershed. Lee now felt that Washington was worthless as the commanding general. He feared that the patriot cause was virtually lost, unless it could be rescued from the abyss, preferably by him.

Lee's key moment of decision occurred late in the day on November 21, when an express rider delivered to him two pieces of correspondence from Washington's army, one from Washington himself and the other from aide-de-camp Colonel Joseph Reed. Lee read his commander's letter first. After informing Lee of the details of the loss of the fort "called by your name," Washington concluded that "I am of the opinion, and the gentlemen about me [meaning his subordinate officers] concur in it, that public interest requires your coming over to this side [of the Hudson River to New Jersey] with the Continental troops."[49] Again, and notably, Washington failed to express his wishes in an explicit order.

Lee then picked up Reed's letter, which Reed had slipped into the express rider's mail pouch without Washington's knowledge. Reed, a prominent Philadelphia lawyer, suggested that Washington's personal staff had lost faith in its commander and viewed him as a vacillating leader. "I do not mean to flatter nor praise you at the expense of any other," wrote Reed, "but I confess I do think that it is entirely owing to you that this army and the liberties of America . . . are not totally cut off." Reed added, "You have decision, a quality often wanting in minds otherwise valuable." He credited Lee's decisiveness for the Continental army's escape from Manhattan over to Kingsbridge, and added, "I have no doubt had you been here, the garrison at [Fort] Washington would now have composed a part of this army."[50]

Reed then delivered a scathing assessment of Washington: "Oh! General—an indecisive mind is one of the greatest misfortunes that can befall an army." Convinced that Washington was unworthy of the top command, Reed wrote that "as soon as the season will admit, I think yourself and some others should go to Congress and form the plan of the new army."[51] He made it clear that others close to Washington shared his shocking views.

After carefully mulling over these two letters and the disasters that had befallen the Continental army during the last few months, Lee reached a momentous conclusion: Washington was not a worthy commander-in-chief and no longer deserved unquestioned obedience. Further, Lee, for the good of the patriot cause, should maintain an independent command for as long as possible.

Lee's mindset at this time is otherwise difficult to determine. It is possible that he also thought that he should replace Washington as commander-in-chief. In order to put himself in the best position to accomplish that goal, Lee may have decided that, to the extent possible, he had to avoid giving up his independent command; if he joined Washington's force he would be subject to Washington's direct authority. Then, Lee may have hoped, when Howe's stronger force crushed Washington's outmanned and beleaguered troops, as then seemed likely, Congress would finally recognize that Washington was not up to the task, and that Lee and those troops that remained were the country's potential saviors. But if Lee could somehow forestall Howe, his promotion might come even sooner.

While Lee was too astute to put these thoughts on paper, his actions and many of his letters in the next month revealed that he likely was aiming for the top command. He had to be careful—while he thought he and his small army could save the patriot cause, he could not disobey Washington's orders outright. To do so would risk not only his hopes of succeeding Washington, but also his present position as second-in-command.

At this time Washington was far from the mythical figure he would later become. To date, his only major success had been driving the British out of Boston, and he had suffered a series of stunning defeats on Long Island, Manhattan, and at Fort Washington. And it was a fact that without the reinforcements from Lee, Washington's troops were no match for Howe's.

On November 22, the day after making his career-changing decision, Lee picked up his pen and wrote to a key constituent, James Bowdoin, president of the Massachusetts Council. Massachusetts was crucial to Lee's future plans. If Washington's army was crushed, as Lee expected, Lee would have to fall back into New England and rely mostly on support from Massachusetts and Connecticut. He began his letter, "Indecision bids fair for tumbling down the goodly fabric of American freedom, and, with it, the rights of mankind.... T'was indecision in our military councils which cost us the garrison at Fort Washington, the consequence of which must be fatal, unless remedied in time by a contrary spirit." Lee's use of Reed's term "indecision" was a clear reference to Washington.[52] The Massachusetts legislature responded to the general's letter, but saw no reason to panic. "With pain we read the disasters that have befallen us, but yet we are not dispirited."[53] To Lee's chagrin, there was no hint of criticizing, let alone replacing, Washington.

By the morning of November 24, two days after receiving Washington's letter, Lee had not moved. He wrote two more letters that day. In the first, to Washington, he acknowledged his superior's recent instructions, but then claimed he was unable to march due to his troops' "wretched condition with respect to shoes, stockings, blankets and which the present bad weather renders more intolerable." These complaints were no doubt true, but Lee's men were no worse off than other Continental forces in the field. Lee also mentioned that a brigade of enemy troops led by Loyalist Robert Rogers, the famous French and Indian War frontier fighter, was nearby, and "in so exposed a situation as to present us the fairest opportunity of carrying them off—if we succeed, it will have a great effect, and amply compensate for two days delay."[54] Lee hoped that Washington would accept at least one of these excuses.

Lee also penned a private response to Joseph Reed's "most obliging, flattering letter." He agreed with Reed about "that fatal indecision of mind which in war is a much greater disqualification than stupidity or even want of personal courage; accident may put a decisive blunder in the right, but eternal defeat and miscarriage must attend the man of the best parts if cursed with indecision."[55] He then explained in more detail why he was not immediately setting out to join forces with Washington.

The next day, Washington, hungry for news from Lee while Reed was away on a mission, mistakenly opened Lee's private letter to Reed and read its shocking contents. The stunned Washington discovered not only that his army's second-in-command was accusing him of "fatal indecision of mind," but also that one of his most important aides, Reed, must have used the same phrase in writing to Lee. Washington was now on his guard, but he wisely informed neither Lee nor Reed that he had read the letter.

On November 24–25 Lee failed in a bid to catch and crush Rogers's corps. Normally, such an effort would have been worthwhile, but when the fate of Washington's army and therefore the fate of the patriot cause lay in the balance, reaching Washington quickly was the higher priority. On November 26, the general received a letter from Washington, who was responding to Lee's earlier November 21 letter to Reed. Washington again urged Lee to come with his division as soon as possible.[56] The commander-in-chief desperately needed reinforcements; his small force was retreating before a powerful British force under Cornwallis, yet he had fewer soldiers in his command than Lee, who was not being attacked.[57] Placed on the defensive, Lee responded immediately, restating his reasons for having not yet rejoined Washington, but adding, "Part of the army has moved on—I set out tomorrow."[58] Six days after receiving instructions to link up with Washington, Lee felt he could delay no longer without risking an accusation of insubordination. But he still had control over how fast he would proceed, and whether his route would include a detour.

Lee made plans for the main part of his command to march some thirty miles north to King's Ferry, just south of Peekskill, where a crossing of the Hudson River could be made without fear of a British attack. After thousands of New York, Massachusetts, and Connecticut state troops and militiamen departed for home following the expirations of their terms of service, his own shrinking division totaled 4,000 men.

Despite informing Washington that the balance of his army would begin the two-day march from North Castle to King's Ferry on November 27,[59] Lee took much longer than that. The Continental 12th Regiment of Massachusetts, for example, did not set out toward Peekskill until the morning of the 29th. Colonel Christopher Lippitt's Regiment of Rhode Islanders left that afternoon. Nor did Lee push his men: these two regiments took a leisurely five days to come within two miles of King's Ferry.[60]

Riding ahead of his slow-moving troops, Lee reached the Peekskill headquarters of General William Heath on November 30. He immediately met with the Massachusetts native and, after asking for a cup of tea, shocked Heath by directing him "to order 2,000 of your men to march with me." But although Lee was his superior officer, Heath refused, citing Washington's orders to protect the Hudson Highlands. Probably expecting this response, Lee replied that he would issue the order himself, stating, "The commander-in-chief is now at distance and does not know what is necessary here so well as I do." He then perused the returns of Heath's regiments and said, "I will take Prescott's and Wyllys's regiments."[61] Lee later justified this act on the grounds that "without taking two regiments from Heath I could not march in force sufficient to the Jerseys, and perhaps the fate of America depends on the competency of my force."[62]

From a distance, meanwhile, Washington's impatience was beginning to show. The night before his meeting with Heath, Lee received a scathing dispatch from the commander-in-chief. "My former letters were so full and explicit, as to the necessity of your marching as early as possible, that it is unnecessary to add more on that head," Washington wrote. "I confess I expected you would have been sooner in motion."[63] In his November 30 response, Lee, after casually offering to "explain my difficulties when we both have leisure," informed his commander that "The day after tomorrow we shall pass the river, when I shall be glad to receive your instructions." Lee was finally willing to cross the Hudson River, but he was still unwilling to rush, as Washington clearly desired. He ended the letter with the observation, "I do assure you . . . that detached generals cannot have too great latitude, unless they are very incompetent indeed."[64]

The next day, December 1, with Prescott's and Wyllys's regiments on the march to Peekskill, and Lee's troops preparing to head out of camp for the Hudson River crossing at King's Ferry, Lee reconsidered his high-handed treatment of Heath, which Washington would surely not appreciate. Early that morning he rode up to the door of the post's headquarters building and called out for the portly Massachusetts general, who ambled up to the door. "Upon further consideration," Lee said, "I have concluded not to take the two regiments with me. You may order them to return to their former posts."[65]

Lee had good reason to conclude that these two regiments were needed more in New Jersey, where the British army had invaded in force, than in the quiet Hudson Highlands. Indeed, on December 7, Washington would change his mind and order Heath to dispatch one of his brigades south to northern New Jersey to annoy and distract Howe.[66] Nevertheless, at this time, Washington's orders to Heath were clear, and Lee had sought to undermine his commander-in-chief's directives.

At Peekskill, Lee left behind a number of sick and lame soldiers. Meanwhile, some New Englanders unwilling to fight in another "country" (New Jersey) had deserted, leaving the general with perhaps 3,000 men.[67] Women camp followers, who washed and mended soldiers' clothing and otherwise made camp life more bearable, were also left behind. Heath vividly recalled the sufferings of Lee's men as they departed: "General Lee took with him into [New Jersey] some of as good troops as any in the service, but many of them were so destitute of shoes that the blood left on the rugged frozen ground, in many places, marked the route they had taken."[68]

Lee informed Washington that he would cross the Hudson River on December 2, but not until December 4 did the last of his troops, using flatboats and scows in blustery conditions, finally cross into New Jersey from King's Ferry.[69] Heavy rains on December 2 and 3 had slowed progress, but still Lee was moving with little haste.[70]

Meanwhile, Washington's army was on the run. In one of the great retreats in American military history, Washington and Greene eluded General Cornwallis and his pursuing British army for more than 170 miles. The day after the November 20 fall of Fort Lee, the American troops evaded fighting Cornwallis, an experienced career officer who was also a member of the House of Lords, by passing over a bridge across the Passaic River and retiring to Newark.[71]

On November 28, Washington's army barely escaped Cornwallis's 4,000 rapidly closing troops. It would have been caught outside Brunswick (now New Brunswick) on December 1 but for an order from General Howe to Cornwallis not to proceed beyond that town, and the Americans' timely destruction of the Raritan River bridge.[72] Nathanael Greene wrote, "when we left Brunswick, we had not 3,000 men, a very pitiful army to trust the liberties of America upon."[73]

Fortunately for Washington, General William Howe continually failed to move aggressively. He instructed Cornwallis to remain in position at Brunswick for several days, which allowed Washington's "flying army" to slip away toward Princeton and Trenton.[74] According to Cornwallis, in a statement made in defense of Howe after the campaign, time was needed to send reinforcements to New Jersey, in part because it was "necessary to pay some attention to a considerable body then passing the [Hudson] River under General Lee."[75] Thus, as Washington and others did not appreciate, Lee's mere presence in New Jersey, late as it was, helped to save Washington's army.

At the same time, Howe refused to change his plans to send an invasion fleet from the East River, off Manhattan, to capture Newport, Rhode Island. With 7,100 troops on board seventy-one transport ships ready to depart, the man Howe had appointed to command the expedition, Lieutenant General Henry Clinton, proposed a new plan, due to the exposed condition of Washington's army and Philadelphia's resulting vulnerability. Clinton proposed two alternatives: land the troops at Amboy, New Jersey, where his army and Howe's could trap Washington in a pincer movement; or ship them to the Chesapeake Bay to seize Philadelphia. But the rigid Howe rejected both suggestions, and Clinton's invasion fleet started for Newport on November 29.[76]

On December 5, a full four days after Cornwallis halted his advance at Brunswick, Howe finally decided to visit Cornwallis in the field to discuss a move on Philadelphia.[77] Meanwhile, Washington, perhaps as anxious as he ever would be during the war, watched as hundreds of his men whose service terms had expired left his army for their homes. Writing to Lee on December 1, Washington had bemoaned, "The force I have with me is infinitely inferior in number and such as cannot give or promise the least successful opposition" to the British army's expected "push to Philadelphia." The desperate commander had urged on Lee: "I must entreat you to hasten your march as much as possible or your arrival may be too late to answer any valuable purpose."[78] Still, Washington refused to issue to his subordinate an outright order.

On December 2, in Philadelphia, a nervous Continental Congress ordered Washington to dispatch an express rider to locate Lee and to discover "where and in what situation he and the army with him are."[79] The next day Washington instructed Lieutenant Colonel Walter Stewart to do just that.[80] In a letter carried by Stewart, the commander-in-chief pointedly stated, "You will readily agree that I have sufficient cause for my anxiety, and to wish for your arrival as soon as possible. . . . The sooner you can join me with your division, the sooner the service will be benefitted." He closed by stating that, "As to bringing any of the troops under General Heath, I cannot consent to it. The posts they are at . . . being of the utmost importance, they must be guarded by good men."[81]

Stewart found Lee on December 4 at Haverstraw, New Jersey, three miles south of King's Ferry. The lieutenant colonel doubtlessly informed Lee of Congress's anxiety, but failed to make an impression. In fact, for continuing to maintain an independent command, Lee offered a new and arguably cogent reason: remaining where he was in order to strike British outposts in the area from behind. Moreover, he declared that since Washington had departed Brunswick, he did not know where to join him. "But although I should not be able to join you at all," Lee wrote in a remarkable response to Washington's entreaties, "the service which I can render you will, I hope, be full as efficacious." The increasingly bold general explained that when General Horatio Gates's reinforcements from Albany reached northern New Jersey, his and Gates's combined force of 5,500 men would "startle the enemy" by "hanging on their flanks or rear."[82]

Lee's soldiers found marching in the hills arduous and the numerous local Tories annoying. New Jersey Loyalists had been

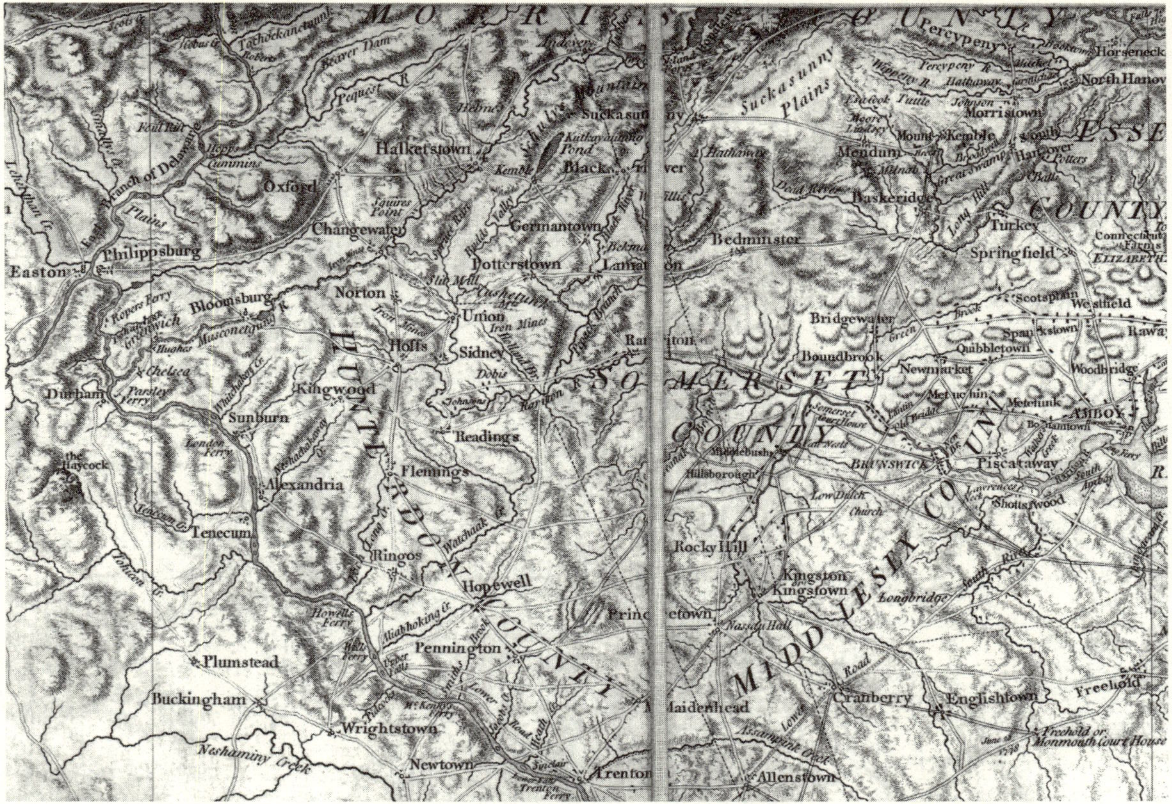

Map of northern New Jersey, showing Morristown, Basking Ridge (center, upper right), Brunswick, Hillsborough (center right), Alexandria (center left), Germantown (center, upper left), Philipsburg, New Jersey, across the Delaware River from Easton, Pennsylvania (far left), and Monmouth Court House (bottom right). From "The Province of New Jersey, divided into East and West, commonly called the Jerseys." By William Faden, London, 1778. (*Library of Congress*)

energized by General Howe's November 30 proclamation offering pardons, and thousands accepted the offer. Lieutenant Joseph Hodgkins of Ipswich, Massachusetts, and the 12th Continental Regiment, wrote to his wife, "This march was very unexpected to us all and the travelling very bad." In another letter he added, "The country is full of them cursed creatures called Tories."[83] Sergeant John Smith of Lippitt's Regiment from Rhode Island wrote, "we stopped to refresh ourselves a little about noon. The inhabitants abused us calling us 'Damn'd Rebels' and would not sell us anything for Continental money. The soldiers killed their fowls and one stole a hive of bees and carried it off with him."[84]

Once Lee's men crossed the Hudson River into New Jersey, they made steady if not speedy progress. Between Haverstraw and Morristown, from December 4 to 10, his army alternated between tramping 7–8 miles in the afternoon and marching all day.[85] There were several reasons for this, including the ragged and barefoot condition of many of his troops; the weather, which delivered either biting cold or muddy roads on which artillery and supply wagons often became stuck; and, most importantly, the troops' need to forage for food in the sparsely populated Watchung Mountains of northwest New Jersey. And, of course, Lee felt no urgency to push his men.

Lee finally reached Pompton Plains on December 7. Riding ahead of his main force, he arrived at Morristown on December 8, about thirty-six miles from the Delaware River crossing at Tinicum in Bucks County, Pennsylvania. Few roads led to Morristown, which sat nestled in the Watchung Mountains. It was therefore easy to defend, particularly in winter snows. Lee's division was down to 2,700 men, mostly Continentals, but he hoped to be reinforced by more than 1,300 local militiamen.

Meanwhile, on December 7, after receiving reinforcements and, as Howe wrote, "finding the advantages that might be gained by pushing on to the Delaware, and the possibility of getting to Philadelphia," Howe ordered his main force to advance. He reached Princeton, which Washington had evacuated the same day.[86] The next day, Howe pushed on to Trenton, but he was again too late. The main part of Washington's army had crossed the Delaware River the day before, and its rear guard slipped across just as Howe entered the town.[87] While the Delaware River provided Washington's force with temporary protection, the powerful British army was now only thirty miles from Philadelphia. "I tremble for Philadelphia," Washington wrote to his cousin, Lund. "Nothing in my opinion but

General Lee's speedy arrival, who has long been expected, though still at a distance (with about 3,000 men) can save it. We have brought over, and destroyed, all the boats we could lay our hands on, upon the Jersey shore for many miles above and below this place; but it is next to impossible to guard a shore for sixty miles with less than half the enemy's numbers."[88]

On December 1, Washington had ordered all vessels on the Delaware River for seventy miles to be seized or destroyed.[89] The move now paid dividends. Sent to locate enough boats to carry Howe's army across the Delaware, British officers found just a handful.[90] Still, if Howe mustered even moderate enterprise, he could yet order the building of flatboats from seized cut boards or have flatboats brought by wagons from his brother's fleet in New York City.[91] Once across the Delaware he would find Washington's force too weak to halt a British march on Philadelphia. Writing on December 8 to John Hancock, president of the Continental Congress, a concerned Washington noted of Lee, "I cannot account for the slowness of his march."[92]

Major General Charles Lee of the Continental army. This idealized portrait probably bears no resemblance to Lee. Published by C. Shepherd in Philadelphia, Oct. 31, 1775. (*Library of Congress*)

After arriving at Morristown that same day, meanwhile, Lee met Colonel Richard Humpton of the 11th Pennsylvania Regiment of Continentals, the second officer sent by Washington to consult with his wayward subordinate.[93] Informed by Humpton that 1,000 Philadelphia Associators under Colonel John Cadwalader had reinforced Washington's army, Lee immediately drafted a letter to his commander, claiming that since Washington's army was now "very strong," Lee's force could "make a better impression by hanging on [the enemy's] rear, for which purpose a good post at Chatham seems the best calculated."[94] Chatham, a small village on the Passaic River, was seven miles southeast of Morristown and eleven miles west of Newark, within easy striking distance of several British outposts. In a similar letter to Congress written the same day, Lee added that his army would "annoy, distract, and consequently weaken [the enemy] in a desultory war," essentially a series of harassing raids.[95]

Lee pushed on to Chatham later on December 8, perhaps to reconnoiter its usefulness and meet with local militia leaders. There he spent the night, possibly at Day's Tavern, the best in the village.[96] Shortly before he retired, however, Major Robert Hoops, the third officer sent by Washington to find Lee, reached the general's quarters with word that Washington's army had been forced to cross the Delaware River. Hoops also delivered a missive from Washington written the prior day stating that his force was inadequate and begging Lee to hurry to join him, lest Philadelphia possibly fall to the British. Hoops further informed Lee that boats to transport his division across the Delaware would be ready for him near Alexandria (now Frenchtown, New Jersey), about thirty-five miles north of Trenton. Writing at about the same time to Hancock, Washington explained that once Hoops informed Lee of the commander-in-chief's desperate situation, Lee "would be convinced of the necessity of his proceeding this way with all the force he can bring."[97] The ever-hopeful Washington was mistaken.

Lee read Howe's intent differently. "I cannot persuade myself that Philadelphia is their object at present," he responded to Washington, whose patience was surely approaching its limit. "It will be difficult, I am afraid, to join you;" Lee added, "but cannot I do you more service by attacking their rear?"[98] Ultimately, Howe would prove Lee correct by failing to advance on Philadelphia that winter. But at this time, Howe was indeed hoping to do so. In any event, it was up to Washington, not Lee, to determine the course of Lee's troops. It was little wonder that Nathanael Greene advised Washington, "I think General Lee must be confined with the lines of some general plan, or else his operations will be independent of yours."[99]

On December 9, Lee received "welcome tidings" from General Heath of developments that could support his plan to maintain and strengthen his independent command in New Jersey. General Gates, commander of American troops at Albany, had dispatched three Continental regiments, about 600 men in total, that had reached Heath at Peekskill, and Gates himself was following with four more Continental regiments.[100] Travelling, in part, on boats down the Hudson River, these regiments had made good time. Lee immediately sent orders for Heath to direct the regiments to combine with Lee's force at Morristown—unaware that Gates already had orders to join Washington.[101] Lee added in his note to Heath, "I am in hopes here to reconquer . . . the Jerseys. It was really in the hands of the enemy before my arrival."[102] Likely under pressure from local patriots, Lee had changed his goal from harassing British outposts to retaking all of New Jersey.

Following Colonel Humpton's return with news of Lee's continuing recalcitrance, Washington tried his best, still short of issuing an order, to dispel any confusion Lee may have had. On December 10, shortly after leading his army across the Delaware River, the commander-in-chief wrote:

> [W]ere it not for the weak and feeble state of the force I have, I should highly approve of your hanging on the rear of the enemy and establishing the post you mention. But when my situation is directly opposite to what you suppose it to be, and when General Howe is pressing forward with the whole of his army . . . to possess himself of Philadelphia, I cannot but request and entreat you, and this too by the advice of all the General officers with me, to march and join me with all your whole force with all possible expedition.[103]

A day later, when Major Hoops returned with Lee's letter in which the latter downplayed the threat to Philadelphia, Washington sent off Colonel Stephen Moylan of Pennsylvania with a letter correcting his subordinate, concluding, "You know the importance of the city of Philadelphia, and the fatal consequences that must attend the loss of it."[104]

Meanwhile, Lee returned to Morristown.[105] After his troops joined him there on December 10, Lee let his men rest for the remainder of that day and the next, despite good marching weather.[106] On December 11 he wrote to his commander to inform him of his new plan to retake New Jersey. First, he tried to excuse his slow progress, explaining, "We have three thousand men here at present, but they are so ill shod that we have been obliged to halt these two days [at Morristown] for want of shoes." Then, oddly, Lee switched to writing in the third person, perhaps thinking the tactic would lessen the blow to Washington:

> General Lee has sent two officers this day, one to inform him where the Delaware [River] can be crossed above Trenton, the other to examine the road towards Burlington, as General Lee thinks he can, without great risk, cross the great Brunswick post road, and by a forced night's march, make his way to the ferry below Burlington. Boats should be sent up

from Philadelphia to receive him. But this scheme he only proposes if the head of the enemy's column actually passes the river. The militia in this part of this province seem sanguine. If they could be sure of an army remaining amongst them, I believe they would raise a very considerable number.[107]

Taking the "great Brunswick post road" and crossing at Burlington would have required Lee's army to pass Princeton, where a British garrison was located. Thus, Lee was apparently contemplating a night march and early morning raid on Princeton, but only, as he said in his letter, "if the head of the enemy's column actually passes the Delaware [River]." Short of that, Lee was contemplating remaining in New Jersey, where more than a thousand militiamen had gathered around Morristown under the command of Colonel Jacob Ford, Jr., of Morris County. Ford and other local militia leaders warned Lee and other Continental officers that without support from the Continental army, "the militia collected will grow dispirited, soon dwindle away, and this state will be lost."[108]

When Lee's December 11 letter reached Washington's headquarters on the night of December 13, its contents confirmed Greene's suspicions, and angered Washington. First, if Lee waited to cross the Delaware River until Howe crossed it, he would rejoin Washington too late to assist in the defense of Philadelphia. Second, the last two lines of Lee's letter made it clear that Lee wanted to remain in New Jersey to help the state's militia prevent the British from taking control of northern New Jersey. Third, Lee was wasting time sending out officers to scout fording sites on the Delaware when Washington had dispatched Major Hoops to Lee for just that purpose.[109]

Meanwhile, on December 11, Howe ordered more troops, this time Colonel Carl von Donop and 400 of his Hessian grenadiers and jaegers, out in search of boats. They too found none, despite searching as far south as Burlington.[110] Even though Howe remained stalled, his looming presence continued to worry the Continental Congress in Philadelphia. On December 12, its members voted to move to Baltimore, and adjourned until December 20.[111]

While Lee did not know it, the potential for his men to strike a blow against the British in New Jersey encouraged some in Congress. Even as he and his fellow delegates prepared to vacate Philadelphia, Pennsylvania's Robert Morris wrote excitedly to inform Silas Deane, Congress's diplomat in France, telling him that

"General Lee crossed the [Hudson] River with a considerable force and is on the march towards the enemy, so that I expect [the enemy] will be driven into winter quarters."[112] In Wilmington, Delaware, meanwhile, Thomas McKean, who had voted for the Declaration of Independence as delegate to the Continental Congress, and then not been reelected, informed Captain Thomas Rodney that "everything was very gloomy and doubtful and that the chief hope that remained was that General Lee, who was on the mountains in the rear of the enemy, would be able to effect some lucky stroke that would prevent the enemy's crossing the Delaware, but if nothing of this sort happened, Congress would be obliged to authorize the commander-in-chief to obtain the best terms that he could from the enemy."[113]

Still, the bottom line was that Washington had repeatedly requested Lee to join his army in Bucks County, Pennsylvania, and Lee had not done so. If Lee's wish to instead strike British or German outposts in northern New Jersey made sense, it was nevertheless against his commander's wishes. And yet there were indications that Lee's intransigence nearly paid off handsomely. According to a rumor that circulated the following year, by about December 10 "it was in contemplation among some of the delegates" to promote Lee "to the supreme command of the army."[114]

As it happened, Washington had by now decided to go on the offensive. Credit for his change of strategy may have rested with Brigadier General William Alexander Stirling, who in a December 12 letter to the general offered to cross the Delaware and cooperate with Lee in an attack on a British outpost.[115] Writing to Gates on December 14, Washington said, "I expect General Lee will be there [Pittstown, northeast of Tinicum, on the Delaware River] this evening or tomorrow, who will then be followed by General Heath and his division. If we can draw our forces together, I trust under the smiles of Providence, we may yet effect an important stroke, or at least prevent General Howe from executing his plan."[116] To Heath, on December 14, Washington wrote tantalizingly, "Here, if we can collect our force speedily, I should hope we may effect something of importance."[117] The commander-in-chief was already thinking of re-crossing the river and attacking unsuspecting British or German positions. But would he do so before Lee?

Drawing of Widow White's Tavern, J. H. Horn. (*Horn, Historic Somerset*)

2

Widow White's Tavern

By December 11, with his troops having rested at Morristown for more than a day, Charles Lee found himself in a bind. He knew that if, after joining Washington, the generals' combined force struck a telling blow against the enemy, credit would go to the commander-in-chief. But if Lee managed to strike a British post on his own, the glory would be all his. Still, the Continental army's second-in-command wanted to avoid the appearance of insubordination. Lee's staff, including his highest-ranking subordinate, Brigadier General John Sullivan, was fully aware of the visits by Stewart, Humpton, and Hoops, as well as the contents of Washington's letters of early December. Realizing that he could no longer ignore Washington's increasingly forceful summonses, Lee ordered Sullivan to depart with his army the following morning. The New Hampshire native would head southwest in the direction of Germantown, on the road to the river crossing near Tinicum.[1] Sullivan issued orders for the army to be ready to march at 8:00 a.m. on December 12.[2]

Beyond Germantown, Lee would be on the left flank of the British army, still in position to pick off a British post to the south, perhaps Princeton or even Brunswick. He had one or two more days to decide whether to proceed west as fast as possible to link up with Washington across the Delaware River, or to tarry a bit longer in New Jersey and try something bold. Keeping his options open, he issued four days' rations to his soldiers.[3]

Because of an overnight snowfall, Lee's army did not set out until 11:00 a.m. The weather warmed up considerably during the day, and melting snow left the roads muddy and nearly impassable for artillery and supply wagons.[4] "Many of our soldiers," recalled Sergeant John Smith, "had [no] shoes to wear and were obliged to lace on their feet the hide of cattle we had killed the day before."[5] Lee's long column snaked its way through the Watchung Mountains with Sullivan at its head and Lee and his small entourage about two miles behind. At some point during the day, a courier arrived and handed to Sullivan Washington's letter of December 10, in which he had urged Lee to cross the Delaware and join his army. Sullivan likely forwarded it to Lee.[6]

Just eight miles out of Morristown, Sullivan halted his column for the night near Vealtown (now Bernardsville), a village in Somerset County some twelve miles short of Germantown. Many of the soldiers pitched their tents in nearby woods.[7] However, the lead regiment, Lippitt's Rhode Islanders, forged ahead five miles west, toward the village of Bedminster. Before stopping for the night himself, Lee sent ahead his recently appointed aide-de-camp, Major William Bradford, Jr., the son of Rhode Island's deputy governor, to order Lippitt's men to retrace their steps to Vealtown. Lippitt's tired men grudgingly did.[8] Why Lee ordered the Rhode Islanders back is not clear. He may have been mulling offensive action for the next day, or he may simply have wanted to concentrate his forces in case the British attacked him in the mountains.

Bradford's brief absence left Lee riding with two officers, both recently arrived, noble-born French volunteers. The first, Captain Jean-Louis de Virnejoux, had received a commission from Congress on September 19, 1776.[9] The second, René-Etienne Henry Vic Gaiault de Boisbertrand, had been a lieutenant colonel in the French cavalry before obtaining a two-year leave to travel to America. During his journey across the Atlantic that October, the ship carrying the thirty-year-old Boisbertrand had been captured off the Atlantic coast by a Rhode Island privateer whose captain was confused about how to handle the Frenchman. Put ashore at Bedford (now New Bedford), Massachusetts, he was brought before Boston officials, who gave him some pocket money and sent him on his way to Philadelphia. He was to deliver to Congress secret messages from French arms suppliers, and request a commission in the Continental army. During his journey, two days earlier, he had fallen in with Lee, and decided to see if he could be "useful."[10] Lee also had accompanying him a guard of about a dozen soldiers.[11]

Lee's experienced aides-de-camp—Jacob Morris, Otway Bird, John Eustace, and Joseph Nourse—no longer accompanied him. The temporarily absent Bradford was probably still too in awe of the general to be useful, as he had been a member of Lee's staff for only a little more than a month.[12] Thus, the general was without bright young advisors at a crucial moment. Before leaving the army a few days earlier, the ill, twenty-two-year-old Nourse, who had been with Lee since the siege of Charleston, confided to Bradford that "there would be warm work" before their superior's force linked up with Washington's.[13]

At a fork in the road, where his troops led by Sullivan had earlier taken the right fork and proceeded to the southwest towards Vealtown, Lee pondered where to spend the night in the lightly inhabited area. There were no large houses whose wealthy families could be imposed upon. Rather than stay at a small private home, he preferred to stay at an inn, where the proprietor would have experience hosting a group of guests and would not expect to be entertained by Lee. After asking for the nearest inn, he was informed it was Widow White's Tavern at the village of Basking Ridge (then called Baskenridge), which was two miles to the southeast on the left fork of the road and about three miles southeast of the main camp of Sullivan and his soldiers.[14] The tavern, perched on a small hill, was the last house at the south end of the village and stood about four-tenths of a mile from the main part of Basking Ridge. Lee decided to spend the evening there.[15]

The inn had undergone several name changes, due to the unfortunate luck of its proprietor, Mary Whitaker, in marrying men who died young. Mary was the daughter of Jonathan Whitaker and Elizabeth Jervis, who owned several sizable tracts of land in Somerset County. Mary had first married Samuel Brown, a Basking Ridge tavern keeper who died in late 1763. In his will, Samuel left the tavern to the local Presbyterian Church, but allowed Mary the use of it during her lifetime. Mary then wed Ebenezer White of Long Island, and changed the name of her former husband's establishment to White's Tavern. Upon White's death (sometime prior to 1776), the inn became known as Widow White's Tavern.[16] Operating an inn was one of the few occupations deemed acceptable for women without a man in the house, and the widow had to make a living. Now, on the evening of December 12, the twice-widowed Mary White, along with a female relative (probably her older sister Elizabeth), welcomed General Lee and his guests into her inn and tried to make them comfortable. Word of the famous Continental officer's presence in tiny Basking Ridge quickly spread.

Widow White's Tavern was not fancy. It likely had simple furnishings, perhaps about ten wooden chairs, a dining table, and a few other wooden tables in the common areas. It probably boasted four bedrooms, each with a bed, small chair, and candle stand. The following summer Ebenezer Hazard, surveyor general of the Continental Post Office, would pass it by while inspecting area roads, and write "I should never have expected to find a General there."[17]

Settling in, the Continental army's second-in-command wrote to the Reverend James Caldwell, an important local patriot who provided good intelligence of British posts and troop movements. In this letter, which has not survived, Lee apparently intimated that Continental troops would be left in New Jersey to support the local militia then gathering at Chatham.[18] After signing it, Lee retired to his bedroom. His aides slept on blankets in the spacious common room in front of its warm fireplace.

At 4:00 a.m. on December 13, Major James Wilkinson, aide-de-camp to General Gates, arrived at Widow White's Tavern, dismounted from his horse, and woke up Mary White, who ushered the tired nineteen-year-old officer into Lee's bedroom. Originally from Maryland, Wilkinson was in Philadelphia studying to be a physician when the war began. He enlisted, and was quickly promoted to captain and assigned to Gates's staff. From Albany, Gates had sent ahead three Continental regiments, which Lee had ordered to join his small army. Gates himself had followed on December 2 with four more Continental regiments, but a blinding snowstorm on the night of December 11 had all but stopped them in the hills of northern New Jersey. Gates had therefore dispatched Wilkinson to find Washington and return with advice as to what route to follow.[19] After discovering at Sussex Court House (now Newton, New Jersey), about seventy-five miles north of Trenton, that Washington had already crossed the Delaware River and that the boats had been removed from its ferries, Wilkinson had instead headed to Morristown. Late on December 12, Wilkinson stopped at a roadside house and found a sleeping Joseph Nourse, who directed him to Lee's overnight residence in Basking Ridge.

Holding a letter from Gates that he felt could be urgent, Wilkinson decided to wake the general. As he later recalled:

> I was presented to the General as he lay in bed, and delivered into his hands the letter of General Gates. He examined the superscription, and observed it was addressed to General Washington, and declined opening it, until I apprised him of the contents and the motives of my visit. He then broke the seal and read it, after which he desired me to take repose. I lay down on my blanket before a comfortable fire, amidst the officers of his suite, for we were not in those days encumbered with beds or baggage.[20]

Lee remained awake. Wilkinson rose at dawn but did not have a chance to meet the busy general until 8:00 a.m. After the young major filled in Lee on developments in northern New York, Lee gave Wilkinson his opinion of Washington's main army, which the general "condemned in strong terms."[21] According to Wilkinson, Lee then began to rant about what he believed were poor decisions made by Washington and his staff during the siege of Boston, and to crow about how he had saved the main army from capture on Manhattan Island.

Lee and Wilkinson were then interrupted by several members of a Connecticut light horse regiment commanded by Colonel Elisha Sheldon. The men raised a litany of complaints: one needed forage for his horse; another needed his horse to be shod; and still another sought overdue pay. Lee, Wilkinson later recalled, treated the soldiers "very irreverently" and shouted out of the window, "Your wants are numerous, but you have not mentioned the last—you want to go home, and shall be indulged, for damn you, you do no good here."[22]

Lee's busy morning continued. Arriving next was Colonel Alexander Scammell, a "remarkable tall man, and an accomplished officer and gentleman."[23] Scammell sought marching orders for General Sullivan. He had been appointed Lee's assistant adjutant general in October of 1776; prior to the promotion, he had served as Sullivan's aide-de-camp. The dashing, twenty-two-year-old native of Mendon (now Milford), Massachusetts, had graduated from Harvard College in 1769 and studied law under Sullivan in New Hampshire.[24] Wilkinson described the scene:

> [A]fter musing a minute or two, [Lee] asked the Colonel if he had with him the manuscript map of the country, which

was produced and spread on a table. It attracted my attention, and I observed General Lee trace with his finger, the route from Vealtown to Pluckemin, thence to Somerset Court House, and on by Rocky Hill to Princeton. He then returned to Pluckemin, and traced the route in the same manner, by Bound Brook to Brunswick, and after a close inspection carelessly said to Scammell, to "tell General Sullivan to move down towards Pluckemin, that I will soon be with him." This was off his route to Alexandria on the Delaware River, where he had been ordered to cross, and directly on that towards Brunswick and Princeton.[25]

Wilkinson knew that Pluckemin was about six miles from Vealtown, and that British-held Princeton was twenty-two miles from there. Gates's aide-de-camp surmised that Lee was planning not to march to join Washington's army, but to launch his own raid on Princeton. Shortly after Scammell departed, Lee sent a second rider galloping off to Pluckemin with a second note for Sullivan.[26] (The contents of this message are unknown, as British troops captured the messenger shortly thereafter.) Lee, meanwhile, had breakfast with Wilkinson, Bradford, and the two French officers, and then ordered his horse saddled.

Before departing the tavern, Lee completed a letter he had started the night before to his friend and fellow former British army officer, General Horatio Gates. The missive, which Lee gave to Wilkinson to deliver, distills Lee's conflicting thoughts at this crucial time:

December 12/13, 1776
My Dear Gates:
 The ingenious maneuver of Fort Washington has unhinged the goodly fabric we had been building. There never was so damned a stroke—entre nous, a certain great man [Washington] is most damnably deficient. He has thrown me into a situation where I have my choices of difficulties. If I stay in this province [New Jersey], I risk myself and army, and if I do not stay the province is lost forever. I have neither guard, cavalry, medicines, money, shoes, or stockings. I must act with the greatest circumspection. Tories are in my front, rear and on my flanks. The mass of the people is strangely contaminated. In short unless something which I do not expect turns up we

are lost. Our counsels have been weak to the last degree. As to what relates to yourself if you think you can be in time to aid the General [Washington] I would have you by all means go. You will at least save your army. It is said the Whigs are determined to set fire to Philadelphia. If they strike this decisive stroke the day will be our own, but unless it is done all chance of liberty in any part of the globe is forever vanished. Adieu, my dear friend. God bless you.
Charles Lee[27]

This letter, containing four slurs against Washington's ability as a general, is yet more evidence that Lee had entirely lost confidence in his commander. It indicates Lee's continued preference for not joining Washington's army, but instead remaining in New Jersey to support the patriot militia and raid an exposed British-held town, perhaps Princeton. While he set forth his dilemma of either joining Washington or remaining to help save what was left of patriot-controlled New Jersey, his orders were to do the former. With a forced march of a day or two, he could lead his men across the Delaware River, as his commander desired. He had no orders to protect New Jersey. This letter also reveals that Lee thought Howe's army still posed a threat to Washington's army, by its reference to the possibility of Gates's regiments arriving in time to aid Washington. It further reveals that Lee believed Philadelphia could still be taken by the British, by his reference to talk of patriots intentionally burning Philadelphia to deprive the British army of winter quarters there. (If Philadelphia was not still under threat of being captured, there would be no need for patriots to consider burning it.) Lee also made it clear in the letter his awareness of the presence of Tories all around him, a point that would later come back to haunt him. Nearly finished with this amazing document, Lee was just minutes from leaving Widow White's Tavern.

The movements of Lee and his army were never far from the thoughts of British commanders chasing Washington. On December 5 General Howe travelled from New York City to Amboy (now Perth Amboy) to meet with Brigadier General James Grant, commander of the British 4th Brigade. Grant informed Howe and his party that Cornwallis had instructed Grant to remain at Amboy in order to cover Cornwallis's rear. Captain Friedrich von Muenchhausen, a Hessian aide-de-camp to General Howe, explained, "This was most necessary since all the information we received regarding the corps of General Lee indicated that he intended to cross the Hudson River and get into the rear and on the right flank of our corps."[28]

Meanwhile, Cornwallis's division, pushing through Brunswick, Princeton, and nearby Pennington, became aware that Lee's army had crossed the Hudson River into northern New Jersey. In his diary entry for December 6 and 7, a British officer stationed in New York City wrote, "Undoubted intelligence received that General Lee had passed into Jersey with a body of troops, supposed to amount to five and twenty hundred or three thousand, and destined for Philadelphia, at least as far as we can tell."[29] This accurate intelligence, probably obtained from an American deserter from Lee's army, was likely quickly passed on by a fast messenger to Generals Howe and Cornwallis.

On December 10, Captain Muenchhausen recorded in his diary, "General Lee, who is in our rear, makes our support line very unsafe. He often sends out raiding parties. Last night one of them captured a small escort with eight baggage wagons."[30] The next day, the German officer added, "The support lines behind us become more and more unsafe because of General Lee, who is very audacious. He has captured several patrols and individual dragoons with letters, and has also taken 700 oxen and nearly 1,000 sheep and hogs from our commissary."[31] Unknown to Muenchhausen, it was Morris County, New Jersey, militia under Colonel Jacob Ford, Jr., not Lee's Continentals, that had raided Woodbridge.[32]

At this time, Howe kept a strong detachment of British and Hessian troops at Trenton, and Cornwallis commanded another powerful detachment about eight miles north, at Pennington.[33] At Pennington, Lee arose as a topic of conversation in Cornwallis's council of war on December 11. Was it Lee's army that had been harassing Howe's supply lines, or was it merely local patriot militia? In manning a series of posts from Brunswick to Trenton and as far south as Burlington, had Howe left himself exposed to an attack by Lee? Was Lee angling to return to New York to protect New England? Or was he headed to join forces with Washington across the Delaware River?

At this point in the council of war stepped forward Lieutenant Colonel William Harcourt, the thirty-three-year-old commander of the 16th (Queen's) Regiment of Light Dragoons, a British cavalry regiment in Cornwallis's army. Harcourt explained how he came to recommend sending a scouting party northward towards Morristown for more intelligence and volunteered to lead it:

> It now appears that General [Lee] had passed the [Hudson] River with a very considerable corps about ten days before. So ill-informed, however, were we of all his motions, that the latest account was positive as to his not having passed the river, and was doubtful whether he had not retreated towards New England. In this situation of affairs, I offered my services to Lord Cornwallis, to procure intelligence of the enemy's situation by the means of a patrol. His Lordship upon this, as indeed upon every other occasion, treated me in the most obliging manner, accepted my offer, and gave me his directions.[34]

Lieutenant Colonel William Harcourt, commander of the 16th Regiment of Light (Queen's) Dragoons. His regimental uniform is scarlet red with dark blue facings. Watercolor miniature by Richard Collins, ca. 1780. (*National Portrait Gallery*)

It was impressive that a lieutenant colonel, never mind an earl's son, had volunteered for such a dangerous mission into enemy territory. Harcourt could have assigned the task to a subordinate officer and no one would have questioned his courage.

William Harcourt was the second son of one of England's most prestigious aristocrats, Simon Harcourt. In 1749 the king had bestowed on the elder Harcourt the titles Earl of Stanton Harcourt and Viscount of Nuneham-Courtney. Simon Harcourt had gained royal favor in 1745 by raising a regiment that helped crush the Scottish rebellion the following year. He had also led the delegation that successfully negotiated the marriage of George III and Princess Charlotte of Mecklenburg-Strelitz in 1761. He had served as ambassador to France from 1768 to 1772, and was then appointed Lord-Lieutenant of Ireland, an important royal post that he still held.[35] As with many of English nobility's "second sons," William chose to pursue a military career. Born on March 20, 1743, he entered the army in 1759 as an ensign in the foot guards. Later that year he joined the 16th Regiment of Dragoons as a captain, and assumed his new duties under the unit's founder and commander, Colonel John Burgoyne.³⁶

As the second son, Harcourt had no rights of inheritance and had to make his own way, albeit with the great advantages of wealth and high social standing. Soon after entering the army, Harcourt accompanied his father to Mecklenburg-Strelitz to escort the future Queen Charlotte to England, and quickly became her friend.³⁷ After a stint as an aide-de-camp to General George Keppel, Earl of Albemarle, during the successful siege of Havana in 1762, he served as the lieutenant colonel of several regiments. He rejoined the 16th Regiment of Light Dragoons as Burgoyne's second-in-command in 1770. When Burgoyne was promoted to the rank of general, Harcourt effectively assumed command of the regiment informally known as "Burgoyne's Light Dragoons."³⁸ Harcourt also took a seat in Parliament, representing the city of Oxford from 1768 to 1774.³⁹

Charles Lee had his own connection to Burgoyne's 16th Regiment. He had led about fifty of its light dragoons, as well as infantry from other regiments, during his successful raid on a Spanish encampment in Portugal in 1762.⁴⁰ On September 12, 1775, the War Office ordered "the 16th (or Queen's) Regiment of Light Dragoons . . . to embark for North America in the ensuing Spring."⁴¹ Although Harcourt's thoughts on the matter cannot be determined, a London newspaper later reported that "Col. Harcourt before he left England expressed hopes that he should take General Lee."⁴²

At the end of June 1776, Harcourt finally embarked from Portsmouth, England, with his regiment of 490 men, along with reinforcing elements of the 17th Regiment of Light Dragoons (most of which was already in America).⁴³ These were the only two British cavalry regiments to serve in the war. Harcourt brought enough horses for only about half of his men, so his regiment included dismounted troopers.⁴⁴ After a stormy voyage of thirteen weeks, during which thirty-nine horses expired and four soldiers died of illness, all but one of Harcourt's transports landed at Halifax, Canada. In September, a Massachusetts privateer captured Harcourt's wayward vessel, which had drifted away in a storm. Harcourt lost about twenty-one soldiers as captives. The remainder of the regiment finally arrived in New York City on October 3, 1776. The cavalrymen, their surviving horses, and the dismounted troopers rested for a week before beginning their service in earnest.⁴⁵

While his men recuperated in New York City from their rough voyage, Harcourt was approached by an extraordinary young officer, twenty-two year-old Banastre Tarleton. By the end of the war he would be one of the most feared cavalry commanders on either side; at this time, he was virtually unknown. The son of a successful merchant and former mayor of Liverpool, he was educated at Oxford, but proved an indifferent student. At age nineteen, upon his father's death, he inherited a sizable fortune, but within a year had gambled most of it away.[46] The October 14, 1780, edition of the *London Chronicle* would note of Tarleton: "Being of a lively disposition and rather involved in his circumstances, he had recourse to the Army, as a profession in which, from his natural activity and courage, he would be sure of making his fortune or dying in the pursuit of it." In 1775, his mother purchased for him a cornet's commission in the British 1st Regiment of Dragoon Guards. (A cornet was the lowest-ranking officer in a dragoon regiment.) Seeking fame, Tarleton persuaded his commanding officer to allow him to volunteer for duty in America.

Banastre Tarleton. Later known for his ruthlessness in the south, Tarleton made his first impression as a soldier leading the advance guard of Harcourt's party on December 13, 1776. Engraving from life-size portrait by Sir Joshua Reynolds, ca. 1782, with an illustration of his dragoons. (*Library of Congress*)

Before heading overseas, Tarleton had the opportunity to show off his martial spirit in one of his favorite haunts, an upscale London gambling establishment. As his biographer wrote:

> Attired in the handsome uniform of the Dragoon Guards, with its scarlet coat, and wearing an enormous saber, he strutted around to the Cocoa Tree. As he and his friends discussed the prospective war in America, the conversation drifted to General Charles Lee. In a burst of excitement, Cornet Tarleton sprang to his feet, swung the great saber over his head, and, to the astonishment of the more pacific visitors to the Cocoa Tree, cried: "With this sword I'll cut off General Lee's head!"[47]

In New York, the glory-seeking Tarleton encountered the dashing and brash dragoons of the 16th Regiment and their ambitious, well-connected commander. He immediately applied to Harcourt for service in his regiment. With one transport of his dragoons still missing, and the balance of his force still recovering from the sea voyage, Harcourt gladly accepted the help. He also selected the promising Tarleton to ride with his men on the December 12 scouting mission to Morristown.

Riding on large, athletic horses, the British mounted dragoons were an intimidating sight. They wore red jackets with blue trim, white breeches, and black leather helmets with horsehair crests. Each man was armed with a saber, a carbine, and sometimes a pair of pistols. Officers carried pistols and single-edged, straight-blade cavalry swords, whose thirty-seven-inch length made them effective against both foot soldiers and mounted men. In addition to Royal Forester carbines, Harcourt armed some of his men with the fine, new 1776 Pattern Rifle.[48] Harcourt's mounted and dismounted troopers joined Howe's army at Flushing, New York, on October 20, in time for the Battle of White Plains. [49]

Though Harcourt's mounted dragoons served mostly as scouts and messengers on patrols, they quickly gained a reputation as killers. On October 23, near Eastchester, New York, American troops bested a Hessian contingent in a sharp clash and took two prisoners. Two days later General Lee marched off, leaving one of the men—a wounded major—in the care of an American surgeon's mate, in a hospital guarded by thirty Rhode Island soldiers. Shortly thereafter, a party of approaching light dragoons panicked the Rhode Islanders, who fled, leaving the hospital unprotected. Some of the dragoons, Lee complained later to Howe, "broke into the house and most inhumanely murdered the wretched mate."[50]

On November 21, Harcourt and his 16th Regiment were ferried across the river to Fort Lee, where, according to Howe, "they scoured the country on the 22nd, as far as the Passaic River, and had found the enemy had abandoned all the intermediate country."[51] But as Tarleton noted on November 23, there was still action to be had: "Lt. Col. Harcourt commanded a reconnoitering party of dragoons and light infantry yesterday. We penetrated 12 miles into to the country . . . where we found the rebels posted. We alarmed them, cut a few sentries down and saw their position. . . . We then retreated without any loss or wound except to one horse's ear."[52] On December 2, ferries carried Harcourt's dragoons from Staten Island to Elizabethtown, New Jersey, where the men joined Cornwallis's army in its pursuit of Washington.[53] Writing home to his father on December 5, Harcourt described a "most fatiguing but very successful expedition under Lord Cornwallis, which has given us possession of a great part of the Jerseys."[54]

A mounted dragoon of the 16th (Queen's) Regiment of Light Dragoons, 1770. Watercolor by Cecil C. P. Lawson, 1956. (*Anne S.K. Brown Military Collection, Brown University*)

The sight of the dragoons of the 16th Regiment, and its sister regiment, the 17th, struck fear in the breasts of American soldiers. But the mounted men began to suffer some casualties. The greatest threat to the British cavalrymen was not from Continental soldiers in large units, but from ambushes by small numbers of local militia hiding behind trees and stone walls. Captain Thomas Stanley of the 17th, then stationed at Amboy, wrote:

> I had a dragoon of my troop killed. The service the dragoons are now employed on is very harassing and a very dangerous one when we patrol the roads and carry expresses from post to post, neither of which duty we can scarce even perform without being shot at. I have within these ten days a man and horse killed, another man wounded and his horse shot dead under him and he was taken by three or four of them who had fired at him. He watched his opportunity and knocked two of them down with the back of his carbine and escaped. My lieutenant has likewise been shot through the thigh, and I got a ball through my great coat. They picked off a good number of us in this shabby method, but it makes the rest of the soldiers twice as fast as any drilling in time of peace.[55]

On December 12, the same day that Harcourt's patrol was to commence, the following order was issued from British-held Trenton: "Small straggling parties, not dressed like soldiers and without officers, not being admissible soldiers, or peaceable inhabitants of the country, who presume to molest or fire upon soldiers, will be immediately hanged without trial as assassins."[56] Harcourt recognized how dangerous a patrol through the New Jersey countryside could be, but he volunteered to lead it.

During the December 11 council of war, Cornwallis provided Harcourt with detailed instructions for the mission. The general had on more than one occasion sent patrols northward in search of intelligence. This time, however, Harcourt and his party would penetrate deeper into northern New Jersey, and spend at least one night in possibly hostile territory. Harcourt was only taking a portion of his regiment with him. His thirty-two troopers—Captain Charles Eustace (of the 33rd Regiment), Captain Thomas Nash, Lieutenant Thomas Leigh, Cornet Banastre Tarleton, Cornet Francis Geary, and twenty-seven sergeants, corporals, and privates—were ordered to be ready to ride the next morning, December 12.[57]

As planned, Harcourt's party galloped out of Pennington and headed northeast toward Morristown. They were joined by at least three other men who were not mentioned in official British dispatches. Two of them were servants, one for Lieutenant Colonel Harcourt and the other for Captain Nash. In addition, Harcourt had at least one local Loyalist guide who knew the roads between Pennington and Morristown. According to a British officer at Brunswick, "Colonel Harcourt met a Yorkshireman" formerly from England, "who was acquainted with the country and had him for a guide."[58] Less reliable reports indicate that the man's name was Richard Witham Stockton, then an officer in a New Jersey Loyalist outfit. Two other local Loyalists, seventeen-year-old William Robbins, and Asher Dunham of Morris County, would later claim to have served as guides.[59]

After riding about eighteen miles without incident, the men stopped for the night just south of Hillsborough (called Somerset Court House by the Americans, and now known as Millstone), on the west bank of the Millstone River, where two companies of Captain Sir James Baird's British 71st Regiment were quartered.[60] Tarleton and a few others went to sleep in a comfortable house, which at 1:00 a.m. mysteriously caught fire and burned to the ground. The men escaped without injury and found new quarters in a barn, where they slept until 5:00 a.m., when they were ordered back onto their saddles.[61]

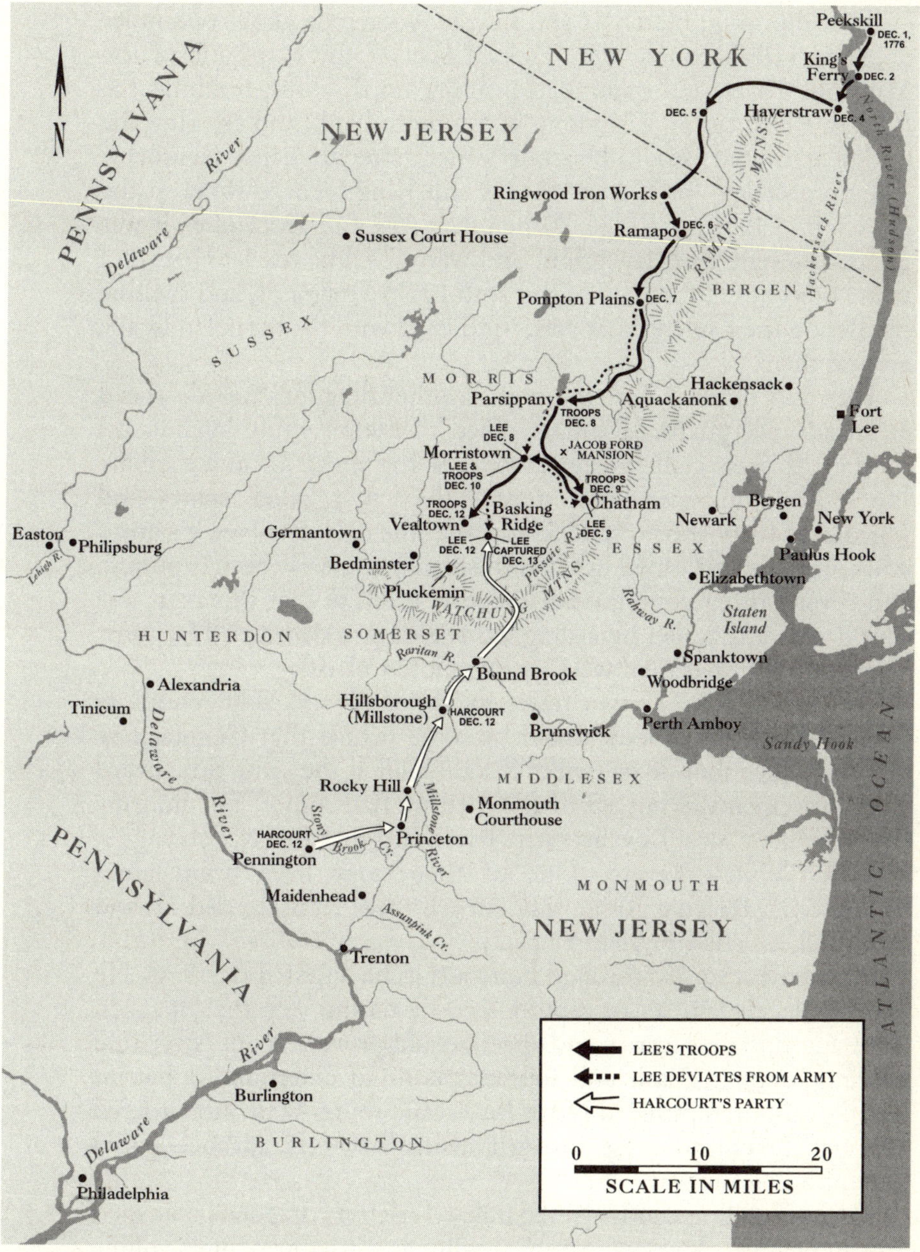

Widow White's Tavern 41

The routes of Charles Lee and William Harcourt's party that converged at Basking Ridge, resulting in the capture of Lee.

That morning, Harcourt and his dragoons rode about two miles north to Hillsborough, then crossed over to the east bank of the Millstone River, and continued heading north. After reaching the Raritan River, riding east along its southern bank, and crossing the bridge at Bound Brook, Harcourt's men entered enemy territory.[62] They proceeded north over what is still King George Road in the direction of Basking Ridge. Although it was mid-December, it was an "exceedingly fine day, bright and warm."[63] The scarlet coats and white breeches of the men of the 16th Light Dragoons, and the fine saddles on their splendid horses, contrasted with the bleak landscape around them.

Harcourt ordered Tarleton and six other dragoons to ride ahead as an advance guard, "a circumstance," Tarleton wrote later to his mother, "I ever shall esteem as one of the most fortunate of my life."[64] Tarleton's men soon spotted their first "rebel" sentry and killed him. (Probably to spare his mother the ugly details of his unit's work, Tarleton informed her that the man had merely been captured. But several other contemporary reports indicate that this man was "cut down" and killed by a dragoon wielding a sword.)[65] Harcourt, Tarleton, and their men were getting close to Lee.

Riding on another two miles in Tarleton's wake, Harcourt, as Tarleton later described, "found by some people that General Lee was not above four or five miles distant, and at the same time heard that our retreat was cut off by the road we had come." The informers were likely local Loyalists who had heard that Lee was staying at Widow White's Tavern. One of them may have been James Compton, a Basking Ridge resident who was later accused of, and admitted, assisting Harcourt's party.[66]

Excitement surged through Harcourt as he digested the news. He quickly decided to try to capture Lee—a daring step that, if taken with appropriate surprise and speed, could prove a coup. After first sending Captain Nash and four dragoons to determine if patriot militia was attempting to block his escape route, Harcourt ordered his detachment to press forward, with Tarleton's advance guard again leading the way.

After travelling another three miles, Tarleton's dragoons managed to capture two American sentries who, as Tarleton wrote, "volunteered" useful intelligence. "The dread of instant death obliged these fellows to inform me, to the best of their knowledge, the situation of General Lee. They told us he was about a mile off, that his guard was not very large and that he was about half a mile in the rear of his

Detail from "A Map Containing Part of the Provinces of New York and New Jersey," by Andrew Skinner, 1781, showing Bound Brook and Brunswick at the bottom, and Pluckemin, Basking Ridge, and Morristown to the north. (*Library of Congress*)

army. These men were so confused that they gave us but an imperfect idea where General Lee was."[67] Harcourt, concerned about pressing forward with Lee's army so close, ordered Tarleton and two other troopers to the top of a rise to see what might await them. Tarleton complied, and later explained what happened next:

> In going to the ground, I observed a Yankee light horseman, at whom I rushed and made prisoner. I brought him in to Colonel Harcourt. The fear of the saber extorted great intelligence, and he told us he had just left General Lee from

whom he had an express message to carry to General Sullivan at Pluckemin. He could not satisfy me exactly as to the strength of General Lee's guard, but confirmed the account of the other two prisoners as to his situation. He said he thought his guard did not consist of above 30 men. He pointed out to us the house where he had left General Lee and mentioned that he [Lee] was going to move directly.[68]

Harcourt quickly pondered the odds of his twenty-four dragoons defeating Lee's guard, reported as roughly thirty men. If his horsemen maintained the element of surprise, he could quickly approach the tavern (which stood about a mile off the main road) and perhaps overcome Lee's guard with sabers before American gunfire could alert any other troops stationed in the area. Harcourt was willing to take the risk, but he sought support from Captain Eustace, Cornwallis's aide-de-camp. Harcourt, Tarleton wrote, "called to Eustace to know whether he thought we were strong enough" and "Eustace replied in the affirmative." Without further delay, Harcourt ordered Tarleton and his advance guard (now five dragoons) toward the tavern. They set out "at full speed."[69]

Another version of this sequence of events was later recorded by Howe's aide, Captain Friedrich von Muenchhausen, who based it on details obtained from an unidentified member of Harcourt's party. Muenchhausen's account matches Tarleton's version in its material facts, but includes some interesting additional details, particularly the threat of hanging as opposed to death by sword:

> The [rebel dragoon] officer was captured in spite of his efforts to escape. Upon being questioned, the officer at first would not admit that General Lee was nearby. But when preparations were made to hang him, he not only confessed, but promised to lead Colonel Harcourt to General Lee's house. Two dragoons, one on each side, rode with the officer, under orders given in his presence, to cut him to pieces if he attempted to lead the Colonel and his dragoons to the wrong house, or into a trap. A cornet with six dragoons [not the five noted by Tarleton] mounted on our best horses were then detached with orders to guard the doors of the house. Harcourt followed some hundred paces behind the detached cornet [Tarleton]. The whole Harcourt party, including the advance detail, proceeded very slowly as long as they were not discovered. When they were close enough for the captured

officer to show them the house where General Lee had his quarters, they dashed in all possible haste toward the house.[70]

By 10:30 a.m., an unsuspecting Lee was ready to depart Widow White's Tavern to rejoin his army. Major Wilkinson glanced out the south-facing window, down the roughly 100-yard-long lane that connected the tavern's grounds with the main road. Woods bordered it on one side, and an orchard the other.[71] According to Wilkinson, he saw:

> [A] party of British dragoons turn a corner of the [lane] at a full charge. Startled at this unexpected spectacle, I exclaimed, "Here, sir, are the British cavalry." "Where?" replied the General, who had signed his letter in the instant. "Around the house," for they had opened files, and encompassed the building. General Lee appeared alarmed, yet collected, and his second observation marked his self-possession: "Where is the guard? Damn the guard, why don't they fire?" After a momentary pause, he turned to me and said, "Do, sir, see what has become of the guard."
>
> The women of the house at this moment entered the room, and proposed to him [Lee] to conceal himself in a bed, which he rejected with evident disgust. I caught up my pistols which lay on the table, thrust the letter he had been writing into my pocket, and passed into a room at the opposite end of the house, where I had seen the guard in the morning. Here I discovered their arms, but the men were absent. I stepped out of the door, and perceived the dragoons chasing them in different directions, and receiving a very uncivil salutation, I returned into the house.[72]

What had become of Lee's guard of about a dozen soldiers? According to Wilkinson, "The morning being cold and the sun bright, they had left their station, crossed the main road, and were sunning themselves on the south side of a house about 200 yards from the tavern, which enabled Harcourt to cut them off from their arms."[73] Spotting the fearsome British dragoons riding furiously towards them with their swords held high, two of the guards had scrambled for their muskets. According to one report, one of them got off a shot before being cut down.[74] Another account stated that the sole sentry at the door, "[h]is piece not being loaded," advanced toward the oncoming dragoons, who "rode up to him and said, don't shoot; if you fire we will blow your brains out."[75] According to William Bradford, Tarleton and five of his dragoons surrounded the house, and, slashing away with their swords, "cut off the arm of one of the guards crying for quarter."[76]

Tarleton's approach had caught some of Lee's other guards some distance from the tavern. They quickly returned, retrieved their muskets, and tried to offer a defense. But the balance of Harcourt's men soon arrived and, led by Lieutenant Leigh, subdued them or chased them off.[77] The dragoons, showing good discipline, were focused on capturing their intended target—Lee—and not on killing his guards. To force Lee from the tavern, they began to riddle it with carbine fire. Harcourt, meanwhile, rode up a nearby hill to reconnoiter for approaching American reinforcements. None were visible. Outside the tavern, Tarleton would later write, he rode up to "[a]n old woman upon her knees" who "begged for her life and told me General Lee was in the house," which "assurance gave me pleasure."[78]

Inside the tavern, Lieutenant Colonel Boisbertrand, Captain de Virnejoux, and Major Bradford kept up a steady return fire, but with pistols that were of little use from a distance. Neither Lee nor Wilkinson joined in the shooting.[79] Still, General Howe would later report that "Harcourt narrowly escaped a shot that went through the tassel of his helmet."[80] Targeting its windows, Harcourt's men reportedly "fired sixty or seventy shot into" the tavern.[81] After about eight minutes, Tarleton fired through its door and yelled to its inhabitants: "I know General Lee is in the house. If he would surrender himself, he and his attendants should be safe, but if my summons was not complied with immediately, the house should be burnt and every person without exception, should be put to the sword."[82]

Immediately following this ominous warning, Boisbertrand, in a panic to escape, rushed out of the building through its back door and headed for the woods north of the tavern. Tarleton galloped after the fleeing Frenchman, and quickly captured him at sword point.[83] Boisbertrand later stated that he had been "slightly wounded in the arm and head" after being "felled with blows from the flat of a sword," presumably by Tarleton.[84] Two other American guards who made a run for it were less fortunate. Harcourt's dragoons cut them down.

Seeing no sign of help from his army, Lee felt that his fate was sealed. "The General saw then that he must submit and after walking the chamber perhaps ten or fifteen minutes, told [me] to go

"The American General Lee taken prisoner by Lieutenant Colonel Harcourt of the English army, in Morris County, New Jersey, 1776." Basking Ridge, where Lee was seized, is actually in Somerset County. This idealized version was engraved by William Hamilton and sculpted by J. Hawkins. First published in Edward Barnard's *History of England*, in 1783. (*Anne S.K. Brown Military Collection, John Hay Library, Brown University*)

down and tell them General Lee would submit," William Bradford recalled later. "[I] went to the door and on opening it a whole volley of shot came on. At the door, [I] spoke loud and opened it again and delivered his orders."[85]

At this point, both Lee and Bradford stepped through the tavern door and walked outside toward Harcourt's troopers. According to Bradford, who had been slightly wounded, "General Lee came forward and surrendered himself as prisoner-of-war, saying he trusted they would use him like a gentleman. Of this, one of them [probably Colonel Harcourt] gave assurance and ordered him instantly to mount."[86] Before doing so, Lee asked permission for Bradford to retrieve his hat and cloak from the tavern. Keenly aware of the need for haste, Harcourt nevertheless generously agreed. Fearing that he too would be taken prisoner, Bradford came up with a ruse to try to fool Harcourt's men. Lee, he wrote, "requested his hat and cloak, and [I] went to fetch it—but changing [my] clothes on [my] return, they did not know [me] from a servant. Laying down the general's hat and cloak, [I] escaped back into the house. They immediately rode off in triumph with the general, leaving a few to get the horses from the stable and take and bring off the rest as captives."[87]

By now James Wilkinson, armed with two pistols, had taken shelter in the tavern's interior (reportedly inside a chimney) and could see neither Lee nor Bradford.[88] But he heard Tarleton's threat to torch the tavern. "Within two minutes I heard it proclaimed, 'Here is the General, he has surrendered,'" he wrote later. "A general shout ensued, the trumpet sounded the assembly, and the unfortunate Lee mounted on my horse, which stood ready at the door, was hurried off in triumph, bareheaded, in his slippers and blanket coat, his collar open, and his shirt very much soiled from several days use."[89]

In Tarleton's version of these events, "General Lee surrendered himself to the sentry I had placed at the front door," while Tarleton and other dragoons were subduing Boisbertrand and the two men who had made a run for the woods. "The prisoner was led to Colonel Harcourt" who "placed his noble prisoner upon a horse and led him off .... The bugle horn was then sounded. I brought up the rear of the men and the French colonel."[90]

Captain von Muenchhausen heard a slightly different story. "Since there was no horse for the French colonel, a servant of Harcourt rode next to him, and was about to take him on his horse with him," he wrote. "The Frenchman protested that riding the same horse with a servant was below his dignity. But after the servant had given him some good nudges in the ribs, probably also an insult to his dignity, he finally gave in and mounted."[91] Another report held that the dragoons treated Boisbertrand "with every... mark of indignity."[92] He was one of the first French officers that the British had captured. The dragoons were probably angry about French involvement in the war—what they viewed as a quarrel among relatives.

Basking Ridge residents north of the tavern were shocked that British dragoons had penetrated so far north. "My father, who was always attentive to every officer of the army, called on General Lee [on December 11], and invited him to breakfast the next day," then-nine-year-old Eliza Morton wrote later. "He accepted; but, as he did not appear at the appointed time, Mr. Morton became impatient, and walked up the hill to meet his expected guest. On his way, he encountered many of the country people running in great consternation, exclaiming, 'The British have come to take General Lee!' My father hurried on, and saw Lee, without hat or cloak, forcibly mounted, and carried off by a troop of horse."[93] The entire assault, culminating with Lee's surrender, had taken only about fifteen minutes. Two of Lee's guards were dead and several others were wounded, including Lee's aides Bradford and the captive Boisbertrand, each of whom had suffered minor injuries.[94] Of the dead guards, one villager recalled that the British dragoons had "used their sabers only" and had "hacked them... terribly."[95] Lee and Boisbertrand were prisoners; Bradford, Wilkinson, and Virnejoux had avoided capture simply by remaining inside the tavern. Injuries to Harcourt's men, Tarleton noted, amounted to "[o]ne horse's leg, which was slightly grazed, and one saddle, which was shot through the pommel."[96]

The fate of the messenger captured while attempting to deliver Lee's message to General Sullivan at Pluckemin—the man who, under the threat of instant death, had guided Harcourt's party to Widow White's Tavern—is unclear. Tarleton reported taking "prisoner" the two sentries who had provided information on Lee's whereabouts, but wrote nothing more of them.[97] Were the three soldiers kept as prisoners? Were they released in return for their cooperation? Were they killed by dragoons? There is no way of knowing.

Harcourt, Tarleton, and their two prisoners sped down the lane back to the main road leading south out of Basking Ridge. The balance of his party quickly followed. There was an unconfirmed report that a few dragoons were left behind "to take charge of the remaining prisoners"—Lee's guards—who, "however, escaped by re-entering the house [Widow White's Tavern] and obliging the enemy to retire...."[98] Harcourt's men remained in considerable danger. The entire countryside would soon be alerted to their presence, and patriot militia would be looking for them. Soon, in fact, Harcourt encountered Captain Nash and his four dragoons, who had briefly skirmished with Americans set on cutting off their retreat. (Nash had his servant taken prisoner in the action.) Harcourt therefore turned off the road, no doubt relying on his Loyalist guide to find a less-traveled course to Hillsborough.

As Lee rode off with his captors, he must have wondered about his future as a prisoner. Since his defection to the American cause, more than one English newspaper had suggested what might become of him if he were ever captured. In the March 30, 1776, edition of London's *General Evening Post*, a poem submitted by "Q" included the ominous lines:

> Ambition's dupe, a lawless faction's *tool*,
> Must live a *madman*, and must die a *fool*,
> Here read thy *character*, thy peril, *Lee*;
> A traitor's name, a traitor's destiny.

In June 1776, a false report that Lee had been captured in Virginia by General Henry Clinton spurred a clamor in the British press for Lee to suffer "a traitor's destiny"—hanging.[99] Lee was no doubt aware that in the aftermath of the Scottish rebellion of 1745–1746, the British had hanged Scot leaders before London mobs.

Lee's final hope was that New Jersey militia guarding roads and villages south of Basking Ridge and north of Hillsborough would intercept Harcourt's party and free him. But the sight of thirty-plus well-armed British dragoons racing by must have been intimidating to locals. Harcourt's troopers, Tarleton recalled, "retreated afterwards thirteen miles through enemy country without any accident. We then forded a river, approached Hillsborough and gave each other congratulations with every symptom of joy."[100]

At Hillsborough, where Sir James Baird's two companies of the 71st Regiment remained, Harcourt's men were safe. There, Harcourt stopped at a Dutch doctor's house to have lunch with his fellow officers, including two surprise visitors, Lieutenant Colonel Charles

Mawhood of the 17th Regiment of Foot and a Major Moyney. As it happened, Moyney and Lee were old friends from Lee's days in the British army. According to one account, "Major Moyney immediately ran out and kissed General Lee with tears in his eyes, and the General told him he never expected to see him in America." These men, Lee included, sat down for a meal.[101]

After the short repast, Harcourt and his party and a "much dispirited Lee"[102] continued on to Cornwallis's headquarters at Pennington, from which the now-jubilant force had departed the previous day. "This is a most miraculous event—it appears like a dream," Tarleton wrote to his mother. "We conducted General Lee and the French colonel to Lord Cornwallis at Pennington. Our day's march [ride] exceeded 60 miles."[103] Cornwallis must have been pleasantly surprised. As prominent Loyalist Joseph Galloway wrote on December 14, Harcourt had been "sent out to reconnoiter General Lee's army and returned with General Lee himself."[104] Harcourt, meanwhile, informed his father of his role in the expedition during which "General Lee became my prisoner," expressing satisfaction that it had been accomplished "without the loss of a single man."[105]

Harcourt's party had indeed been fortunate, a fact made abundantly clear the next day when a reconnaissance force led by Cornet Francis Geary was ambushed by New Jersey militia near Flemington, New Jersey. Geary, the son of Admiral Sir Francis Geary of the Royal Navy, was shot through the forehead and killed.[104] Evan Evans, a private in the 16th Regiment of Light Dragoons, was also killed.[107]

Meanwhile, back at Basking Ridge, locals had the sad task of burying Lee's two dead guards. One woman later recalled that Tarleton's dragoons had "hacked them so terribly that it was found very difficult to remove their bodies to the graveyard, and they were put in boxes and interred in the field where they lay."[108] Eliza Morton, who lived a half-mile from Widow White's Tavern, recalled that one of the wounded guardsmen, who had been slashed by a sword, "was brought down to our house, where he was taken care of until he was carried on a litter to a surgeon at Mendon; and after three months he recovered, and came to thank my mother for her kindness to him."[109]

3

A Severe Blow to the Cause

As soon as Harcourt and his dragoons galloped away from Widow White's Tavern, Majors Wilkinson and Bradford emerged from the shot-up building, found horses, and raced off to convey the news to General Sullivan. After riding two miles to the northwest, Lee's anxious aides came across the entire division, in parade formation and ready to march. The slightly wounded Bradford rode up to the head of the column to greet Sullivan and inform him of the morning's shocking developments. Sullivan was stunned at suddenly finding himself commander of the division. According to Private John Howland of Lippitt's Regiment of Rhode Islanders, news of Lee's fate "spread through the whole line." Hearing the murmurings and knowing the cause, Howland recalled, Sullivan then "rode through the line giving orders, to show that we still had a commander left."[1] The general also dispatched some light horsemen to chase down Lee and his captors. David How, an eighteen-year-old private in the 16th Regiment of Massachusetts Continentals, wrote that he and other men from his regiment "went with a party to pursue them and went 8 miles but were too late."[2]

Wilkinson, who also met with Sullivan later that morning of December 13, wrote, "I had not examined General Lee's letter, but believing a knowledge of the contents might be useful to General Sullivan, who succeeded him in command, I handed it to him, who after the perusal, returned it with his thanks, and advised me to rejoin General Gates without delay."³ Sullivan, who must have been further surprised by the contents of Lee's remarkable letter to Gates, pondered what to do next. He had orders from Lee to march to Germantown, but he held letters from Washington to Lee entreating the latter to march his division to the Delaware River crossing at Tinicum as expeditiously as possible. (Sullivan never received Lee's orders to march to Pluckemin, since the courier carrying them had been captured by Tarleton.) Sullivan decided to march as planned southwest to the small village of Germantown and then link up with Washington. The New Hampshire general issued his orders, and as Sergeant John Smith noted, "the whole division marched forward to Germantown . . . exceeding tiresome, as the road was full of stones and very muddy."⁴ The men, recalled Lieutenant Stephen Olney of Hitchcock's Regiment from Rhode Island, marched with "dejected spirits," knowing that their commander was a captive of the enemy.⁵

As the army marched, Colonel Stephen Moylan, sent by Washington on December 11 to urge Lee on, caught up to Sullivan. Washington probably knew that Moylan was a friend of Lee's; it was he who had nicknamed Lee "Naso." Moylan had heard rumors that a sizable British force was looking to cut off Lee's division before it could reach the Delaware River. To minimize this risk, Moylan recommended to Sullivan that the next day he march his men, without their baggage, eighteen miles to the ferry at Tinicum, where "the troops could be got across in the night." The troops' baggage could be sent higher up to Philipsburg, New Jersey, and ferried from there across the Delaware River to Easton, Pennsylvania.⁶ Sullivan instead decided on a more conservative approach, taking both his troops and their baggage on the more northerly (and longer) route towards Easton and crossing the river there. On December 15 Sullivan wrote, "I have altered my route to Easton, where I now intend to cross the Delaware if possible this night, as I have intelligence of a large body of the enemy being about twenty miles yesterday afternoon on my left."⁷ According to Lieutenant Olney, this redirection "to avoid the enemy" resulted in Sullivan's men "making about three days march more than by the direct road" to Tinicum.⁸

If Sullivan's choice of course was open to question, his aggressive spirit was not. The brigadier general had his troops marching every day and for more hours than Lee ever had. After reaching

Germantown on December 14, he wrote to General Heath, "I beg you to hasten your march as fast as possible as General Washington writes in the most pressing manner for our troops to come on."[9] Unable to spare much time for foraging, Sullivan had difficulty providing sufficient food for the men, some of whose daily rations were only "a pint of flour per man." Private Howland repeated one soldier's bitter complaint: "If Congress can't give us bread and meat, they better make peace, and every man can go and look out for himself."[10] Sergeant John Smith of Lippitt's Rhode Islanders recalled, "Many of our men . . . whose shoes were worn out, repaired to the butcher's yard, and cut out a piece of raw hide, which they laced with strips of the same skin about their feet . . . . [but] as soon as my moccasins became frozen, they chafed my toes till they bled."[11]

On the morning of December 14, meanwhile, Wilkinson, who had set out north in search of General Gates and his column, found both at Sussex Court House. Wilkinson's news of Lee's capture "afflicted Gates profoundly," as the two men "had been long acquainted, had served together as British officers, and were personally attached."[12] Like Sullivan, Gates ordered his troops to take a northerly route to the Delaware River and to cross at Easton, Pennsylvania. Strangely, Gates left his division under the command of General Benedict Arnold, and with a small guard continued farther north to cross the Delaware above Easton. It appears that Gates wanted to be as far away from British dragoons as possible, in order to avoid Lee's fate. Along with his guards, Major Wilkinson, and his aide, John Trumbull, Jr., Gates decided to spend that night at a private residence in the western New Jersey mountains. To prevent word of his presence leaking out to local Tories, the Continental general introduced himself as "Captain Smith of Berkley, Virginia." According to Wilkinson, when the head of the household, a Jewish man named Levy, turned to Trumbull and asked if he hadn't seen him some time ago in Connecticut, Gates cut in, "No! He is a neighbor's son in Berkley." But Gates's suspicion was now fully aroused. Despite the poor weather, he now "ordered the horses to be saddled," and, recalled Wilkinson, the men "made a perilous passage of the river, through floating ice, and marched until midnight before we lay down in a dirty stove room which almost suffocated me."[13]

Sullivan's army marched into Germantown on the evening of December 13. Wasting no time, the general dashed off the following letter for immediate delivery to Washington:

Brigadier General John Sullivan, left, who assumed command of Lee's division after Lee's capture. Print from a portrait once in the possession of the Sullivan family. Major General Horatio Gates, right. Like Lee, he was a former officer in the British army. Printed for T. Robson, Newcastle upon Tyne, 1780. (*Library of Congress*)

My Dear General: It gives me the most pungent pain to inform your Excellency of the sad stroke America must feel in the loss of General Lee, who was this morning taken by the enemy near Vealtown. He ordered me yesterday morning to march for this place early, which I did, and by some fatality he was induced to go to [Basking Ridge], nearer the enemy by three miles than we were. Some Tories doubtless gave information, and this morning seventy of the light horse surrounded the house, and after a gallant resistance by him and his domestics, he was made a prisoner. I have taken every step to regain him, but almost despair of it. I received your Excellency's letters to him of the 10th and 11th instant, and shall endeavor to join the Army as soon as possible. . . . Dear General, I most heartily sympathize with you and my country in this affecting loss; and am your most obedient servant.[14]

If Lee's behavior had severely tested him, George Washington was nevertheless shaken by the news. To his cousin Lund Washington, the commander-in-chief wrote, "Our cause has also received a severe blow in the captivity of General Lee—unhappy man! Taken by his own imprudence! Going three or four miles from his own camp to lodge, and within 20 of the enemy."[15] Washington conveyed the "melancholy intelligence" to Congress, adding that "I sincerely regret General Lee's unhappy fate, and feel much for the loss of my country in his captivity."[16] The president of Congress, John Hancock, confirmed receipt of Washington's letter from Baltimore, and sadly concurred. "His loss must be extremely regretted by every friend to this country."[17] To Robert Morris, Hancock wrote, "I am afraid his loss will be severely felt, as he was, in a great measure, the idol of the officers, and possessed still more the confidence of the soldiery."[18] Lee's capture was no less disappointing to Nathanael Greene, who had received his own share of Lee's sniping for refusing to abandon Fort Washington. Greene wrote to his wife Catherine that Lee's capture "is a great loss to the American States, as he is a most consummate general," and told his cousin, Colonel Christopher Greene, that the loss was "more so as the hearts and confidence of the people are much bound up in him."[19]

At the same time, John Trumbull, Jr., the Connecticut governor's son who was marching with Gates's division, shared with his father a more telling view held by many other young Continental officers. "This is a misfortune that cannot be remedied, as we have no officer in the army of equal experience and merit." Trumbull believed that Lee's capture "deprived us of the best, almost only officer, who could rescue us from a situation so nigh desperate."[20] James Thacher, a physician from Plymouth, Massachusetts, serving in a Continental regiment, echoed Trumbull, writing: "The loss of this favorite general officer, it is feared, will be attended with very serious consequences, as respects the American Cause. . . . Such is now the gloomy aspect of our affairs that the whole country has taken the alarm; strong apprehensions are entertained that the British will soon have it in their power to vanquish the whole of the remains of the Continental army."[21] In March 1777, Boston's *New England Chronicle* would neatly summarize Lee's valuable, early war contributions to the patriot cause:

> It is impossible for an American to reflect upon the important services this illustrious general has rendered to the United States, by rousing and directing their military spirit in the beginning of the controversy; by forming their armies; by exciting a spirit of emulation and laudable ambition among their officers; by his attention to the health, clothing, etc. of

their soldiers; and lastly, by his zeal in inculcating the principles of liberty and good government upon all orders and classes of men.[22]

In the immediate wake of Lee's capture, other reactions were less grim. "This is a loss for us but I hope not so great a loss as people in general imagine," commented Congressional delegate William Whipple to his New Hampshire colleague, Josiah Bartlett.[23] Private John Howland of Lippitt's Regiment wrote, "I confess it was not a subject of any grief to me, as I had known him in Providence before he was appointed to our army, and thought we could manufacture as good generals out of American stuff as he was." Howland conceded, however, that his view "was not the prevalent opinion."[24] When Colonel John Cadwalader of Philadelphia grumbled on December 22 that Lee's "capture had damped the spirit of the army very much, and everything looked very gloomy," Captain Thomas Rodney of Delaware pointedly disagreed. "I did not view his capture as unfavorable," he asserted, "but as an advantage—that too much confidence had been put in General Lee, that this must have greatly embarrassed the commander-in-chief, as he was afraid to do anything without consulting General Lee, but now he would be at liberty to exert his own talents."[25] Along the same lines, Nathanael Greene considered Lee's capture part of God's plan, "as if he meant the freedom of America should be established by Americans only."[26]

Some patriots, stunned at how easily an experienced officer (and an ex-British officer, at that) such as Lee had been captured, saw something much darker in the affair. Lieutenant Colonel Samuel Blachley Webb of the Connecticut Continental line believed that "we shall find it hard work to convince many officers and soldiers that he is not a traitor."[27] After the war David Ramsey, in his 1789 history of the American Revolution, summarized this sentiment:

> [Lee] had been repeatedly ordered to come forward with his division and join General Washington, but these orders were not obeyed. This circumstance, and the dangerous crisis of public affairs, together with his being alone at some distance, from the troops which he commanded, begat suspicions that he chose to fall into the hands of the British. Though these apprehensions were without foundation, they produced the same extensive mischief, as if they had been realities. The Americans had reposed extravagant confidence in his military

talents, and experience of regular European war. Merely to have lost such an idol of the states at any time, would have been distressful, but losing him under circumstances, which favored an opinion that, despairing of the American cause, he chose to be taken a prisoner, was to many an extinguishment of every hope.[28]

Elbridge Gerry, a young Massachusetts delegate to the Continental Congress, confessed to James Warren that he was "at a loss to account" for Lee's capture, adding that "Time will instruct us further on the matter and may remove every suspicion unfavorable to his character."[29]

Other Continental officers discussed the version of Lee's capture reported by Captain Virnejoux, to whom Sullivan in his December 13 letter to Washington had indicated had "behaved with great bravery in defending the General; and had his advice been taken, the General would have escaped."[30] Virnejoux, upon the appearance of Tarleton's troopers, had exchanged fire with them from within the tavern, refusing to surrender or flee. Had Boisbertrand, Bradford, Wilkinson, and even Lee done the same, they might have been able to hold off their attackers until alerted American troops reached the area. But neither Wilkinson nor Lee fired a shot. And Boisbertrand's efforts ceased with his escape from the tavern.

Thirteen months later, on January 20, 1778, at Scott's Farm, between the main American camp at Valley Forge and British-occupied Philadelphia, Captain Henry "Light Horse Harry" Lee of the Continental cavalry and some ten of his of his men rested in a stone house. They would soon demonstrate how a house could be successfully defended by a small group of determined soldiers. Obtaining information of Lee's location, General Howe sent from Philadelphia to surprise him a detachment of cavalry (either forty or eighty men, the reports conflict), under the command of Major Richard Crewe of the 17th Dragoons and with the assistance of Captain Banastre Tarleton. Alerted to the arrival of the dragoons, Lee and eight of his troopers grabbed their weapons, manned windows and doors inside the stone house, and began firing at their attackers. A tenth soldier, like Boisbertrand at Widow White's Tavern, panicked and fled the house, resulting in his capture. Some of Crewe's dragoons rushed the farm house and attempted to climb through unmanned windows, where hand-to-hand fighting ensued.[31] Crewe then ordered Captain

Tarleton to drive the horses of Lee's cavalrymen from nearby stables. Tarleton and his detachment of dragoons charged, as they had borne down on Widow White's Tavern a year earlier. "But Harry Lee was no Charles Lee," as Tarleton's biographer wrote.[32] Well-aimed fire from the stone house drove off Tarleton and his men, saving Lee's horses. A fellow British officer wrote that Tarleton "miraculously escaped with his life, having his horse wounded in three places, his helmet shot off his head, and shot through his light dragoon jacket."[33] Crewe then called off the attack, taking with him a wounded officer and a sergeant. But he left behind two dead and four wounded, one of them mortally. Lee's men suffered just three wounded.[34]

Many more Americans, sure of Lee's loyalty to the patriot cause, looked for another explanation for his capture—Tory treachery. One story was passed on by William Bradford, shortly after the major rode into Morristown on December 13, to Joseph Trumbull, a Continental commissary and another son of Governor Trumbull's. In a December 17 letter to his father, the commissary wrote that Bradford had informed him that Harcourt's party was "led by a Tory, who was with the General complaining of the loss of a horse taken by the army the evening before. He found out where the General was to lodge and breakfast, and that he was to be at this tavern [Widow White's] about noon. He left them, and rode eighteen miles in the night to Brunswick, and returned with the party of light horse."[35] This story soon evolved into a version that was widely circulated in American newspapers (because it was first printed in a Hartford, Connecticut, newspaper on December 23, 1776, its source was probably also Joseph Trumbull): "Intelligence of General Lee's unguarded situation was given to the enemy last night, by an inhabitant of Basking Ridge, personally known to the general, and who had made great pretensions of friendship for the American cause, though at heart the greatest villain that ever existed. This Judas rode all the preceding night to carry the intelligence, and served as a pilot to conduct the enemy, and came personally with them to the house where the general was taken."[36]

This account is likely untrue. All evidence indicates that Harcourt learned of Lee's presence at Basking Ridge from local Tory sympathizers while out searching for the general's army. The fact that Bradford reported this version to Trumbull on the day of Lee's capture gives it some credibility, yet he apparently made no mention of the unidentified Tory a few weeks later when he gave a full account of the raid to the Reverend Ezra Stiles.[37] And Harcourt's party left from Pennington, not Brunswick. Moreover, if Harcourt had known from the outset of his trip that Lee was at Basking Ridge, he likely would have forced his men to ride all night to make sure they nabbed their prey. It is possible, however, that this mysterious Tory did exist. He may simply have been one of the Loyalist sympathizers who met up with Harcourt's party on its way north on the morning of December 13.

A similar version of this story was told by Brigadier General Adam Stephen to Thomas Jefferson in a letter written about December 20. Stephen was then with Washington's army on the western side of the Delaware River. Stephen wrote that Lee had "lodged the night before at a house recommended to him by a Colonel Vanhorn, a person in the enemy's service, who was appointed to sign pardons" for New Jersey residents willing to sign the oath of allegiance to the British Crown. Stephen also wrote that the British troopers were "supposed to be detached by the advice of Vanhorn."[38] This Vanhorn could have been Colonel Philip Vanhorn, who was thought to have harbored Loyalist sympathies, but who also had the respect of both sides. One of his daughters even married Lee's friend, Colonel Stephen Moylan.[39] There is no indication that this Vanhorn, or anyone by that name, was otherwise blamed or punished for this alleged misdeed. He might simply have innocently recommended Widow White's Tavern to Lee, thus giving rise to this story.

Another story with a Tory connection would soon emerge. This one included a name, Major Richard Witham Stockton of the New Jersey Volunteers, a Loyalist unit.[40] On March 2, 1777, Colonel Hugh Hughes, a New York deputy quartermaster general, wrote: "A few days since a part of General Putnam's division attacked a party of the enemy about three miles from Brunswick and made 60 prisoners, among whom is Stockton who led the party who took General Lee."[41] At about the same time, a New England newspaper printed the letter of an unidentified American officer, who wrote: "I have the pleasure to acquaint you, that a few days ago a party of General Putnam's division, attacked and defeated a party of Tory soldiers, in Monmouth, killed a number, and took about 40, with their arms, and one Major Stockton, an infamous Tory who commanded them." The newspaper's editors then added in italics, "*The above Major Stockton is the identical villain who betrayed his*

Excellency General Lee into the hands of the enemy."[42] Shortly thereafter an unidentified Tory wrote from Philadelphia: "Major Stockton was brought prisoner here during my absence to Lancaster, as were the men who were taken with him near Brunswick. They threaten the major very hard, as they say he assisted in taking Lee. He was brought to this city in a wagon, with his back towards the horse, in irons, and a drum going before him, beating the Rogue's March."[43] Called "Double Dick" by his enemies, Stockton's skill as a guide had also earned him a more complimentary sobriquet, the "Famous Land Pilot."[44] But it would appear that the accusations made against Stockton, after his capture at Bennet's Neck, New Jersey, on February 18, 1777, were false. Apart from these March 1777 references, there is no evidence in either British or American records of Stockton having served as a guide for Harcourt. When patriot authorities interrogated him, Stockton denied any role in Lee's seizure.[45] In any event, as a commissioned officer of a Loyalist regiment in the British army, both at the time of Lee's and his own capture, Stockton could not have been prosecuted in court for any role he may have played at Basking Ridge.

Stockton's captors may have focused on the wrong man. After the war Stockton's subordinate in the New Jersey Volunteers, Captain Asher Dunham of Hanover, New Jersey, who was captured with Stockton at Bennet's Neck, submitted a claim for compensation from the British government. He stated that "in November 1776 he joined the Royal Army at New Brunswick in New Jersey, and gave them every intelligence and rendered them every other service he was capable of." Dunham added that he "was at the time frequently employed by General Skinner and others to procure information for the Royal Army, that he was in the country on that service at the time Colonel Harcourt took the rebel Major General Lee, and did actually join him on that occasion."[46] It is impossible to confirm Dunham's claim. If it was true, he must not have divulged it to patriot authorities. In any event, Dunham shared Stockton's fate: he was, as he later described it, "marched in irons from Princeton to Philadelphia gaol [jail]" and "closely imprisoned in different gaols until sometime in the month of August 1778," when he was exchanged.[47]

Shortly after Lee's capture, Captain Thomas Rodney met the physician to whose home Lee had been brought upon Harcourt's return to Hillsborough. The doctor, according to Rodney, recalled that during the meal with Lieutenant Colonel Mawhood:

General Lee requested that the man who had betrayed him should be brought in, and when the General saw him he abused him as a villain worth the punishment of the most base and inhuman traitor. The doctor could not remember the villain's name but said that he was a Continental officer dressed in blue faced with red and wore a brown cloak, lined with blue baize; that he heard him [the deserter] tell the Colonel, that he had been in the Continental service but that he had got tired of it, and had lately given the British army all the information in his power, and now that he had informed the light horse of General Lee, and had gone with them, and shown them where he was so that they had him in their possession, he hoped they would remember and reward him. The doctor says that he took such particular notice of the villain that though he forgot his name he will never forget his face.[48]

The fact that Lee did dine with British officers at Hillsborough gives the physician's story some credibility. But there is no other evidence of this purported Continental deserter's existence. Lee's surviving letters do not mention him. And the contemporary accounts of Harcourt, Tarleton, Muenchhausen, Howe, and others are consistent in stating that Harcourt's mission was simply to seek intelligence of Lee's army, and that the he discovered Lee's quarters by chance. However, as with the mysterious Tory described above, if this deserter did exist, he may have met up with Harcourt's party on its way northward the morning of December 13.

That one or more Tories south of Basking Ridge provided word of Lee's location was confirmed by Washington and others. In his note to Lund Washington shortly after Lee's capture, Washington alluded to "a rascally Tory" giving "notice" of Lee's presence at Basking Ridge. "A large part of the Jerseys have given every proof of disaffection" from the patriot cause, Washington further complained.[49] Dr. Thacher, in his diary, noted that "information" of Lee "lodging at a house three or four miles from his troops . . . was, by some Tories, communicated to Colonel Harcourt of the British light horse."[50] Thacher's information was likely the most accurate. "Oh! What a damn'd sneaking way of being kidnapped. I can't bear to think of it," wrote Dr. William Shippen, an army physician then tending to some of Lee's former soldiers.[51]

One of the civilians whom Harcourt and Tarleton had grabbed and interrogated on their way toward Widow White's Tavern was soon identified. He was James Compton of Basking Ridge itself. Brought before the New Jersey Council of Safety on August 29, 1777, to be questioned about various suspicious activities, Compton "acknowledged to have been at the taking of General Lee but says the British light horsemen forced him to go with them for that purpose, threatening to kill him on refusal."[52] Compton's story may have been true. But, given his Tory leanings, he may also have voluntarily provided the information.

Perhaps the most shocking aspect of Lee leaving himself so vulnerable was that he knew full well how many Tories resided in northern New Jersey. Moreover, he had gained a reputation for dealing harshly with them. According to Lieutenant Colonel Webb, Washington was "much surprised General Lee should venture to lodge from camp in a country where he must have known we had many enemies."[53] Throughout the war, Tories had passed on important local intelligence to the British army. Lee was aware of that, which in part explains why he handled them sternly. Indeed, in his last letter to Gates, written at Widow White's Tavern, he had observed with alarming prescience, "I must act with the greatest circumspection—Tories are in my front, rear and on my flanks—the mass of the people is strangely contaminated." And yet, with British army outposts no more than twenty miles away, and both Cornwallis and Howe having dragoons at their disposal, Lee demonstrated alarming "imprudence," as Washington described it. The American Commissary of Prisoners, Elias Boudinot, who would visit Lee in his captivity, was harsh but accurate in ascribing Lee's capture to the general's "own extreme negligence & folly."[54]

According to a legend born a few years later, Lee's "folly" was staying at Widow White's Tavern in order to sleep with a local woman. In late August 1781, while French forces and Washington's main army were marching through New Jersey on their way to Yorktown, Virginia, a French officer named Baron Ludwig von Closen took a short detour to visit the famous tavern "to learn the circumstances that could have caused General Lee to have fallen into the hands of the English." There Closen was informed "that believing himself to be secure, since he [Lee] was 40 miles from the English cantonment, he preferred to spend the night there with a simple guard consisting of a corporal and four men *since he was rather smitten by the lady of the house.* One of the lady's cousins, who was jealous of him, went underhandedly to Colonel Harcourt . . . that the general was in this house with a small guard.... This poor General Lee... will be blamed for this eternally."55 This version of Lee's capture does not make clear how Lee could have been smitten with the "lady of the house," since he had never before visited Basking Ridge or the immediate area. The story erroneously held that Harcourt broke down the tavern door prior to taking Lee prisoner inside, and that Lee's aide-de-camp (presumably Major Bradford) escaped out of a window.

Lee would have been chagrined to hear that some were comparing the disasters at Fort Washington and Fort Lee, for which Lee had heaped scorn on Washington, with Lee's capture, for which Lee himself was most responsible. "A fatality strange indeed for some time past hath seemed to attend our affairs," wrote William Ellery, a Rhode Island delegate to the Continental Congress. "The loss of Fort Washington, where 2600 of our men were captivated in an inglorious manner, the loss of Fort Lee by surprise, with a great quantity of stores, and the capture of the General who was honored by his name being given to that fort, and in short all our affairs have in a strange manner proceeded."56

While some Americans wondered about Lee's mindset at the time of his capture, others dwelt on the disrespect with which they thought Lee had been treated. One report published in American newspapers focused on British arrogance after Lee had been brought to British headquarters at Brunswick:

> The enemy showed an ungenerous—nay, boyish triumph—after they had got him secure at Brunswick, by making his horse drunk while they toasted their King till they were in the same condition. A band or two of music played all night to proclaim their joy for this important acquisition. They say we cannot now stand another campaign. Mistaken fools! To think the fate of America depended on one man. They will find ere long that it has no other effect than to urge us on to a noble revenge.57

Some patriots harped on Harcourt's purported failure to treat Lee like a gentleman. Mercy Warren, in her early history of the American Revolution, wrote that "Lee was not suffered to take either hat or cloak and thus in a ruffian-like manner, was he conducted to British headquarters."58 Even Washington complained to a relative that Harcourt's party had carried off Lee "with every mark of indignity—not even suffering him to get his hat, or surtout coat."⁵⁹ To Washington, who was always extremely sensitive to any slights to his gentlemanly status, Lee's treatment constituted the ultimate insult. The young, more rash, John Trumbull, Jr., wrote to his father, "The inhuman rascals would not permit the General to take his hat and coat, but carried him off almost naked."⁶⁰

Such reports were largely unfounded. Wilkinson recalled seeing Lee "hurried off in triumph, bareheaded, in his slippers and blanket coat, his collar open, and his shirt very much soiled."⁶¹ But Wilkinson was probably describing Lee's appearance shortly before he stepped out of the tavern to surrender to Harcourt, when he last laid eyes on the general. The closest witness to Lee's departure was William Bradford, who subsequently informed Reverend Ezra Stiles that after being ordered to mount a horse, Lee "requested his hat and cloak." Bradford stated that, as he had accompanied Lee outside, he was then permitted by Harcourt to retrieve from the tavern Lee's hat and cloak, and that he did so, laying both down on the ground next to the general.⁶² It is possible, however, that Harcourt, in his haste to leave the area, simply ordered Lee's garments brought along. According to an account supplied to a British naval officer, Harcourt indeed did not give Lee "time to put his hat on."⁶³

Another version of Lee's state of dress when he left the tavern appeared in a letter written on December 21, 1776, by an unknown American author. "The General came down without his hat or side coat," the writer claimed, and said, "I hope you will use me like a gentleman; let me get my hat and coat." The Captain [presumably Colonel Harcourt] said, "General Lee, I know you well. I know you are a gentleman—you shall be used as such. I know you too well to suffer you to go for your hat and coat," and ordered him to mount.⁶⁴ This account, when considered alongside Bradford's, is also credible. Harcourt may not have wanted to risk Lee slipping away, and instead dispatched Bradford to fetch the general's hat and coat. In fact, Harcourt would have been justified in denying Lee his hat and coat, due simply to the strained circumstances. As British major general James Robertson wrote to Lieutenant General Henry Clinton on December 19, Lee "came to the door without a hat; he was not allowed time to get this nor to put on his surtout coat, the firing having alarmed the enemy."⁶⁵

Regardless, at some point, Lee evidently did put on his hat and coat, based on the recollections of Ensign Martin Hunter, in the light infantry of the British 52nd Regiment, who described seeing the captured general on his arrival at Pennington on December 13. "General Lee was brought in behind a dragoon—so dirty and ungentlemanlike a looking general I never saw before," Hunter wrote. "Everybody, of course, turned out to look at him. He had on an old blue coat turned up with red, an old cocked hat, and greasy leather breeches."[66] If Lee was dressed in his usual slovenly manner, his honor at least had remained unbruised.

Sketchy American reports also tended to exaggerate the number of dragoons in Harcourt's party, putting the number at seventy.[67] Fault for this lay, in part, with Bradford. The major had given that estimate to General Sullivan, who relayed it to Washington.[68] Bradford later reduced that figure to "about fifty."[69] The actual number was just thirty-three.

Word of Lee's capture thrilled officers in the British army in America. Captain Friedrich von Muenchhausen, of Howe's staff, wrote in his diary, "Victoria! We have taken General Lee, the only rebel general whom we had cause to fear. . . . for as to his ability and knowledge of the art of warfare, he is undoubtedly the first general."[70] The wife of a captain in the Scottish 71st Regiment, while writing a letter in New York City, was interrupted with the stunning news. "This instant five or six officers came running into the room to tell me that the infernal rebel Lee is taken for certain," she wrote, "which gives us all joy that such a villain is in custody."[71] British officers were rightfully proud of their army's feat and surprised by the ease of Lee's capture. "It is very remarkable that this great hero should allow himself to be taken without any great resistance by so small a party of dragoons . . . within 500 yards of his own camp where he had 4,000 men," wrote one.[72]

Some British observers, raised as they were in a stratified society and tending to see events as led by great men, thought Lee's capture would end the war. The pleased Lieutenant Colonel Harcourt himself, in a December 17 letter to his brother, George Simon Harcourt, Viscount Nuneham, wrote that after the brilliant New Jersey campaign and his capture of the "most active and most enterprising of the enemy's generals . . . it seems to be the universal opinion the rebels will no longer refuse treating upon the terms which have been offered them."[73] Lieutenant General Clinton thought that Washington had no military ideas except those that Lee had put into his head.74 Captain Charles Fielding, commander of the 32-gun frigate *Diamond* stationed off Newport, Rhode Island, opined, "I think they [the rebels] cannot stand long, as Lee was their chief man."75

Harcourt's fellow officers celebrated the lieutenant colonel's role in Lee's capture. Shortly after the raiders returned to Brunswick, General Howe praised "the readiness with which Lieut.-Colonel Harcourt undertook the command of the detachment that made General Lee a prisoner, as of the address and gallantry manifested by him on that critical occasion."76 An unidentified British officer penned a letter extolling "Colonel Harcourt, whose bravery and address upon this occasion forms at present the general conversation of the camp."77 Another officer, in a letter published in the March 4, 1777, edition of London's *St. James's Chronicle*, gushed, "Colonel Harcourt's activity in this affair, as on every other since his arrival, merits the highest ecumenisms."

Naturally bitter toward a man who had turned against the army that had molded him from 1744 through 1763, British officers eagerly discussed Lee's fate. "I am happy to hear that Mr. Lee is in custody," crowed one, "and I will be still happier to hear in the next accounts from New York that he has been tried as a deserter, condemned and hanged."78 Another, stationed in New York agreed, stating "It is the general opinion that General Lee will be tried as a deserter."79 Another officer, serving in the 64th Regiment, assured his friend in London, that Lee "will be destined to the cord."80 Still another officer, stationed in Newport, Rhode Island, wrote to a friend in Edinburgh that he hoped Lee "will meet the fate he deserves."81 Perhaps the most pointed comments published on Lee's future, however, were penned by an unidentified officer in the 6th Regiment who had participated in the New Jersey campaign. "Had I been fortunate as to have the command of a party that took Lieut. Col. Lee, or any man that ever served in our Army," he offered, "he should neither appear before any tribunal erected by the laws of England, nor can I conceive that in putting him in instant death I could injure my character as a man or officer; he has no claim to mercy as a prisoner, his offense is too heinous."82

It was a matter of great speculation among British and German officers whether Lee, when he surrendered, conducted himself with the honor befitting a gentleman. General William Howe, in a letter to General Clinton, stated that "General Lee made his appearance at the door, begging for his life."[83] Both Captain Muenchhausen and Major Stephen Kemble stated that Lee asked that his life "be spared."[84] Captain Thomas Harris, later Lord Harris, of the 28th Regiment, claimed that "Lee behaved as cowardly in this transaction as he had dishonorably in every other. After firing one or two shots from the house, he came out and entreated our troops to spare his life." Harris continued, "Had he behaved with proper spirit, I should have pitied him."[85] Two other British officers also claimed that Lee "begged for his life, which Colonel Harcourt gave him."[86] They may have read the December 23 edition of the *New York Gazette and Weekly Mercury*, published by Loyalist Hugh Gaine, in which it was asserted that "Lee, fearful of being put to the sword, begged his life in a manner which shows that where just and loyal principles are not, true courage is never to be found. His life was granted by the brave commander for further consideration."[87]

The idea that the American general begged for his life, however, is not supported by the statements of William Bradford, William Harcourt, and Banastre Tarleton, who likely would have mentioned such extreme behavior. The most reliable of the American accounts, by Bradford, reported that "General Lee came forward and surrendered himself as prisoner-of-war, saying he trusted they would use him like a gentleman. Of this, one of them [presumably Harcourt] gave assurance and ordered him instantly to mount."[88] Lee's request to be treated as a gentleman does not seem to have been unreasonable, but even here some British officers would have found it offensive that Lee would have questioned Harcourt's honor.

As for Lee's internal response to his predicament, Bradford told patriot minister Ezra Stiles that "He whose courage never failed before, when he walked out and surrendered himself, lost all the blood from his face and was pale with ____."[89] In retelling the story Stiles left the last word blank. Bradford had presumably used the word "fright" or something similar.

Of course, Loyalists were thrilled that the hated Lee had been snatched back from his adopted army. Prominent Pennsylvania Loyalist Joseph Galloway wrote that the capture "has done Colonel Harcourt immortal honors." He added, with not a little exaggeration, "Indeed, history gives no account of a more brave and successful maneuver."[90]

On Tuesday, February 12, 1777, Captain James Wallace, commander of the 50-gun HMS *Experiment*, arrived at Lord George Germain's house at Pall Mall, in London, having carried across the Atlantic Ocean the latest dispatches from America. They included the stunning news of Lee's capture.[91] Many British newspapers exaggerated the importance of Lee's demise. "The capture of General Lee must greatly accelerate the ruin of the Americans," one asserted. "In the plenitude of their power, and the infancy of the war, they had but three generals, Montgomery, Lee and Washington, who had seen service, or know the art militarily systematically. They are now reduced to *one*, and at a time when they are driven out of their principal towns, the credit of their finances impaired, and their general resources but *few* indeed."[92] In summarizing the events of 1777, the British *Annual Register* noted of Lee's capture: "The rejoicing in Great Britain on this occasion was equal at least to the dejection of the Americans. It was conjectured that some personal animosities between this general and several officers in the army, as well as persons of power at court, contributed not a little to the triumph and exultation of that time."[93]

In their rush to cover the story in the weeks that followed, English newspaper reports stretched to include the fanciful. In one account, "Colonel Harcourt rushed into the house with a brace of pistols, and found General Lee in a room sitting with his sword lying on the table."[94] In another, "Lee killed two of the light horse and then surrendered; his aides-de-camp, two Frenchmen, were cut to pieces, as they would not surrender."[95] Another story had Lee confined on board a British warship in the English Channel and saying to Harcourt upon his capture, "he intended to take the benefit of the proclamation"—Howe's offer of a pardon if the individual pledged himself to the King—but Lee was informed "it was then too late."[96] This spurious account led one correspondent to question Lee's "presence of mind," as if no gentlemen officer would deign to seek such a pardon.[97] A still more elaborate story played on Lee's reputation for erratic behavior. "General Lee . . . fell on his knees to Colonel Harcourt, with his sword in his hand," went this version. "Suddenly, however, recovering his panic, he flew into a violent rant of his having for a moment attained the supreme command. He gave many signs of wildness, and of a mind not perfectly right."[98]

Somehow, the *Morning Chronicle and London Advertiser* got hold of a copy of a letter purportedly written by Lee following his capture, and published it on February 19, 1777. Its editors wrote:

The following is a genuine copy of a letter, sent by General Lee, after he was taken by Colonel Harcourt, to his old friend, Captain Kennedy, in our army: "The amazing alertness of Colonel Harcourt, and the poltroonery of my guard, have thrown me into the hands of your army; whatever may be my fate, I hope to sustain it with fortitude; sure no man was ever engaged in a better cause; but fate seems determined there shall be no freedom, and a horrid, gloomy slavery universal."

Two days later, the newspaper retracted its claim that the letter was legitimate, informing its readers, "The letter laid before the public, as if written by General Lee to Captain K__, is suspected to be an imposition, as by comparing it with the speech, attributed to Caractacus, when before Claudius, may more evidently appear."[99] The newspaper's editors assumed that its readers were familiar with the story of Caractacus, the British king who, after being captured by the Romans in 50 A.D., reportedly convinced Emperor Claudius to pardon him. Historians have since almost universally dismissed Lee's letter as a forgery. However, the author has uncovered new information indicating that Lee likely did pen this sentence to his old friend Primrose Kennedy, then a captain in the 44th Regiment recovering from illness in England.[100]

Lee's fate would continue to be the subject of intense scrutiny in England, as it was with British officers in North America. The February 15 edition of the *Morning Post and Daily Advertiser* repeated the rumors that "Mr. Lee will be tried and executed almost as soon as he arrives" in England, but then called this view "an erroneous notion." Instead, it reported, "General Lee, we hear, will be confined in the Tower" and his court-martial will be delayed "till the American rebellion is finally subdued." Two days later, the newspaper offered a correction: "It is now confidently asserted that General Lee is not coming over to England, but the orders are already dispatched to General Howe to try him by martial law, and first for breach of a certain section of the articles of war in flying his colors as an English officer and aiding and assisting the enemy in the rebellion attacking men of the King's forces." The implication was that Lee would be found guilty and hanged in America.

On February 23, Lord George Germain received a letter from Howe, dated December 20, 1776, addressing the topic of treating Lee as a military deserter, subject to hanging. Upon receiving the news of Lee's capture, Howe had ordered his judge advocate general to Brunswick to prosecute his new prisoner on a charge of desertion.[101] But in one of Howe's councils, an officer had recalled the newspaper report of Lee resigning his British commission as a lieutenant colonel prior to assuming his position as general in the Continental army. This raised the question of whether Lee could be classified as a deserter. Nor was it clear whether an officer who was on half-pay and therefore on temporary retirement could be considered a deserter.[102] If Howe acted precipitously and Lee was hanged after a hasty court-martial, the British commander-in-chief might be vilified not only in American newspapers, but in some British publications as well. Furthermore, if an English court later concluded that Lee had properly resigned and never should have been court-martialed in the first place, let alone hanged, Howe risked facing a lawsuit and paying hefty damages.

General Howe was willing to take the time needed to seek a judicial determination from London. In his February 20 letter to Germain, he wrote: "General Lee, being considered in the light of a deserter, is kept a close prisoner but I do not bring him to trial as a doubt has arose whether by a public resignation of his half-pay prior to his entry into the rebel army he is still amenable to the military law as a deserter, upon which point I shall wait for information; and if the decision should be for a trial upon this ground, I beg to have the judges' opinions to lay before the court."[103] The careful Howe wanted to be protected by a court's written decision before he tried Lee as a deserter and, if convicted, hanged him.

At a meeting of the British Cabinet on February 25, Lee's fate was decided: "Sir William Howe to be directed to send Major-General Lee prisoner to England."[104] On March 3, Lord Germain responded to Howe, "As you have difficulties about bringing General Lee to a trial in America, it is his Majesty's pleasure that you send him to Great Britain by the first ship of war."[105] Lee would be tried by a military court in England as a deserter. Howe would be relieved of the responsibility for the court-martial and his request for a written legal opinion could be conveniently ignored.

In Great Britain, the hero of the day was Lieutenant Colonel William Harcourt. Howe shared details of the raid in a December 20, 1776, dispatch to Lord Germain. "Being confident this gallant action will not escape his Majesty's gracious attention, it is needless for me to recommend Lieutenant Colonel Harcourt to the King's notice upon this occasion."[106] Howe's recommendation was indeed not necessary. When news of Lee's capture reached London on February 12, King George III was holding a levee at the Queen's Palace at St. James's Park, at which were present a host of dignitaries, including foreign ministers, most of the officers of state, the Duke of Hamilton, Lords Derby, Spencer, and Sandwich—and Lord Earl Harcourt, William Harcourt's father.[107] The March 1, 1777, edition of the *London Evening Post* reported that "Upon Lord Harcourt going to the levee after the news of General Lee's being taken, the King came eagerly to him: 'Oh! My Lord! Your son has behaved with the utmost gallantry; it gives me the utmost pleasure, and I doubt not it does the same to you,' which pleased his Lordship not a little. His Majesty added, 'I shall take care of Colonel Harcourt; leave his fortune to my care.'"[108]

Lord Germain was equally effusive in his praise of Lee's captor, telling Howe, "The behavior of Lieutenant Colonel Harcourt, in taking General Lee, has done him infinite honor, and could not (as you justly observe) escape his Majesty's attention. I have it consequently in express command to signify, through you, his royal approbation, as well of the readiness with which the colonel undertook the command of the detachment, as of the address and gallantry which he manifested on that critical occasion."[109] Understandably, Harcourt expected that a promotion would soon be coming his way.

Neither King George III, Lord Germain, or Lieutenant Colonel Harcourt could know that, as so often is the case with history-making events, Lee's capture had unintended consequences. Each man felt that Lee's capture would shorten the war. Instead, the divisive general's capture made possible Washington's pivotal, perhaps war-saving victories at Trenton on December 26 and Princeton on January 3.

One day after Lee's seizure, on December 14, Howe, still stymied from crossing the Delaware River by a lack of flatboats, concluded that he would be unable to threaten Philadelphia in the current campaign. With "the weather having become too severe to keep the field," he ordered his troops, then concentrated in two wings at Trenton and Pennington, to disperse and seek shelter in towns spread across middle and northern New Jersey.[110] As Howe explained to General Clinton in a December 21 letter, the British army "could not penetrate" beyond Trenton, "the Rebels having burnt and destroyed all the boats upon the Delaware [River] for many miles up, as soon as their army had passed. The season being too far advanced to remain longer in the field, a considerable corps of the army is gone into cantonments in the Jerseys."111 Howe conceded on December 20 in a letter to Germain, "The chain, I own, is rather too extensive, but ... I conclude the troops will be in perfect security."112 The 16th Regiment of Light Dragoons settled in for the winter at Brunswick and Princeton.

Meanwhile, Brigadier General John Sullivan's Continental troops, now numbering just 2,500, marched throughout most of December 14 and 15, before beginning to cross a swift-flowing, 500-yard-wide stretch of the Delaware River from the ferry landing at Philipsburg, New Jersey, opposite Easton, Pennsylvania. The bulk of the army was across by December 16.113 The next morning, "in good spirits and much pleased with their General Sullivan," they marched nine miles south to the small town of Bethlehem, arriving in the evening.114 There they found recuperating Gates, his staff, and his three Continental regiments totalling 600 men, who had crossed the river one day ahead of them.115

George III, king of England. Mezzotint by E. Fisher from painting by Benjamin West, published in 1778. (*National Archives*)

Brigadier General William Stirling, who in a December 12 letter to Washington had offered to cross the Delaware and cooperate with Lee in an attack on a British outpost, also entered Easton on December 16. "I came from Headquarters in hopes of effecting a junction of the troops under the command of yourself, General Gates and General Sullivan," he informed General Heath, "and attempting something on the enemy, but that is now too late, as the troops under General Sullivan and General Gates are already on the west side of the Delaware." Stirling advised Heath, whose troops were still on the march through northern New Jersey, to make the river crossing at Easton as well.116

Gates's division departed Easton on December 16 and 17, with Sullivan's force following. The hungry, poorly clothed, and tired soldiers crossed the Lehigh River and headed south. Most of them joined Washington's army at Bristol, Pennsylvania, on December 21 and 22.[117] Seeing his force double in size emboldened Washington to consider a rare, winter-time raid across the Delaware, before enlistments of many of his men could expire at the end of the year. Transporting his army across the icy river on a stormy Christmas night, Washington shocked the enemy—and many of his fellow countrymen—by delivering a surprise attack on the isolated Hessian garrison at Trenton. At a cost of a dozen men, Washington's Americans killed or wounded 105 and captured 890 of the enemy. Then, brilliantly side-stepping a powerful force under General Cornwallis sent by Howe to track him down, Washington re-crossed the river and punished British regulars under Lieutenant Colonel Charles Mawhood at Princeton on January 3. Having inflicted two embarrassing defeats on the British army, Washington left Princeton on January 3 and marched his army north toward Rocky Hill, a small town thirteen miles southwest of Brunswick.[118]

All the while, Lee remained under heavy guard at Brunswick. But he was far from being out of American reach. On December 31, Colonel John Cadwalader learned that just 250 British troops held Brunswick, and boldly decided on a raid in force to free Lee. The force he assembled, recalled Joseph Reed, included "about 500 Rhode Island troops, a part of the detachment commanded by General Lee before his capture . . . without shoes or blankets and otherwise in a wretched plight for a winter campaign."[119] But he also had fresh, well-provisioned and supplied militia from Philadelphia. One of the officers assigned to the task, Captain Thomas Rodney of Delaware, wrote:

> This morning by day light our light troops were ordered to make a forced march to-day, and surprise the town in the dead of night, and bring him [Lee] off. We accordingly set off, and pushed on to Cranberry from whence we were to go on horseback after night and execute the plan. This is a little village scattered on both sides of the road, about 12 miles from Allentown. We stayed here and refreshed ourselves until dark, waiting the return of two spies, who had been sent to reconnoiter Brunswick and the British troops that were on their way from Amboy. On their return they brought accounts that these troops had become alarmed and had gone to reinforce Brunswick with 1,500 men, which rendered our plan abortive,

and being but five miles from the enemy we held a council of war and concluded it best to return. . . . We accordingly marched back to Allentown through a very dark night and roads half leg deep which worried the troops exceedingly.[120]

Colonel John Cadwalader, commander of an American force that nearly tried to free Lee from his captivity at Brunswick. (*Stryker, Battles of Trenton and Princeton*)

By January 2, however, British forces at Brunswick had been dramatically reduced. At least some of those who remained resented looking after the prized general. As Irish-born Lieutenant Loftus Cliffe of the 46th Regiment wrote to a relative in Britain, "we are here with a battalion of the Guards to prevent Mr. Lee's rescue; I wish he was shot or hanged."[121] Perhaps Lieutenant Cliffe sensed how near Washington's army was. Cornwallis certainly did. Early on January 3, after hearing of Washington's attack at Princeton, Cornwallis's column, led by the 16th Light Dragoons, marched after the Americans, but reached Princeton an hour too late. At 4:30 p.m., Cornwallis ordered the bulk of his column out on a forced march sixteen miles to Brunswick in case, one British officer wrote, "George Washington marched to possess it or to recover General Lee."[122]

At Brunswick, Brigadier General Edward Mathew took the precaution of sending Lee north across the Raritan River, accompanied by guards and as many of the army's war stores (as well as the cash for paying the troops) as his wagons could carry.[123] British concern was well founded. Washington, learning of Cornwallis's approach, had taken his men northeastward toward Brunswick. "We at first intended to have made a forced march to Brunswick at which place was the baggage of their whole army and General Lee—but our men, having been without either rest, rum or provision for two nights and days, were unequal to the task of marching 17 miles further," General Henry Knox wrote. "If we could have procured 1,000 fresh men at Princeton to have pushed for Brunswick we should have struck one of the most brilliant strokes in all history."[124]

Instead, Washington altered course, and led his exhausted and hungry troops north to Somerset Court House (now Millstone).

They arrived in the evening and slept on frozen ground.[125] Meanwhile, at about 6:00 a.m. on January 4, the vanguard of Cornwallis's exhausted troops reached Brunswick, where all was quiet.[126] Lee eventually returned to his cell at Brunswick. On January 5, Washington's reenergized soldiers marched through Bound Brook and on to Pluckemin. The following day they continued through Vealtown, past Basking Ridge, and into winter quarters at Morristown.[127]

The string of defeats and retreats that filled the second half of 1776 had left the American army and the patriot cause on the verge of disintegration. But Washington's twin victories at Trenton and Princeton restored American morale. In a January 7 letter to Robert Morris, Colonel Stephen Moylan wrote, "if we only had five hundred fresh men, there is very little doubt we should have destroyed all their [British] stores and baggage at Brunswick . . . and probably have retaken poor Naso. But let us not repine—it was glorious," he wrote of Washington's stunning successes. "The consequences must be great. America will—by God—it must be free."[128] Nicholas Creswell, a Loyalist who had moved from his native Virginia to New York City, recognized an immediate change in the American spirit. "The minds of the people are much altered," he wrote. "A few days ago they had given up the cause for lost. Their late successes have turned the scale and now *they are all liberty mad again*. . . . This has given them new spirits, got them fresh succors and will prolong the war, perhaps for two years. They have recovered their panic and it will not be an easy matter to throw them into confusion again."[129] Writing from Brunswick on January 13, William Harcourt now admitted to his father, "I must own that I was once sanguine enough to think that this disagreeable war drew near to a conclusion, and that the uninterrupted success our arms had met with in the Jerseys would soon oblige the rebels to make their submission. Such, however, are the sudden turns in war that I think we may now reckon with certainty upon another campaign."[130]

Lee's capture had appeared to be a major blow to the American cause. But it had likely made Washington's victories at Trenton and Princeton possible. If Harcourt and his men had not found him on the morning of December 13, he probably would have attacked the British on his own, perhaps either at Brunswick or Princeton. But the results might have been disastrous. The British were acutely aware of his presence; indeed, that was the very reason for Harcourt's patrol of December 12–13. Even if Lee had succeeded, he may have had difficulty getting his troops safely back across the Delaware River to rejoin Washington's army. In any event, such a raid would have alerted Howe and his commanders to the dangers of more surprise raids; as a result, the stunning success at Trenton may never have occurred. By contrast, the British never saw Washington's moves coming. True, the fierce Christmas snowstorm had helped mask his troops' movements and kept wary Loyalist lookouts inside their homes. But as Private John Howland of Lippitt's Regiment later noted, "Knowing that for a considerable time before there had been no American troops in Jersey, [the Hessians at Trenton] had little reason to expect being attacked by an enemy from Pennsylvania."[131]

If Lee had rejoined Washington in time to participate in councils of war prior to the Trenton attack, he might have argued, perhaps convincingly, against a surprise attack on the Hessian garrison. If so, he would not have been alone. After delivering his own troops to Washington, Horatio Gates had, shockingly, left the army on December 23. He was bound for Baltimore, determined to share his concerns over Washington's leadership with the Continental Congress. Gates believed that while Washington remained north of Philadelphia, Howe "would privately construct bateaux, pass the Delaware in [Washington's] rear, and take possession of Philadelphia before he was aware of the movement." Gates recommended that Washington "retire to the south of the Susquehanna, and there form an army."[132] The absence of both Lee and Gates from Washington's camp, then, proved a blessing for the patriot cause.

Not all British military men saw the American victories as a momentum shifter. Comparing Harcourt's capture of Lee with the loss of Trenton, one officer wrote, "the last is disagreeable, but it is more than counterbalanced by the former, which I think is likely to turn out one of the luckiest circumstances of the war."[133] In a French newspaper, an American dismissed such sentiment, accusing British government leaders of "most pompously blowing up the taking of Gen. Lee, and endeavoring by that means" to downplay the losses at Trenton and Princeton.[134]

Of all the reactions to Lee's capture, two stand out as especially prescient. One, quoted above, was by Captain Thomas Rodney, who observed even before Trenton that Lee's capture would benefit the patriot cause by forcing Washington to rely less on his more experienced subordinate, and become more assertive. The other was by Sir Joseph York, then the British minister at The Hague, who had assisted Lee in several pre-war squabbles in Europe. When York first heard of Lee's capture, he was "convinced, from what I have seen and known of him, that he was the worst present which could be made to an army." After hearing about the debacles at Trenton and Princeton, he wrote: "I was one of those who expressed a sincere concern at the taking of Lee . . . it is impossible but Lee must puzzle everything he meddles in, and he was the worst present the British could receive. My opinion has been verified much sooner that I wished, as the only stroke . . . which they have struck happened after his being made prisoner."[135] Washington's late-December victories, the British minister noted, enabled the Americans to "find that he [Lee] was not the only efficient officer in the American service."[136]

That had long been clear to some. From Boston, Hannah Winthrop triumphantly wrote to her friend Mercy Warren, "Let us my friend enjoy this victory, and though a skillful general has been meanly kidnapped let us not think the fate of America hangs on the prowess of a single person."[137] On January 6, William Gordon, a friend of Washington in Massachusetts, wrote to the general to "congratulate your Excellency for and on the success of our army [the surprise attack at Trenton]. The enemy will from hence see that we were not wholly dependent upon the abilities of Lee, and that we have generals still remaining who have skill to plan, together with courage and conduct, to execute. It will be a fine regale to his [Lee's] honor in his confinement, and I heartily wish he may often have the like, till we have the wherewithal to exchange for him."[138]

4

A Prisoner of High Value

After Harcourt and his party brought Charles Lee to Pennington on December 13, the prisoner was moved to Princeton on December 14 and then, probably the next day, to Brunswick where he was confined under close guard. At first, Lee reportedly was "defiant" and "acted very impudently."[1] One British officer noted that "He behaved with great insolence the first 24 hours."[2] Another recalled that Lee became "dejected," and failed to recover from the shock of capture for several days. Meanwhile he praised his own leadership at Charleston, lauded American soldiers as "the best troops in the world," and ascribed American defeats to "bad luck." He constantly asked what General William Howe would do with him, and declared that he expected to be exchanged for British officers held as prisoners by the American army, in accordance with military custom.[3]

Upon learning of the arrival of Howe and his staff in Princeton the afternoon of December 14, Lee immediately made several verbal and written requests to meet with the commanding general. Howe refused to cooperate, returning Lee's two letters "unopened and enclosed under a cover directed to 'Lieutenant Colonel Lee.'"[4] Lee's mood then immediately darkened; he realized what this meant. Howe had addressed Lee by his last rank in the British army, and therefore still considered Lee an officer in British military service. Thus, in Howe's eyes Lee was a deserter—and one who had taken up arms against his own king. Lee had no illusions about what conviction for these offenses meant for him: death. According to a report that circulated among British officers, "when he [Lee] received a message, directed to him as Lieut. Col. Lee (the rank he holds in our army) he showed the greatest marks of apprehension; as he then concluded he was to be treated as an English officer, deserting, and in arms against the King."[5] Colonel Harcourt concluded that the captive general was "at least as anxious as one could imagine him" for the preservation of "his life."[6]

Under one type of parole, it was the policy of both the American and British armies to permit captured officers to be released from close confinement and to move freely within a specific town, on condition that they swear as gentlemen not to try to escape. On December 14, Howe's aide, Captain Muenchhausen, met with Lee and recorded the following in his diary:

> He [Lee] has begged to be paroled and vouches that he would not attempt to escape, so that it would not be necessary to keep a strong guard over him. The answer to all this was that a man such as he, whose life was in danger because he could be considered a British deserter as well as a rebel, could not possibly be trusted to keep his parole. As a result, he is not allowed to write letters, and one officer and two sentries are continuously in the room with him, in addition to many other sentries being posted around the house in which he is kept. This is very annoying to Lee.[7]

On December 20, Howe had written to his civilian superior in London, Lord Germain, informing him that he would not bring Lee to trial until it was determined if Lee's resignation from the army prior to assuming his position as general in the Continental army meant that he could not be classified as a deserter under British military law.[8] Howe had also added, "Deserters are excluded in my agreement with the enemy for the exchange of prisoners."[9] The general made his position on Lee equally clear in a December 21 letter to General Clinton. "As I look upon him in the light of a deserter from the service," he wrote, "he is kept a close prisoner at Brunswick, where Major General Grant now commands."[10]

Consistent with his view of Lee, Howe deemed his captive ineligible for exchange. For the moment, the issue was academic, since the Americans had no British prisoners of Lee's rank to suit an exchange. Moreover, as Howe refused to parole Lee within Brunswick, he naturally did not even consider the second type of parole, which permitted the officer to return home on the condition that he not take up arms again until he was formally exchanged. Until Lee's status was officially determined in London, Howe kept him confined to one or two rooms.

General Sir William Howe. Howe served as commander-in-chief of the British forces in North American from 1775 to 1778. Print published in London in 1785. (*Library of Congress*)

Lee sent a request to Major General James Grant for money, but was refused on the ground that he did not lack necessaries. Grant wrote that Lee "is astonished I am civil to him." Lee was anxious about his life, mused Grant, and wrote him often. The British general was unable to resent a man writing out of fear of being hanged.[11] Others at Brunswick were not so understanding. As a result of his being "very meanly dressed," Lee, according to an unidentified British officer, requested a tailor to mend his clothes, but no one "would work for so great a rascal (as the gentlemen tailors called him)."[12]

With the battles at Trenton and Princeton over, and the threat of an American raid-in-force against Brunswick ended, Lee was now a prisoner for the long term. On January 13, 1777, Howe had his high-value captive moved from Brunswick to Amboy, and then carried by the armed schooner *Alert* to New York City, where Lee was "put into the custody of a strong guard."[13] The British had made New York City their headquarters in America, and kept most of their prisoners there. Lee was fortunate that he was a Continental officer and not an ordinary soldier. Approximately 5,000 rank-and-file Americans captured during the battles of Brooklyn and White Plains, and the seizure of Fort Washington, were not as lucky. Indeed, they were victims of a massive human rights disaster.

These captives, shocked by battle and roughed up by their British captors, had been herded into empty New York sugar houses, churches, and other public buildings, or onto prison ships off of Brooklyn. Given little or rotten food lacking in nutrition, the prisoners quickly weakened, and became vulnerable to disease and starvation. They were further subjected to foul water, overcrowding, and scant clothing, blankets, and firewood in the brutally cold winter months. They began to die by the cartload.

Henry Franklin, a Quaker who visited a New York City church two days after the fall of Fort Washington, testified that prisoners were already fighting over scraps of food. Private Thomas Boyd of West Caln, Pennsylvania, recalled worm-filled food, putrid water, beatings by guards, the rancid smell of urine and excrement, and so much sickness that burial parties would remove ten or twenty bodies from his jail every morning.[14] When New Jersey militia captain Edward Boylston was thrown into a sugar house in January 1777, he immediately found that "there was not a place to lie down for rest, day nor night, but upon the excrements of the prisoners. . . . With yellow fever, want and suffering the prisoners were dying constantly, and it was impossible to move without stumbling over the dead and dying."[15] Samuel Young, a private captured at Fort Washington, wrote of the terrible conditions that he and his fellow prisoners endured, first in a New York church and then on board a ship in the harbor. In a December 15, 1776, deposition, Young stated that "great numbers died in this confinement, sometimes three, sometimes four, and more, every day, and one day nine died; and that they themselves are in a frail state of health, occasioned by this barbarous usage; and many of them who were released died upon the road before they reached home."[16]

Historian Edwin Burrows, who studied the plight of American prisoners in New York City during the Revolutionary War, concluded that the death rate in city prisons was an astounding 50 to 70 percent. Burrows persuasively rejected arguments that while Americans may have suffered in British prisons, the British were blameless. Burrows did not claim that the British *intended* the deaths of so many captives, as many Americans argued during the war. Instead, he concluded that the deaths were the result of "something well beyond the usual brutalities and misfortunes of war—a lethal convergence, as it were, of obstinacy, condescension, corruption, mendacity, and indifference. Although the British did not deliberately kill American prisoners in New York, they might as well have done."[17]

Some historians, while recognizing the horrid prison conditions, have claimed that the Americans treated British prisoners with similar cruelty. In general, however, this was not true. Burrows found that while Americans often talked about retaliating against their British prisoners, they did not. He estimated that of 35,800 American war-related deaths, roughly half occurred in New York City prisons or prison ships.[18] British soldiers and sailors captured by the Americans did not suffer anywhere near this level.

Part of the problem was that British authorities viewed the war not as one of liberation, as the Americans did, but as a rebellion against recognized authority fought by traitors. Parliament, the British administration, and the British army had a long history of crushing, with little mercy, rebellions in Ireland and Scotland. Even Captain Frederick Mackenzie of the Royal Welch Fusiliers, typically a reasonable and sensible British officer, wrote after the Battle of Brooklyn, "Rebels taken in arms forfeit their lives by the laws of all countries."[19] Not every Englishman agreed. In Parliament, Charles Fox, who had opposed harsh treatment of American colonists, pointed out that "all the great asserters of liberty, the saviors of their country . . . had been called rebels."[20]

While the legal status of captured "rebels" remained uncertain, Burrows found British commanders had a free hand, with disastrous consequences for the prisoners. Caroline Cox, another authority on British treatment of patriot prisoners, agreed, writing "The British were reluctant to do anything that appeared to recognize formally the Continental army or any other colonial soldiers." Cox added that for the British this was not a war against another sovereign country, such as France. Rather, it was a war "against domestic rebels. They saw their captives as traitors who should be tried for treason and not as prisoners" of a sovereign country with rights to be treated with respect and dignity.[21] The Continental Congress felt that "England ought to be obliged to treat and acknowledge us as an independent state, at least so far as respects prisoners of war." But delegates soon realized that they might be required to impose the doctrine of retaliation on British military captives in order to insure fair treatment of American prisoners.[22]

American officers, at least those who were recognized by British military authorities as officers, fared better. An officer, it was thought, was a gentleman, a man of taste and breeding above common, ordinary folk. Based on vestiges of knighthood from the Middle Ages, it was thought that a gentleman could be trusted to keep his promise not to escape before being exchanged. Thus, officers could be paroled within a town and kept in cleaner and less-crowded housing with other officers. On rare occasions, they were even permitted to return to their homes on the promise of not taking up arms until they were formally exchanged. The system of parole thus benefited captive British officers, who expected, and in fact received, just such treatment from the Americans. Charles Lee hoped to be treated similarly.

When the war began, British authorities were not sure whether captured American officers should be treated as rebels with no rights or as gentlemen with customary rights. British officers laughed at the pretensions of American militia officers, whom they could not distinguish from rank-and-file soldiers, and sometimes ended up treating them as ordinary privates. Captured privateer captains who had wreaked havoc on British commercial and military supply vessels were considered nothing less than pirates. Such men were simply thrown into prisons along with common sailors. The question for British military authorities was whether Continental army officers, such as Charles Lee, were to be treated with leniency and entitled to parole within the towns in which they were held.

The case of Colonel Ethan Allen exemplified the British army's early war quandary. Allen, a former ironmaster, first rose to prominence as the leader of the rough-and-tumble Green Mountain Boys, who prior to the war had fought to keep powerful New York claimants out of what would become Vermont. In May 1775 Allen led a party of about eighty-five men in seizing Fort Ticonderoga, whose cannon would later be used to drive the British army from Boston. But then the overconfident Allen and a handful of men made a premature incursion into Canada, ahead of Brigadier General Richard Montgomery's invasion force. Allen and his small band were captured outside of Montreal and then sent to the second-in-command of British troops in Canada, the rebel-hating and sometimes cruel Brigadier General Richard Prescott.

Prescott's name would soon be well known among the "rebels" he hated. The lieutenant colonel of the 7th Regiment of Foot (the Royal Fusiliers), Prescott was appointed Brigadier General in North America and posted to Canada in early 1775.[23] Prescott steadfastly viewed resisters to British authority as traitors and common criminals. In October, with General Richard Montgomery's army laying siege to nearby St. John's and eyeing Montreal next, Sir Guy Carleton, the British military commander and governor of Canada, ordered Prescott to take into custody Thomas Walker, an American merchant who had moved from Boston to Montreal in 1763. Walker had been caught providing support to the American cause. British authorities certainly had a right to arrest such a man, but Prescott seemed to delight in punishing him. At 2:00 a.m. on October 5, 1775, a squad of fifty soldiers sent by Prescott seized Walker and burned his house to the ground. They hauled their prisoner to British-held Montreal. When Walker arrived at the riverfront near the Montreal barracks, Prescott, "in great wrath, came down upon the beach," where he ordered his troops to surround Walker, and for the prisoner's arms to be "pinioned." Then Prescott accosted him. "You are a traitor and a villain you scoundrel, to betray your country; but the laws of your country have overtaken you at last—you shall have the justice of this country," he screamed. Prescott ordered Walker placed in heavy irons, calling out to the blacksmith "to rivet them well," which caused his prisoner "inexpressible pain." Walker was then confined to a room "in irons, for thirty-three days and nights, without fire or candle for a long while," and without visits from his wife or any friend. Walker was freed by Montgomery's men in early November.24

Major General Richard Prescott commanded the British garrison at Newport and on Aquidneck Island until his capture on July 12, 1777. (*New England Magazine, Sept. 1894*)

On the morning of September 25, 1775, the captive Ethan Allen appeared before Prescott under heavy guard and identified himself as "Colonel Allen, who took Ticonderoga." The British general, according to Allen, "shook his cane over my head, calling me many hard names, among which he frequently used the word 'rebel,' and put himself in a great rage." Prescott blustered, "I will not execute you now, but you shall grace a halter at Tyburn, God damn ye." In other words, Allen would hang in the principal place in London for executing criminals.25 Prescott then confined Allen aboard the schooner *Gaspée*, where guards who referred to him as a criminal shackled his hands and feet with thirty pounds of iron bars. A British midshipman later confessed that the *Gaspée's* captain had ordered him to "put a pair of irons on Allen's legs, which he wore for seven or eight days, during which he was kept by the Boatswain's Cabin. Afterwards the irons were taken off his legs in the morning and handcuffs were put on his hands, which was the practice for some considerable time. Then only one leg was ironed in the night and handcuffs in the day."[26] On the first day of his confinement the shocked Allen addressed a letter to Prescott in which he protested that he had expected "honorable and humane treatment, as an officer of my rank and merit should have" and compared his own good treatment of British officers that he personally had captured at Fort Ticonderoga. But Allen's complaints went unheeded, and he remained bound in heavy irons for the next six weeks.[27]

On November 11, Carleton, who also ignored pleas from Allen for better treatment, put the Vermonter and his men aboard the 16-gun sloop *Adamant*, which was bound for England. The ship's captain threw Allen and thirty-six other prisoners into the vessel's dark and dank, twenty-two-by-twenty-two-foot hold for the forty-day journey. The captives were soon overwhelmed with diarrhea, fever, lice, and intolerable thirst. "When we asked for water, we were, most commonly, instead of obtaining it, insulted and derided," Allen later wrote.[28]

Two months after capturing Allen, Prescott along with most of his 7th Regiment, was taken prisoner by General Montgomery's advancing army on board the schooner *Gaspée* as it tried to slip down the St. Lawrence River to Quebec.[29] Prescott found the tables had turned. Hearing of Prescott's harsh treatment of Allen, Montgomery, according to Robert R. Livingston of New York, "resented his conduct so highly as to refuse to see him or any of the officers of his party."[30] Montgomery sent the British general to Fort Ticonderoga. There, Prescott was interviewed by the quasi-aristocratic Major General Philip Schuyler of New York, to whom Montgomery had written with details of Prescott's behavior. On November 30, Schuyler replied: "Prescott arrived and was in my room half an hour before I received your letter. I believe he could easily perceive that I knew his character, and I had an opportunity this morning to write him a line, which I declared that I thought it a duty incumbent on every honest man to do to others as he would wish to be done by, that upon this principle we had always paid attention to those whom the fortune of war had put into our power."[31]

Prescott's reputation quickly became known to both Congress and George Washington.[32] On December 18, the commander-in-chief wrote to General William Howe, then commander of the British forces defending Boston, about "a circumstance which, were it not so well authenticated, I should scarcely think credible." Washington had been informed, he wrote, that Allen "has been treated without regard to decency, humanity, or the rules of war—that he has been thrown into irons, and suffers all the hardships inflicted upon common felons." Washington assured Howe "that whatever treatment Colonel Allen receives, whatever fate he undergoes, such exactly shall be the treatment and fate of Brigadier Prescott, now in our hands." The American commander-in-chief warned, "The law of retaliation is not only justifiable . . . but absolutely a duty."[33] Without prompting from Congress, Washington was making Allen's ordeal the test case for American-British prisoner-of-war policies, particularly with respect to the treatment of officers. Howe refused to discuss the matter with Washington, but informed his London superiors of the threat of retaliation and sought instructions as to how to respond.[34]

British treatment of Ethan Allen particularly outraged the Continental Congress, which had by now returned to Philadelphia. It immediately ordered General Schuyler to confine Prescott in close custody, but not to put him in irons until it received clarification as to how Allen had been treated.[35] Prescott arrived in Philadelphia under a strong guard on January 24, and the next day was brought before Congress to explain his "cruelty to Colonel Ethan Allen and others."[36] Prescott uncharacteristically behaved "modestly," admitting he had placed Allen in irons, while offering as a defense "the commands of Carleton, his superior officer."[37]

Congress also heard testimony from Lieutenant Colonel Edward Antill, an American-born Quebec resident who had joined the Continental army's 2nd Canadian Regiment. Antill accused Prescott of "great malevolence and bad behavior" toward "our people."[38] Congress subsequently instructed that Prescott be taken to well-appointed City Tavern, where other British officers were residing in comfort. Then, after some discussion, Congress's rankled delegates agreed that retaliation against Prescott was appropriate. On January 29, it voted to order the British general to be "kept in close confinement in the gaol [jail] of Philadelphia."[39] As Virginia's Thomas Jefferson explained, the delegates directed "Brigadier General Prescott to be bound in irons, and confined in close jail, there to experience corresponding miseries with those which shall be inflicted on Mr. Allen. His life shall answer for that of Allen . . . as for those of the brave men captivated with him."⁴⁰

A letter written by an unidentified British officer (probably of the 7th Regiment) and published in English newspapers subsequently made Prescott's predicament public knowledge. The officer's story began on January 30 in a City Tavern room, where he, Prescott, and several other officers were dining when an American army captain, supported by thirty soldiers,

> came into the room, and said he was ordered by the Congress to carry General Prescott immediately to the common gaol. The General submitted to his fate. The room in which they lodged him, was cold and damp, bare walls, no fireplace, the furniture nothing but a chair and a truckle-bed. From the unwholesomeness of this situation, and other hardships, the wounds he had received in former services broke out afresh, and reduced him to so low a state that his death seemed inevitable. Major [Charles] Preston, who was also a prisoner, went to [John] Hancock, the President of the Congress, and told him, that if they were determined to sacrifice his brother officer to their resentment, it would be an act of humanity to dispatch him immediately, and not suffer him to linger in misery. Upon this representation Doctor Cadwalader was sent to visit him, who, by his humane account of the General's case, and other kind offices, obtained leave for his removal to his former lodgings in the town, with sentinels to guard him. This severe treatment the Congress declared was intended as retaliation for the imprisonment of Ethan Allen.⁴¹

As recorded by the official diarist of the Continental Congress, on February 5, Dr. Thomas Cadwalader, a respected Philadelphia physician, verified "that General Prescott's wound (received at the Battle of Fontenoy [in 1745]) is bad, his room in jail damp and his case dangerous," and that Prescott was removed from the common jail and "indulged with liberty to take lodgings in the City Tavern under a guard from the barracks."⁴² Prescott spent only about a week in Philadelphia's common jail.

A month later, Samuel Adams and two other delegates to the Continental Congress spent an hour with Prescott at City Tavern, listening to the general's complaints of his mild inconveniences.⁴³ On March 16, a Philadelphia newspaper quoted an unidentified patriot who compared the differing treatment of Colonel Allen and General Prescott:

> [W]e are assured by a gentleman, now in this city, that he saw him [Ethan Allen] in England, confined in a loathsome gaol, and suffering under a heavy lead of irons. How different the situation of Allen and Prescott—the first, taken fighting for his life, liberty and property, is treated as a villain, while the other, taken fighting to support the cruel edicts of a tyrannical ministry, whose aim is to rob and enslave, is lodged at a first rate tavern in this city, and fed with the best markets afford. Oh! George! Who is the savage? After this, can any man blame the Americans should they retaliate?[44]

In April, Thomas Walker, seeking revenge, travelled to Philadelphia to share with Congress his story of abuse at General Prescott's hands. Disgusted to find that Prescott was "lodged in the best tavern of the place, walking or riding at large through Philadelphia" and "feasting with gentlemen of the first rank," Walker delivered his testimony, and then quickly returned to Montreal.[45]

At the end of August 1776, Prescott, recently promoted to major general in North America only, was brought to Reading, Massachusetts, paroled, and allowed to move freely around the town. The following month he was exchanged for Major General John Sullivan, who had been captured at the Battle of Brooklyn, on Long Island. As Howe's secretary, Abraham Serle, then aboard the 64-gun flagship *Eagle*, wrote on September 24, 1776, "General Prescott came on board in the afternoon to his great joy. He says, the rebels behaved but indifferently to him, and even sent him to gaol, after they had heard of the defeat in Long Island."[46] Prescott apparently did not mention that his short confinement in Philadelphia's common jail had been in retaliation for his own confinement of Ethan Allen.

Meanwhile, Allen and his men arrived in England a few days before Christmas and were whisked off to a prison, at Pendennis Castle, near Falmouth, where they were placed in irons. Aware now of Congress's threat of retaliation against Prescott and other British officers, Lord George Germain and King George III reconsidered how they would deal with Allen and other rebel officers. The debate spilled over into Parliament as well as the press. Historian D. K. Abbass has written: "Allen's capture focused the debate in Parliament over whether or not the colonies were in revolt, and if so Allen should be treated as a traitor [and hanged]. Some in

Parliament argued that the colonies were not in revolt, but in any case they admitted that the Americans held more prisoners in North America than did the British, and that the Americans could be used for later exchange."[47] When members of the opposition to Germain's cabinet obtained a writ of habeas corpus, which meant that Allen would either have to be formally charged in an English court or released, Germain became concerned that Allen had become so popular that no English jury would convict him. Germain therefore had Allen and his men shipped back to North America, beyond the reach of meddlesome English judges, where they could be exchanged on a case-by-case basis for "his Majesty's officers and loyal subjects" who found themselves "in the disgraceful situation of being prisoners to the rebels."[48]

The journey home, followed by a stay in a Halifax, Canada, jail, worsened Allen's condition. Weakened by a dangerous fever, the stubborn Vermonter finally conceded that "the malignant hand of Britain had greatly reduced my constitution, stroke by stroke."[49] In October 1776, Allen and those of his men who survived were sent to New York City on a ship whose captain, Richard Smith, handled American prisoners with more discretion.[50] Allen wrote that Captain Smith "assured me that I should be treated as a gentleman," which, after all the indignities, he had suffered, "drew tears from my eyes."[51] Once in New York, Allen was briefly confined in a "filthy church," but was then finally accorded the treatment of an officer. He was paroled, allowed to live in a house with other American officers, and allowed his freedom within the city.[52] General Howe's policy was now to treat at least captive Continental army officers as gentlemen.

When he arrived in New York City on January 13, Charles Lee hoped for the type of even-handed treatment that Allen was finally receiving. The British, however, considered him a special case, due to his service in the British army. Until it was determined whether or not his resignation was enough to save him from the gallows, he would be confined to one or two rooms under a heavy guard. It appears that by day at least one British officer or guard remained in the room with Lee, a violation of privacy that must have greatly annoyed the American general. Even Britain's *Annual Register*, in summarizing the events of 1777, commented that Lee was "watched and guarded with all that strictures and jealousy which even a state criminal of the first magnitude could have experienced."[53]

Lee's surroundings were nevertheless comfortable. While waiting for his civilian superiors to decide Lee's legal status, Howe had him detained in a room in New York City Hall, which, groused Loyalist historian Thomas Jones, ranked as "one of the genteelest public rooms in the city." A sentry, wrote Jones, stood at the door. Lee had ample firewood and candles, as well as permission to order a daily dinner from the City Arms, a nearby tavern, sufficient for six people, with what liquor he wanted. He had the privilege of asking five friends to dine with him each day. "This," complained Jones, "was all furnished at the expense of the [British] nation."[54] Arch-Loyalist William Franklin, the last royal governor of New Jersey and Benjamin Franklin's only, albeit illegitimate, son, complained to Lord Germain that "General Lee (who in justice was not entitled to be considered as a prisoner of war or in any other light than as a deserter) had a table kept for him at the expense of at least thirty shillings sterling per day to the Crown."[55]

At first, Lee stayed out of trouble and avoided controversy. On January 20, 1777, a British officer wrote to a superior in England, "Lee is here, and has been visited by General [James] Robertson and some more principal people; he is cheerful, and talks a good deal of his travels through Europe, but never touches on American politics."[56] The Continental Congress, meanwhile, worked to ensure that Lee was treated properly, and to arrange for his exchange as quickly as possible. During a December 20, 1776, meeting in Baltimore, Congress enacted a resolution requesting its President, John Hancock, to "write to General Washington, and desire him to send a flag to General Howe, and enquire in what manner General Lee . . . is treated; and if he finds that he is not treated agreeable to his rank and character, to send a remonstrance to General Howe on the subject."[57] After this letter was sent, one of Lee's aides-de-camp, Major John Eustace, told members of Congress of Lee "having addressed two letters to General Howe, received them back unopened, and enclosed under a cover directed to *Lieutenant Colonel Lee.*"[58] The delegates knew what this meant. Virginia's Richard Henry Lee expressed outrage that the "wicked enemy" was "actually preparing to try General Lee by a special court martial" after refusing to accept "that gentleman's resignation of his commission."[59]

Congress addressed Lee's situation on January 6, 1777. In the preamble to a resolution that he had drafted, Richard Henry Lee stated: "Congress being informed that Major General Lee hath, since his captivity, been committed to custody of the Provost, instead of being enlarged upon his parole, according to the humane practice that has taken place with officers of the enemy who have fallen into the hands of the American troops, a treatment totally unworthy of that gentleman's eminent qualifications, and his rank in the service of these United States."[60] The resolution requested that Washington offer to exchange Lee for the five surviving Hessian field officers captured at Trenton. If the offer was not accepted, and Lee's confinement continued, the resolution required the commander-in-chief to apply "the principles of retaliation" to the five Hessian officers, along with Lieutenant Colonel Archibald Campbell, then in prison outside Boston, "in order that the same treatment which General Lee shall receive may be exactly inflicted upon their persons."[61]

Writing from his army's winter camp at Morristown, New Jersey, on January 13, Washington informed Howe of his offer to exchange Lee for the Hessian field officers. Based on the well-established practice that captors could refuse a proffered exchange unless the captive officer was exchanged for an officer of the same rank, the American general probably did not expect the offer to be accepted. He did believe, however, that Howe's rejection of it could sow dissatisfaction in the ranks of Howe's German allies, who would surely be disappointed that their fellow officers would not be released. If the exchange was not agreed to, Washington wrote, Congress would demand that Lee be given "his liberty upon parole, within certain bounds, as has ever been granted to your officers in our custody." The American general continued,

> I am informed from good authority that your reason for keeping him [Lee] in stricter confinement than usual is that you do not look upon him in the light of a common prisoner of war, but as a deserter from the British service, as his resignation was never accepted, and that you intend to try him by court martial.... I must give you warning that Major General Lee is looked upon as an officer belonging to and under the protection of the United States of America and that any violence which you may commit upon his life or liberty will be severely retaliated upon the lives or liberties of the British officers or those of their foreign allies at present in our hands.[62]

Ten days later, on January 23, Howe forcefully responded to Washington—rejecting the proposed exchange, but also indicating that Lee was safe for the moment. "I shall not make any further comment upon it than to assure you, that your threats of retaliating upon the innocent such punishment, as may be decreed in the circumstances of Mr. Lee by the laws of his country, will not divert me from my duty in any respect," he declared. "At the same time you may rest satisfied that the proceedings against him will not be precipitated."63 Howe was trying to place Lee in a unique category—in between a prisoner of war entitled to the rights of a captive officer and a deserter under English law.

Lieutenant Colonel Archibald Campbell. In 1777, in retaliation for Lee's imprisonment, he was imprisoned in conditions that even George Washington described as "shocking to humanity." The portrait shows Campbell in India about 1770. Artist unknown, possibly by Allan Ramsay. (*Walcott, Sir Archibald Campbell*)

Congress thought that Howe intended to court-martial Lee. Nor did it approve of Lee's ongoing confinement to one or two rooms. On February 20, Congress adopted a measure directing the Board of War "immediately to order the five Hessian field officers and Lieutenant Colonel Campbell into safe and close custody, it being the unalterable resolution to retaliate on them the same punishment as may be inflicted on the person of General Lee." The resolution further sought to "teach our cruel enemies to regard the laws of nations and the rights of humanity and that Congress not only lament, but would willingly avoid, the necessity of this just retaliation."64 Thus, Congress relied on the "law of nations" as authority for its drastic action. During the pre-vote debate, one delegate observed that "Retaliation is the only instrument whereby nations can compel observance of that law, and America [as an independent country] ought therefore firmly to retaliate when the law of nations was violated."65

Once the Board of War's order reached Dumfries, Virginia, where the five Hessian officers were being held, they were subject to house arrest. American prison authorities "placed sentries before their quarters," but there are no surviving reports of their having suffered abuse or discomfort.66 The brunt of American retaliation instead fell upon Lieutenant Colonel Archibald Campbell. Born in

1739 into a prominent family at Inverary, Argyll, Scotland, Campbell had served as a captain-lieutenant in the Corps of Engineers in the Caribbean during the Seven Years' War, and then as chief engineer in Bengal, India, from 1768 to 1772. After becoming wealthy trading in silks in India, he purchased an estate at Inverneill, in Argyll, and then represented the Stirling Burghs in Parliament from 1774 through 1780. In November 1775, after helping to recruit the 71st Regiment (also known as Frasier's Highlanders) for service in North America, he was appointed its lieutenant colonel. His battalion sailed from Scotland in the spring of 1776, but he and more than 100 officers and soldiers were captured in Boston Harbor on June 16 when his transport ship entered that port. Campbell's superiors had not informed him that Howe had evacuated the town in March.[67]

Campbell and his fellow Scottish gentlemen officers must have been concerned about how the comparably uncouth rebels would treat them. The Continental Congress had set the policy in such matters for Massachusetts and the other twelve states. Only a few weeks earlier, on May 21, 1776, it had ordered that all persons taken in arms on board any prize vessel (as well as military captives taken on land) should be treated as prisoners of war, "but with humanity." In addition, it had determined that paroled enemy officers would not be permitted to reside in or near any seaport town or public post road. They would instead be sent to more remote inland towns, from which escape and rescue with the assistance of the British navy would be more difficult. Congress further ordered that officers agreeing to paroles would be allowed to move freely within the borders of their towns, and that soldiers would be permitted to work at trades to support themselves.[68]

At first, Campbell was treated decently by his captors. He informed Howe that "we have experienced the utmost civility and good treatment from the people of power at Boston."[69] In late June Campbell was sent to Reading, where he took up residence (with five other officers) in the home of Captain Nathan Parker. He had the freedom to travel up to six miles from town, and the use of five of his personal servants.[70] But when news of Lee's incarceration and Congress's January 6, 1777, resolution reached Boston, Campbell's situation changed dramatically. The resolution required the Massachusetts Council, the state's upper legislative body, to "detain Lieutenant Colonel Campbell, and keep him in safe custody till the further order of Congress."[71] On January 31, the Council ordered the sheriff of Middlesex County to place Campbell "in safe custody until the further order of the Council."[72] A member of the Council explained the rationale for its decision:

> I am sorry to inform you that we have been compelled, contrary to our inclinations, to deprive Colonel Campbell of that liberty with which he has been indulged ever since his captivity. If he feels a melancholy change in his situation, he must thank his friends for it. We have at all times shown the strongest disposition to soften the miseries of war. . . . But humanity carried beyond a certain point degenerates into weakness. The conduct of our enemies not only justifies severity, but makes it sometimes absolutely necessary. . . . As they have shown themselves deaf to the voice of reason, retaliation is the only means of redress left in our power.[73]

The Massachusetts Council believed that "General Lee was put into close confinement," which meant that he was confined to a single cell and restrained with chains.[74] Dr. James Thacher of Massachusetts heard that Lee was suffering "in close confinement in the Provost as a prisoner in New York."[75] That meant a single room in a filthy, military jail cell. This, in fact, was untrue, but the Massachusetts Council did not know that yet. Still, the sheriff, James Prescott, aware of Congress's edict that Lee and Campbell receive "the same treatment," threw Campbell into Concord's common jail on February 1. Adding to Campbell's discomfort, the Massachusetts Council refused to allow any of his servants to accompany him.[76]

Built in 1755 and bordering the West Burying Ground on Concord's main street, the two-story, wooden building's jail cells were awful places to deposit any human being, never mind a member of Parliament.[77] In a February 4 letter of protest sent to George Washington, Campbell described the gruesome conditions:

> I am lodged in a dungeon of about twelve or thirteen feet square, doubly planked and spiked on every side, the sides black with grease and litter of successive criminals and completely hung round with cobwebs. Two small windows or port holes, not glazed but strongly grated with iron on the inside and well barricaded with shutters on the out, introduce a gloomy light to the apartment. Two doors, doubly planked and

locked, shut me from the prisoners' yard, and the gaoler has received express orders against my going into it, even for the necessary calls of nature, and a hole near the middle of these doors serves either to admit any victuals or gratify the gaping curiosity of spectators. In the corner of the room, boxed up within a partition, stands a necessary house, uncovered which does not seem to have been emptied since its first hour of its being consecrated. . . . The loathsome black hole, decorated with chains, and iron rings well riveted and clinched, is granted me for an inner chamber, from whence a notorious felon was but the moment before removed to make way for me, and whose litter and excrement still actually remain.[78]

In a February 14 letter addressed to General Howe, Campbell described the same conditions, concluding that "With respect to your Excellency's treatment of General Lee, I can scarcely believe it similar to mine."[79] The Loyalist historian Thomas Jones later bitterly wrote, "What a contrast between the usage of the two prisoners! Lee, living in genteel apartments, supplied at the expense of the nation with all the luxuries that New York could afford, had his friends to dine with him, his servant to attend him, a good bed to sleep upon, into which he tumbled jovially mellow every night."[80]

Washington received Campbell's February 4 letter at Morristown. On February 27 he also received a rare letter from General Howe, who complained of Campbell's treatment.[81] In response, Washington wrote to James Bowdoin, the president of the Massachusetts Council, describing "the severity of [Campbell's] confinement, as is scarce ever inflicted upon the most atrocious criminals." The Virginian pointed out that Lee was "confined to a commodious house with genteel accommodations" and that the "same" treatment accorded to Lee was to be given the British officer.[82] On March 1, Washington penned a letter to John Hancock, pointing out the disparity in the officers' treatment and requesting that Campbell be placed in a situation more comparable to Lee's.[83] Shortly thereafter, Francis Dana, a member of the Massachusetts Council, inspected the Concord jail. Campbell was then moved to better quarters—a single room in the jailer's tavern in Concord. He was allowed one servant.[84] Word subsequently reached Boston that the "account of General Lee's being confined in close gaol, in New York, is a mistake."[85]

The Old Jail in Concord that briefly held Lieutenant Colonel Campbell. From a watercolor drawing held by the Concord Free Public Library, and possibly made by Campbell himself while a prisoner. (*Walcott, Sir Archibald Campbell*)

Campbell remained unhappy, and on April 13 wrote General William Heath, then the commanding general in the Boston theater, "At present I am only allowed the space of 50 yards to walk in, and as my confinement is at a tavern on the public road, I am unavoidably exposed to tumultuous noise, and the unmerited insults of the lower class of passengers."[86] Campbell requested that he be moved to a house in Reading with a single sentry—a situation akin to Lee's.[87] But Campbell's complaints and requests went unheeded. Howe wrote to Washington, criticizing Campbell's being "exposed to daily insult from the deluded populace" and calling the officer's treatment "repugnant to every sentiment of humanity and highly unworthy of the character you profess."[88]

In all, Campbell spent thirty-four days in the dank, dark, and dirty Concord jail cell.[89] Placing officers such as Campbell and Prescott in a "loathsome" common jail for short stays as retaliation for poor treatment of American prisoners attracted criticism from British leaders then, and from some historians later. But it should be kept in mind that the most serious crisis affecting the health of prisoners was in fetid, crowded, and cold New York City prison ships, and churches and sugar houses used as prisons for thousands of Americans, where dozens of them died daily. American leaders mainly used the mere threat of eye-for-an-eye treatment with captured officers, but it worked. By March 18, Lieutenant Colonel Harcourt was writing to his brother that Lee's "life . . . is effectually secured by the threats of retaliation."[90]

The question of retaliation sparked debate among patriots, including an exchange of letters between Abigail and John Adams. In May, Abigail wrote that "The recital of the inhuman and brutal treatment of those poor creatures who have fallen into [British] hands freezes me with horror." Yet she favored a humane approach:

> Let them reproach us ever so much for our kindness and tenderness to those who have fallen into our hands. I hope it will never provoke us to retaliate against their cruelties. Let us ... keep in mind the precepts of Him who hath commanded us to love our enemies and to exercise towards them acts of humanity, benevolence, and kindness, even when they spitefully use us.... If our cause is just, it will be best supported by justice and righteousness. Though we have many other crimes to answer for, that of cruelty to our enemies is not chargeable upon Americans, and I hope never will be.[91]

Her husband responded, "I admire your sentiments concerning revenge." But he disagreed. "Retaliation we must practice, in some instances, in order to make our barbarous foes respect in some degree the rights of humanity," he wrote. "But this will never be done without the most palpable necessity. The apprehension of retaliation alone will restrain them from cruelties which would disgrace savages. To omit it then would be cruelty to ourselves, our officers and men."[92]

As a result of differing British and American views as to how Lee should be treated, prisoner exchanges ground to a halt. On April 21, Howe proposed restarting the process, despite "Mr. Lee, now professed to be a principal motive for your refusal to continue the exchange of prisoners."[93] But with Howe holding firm on considering Lee as ineligible for exchange, Washington ignored the request, as well as identical pleas made by Howe on May 22 and June 5.[94] Howe's aide, Captain Muenchhausen, complained in his diary on June 8 that "the Americans would not exchange anyone, even though they owed the British army 2,100 men."[95] Finally, on June 10, Washington consented to a partial exchange, excepting Colonel Campbell and the five Hessian field officers.[96] Howe, wanting Campbell back desperately, did not bother to respond.

After Howe received Lord Germain's March 3 letter requesting, in the name of George III, to send Lee to England to stand trial there, Howe responded to Germain on June 3. "Some material points respecting the situation of General Lee being still in discussion with Mr. Washington, in consequence of the agreement entered into for the exchange of prisoners, I venture for the present to postpone General Lee's departure for Great Britain," he wrote.[97] Howe's rebuff of a clear order to send Lee to England was remarkable. And it was Congress's firm stance that had produced it.

Meanwhile, Boisbertrand, who was captured at Widow White's Tavern and carried with Lee to Brunswick and then New York, was having a miserable time. At Brunswick, an English officer wrote that he had seen Boisbertrand and "provided him with quarters, where he was taken good care of, and supplied him with necessaries, and he was at liberty to walk about."[98] However, Boisbertrand's prospects dimmed after meeting with Howe, who, according to the Frenchman's account, "railed at him ungenerously." He was, he wrote afterward, "taken to a dreadful prison in New York," where he remained "for two months without change of linen, sleeping on the floor in a wretched blanket, fed on moldy biscuit and salt pork, both in small quantities." As Boisbertrand bitterly recalled later, "It can easily be guessed that itch, vermin and scurvy were the result of this" treatment.[99] Howe and British prison authorities at New York refused to treat Boisbertrand as a gentleman officer befitting his military and social rank. Since France was not then officially at war with Great Britain, they likely wanted to discourage other French officers from assisting the patriot cause. The British did not have to treat Boisbertrand as a Continental army officer because the Frenchman had not yet received his commission from Congress. He had made the mistake of not travelling straight to Philadelphia to obtain his commission before joining the American army.

After several weeks in his New York cell, the French lieutenant colonel was sent to England. Arriving in April 1777, he was committed to Forton prison, where numerous American sailors were confined in passable conditions. Nonetheless, Boisbertrand complained, "An entire volume would be necessary to depict the outrages and cruelties which [I] had to suffer in the hands of the proud English."[100] He managed to escape on July 23, 1778, and make his way to France. But he then discovered that he had lost both his position as lieutenant colonel in the French cavalry and his hereditary post, since he had overstayed his permitted two-year leave while confined in prison. Boisbertrand used influential contacts in France to try to persuade Congress to appoint him as a brigadier general in the Continental army, but he did not succeed.[101] He never rejoined the French army or held an important post again.

Boisbertrand's life is a reminder that not all French officers met with success in America, and a lesson on how a split-second decision can change one's life forever. Had Boisbertrand not fled Widow White's Tavern on December 12, he probably would not have been captured. In all likelihood he would have then made his way to Philadelphia, met with the Continental Congress, and been given an army commission, probably as a colonel. Instead of starting on a path that might have led to success and glory, Boisbertrand made the decision to flee the tavern and his life turned out very differently.

Shortly after his capture, Charles Lee experienced a dramatic transformation. Since the war's outset he had ranked among the most ardent patriot leaders, and had even advocated a complete break from Britain months before the adoption of the Declaration of Independence. Suddenly, he no longer believed the Americans could win the war, and thought that they should renounce their claimed independence and return to King George III's rule.

In February 1777 Lee was permitted to write to the Continental Congress and request that an American delegation be sent to meet with him in New York City, where he remained a British prisoner. The idea was to negotiate an end to hostilities. Congress rejected the proposal outright. The following month he did what can only be described as treasonous: he drafted and submitted a military plan for the Howe brothers to quickly defeat the American army. The next year, while still a prisoner, he offered to mediate an end to the war. Why Lee underwent this dramatic transformation is beyond the scope of this book.*

After the heady events of February and March, Lee returned to the monotonous routine of life as a prisoner confined to two rooms. Howe did finally allow his prisoner the use of one servant, and Lee wrote to his loyal Italian servant, Giuseppe Minghini, requesting that he join him in New York. Lee also asked Minghini to bring the general's summer clothes, several books, and any of his dogs.[102] Minghini complied, minus the dogs, which were in Virginia.[103]

On May 7, 1777, Lee wrote the following letter expressly for the eyes of patriot leaders in Boston:

---

*The author plans to address Lee's alleged treason in depth in a future book on Charles Lee.

It is with greatest concern (although it is somewhat flattering to me) that I learn that a misrepresentation of the treatment I receive has been the occasion of Colonel Campbell and some other gentlemen prisoners with you being closely confined and in other subjects harshly dealt with. Sir William Howe as a servant of the public thinks it incumbent upon him to guard me securely, but I give you my word and honor that from the beginning I have been treated with tenderness, generosity and respect. Gratitude, truth and humanity impose it upon me as a duty to undeceive you on this head. . . . I flatter myself and am persuaded that the moment you receive this note, Colonel Campbell and the other gentlemen will be put in the situation their rank and character entitle 'em to.[104]

On May 19, Lee wrote to Robert Morris in Philadelphia, "I have no occasion for money at present as my table is very handsomely kept by the General, who has indeed treated me in all respects with kindness, generosity and tenderness."[105] Lee fully anticipated that Morris would share the contents of his letter with Congressional delegates in the city, which Morris did. On June 2 Congress enacted the following resolution: "That a letter be written to the Council of Massachusetts Bay, and to the governor and Council of Virginia, acquainting them, that Congress have received information, that General Lee is treated by General Howe with kindness, generosity and tenderness, and desiring the former to treat Colonel Campbell, and the latter to treat the five Hessian officers, with kindness, generosity, and tenderness, consistent with the confinement and safe custody of their persons."[106]

In a May 26 letter, Campbell, noting the month's reports of Lee's good treatment, again complained of the "unavoidable interference with passengers and other visitors, to whose insults I am even at this hour exposed by my residence at a tavern upon the public road."[107] Congress's June measure would have justified granting Lieutenant Colonel Campbell's request to be moved out of the crowded tavern that he despised, but another development regarding Lee's subsequent confinement quashed that prospect.

On June 4, General Howe suddenly had Lee moved "under a strong guard at six o'clock in the morning" to a room below decks on the 50-gun warship *Centurion*, then anchored in New York Harbor.[108] Lee was "permitted to walk the quarter deck" for parts of each day.[109] According to one British officer, Lee's transfer was ordered for "security" reasons.[110] Bound for Philadelphia with most of his forces, Howe apparently thought that in the event of an American attack on New York City, Lee would be more secure on a warship, which, if necessary, could escape to sea. Indeed, General Henry Clinton, who assumed command at New York after Howe's departure, temporarily moved his own headquarters to a British ship in New York Harbor.[111]

The day of Lee's move coincided with "every possible demonstration of joy" celebrating King George III's fortieth birthday. A New York newspaper reported, "At one o'clock, a royal salute was fired from Fort George, which was answered by all his Majesty's ships in the harbor, as well as merchantmen, to the amount of about 500 sail. After which his Excellency Admiral Lord Howe, and General Sir William Howe, with the principal officers of the Navy and the Army, dined together at his Lordship's house in Hanover Square, where an elegant entertainment was provided."[112] Lee could not help but hear the gunfire, which also echoed from the *Centurion*. An officer wrote in the ship's log for that day, "at 1 p.m. fired 21 guns in commemoration of his Majesty's birthday."[113]

The Royal Navy's Captain John Bowater, whose duty it was to oversee Lee's guard and sometimes even be his companion, hated both Lee and his new job.[114] Nor, apparently, did he treat Lee with the respect the prisoner desired. To General Clinton, who had known Lee prior to the war, the American general wrote two months later, "I am in my present situation subject to such abominable insults that I most earnestly request you to change the place of my confinement, even to a common prison."[115] Clinton promised he would do all he could for Lee, consistent with Howe's orders.[116] For now, however, he could not move the general from the ship without new instructions.

When news of Lee's transfer to the *Centurion* reached Philadelphia, Congress concluded that Howe must be readying his captive for a trip to England. On June 10, Congress passed a resolution warning that such treatment of any person employed in the service of the United States would produce reciprocal treatment of British prisoners in American hands. In addition, it made clear its determination to retain both Lieutenant Colonel Campbell and the Hessian field officers taken at Trenton until the British recognized Lee as exchange eligible.[117] Washington immediately fired off a letter to Howe, repeating these points.[118]

Congress's threat had the desired effect. In a July 6 letter to Lord Germain, Howe wrote: "I have judged it expedient to detain him [Lee] here until I am honored with his Majesty's further pleasure, being apprehensive, were he sent to Britain, that the close confinement of the Hessian officers would be the consequence, which might probably occasion much discontent among the foreign [i.e., German] troops not to be remedied, and be attributed to my sending home General Lee."[119] Even Britain's *Annual Register* admired Congress's "firm and undaunted resolution."[120]

In his June 10 letter to Howe, Washington stated that he desired only that "General Lee be declared exchangeable, when we shall have an officer of yours of equal rank in our possession."[121] At the time, the matter was moot; the American army had no such captive. But that was about to change.

British frigates are in the middle channel in Narragansett Bay, having dispatched boats filled with soldiers ready to land on shore and occupy Newport and the rest of Aquidneck Island. Some of these same frigates later served in a blockade of Narragansett Bay. "The Attack of Rhode Island, December 8th, 1776," a watercolor by Irwin Bevan (1852–1940). (*Mariners' Museum*)

5

Richard Prescott Commands

Charles Lee's fate would be decided neither in London nor in negotiations between the commanders-in-chief of the American and British armies, but in the seemingly insignificant, and inactive, Rhode Island theater of war. The state had been occupied since December 8, 1776, when 7,100 British, Hessian, and Tory troops, commanded by Lieutenant General Henry Clinton and delivered by a fleet of seventy-one warships and transport vessels, invaded Aquidneck Island. Patriot troops, no match for this overwhelming land and sea force, evacuated the island, allowing Clinton's troops to land without resistance. Newport—prior to the war the fifth-most important American city behind Philadelphia, Boston, New York, and Charleston—fell the same day.

In short order British forces occupied all of Aquidneck Island, which was just fourteen miles long and two miles wide, and small Conanicut Island (also called Jamestown), opposite Newport Harbor. His job quickly and easily completed, Clinton departed, leaving command of the British garrison to Lieutenant General Hugh, Earl Percy. Percy's second-in-command was the now-well-known Major General Richard Prescott, who had returned to service after being exchanged for Brigadier General John Sullivan in September.

Commodore Sir Peter Parker, commanding British naval forces at Newport, immediately stationed frigates in the three entrances to Narragansett Bay, thus keeping commercial vessels out of Providence, Bristol, Swansea, and other port towns in upper Narragansett Bay. The blockade also bottled up Continental navy ships and pesky privateers at Providence. Some Rhode Island vessels that tried to slip out of the bay were captured, and their crews placed on prison ships in Newport Harbor. Meanwhile, Admiral Richard Howe, brother of General William Howe, brought more warships to Rhode Island to spend the winter in Newport's ice-free harbor. "I am very much pleased with the good news you have sent unto me, which secures an excellent port for the ships," King George III wrote to the Earl of Sandwich.[1]

Still, the British only occupied about one-quarter of the state. The rest of Rhode Island, and neighboring Bristol and Dartmouth counties in Massachusetts, were firmly in the patriot camp. This was confirmed by a Loyalist spy, who informed General Percy that in Providence, "the inhabitants are notorious rebels, scarcely a loyal subject to be found." East of Narragansett Bay, the spy found Bristol's inhabitants were "disloyal." In Taunton, Massachusetts, "a fine village," the inhabitants were all "rebels, except a few at Swansea called Quakers." It was the same throughout the rest of southeastern New England.[2]

On December 7, when Parker's fleet had sailed into Narragansett Bay, Rhode Island governor Nicholas Cooke had issued a proclamation informing "all the brave inhabitants of New England" that enemy troops were set to invade Newport. "If they get a lodgment in this town, they will soon penetrate the country," he warned. Cooke urgently called on New England men to "come properly armed, with the necessary accoutrements, and with blankets, knapsacks, and such provisions as you can bring with you."[3] In response, 6,000 Massachusetts, Connecticut, and Rhode Island state troops and militia men flocked to camps at Providence, Warwick, Bristol, and Tiverton, surrounding Aquidneck Island. While the call-up helped to prevent an immediate British assault on Providence, New England patriots were not yet sufficiently strong or organized to mount a serious campaign to retake Newport.

Despite entreaties from Rhode Island politicians, George Washington declined to send any Continental troops to the area. He wanted to keep his regulars where they were most needed, before

General Howe's main army in New Jersey, and to help forestall a British army descending from northern New York toward Albany.

Washington did send to Rhode Island two Continental officers to take command of American forces, Brigadier Generals Joseph Spencer and Benedict Arnold. The sixty-three-year-old Spencer, senior in command, hailed from East Haddam, Connecticut, and had gained a reputation commanding two regiments in the Battle of Bunker Hill. Born and raised in Norwich, Connecticut, Arnold had already shown himself to be arguably the most talented field officer in the entire American army. Upon reaching Providence on January 12, 1777, Arnold wrote to Washington that "people in general are in high spirits" and that it seemed to be a "favorable" time "to dislodge the enemy from the country."[4]

On March 1, the Rhode Island General Assembly tried to spur action by offering rewards to American soldiers for each enemy soldier "taken prisoner and brought off" Rhode Island, within fifteen days. The reward was based on the rank of the prisoner: "one thousand dollars for every British or foreign general officer, two hundred dollars for a colonel," down to "twenty dollars for every private." The reward was to be "equally divided between officers and privates" who had effected the capture.[5]

Soon, however, reality crept in. Spencer and Arnold could not raise a sufficient force of New England soldiers to seriously threaten British forces at Newport. On March 2, 1777, with the enlistments of most of the Massachusetts and Connecticut militia about to expire, New England officers held a council of war. Agreeing with Arnold that there was "no reasonable prospect of succeeding against 4,000 well-disciplined troops,"[6] the officers decided to end their efforts and send their troops home.

The British had their own problems in Newport. Initially, Howe had occupied the city as part of a larger plan for his main army in New York City to meet in Albany with the British army descending through upstate New York from Canada. With those two armies cutting off New England from the rest of the colonies, a third British army, with 10,000 men in Newport, could march north to seize Providence and then proceed "into the country towards Boston and, if possible, reduce that town."[7] But this plan was set aside almost immediately after Lord George Germain refused to provide Howe with the additional troops needed to carry it out.[8] Instead, Howe turned his attention to seizing New Jersey, and later,

Philadelphia. That meant Howe subtracting troops from the garrison at Newport, leaving only about 4,300 men to defend the port and the rest of Aquidneck Island. In May 1777, an angry General Percy departed Newport for England, upset with Howe for leaving him too few troops for offensive operations, among other reasons. Howe, seeing little threat to Newport, then ordered three more Newport-based regiments to join his main army in New York. Percy's departure, meanwhile, left Major General Richard Prescott in command of British forces in Rhode Island.[9]

With the British presence now limited to two islands in Narragansett Bay, a few regiments of Rhode Island and Massachusetts troops took up posts at Howland's Ferry in Tiverton, Bristol Neck, at the southern tip of Bristol County, and other locations opposite Aquidneck Island. When members of these units began launching small-scale raids onto the island, Prescott and his men realized that they were surrounded by hostile forces.

On June 20, 1777, Lieutenant Colonel William Barton, a relatively unknown but energetic twenty-nine-year-old officer, sat deep in thought in his headquarters in Tiverton, Rhode Island. Born and raised in the seafaring village of Warren on May 26, 1748, Barton received a limited education. He later began a career as a hat maker in his own shop on Providence's west side. Based on an advertisement in the October 10, 1772, edition of the *Providence Gazette* offering a reward to anyone who apprehended the thieves who had twice broken into his store, it could be inferred that Barton had a modest business. The first robbery cost him "five new beaver hats, not colored; one second hand hat in the new fashion; and one cloth surtout [coat] with basket buttons." In the second he lost "three beaver hats, one of them colored, but not finished; two napped castors, one of them not looped; a parcel of looping; and some silver cord." On the domestic front, Barton married Rhoda Carver of Bridgewater, Massachusetts, on April 26, 1771. The couple's first two children, both sons, were born in December of 1771 and 1773.[10]

When war broke out in 1775, Barton, a firm patriot but lacking military experience, joined a Providence militia company as a corporal.[11] Powerfully built, with a wide body, a large head, and a square jaw, he proved a natural leader and quickly rose in rank. In August of 1775, he was appointed adjutant of a Providence County militia regiment. Then, with the formation of the first state regiment, Barton was named captain-lieutenant of a company. He eventually became its captain.[12] His patriotic fervor was so strong that he named his third son, born in February 1776, George Washington Barton.[13] Trying to earn some extra money to support his growing family, he placed an advertisement in the *Providence Gazette* assuring his old customers that even though he was in the service of "the American army," his shop was still open and being run by a good hatter.[14]

William Barton, in his uniform as colonel of the Continental army during the Revolutionary War. Portrait by James Sullivan Lincoln, 1857, from an earlier portrait done about 1788 by an unknown artist, in the possession of the Rhode Island Historical Society. (*Brown University Portrait Collection*)

Barton first came to public notice through his dealings with Captain James Wallace, commander of a small flotilla of British warships, including the frigate HMS *Rose*. In the months after the Battles of Lexington and Concord, Wallace's ships had terrorized Newport and other towns along Narragansett Bay, and even shelled Bristol. With Rhode Island not yet on war footing, Wallace reigned unchallenged in the colony's waters.

Barton, then the commander of a company stationed on Aquidneck Island, thought up a dual-purpose plan. If it worked, it would both embarrass Wallace and stop runaway slaves from providing him with intelligence that he could use to raid coastal farms. On the evening of January 8, 1776, Barton ordered an African-American man to hail the *Rose* from Brenton Point, just south of Newport. Assuming that the man was another runaway slave who could provide useful information, Wallace sent a midshipman and two sailors in a small boat to fetch him. But as soon as they came ashore, Barton and twenty of his men sprang out from their hiding places and captured them. An enraged Wallace ordered one of his ships to shell the western coast of Narragansett Bay, but, as Newport's Reverend Ezra Stiles, pastor of the First Congregational Church and a firm patriot, wrote in his diary, the "foolish" display of "thunder and lightning" did no damage.[15] Barton resigned from his command in March 1776. Four months later he was appointed major of Rhode Island's newly formed state brigade.[16]

In December, immediately after Clinton occupied Newport, the Rhode Island General Assembly organized an artillery regiment and two infantry regiments, enlisting officers and soldiers for fifteen months.[17] The men in these state regiments would have less experience than those in Continental regiments, but more than those in militia companies, which received only haphazard training. Barton was selected as a lieutenant colonel of the 1st Rhode Island State Regiment, serving under Colonel Joseph Stanton, a successful farmer from Charlestown, Rhode Island.[18]

Barton's regiment was stationed at Tiverton, Rhode Island, opposite Howland's Ferry, the British army's northern outpost on Aquidneck Island. Between these two camps flowed the Sakonnet Channel (now called the Sakonnet River). News of Charles Lee's December 13 capture disturbed Barton, who admitted that he had "a very high opinion of the General's abilities." He later wrote that while at Tiverton, "I used the greatest endeavors to get intelligence of some British officer of the same rank with Major General Lee whom I might surprise and thus effect an exchange of that great man."[19]

On June 20, 1777, Barton learned something that set his mind spinning. At his Tiverton headquarters, Barton interrogated Paul Coffin,[20] a civilian who had recently escaped from Aquidneck Island. It was not uncommon for civilians to use boats to slip away from the British-occupied island, and, when they did, for patriot officers to detain them and try to obtain useful intelligence. The obliging Coffin informed Barton that Major General Prescott, who normally maintained his headquarters and residence at John Banister's house in Newport, was spending nights at the commodious farm house of Henry John Overing in Middletown, about five miles north of Newport. A few days later, a British deserter confirmed Coffin's report.

Finally, Barton had the intelligence he had been desperately seeking. He began to plan a daring operation. Under cover of darkness, whaleboats would carry him and a small body of troops across Narragansett Bay to Aquidneck Island. They would quickly grab Prescott, and then spirit him back to the mainland. This simple plan was fraught with risk: a single warning shot fired by a sentry in a guard boat or at a post on land would likely ruin the operation. Worse, the entire party could wind up in a British prison ship. Barton feared that "if our plan should be blasted, that my country would reprobate my conduct as rash and imprudent."[21] But the former hatter thought that trying to free Lee was worth the risk. Widespread American hatred of Prescott provided an additional inducement.

Rhode Island patriots had a soft spot for Lee, who had formed two connections with the state after becoming a major general in the Continental army. He first visited Rhode Island in December 1775, taking time off from the Americans' siege of Boston. He arrived amid Captain Wallace's reign of terror in Narragansett Bay, at a time when control of Newport was constantly changing between Tories and patriots. On Christmas day, Lee entered Newport with a company of 100 Virginia riflemen. He then called in eight prominent Loyalists—including Joseph Wanton, Rhode Island's former deputy governor and son of the ex-governor—and required them to take an oath not to assist the King's troops. Wanton and two others refused, and were arrested and sent to Providence. "The General's presence here strikes awe through the Tories," wrote Reverend Ezra Stiles. "They are as obsequious and submissive as possible."[22] Lee toured parts of Aquidneck Island and recommended sites for fortifications, and talked of sending two regiments to be stationed in Newport. Lee's visit enraged the lurking Captain Wallace, but stiffened the resolve of Newport's and Providence's patriot elite.[23] Lee's firmness also thoroughly impressed Captain William Barton, who was then stationed in Newport.

When the British fleet poured into Narragansett Bay on December 7, Governor Cooke wrote immediately to Lee, asking for experienced men with which to bolster Rhode Island's officer corps. From Pompton Plains, New Jersey, Lee immediately sent Cooke two officers: Rhode Island native Colonel James Varnum of the Continental army, and a recently arrived French volunteer and engineer named Francois Lellorquis de Malmedy. At the same time, however, Lee managed to insult New England's senior officers. In attempting to persuade Cooke (and ultimately the Rhode Island General Assembly) to appoint Malmedy as a state brigadier general, he pointed out that while New England's rank-and-file soldiers and young officers showed "activity and fire," the quality of New England's top commanders was poor. "Due to a certain rustiness of mind and temperament, you have no man with you capable of conducting an army."[24] Despite the insult, or perhaps because of it, the General Assembly went along with Lee's recommendation.[25] But after General Nathanael Greene read Lee's letter, he exploded in anger, complaining that it "contains some infamous and very illiberal reflections upon the genius of all the New England States.... There are as many men of spirit, activity, and understanding in New England as in any part of the world, according to their numbers."[26] Malmedy was an accomplished engineer, something that Rhode Island desperately needed in order to prepare defensive fortifications. Lee could have narrowed his critique of New England officers to engineers, rather than painting with such a broad brush.

Despite Lee's stunning lack of tact, Rhode Island patriots generally still admired him in June 1777. And they despised British general Richard Prescott for his cruelty toward Newport inhabitants. Prescott's harshness may have been the product of still-fresh recollections of his treatment at the hands of the Americans.[27] Prescott deeply detested patriots, whom he considered vile traitors to the Crown. This was the same man who had screamed in the face of Ethan Allen that he would be hanged, and then clapped him in irons. To Thomas Walker he had blared, "traitor and a villain you scoundrel, to betray your country," before tightening Walker's wrist irons enough to cause him "inexpressible pain." Once Prescott assumed command of the Newport garrison on May 5, 1777, he was in an ideal position to punish all "rebels" who crossed his path.[28]

Born in England in 1725, Prescott began his long military career as a young man. He was wounded in the arm during the British army's loss to the French in the May 11, 1745, Battle of Fontenoy. This wound would never completely heal; it was the same one that caused the Continental Congress to have him removed from Philadelphia's common jail. After recovering enough to return to service, he steadily rose through the ranks, receiving a lieutenant colonelcy with the 50th Regiment in Germany during the Seven Years' War. In late 1761, he was appointed lieutenant colonel of the 7th Regiment of Foot (also called the Royal Fusiliers). Patiently waiting his turn, he served in Canada as a brigadier general in North America only in 1775 and became full colonel of the 7th Regiment in November of 1776. Posted to Montreal he and all but seventy-five of his men were captured by General Montgomery's invading force.[29] From that ordeal he had emerged in the fall of 1776. Now fifty-two years old, Prescott had shown himself to be a competent officer, but he had displayed neither original thinking nor inspired leadership.

Prescott was one of a party of British officers—a small one to be sure—who took an exceptionally hard line against patriots. Perhaps it is surprising there were not more like them. After all, from the British perspective, "patriots" were nothing more than treasonous rebels and criminal traitors. The last time England had faced a major rebellion, in Scotland in 1745–1746, it had been ruthlessly crushed. After the April 16, 1745, Battle of Culloden, hundreds of wounded Highlanders on and near the field of battle were bayoneted to death, and in the battle's aftermath eighty-eight rebels were hanged for treason. Some were drawn and quartered.[30]

These British hardliners included a captain in the King's Own Regiment, who described Americans as "upstart vagabonds, the dregs and scorn of the human species," and declared that Crown rule must be reestablished even if it required "almost extirpating the present rebellious race."[31] Following the June 17, 1775, Battle of Bunker Hill, which claimed the life of popular Massachusetts physician and patriot leader Joseph Warren, Americans mourned the loss. But Captain Walter Sloane Laurie of the British 43rd Regiment callously wrote of him, "I found [Warren] among the slain, and stuffed the scoundrel with another rebel into one hole, and there he and his seditious principles may remain."[32] In October 1775, Royal Navy Lieutenant Henry Mowatt accused the people of Falmouth (now Portland), Maine, of being "guilty of the most unpardonable rebellion" and failing "a dutiful and grateful return to your King and parent state." He then had his small flotilla of warships fire heated cannonballs and incendiary shot into the town, sparking a devastating fire that destroyed some 130 houses.[33]

General Prescott's extreme hatred of "rebels" sometimes drew ridicule. In 1775, Brigadier General Benedict Arnold's successful defense of northern New York so upset Prescott that he offered a 1,000-guinea reward for Arnold's capture. The *Annual Register* later noted that "General Prescott ... had carried matters to such a length as to set a price upon Arnold, and offer a reward for taking his person, as if he had been a common out-law or robber; an insult which Arnold immediately returned, by setting an inferior price upon the General's person."[34] Englishmen tittered at and admired Arnold's cleverness in offering the lower reward even if Arnold himself was a "rebel."[35]

Prescott's contempt for American patriots can further be seen in his treatment of two prisoners taken shortly after the British occupied Newport. One of them was a Portsmouth militia captain named Burrington Anthony, said to be one of the largest and stoutest men in Rhode Island. Spotted in military dress and carrying a weapon, Anthony was arrested and placed in what had been the Newport County jail. (The British had turned it into a prison called the Provost.) There, Prescott verbally abused him. Thomas Durfee, then a boy in whose home Prescott was temporarily quartered, recalled the general repeatedly saying "damn him [Anthony]" and that Anthony "would be hung." Despite this threat, Anthony refused to sign an oath of allegiance to King George III and, in fact, verbally sparred with his British captors. Anthony was kept in jail for almost a year before he was finally released and allowed to leave Aquidneck Island.[36]

Another incident involved a crewman of an American privateer who was captured and imprisoned in Newport in early 1777. He was brought before the town's three British commanders: General Percy, General Prescott, and Commodore Parker. A Boston newspaper reported the following exchange:

> Says Prescott, "What are you?" "I have been a lieutenant of a privateer." "A lieutenant of a privateer, ha! Damn your blood, one of the damn'd thieves," and immediately made up to him and hit him a knock in the jaws, and said he should be hanged. . . . [Prescott] added, "Yes, damn you, I have been a prisoner among you and know how I was treated;" and hit him another knock. Lord Percy desired [Prescott] not to proceed in that way, as he [the lieutenant] was a prisoner; [Prescott] told the prisoner he should be chained neck and heels, and be fed with nothing but oatmeal and water, and while he lived his life should be miserable, and hit him another knock, which Lord Percy again disapproved of, and ordered him to be put into prison, which he said was enough without blows or irons.[37]

Reflecting American outrage, the *Independent Chronicle* called Prescott a "blustering coward." While it cannot be said with certainty that the assault occurred, the incident sounds credible, particularly in light of his treatment of Anthony. Prescott and other British officers did not consider privateer crews legitimate seamen. Indeed, when he ordered his blockade of Narragansett Bay, Parker expressed satisfaction that his efforts had "put an effectual stop to any further mischief from that nest of pirates."[38]

American prisoners placed aboard British prison ships in Newport Harbor were given scanty, poor-quality food and little fresh water, and were in general treated badly. On January 25, 1777, the *Providence Gazette* reported that "A number of Americans have lately arrived here from Newport in a flag of truce, having been exchanged there: one of them is since dead, and some others cannot long survive, owing to the inhuman treatment they received from the enemy." Providence doctor Isaac Senter described other freed prisoners who had arrived from Newport prison ships the next month as "run over with vermin, half rotten with scurvy and putrid fever. Some of their extremities were frozen and almost rotten through neglect." Senter informed his Providence readers that the prisoners had been confined in a ship's hold "where they were half-starved, and denied even light for a number of days." "To complete their misery," Senter added, "they did not fail to receive the kicks, cuffs, and bruises of the soldiery, when opportunity offered, who upbraided them with the epithet of 'damn'd Yankee Rebels.'"[39] Prescott, as commander of the Newport garrison, bore some responsibility for this even if most of the blame lay with the naval commanders who operated the prison ships.

Prescott was known to strike Newport Quaker men with his cane for failing to doff their hats in respect when he approached.[40] On one occasion, Elisha Anthony was passing Prescott on a Newport street when Prescott reportedly asked loudly "why he did not take his hat off!" Anthony responded that, "it was against his principle to show those signs of respect to man." Prescott then ordered his servant to knock off Anthony's hat, which he did.[41] Another time, as Prescott was riding out of town to his country quarters, he saw another Quaker who failed to doff his hat. The general dashed up to him, pressed him against a stone wall, knocked off his hat, and then put him under guard.[42]

Prescott's iron-handed rule included banishing civilians to filthy jails and permitting the destruction of unoccupied patriot houses in Newport.[43] The following story was told to an early historian of the Revolutionary War, probably by a child of the abused father:

> Prescott caused many citizens of Newport to be imprisoned, some of them for months, without any assigned reason. Among others he deprived of liberty was William Tripp, a very respectable citizen. He had a large and interesting family, but the tyrant would not allow him to hold any communication with them, either written or verbal. The first intelligence he received from them was by a letter, baked in a loaf of bread, which was sent to him by his wife. In this way a correspondence

was kept up during his confinement of many months. During his incarceration, his wife sought an audience with the general to intercede for the liberty of her husband, or to obtain a personal interview with him. She applied to a Captain [Henry] Savage [an aide to Prescott], through whom alone an interview with the general could be obtained. She was directed to call the following day, when the savage by name and nature, echoing his master's words, roughly denied her petition for an interview with the general, and with fiendish exultation informed her, as he shut the door violently in her face, that he expected her husband would be hung as a rebel in less than a week![44]

While Tripp was not hanged, Prescott and his aides apparently relished terrorizing civilians.

One apocryphal story that circulated about Prescott involved a local farmer, Thomas Austin, who refused to allow his team of oxen to pull Royal Artillery pieces across Aquidneck Island. Prescott reportedly ordered that Austin be given 300 lashes with a leather whip, which could rip pieces of flesh off the victim's skin after only a few strokes. Indeed, after just a few, attending physicians declared that Austin would never survive 300 strokes. Only then did Prescott release him. Austin later reportedly escaped from the island, arriving at the American army's camp in nearby Tiverton.[45] This flogging probably did not occur. If it had, British, German, and American diarists and other observers would likely have recorded it. Nonetheless, convincing stories like Austin's quickly made the rounds, and deepened local hatred of the British commander.

The hostility of Newport residents toward Prescott was remarked on by the general's own soldiers. "Because he was rather strict, he was not well liked in the city, where there were rebels, in Newport, just as in Providence,"[46] noted one Hessian. Another Hessian observed that Prescott "did not treat the locally born inhabitants well because he had been a prisoner of the rebels previously and had experienced much hardship. As soon as he had the least opportunity to blame someone for something, he placed them in jail. Therefore, the people on the island had the greatest hatred for him, which they also displayed in every opportunity."[47] Even British navy captain John Bowater, overseeing Lee's captivity on board the *Centurion* in New York Harbor, heard that Prescott "treated the inhabitants with great severity."[48]

Prescott's reputation for cruelty combined with his sudden, close proximity to patriot positions, made him the perfect target for Lieutenant Colonel Barton. In retrospect it does appear that Prescott's abuse of patriots was more verbal than physical. Regardless, the mix of fact and rumor helped drive events. He was, at the least, a petty tyrant.

As Barton had learned, Prescott had changed his evening sleeping quarters from the John Banister residence in the heart of Newport to the spacious home of Henry John Overing, about five miles north in lightly populated Middletown. On a working farm with several outbuildings, Overing's main house was located on Aquidneck's western edge, almost a mile from Narragansett Bay. It stood just east of the West Road, one of two main island thoroughfares that stretched from Newport to the island's northern tip at Bristol Ferry. (The other road, called the East Road, ran up the island's east coast.) From British and Hessian deserters Barton learned that Prescott's defenses were weakest along the island's western side—where the Overing house sat. Prescott's defensive positioning was the result of his own, deliberate planning.

Upon assuming command of the British garrison on May 6, 1777, Prescott considered where to station his roughly 3,500 soldiers—three British and four German regiments (each of which included about 400 men), and elite British grenadier and light infantry companies and Hessian chasseurs.[49] With most of the American troops posted near Tiverton and Bristol Ferry, it made sense to shift some units to the island's eastern and northern parts, to guard against raids launched from there.

Prescott could also not ignore the fact that virtually all of the action on Aquidneck Island up to that time had occurred in the vicinity of Howland's Ferry, on the east side of Aquidneck Island, just below the northern tip of the island and opposite the main camp of the Americans across the Sakonnet Channel. (Both the American side of the ferry on Tiverton and the British side of the ferry on Portsmouth were called Howland's Ferry.) American raids had particularly annoyed the small detachments of British and Hessian troops who manned the guard houses and sentry posts at the northern end of Aquidneck Island. As early as mid-December 1776 one Hessian soldier had complained that his detachment was "constantly disturbed."[50] A Hessian officer noted the startling proximity of the Americans just across the narrow channel. "Because they can fire [artillery] shot almost into our camp," he wrote, "we are kept in a continual state of alarm."⁵¹ American harassment continued into the winter months, as an officer of the von Huyn Regiment described in early 1777: "They frequently attacked our detachments and made several attempts to land, so that several times, especially during the night, signals were given by firing guns and setting alarm poles on fire for the regiments to turn out immediately."⁵²

On February 22, the Rhode Island state navy row galley *Spitfire*, carrying eight cannon and sixteen swivel guns and commanded by Captain Isaac Tyler,⁵³ provided cover for some 400 Americans aiming to land on the west side of Common Fence Point, apparently with the goal of repeating the prior day's success in removing hay. At about 10:00 a.m., the *Spitfire* ventured out of nearby Nannaquaket Creek and stationed itself in the Sakonnet Channel, about 200 yards in front of a British guard house, south of Common Fence Point. In response, Royal artillerymen moved two 6-pounder cannon up to the shoreline; Hessian soldiers brought up four more. The *Spitfire* opened fire on the guard house, but return fire from the opposing artillerymen breached the ship's hull and injured some of the crew. Eventually, Captain Tyler ordered his galley to withdraw. Meanwhile, British and Hessian guards met the Americans and drove them back to their boats.⁵⁴ The *Providence Gazette* subsequently reported that the *Spitfire* was "considerably damaged in her hull and rigging, and had seven men wounded, one of them mortally."⁵⁵ But the raid-in-force had alarmed the British.

On March 18, shortly before a number of Massachusetts militiamen in General James Varnum's brigade were to be sent back home after the attempt to recapture Newport had been called off, about twenty-five of them from Wrentham were so eager for action that they staged an unauthorized daylight raid. At 11:00 a.m. they rowed in three whaleboats the 200 yards from Howland's Ferry to the opposite shoreline on Aquidneck Island and, after landing, rushed a short way to a small bridge over a stream. On the other side of the bridge were British guards, supported by an artillery piece that had its side of the bridge within its range. The Wrentham men, staying on their side of the bridge, fired at the British troops, causing them to retire. Upon hearing the firing, Captain John Topham and twenty-five of his men of the 1st Rhode Island State Regiment took three more whaleboats over to the scene of action. The British also sent a small party of soldiers toward the bridge, hoping to lure opposing troops into crossing to where they would be within artillery range. But the New Englanders did not fall for the decoy and soon returned, with no damage done on either side.⁵⁶

The commander of the Rhode Island theater, General Joseph Spencer, informed the Continental Congress that "Since I have given up the hopes of being supplied with troops sufficient to make a descent on Rhode Island [meaning Aquidneck Island], I have encouraged parties in going on to take some of their guards."⁵⁷ As the weather warmed in 1777, Americans began more frequently sending troops in whaleboats over to Common Fence Point and other parts of the northern Aquidneck Island at night. While there, under cover of darkness, the Americans would harass the British and Hessian guards, or assist willing British and Hessian troops to desert to the American side, rowing them to the mainland.

On the night of Sunday, April 27, a sergeant from the British 43rd Regiment deserted his post at the northern end of Aquidneck Island. Americans in row boats picked him up. The British sergeant, on his way to safety, probably informed the Americans that his regiment would likely send out a detachment to search for him. Seeing an opportunity, later that night about sixteen American troops rowed quietly back over to Aquidneck Island, led by Captain Samuel Phillips of Updike's Newtown (now Wickford) in North Kingstown. The Americans lay in ambush and sure enough soon spotted a small detachment of fifteen British troops sent to search for the deserter, commanded by a young ensign, John M. Clarke of the 43rd Regiment. The Americans surprised the British and put them to flight, except for Ensign Clarke, who was captured.⁵⁸

Prescott, increasingly concerned about these raids on the northeastern part of Aquidneck Island, arrived at a new plan to move troops to the northeast to more effectively counter them. On May 24, he directed Brigadier General Francis Smith, commanding the troops in this area, to relocate the British 22nd and 43rd Regiments from civilian houses on the west side of the island north to camps just above Windmill Hill (which the Americans called Butts Hill), in Portsmouth. The British had recently constructed a redoubt atop Windmill Hill, where Prescott's main upper-island fortifications lay.⁵⁹ Smith complied, and also moved the German Landgrave and von Ditfurth Regiments to the area.⁶⁰ To the south of the hill Smith also placed an artillery battery, whose guns could be quickly moved along a secondary road to either the West or East roads. In addition, Smith ordered pickets to patrol to the east and west of Windmill

Hill. These troops could quickly respond to a raid-in-force to any spot on the island's northern coast. On June 17, Smith further ordered the soldiers of the 22nd Regiment to "strike their tents" and move, with two six-pounder cannon, a few miles southeast to Quaker Hill. There they took up positions next to the Quaker meetinghouse at the intersection of Middle Road, Hedley Street, and the East Road.[61]

Guard houses and advanced sentry posts were manned near Howland's Ferry and at other posts in northeastern Portsmouth. The men assigned to these advanced posts were relieved every twenty-four hours. Artillery redoubts were manned by Royal artillerymen at Bristol Ferry, on the northern coast of Aquidneck Island, and at Fogland Ferry, the mid-way point between Newport and the northern tip of Aquidneck Island on its east coast, fronting the Sakonnet Channel. General Smith ordered the grenadiers and light infantry companies of the 54th Regiment, commanded by Captain Thomas Coore, to camp nearby. From Fogland Ferry, Smith also ordered Coore to post fifteen infantrymen at all times there on "constant patrols going during the night, along the coast, to the right and left."[62] "[A]ll these different encampments," Prescott explained, "were connected by pickets, night posts and patrols."[63] To provide further support and to interrupt attempts by Americans to send whaleboats and flatboats across the channel, the sloop-of-war *Kingsfisher* sat anchored off of Black Point in the Sakonnet Channel.

Emphasizing how determined the British were to defend the island's northern and eastern sectors, Smith ordered that "no officer on any account to lie out of camp [that is, to stay in a house away from camp], nor is any officer to leave the encampment in the day, without leave from the commanding officer of the regiment, who will take care not to permit too many to be absent at a time."[64] This order irritated Smith's subordinate officers, who relished the comforts of sleeping at night in nearby civilian houses. To the south, meanwhile, Prescott kept the German von Huyn and von Bunau Regiments on heights to the north of Newport, probably at or near Tonomy Hill. From here, he could quickly dispatch troops into town to protect vital supplies of food, munitions, wood, and hay from patriot sympathizers.[65] Hessian chasseurs—hand-picked soldiers from myriad German regiments—were shifted from Conanicut Island to a new camp south of Newport, on Brenton Neck. To keep Conanicut Island's hay-harvesting operations going, elements of the British 54th Regiment immediately replaced them.[66]

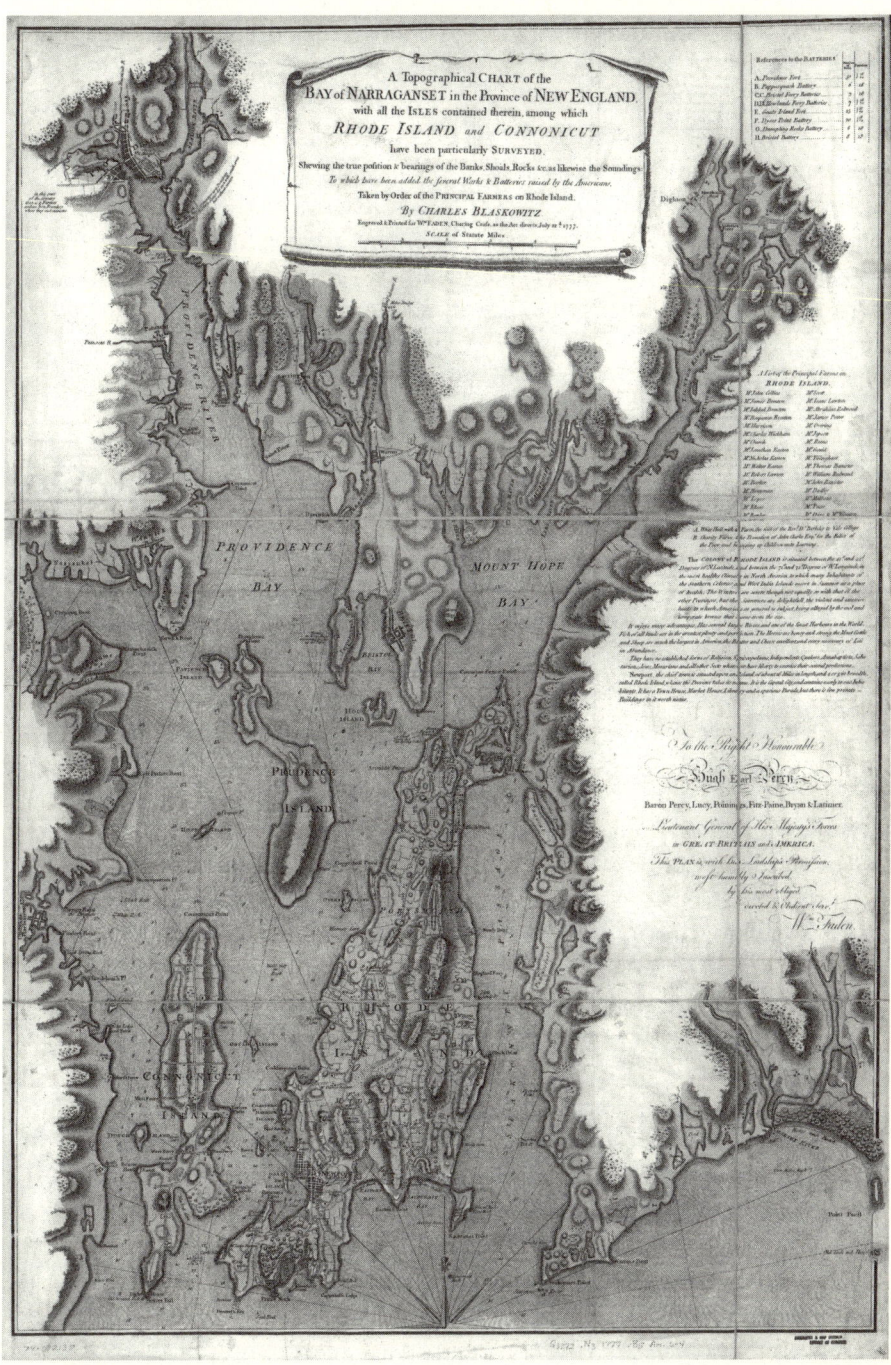

"A Topographical Chart of the Bay of Narragansett," by Charles Blaskowitz, London, 1777. (*Library of Congress*)

To protect Aquidneck Island's western side, General Prescott chose to rely on five navy frigates positioned in Narragansett Bay's west and middle channels. Three of them, the 50-gun HMS *Chatham*, the 32-gun HMS *Diamond*, and the 32-gun HMS *Lark*, were anchored just off the island's west coast, in a line running south to north. The northernmost ship, the *Lark*, protected the flank of the British fortifications at Windmill Hill. The 50-gun HMS *Renown* and the 32-gun HMS *Greyhound* sat west of Prudence Island. Each night, guard boats dispatched from the ships patrolled the waters around them. The British warships intimidated but great gaps lay between them. The *Chatham* was stationed about two-and-one-half miles from the *Diamond*, which was anchored about two miles from the *Lark*. Roughly five miles separated the *Renown* from the *Greyhound*.[67] The main task of the British frigates was to prevent American ships from entering and leaving Narragansett Bay. The gaps between the warships did not prevent Royal Navy officers from successfully accomplishing this goal.

On May 26, Prescott had Smith issue the following order: "headquarters are fixed at Mr. Overings, on the West Road."[68] Prescott would continue to work out of Newport by day, when an American raid was highly unlikely. The Overing house was just four miles south of the main British encampment at Windmill Hill, and from there, Prescott could respond to a night-time incursion with greater dispatch. The general kept two bedrooms in the house. He gave the second to his aide-de-camp, Lieutenant William Barrington of the 7th Regiment—Prescott's regiment. Barrington, the nephew of Lord William Barrington, the British secretary of war, had been captured along with Prescott in October 1775 and freed in late August 1776.[69] Confident in their preparations, neither Smith nor Prescott ordered any patrols along the island's western shoreline. Prescott's Overing farm guard consisted of just one corporal and nine privates stationed at a nearby guard house. Detailed as messengers, four cavalrymen of the British 17th Dragoons were posted in a house just to the south.[70]

Prescott had left himself extremely vulnerable—a fact to which his subordinates repeatedly alerted him. According to one British officer, Prescott "was frequently told of the impropriety of his situation, but despised advice."[71] He may have taken comfort in the fact that his predecessor, Lord Percy, had made his evening quarters at the Stoddard house, just a quarter-mile west of the Overing house.

Moreover, General Francis Smith had previously stayed on merchant William Redwood's estate, which lay just to the north.[72] Smith was in fact still dining at Redwood's house. But he slept in a home much closer to British positions at Windmill Hill.[73]

As if to test Prescott's recent troop dispositions, some fifty New England troops based in Tiverton slipped onto Aquidneck Island's northern coast on the night of June 9. Their target was a British guard house at Common Fence Point. The raiders advanced in three groups, one of which was spotted by a British sentry, who sounded the alarm with a musket shot. The Americans rushed forward on the sentries, who retreated back to their guard house. The Americans reached the guard house and started to fire their muskets, loaded with ball and three buckshot each, at the British troops from the 54th and 22nd Regiments who were streaming out to get their muskets. These shots killed one British soldier instantly and wounded three others. The British guards recovered their composure and began to return a brisk fire. This unnerved the Americans, who then retreated back to their boats. Once they had time to organize, the British sent out patrols to find the Americans, but all they could hear were the oars of their whaleboats going back to the mainland. Two of the wounded British soldiers died the following day.[74]

To the Americans, while the June 9 raid did not achieve the goal of overrunning the guard post, it was a success. It spurred them to attempt several more night-time incursions across the Sakonnet Channel in the next two weeks.[75] These raids annoyed the British command. The three troops who died on June 9 were the first British or Hessian army soldiers to die in combat in the Rhode Island theater. Prescott responded by building a fortified redoubt on Common Fence Point.[76] About ten days after the June 9 raid, Coffin made his escape from Aquidneck Island and then met with Barton.

6

The Overing House Raid

Barton had a rough plan for capturing General Prescott. To execute it successfully, he needed precise intelligence about the Overing house and its immediate surroundings. And it was readily available.

Barton was fortunate that a slave named Quako Honeyman had recently escaped from Aquidneck Island and offered the Americans just what they needed to know. Quako had been a slave of James Honeyman, who prior to the war had been a prominent Newport attorney. Shortly after the British occupied the city, Honeyman leased Quako to an unidentified British regiment or officer. Quako's duties included waiting on Prescott at the Overing house. But when James Honeyman tried to sell Quako to Lieutenant Colonel John Campbell of the British 22nd Regiment, the slave fled to the mainland, perhaps fearing that he would eventually be sent to the dreaded Caribbean. Interrogated by the Rhode Island Council of War shortly after his escape, Quako, "by the information he then gave" rendered "great and essential services to this state."[1] The information he provided included precise details about Prescott's nightly habits and the routines of his guards.[2] In turn, Quako was allowed, temporarily at least, to roam the mainland as a free man.[3]

Barton got still more information from British army deserters, who informed him that each morning a detachment of a sergeant or corporal and ten privates marched to the Overing house to relieve the troops sent the prior morning.[4] Barton must have been pleased that Prescott had such a small detachment guarding the general's nighttime headquarters. Barton himself knew the area around the Overing house, as he had been quartered in a house opposite it earlier in the war, before Clinton's invasion force had arrived. Accordingly, he knew the Overing family as well.[5]

Henry John Overing was born in 1731 in Boston, Massachusetts. He married Mary Whitehorne, the daughter of prominent Newport merchant and distiller Jonathan G. Whitehorne, in South Kingstown in 1755.[6] Overing took up his father-in-law's line of work and earned additional money from his sugar baking business. He imported raw sugar from the Caribbean, refined it, and sold it in loaves.[7] Overing had great success—he even had his own wharf named after him in Newport Harbor.[8] He maintained a home at the lower (southern) end of Thames Street, near his wharf and sugar house.[9] According to a 1774 census, Overing's residence housed fourteen persons—two adult white males (Henry and his son John); two adult white females (Henry's wife, Mary, and daughter Henrietta); two white children (son Henry and daughter Mary); and eight black slaves or free servants.[10] As sugar refining was grueling, labor-intensive work, many of the Overing slaves probably worked in that business. The names of all of his slaves or servants are not known, but a 1783 inventory of Overing's "property" indicates that four slaves were named Cato, Tobey, Robin, and Pomp. A 1783 inventory of the Overing house lists several mahogany chairs, tables, and beds (some likely made by local master craftsmen John Goddard and Christopher Townsend), as well as several dozen china dishes, and a few carpets and tea chests.[11] The Overings had the trappings of one of the wealthiest families in Newport.

In 1771, Henry John Overing purchased a 55-acre farm in Middletown. His family spent considerable time there, particularly during the summer, as it contained a "large mansion house and other buildings."[12] As of the 1774 census, three black slaves or free servants and one white male adult (probably the farm's hired overseer) resided on the farm.[13] Three years later a British military map listed the Overing property as one of the "principal farms" on Aquidneck Island.[14] Its impressive chief residence, probably built sometime between 1725 and 1750 by prominent Newport merchant Jonathan Nichols, was one of the largest houses in the area.[15]

There was no doubt as to Henry John Overing's loyalties. On January 27, 1777, shortly after the British occupation of Newport, he took an oath to the British Crown.[16] He and his family attended Newport's Trinity Church, a bastion of Loyalist support.[17] Handsome young British officers had even begun wooing their seventeen-year-old daughter, Henrietta. Overing's nineteen-year-old son Henry would, in 1779, join the British 54th Regiment, then stationed on Aquidneck Island, and quickly rise to the rank of lieutenant.[18] Barton could expect no assistance from the Overing family.

Crucially, Barton needed to maintain secrecy about his plans. He knew that the British often gleaned information about American operations from deserters, freed prisoners, and Loyalist civilians who escaped from the mainland to Aquidneck Island, as well as spies. Even with his superiors and his fellow officers assigned to the raid, he divulged information only on a need-to-know basis.

In late June, Barton formally presented his plan for Prescott's capture to his superior, Colonel Joseph Stanton. Stanton's 1st Rhode Island State Regiment, in which Barton served as lieutenant colonel, was then stationed in Tiverton, near Howland's Ferry. Stanton issued Barton written orders to support his project, but did not refer specifically to Prescott as a target, so as to keep it secret, even from Stanton's own aides. "You will proceed to the Island of Newport [Aquidneck Island], and attack the enemy when and where you think proper," Stanton wrote. "Make report to me of your proceedings."[19] Rhode Island governor Nicholas Cooke was also informed of the plan.[20] It does not appear that the commander of American forces in the Rhode Island theater of war, Major General Joseph Spencer of the Continental army, was informed. This was to be a strictly Rhode Island state affair.

Barton wasted no time. He asked five regimental officers to volunteer for a secret and dangerous mission, the details of which he did not disclose. According to Barton's later account of the mission, Captain Samuel Phillips (who had been behind the April capture of Ensign John M. Clarke on Aquidneck Island), Lieutenant James Potter, Lieutenant Joshua Babcock, and Ensigns Andrew Stanton and John Wielcocks "all considered to go."[21] Barton's subordinates located five whaleboats, and in a few days "had them fitted in the best possible manner." For this type of mission, whaleboats were ideal: they rode low in the water, did not rely on fickle winds, and required no additional manpower, as Rhode Island's regiments were filled with men with rowing experience.

The Overing house, headquarters of General Prescott, from May to July of 1777. Still standing today, it is now known as the Nichols-Overing House, and is maintained by the Newport Restoration Foundation. (*Newport Restoration Foundation*)

Out of concern for secrecy, Barton delayed asking for rank-and-file volunteers. Then, in early July, he personally appealed to the 1st Rhode Island Regiment. "Brother soldiers," he boomed, "I am about to undertake an enterprise against the enemy. I wish to have about forty volunteers and those who dare to risk their lives with me on this occasion will advance two paces to the front."[22] At this, Barton later reported, the "whole regiment" stepped forward. Barton expressed his gratitude, and then went through the ranks picking out experienced rowers. He also selected four former Aquidneck Island residents to serve as guides. They included Samuel Cory, a veteran of the battles of White Plains and Princeton who before the war had resided near the Overing house.[23] Most of Barton's new force came from his regiment. But word of the mission leaked, producing four more volunteers from Colonel Robert Elliot's Rhode Island State Artillery Regiment and three from Colonel Archibald Crary's 2nd Rhode Island State Regiment. Cory, in fact, was a member of Major Nathan Munroe's Rhode Island state boat service company.[24] Barton's party ultimately included about forty-eight men, including officers.[25]

At least two volunteers were persons of color. Jack Sisson, a former slave from South Kingstown, participated as a boat steerer.[26]

Daniel Page, a Native American from either the Narragansett tribe of Rhode Island or the Pocasset band of the Wampanoag tribe of Massachusetts (it is not clear which), would steer Barton's own whaleboat.[27] A third man, connected to Barton, also apparently played an important role. It is not clear if this man was Sisson, a twenty-two-year-old slave from South Kingstown named Guy Watson, or a slave or servant named Prince Goodwin from Plymouth, Massachusetts.[28]

Barton and his men spent much of July 4, 1777, in Tiverton, preparing for their raid and enjoying the boom of cannon fired in celebration rather than anger. Across the channel, British major Frederick Mackenzie wrote in his diary:

> This being the first anniversary of the declaration of the independency of the rebel colonies, they ushered in the morning at Providence by firing thirteen cannon (one for each colony we suppose). At 12 o'clock the three rebel frigates that lie at and near Providence fired three guns each, and at one o'clock, thirteen guns were fired from their fort at Howland's Ferry. At sunset, the rebel frigates fired another round of thirteen guns each, one after the other. As the evening was very still and fine, the echo of the guns down the bay had a very grand effect, the report of each being repeated three or four times. Several guns were fired during the day, from other places in the adjacent country.[29]

That evening, Barton's raiding party—with eight men, one officer, and provisions in each of the five whaleboats—departed Howland's Ferry for the port of Bristol. The boats proceeded west through the narrow channel, and then veered north into Narragansett Bay. Night travel was necessary so as not to be spotted by the crew of the 32-gun *Lark* a few miles to the south, or by British artillerists manning a battery at the northern end of Aquidneck Island. A thunderstorm over Mount Hope Bay provided additional cover, but it also dispersed the boats. At 1:00 a.m. Barton's boat reached Bristol, where he waited for the others to arrive.

At the headquarters of Rhode Island troops stationed at Bristol, Barton found a British deserter who had just slipped off of Aquidneck Island. The curious American officer "questioned him concerning the enemy's position, whether there had been any alteration in the British encampments within the last few days; he said there had not." Barton was briefly shaken when the deserter insisted that Prescott still maintained a headquarters in Newport. But he soon became convinced that the man simply did not know about Prescott's new overnight arrangements.

By 8:00 a.m. on July 5, the rest of Barton's boats had arrived safely at Bristol. That evening, Barton took his officers to nearby Hog Island, where for the first time he informed them of his plans and the intelligence he had acquired. Although "surprised," he wrote, the officers "readily consented to what I had proposed" and further agreed to "the most solemn charge not to communicate to anyone the least hint of our enterprise."[30] From Hog Island they eyed the British ships anchored in the middle channel, and the British troop positions on the opposite shores. They could not see the beach on which they hoped to land.

After returning from Hog Island, Barton decided not to launch his raid from Bristol, despite its close proximity to Middletown and the Overing house. Instead, he chose a longer but safer route from Warwick Neck, located west of Prudence Island. This course would keep Barton's little flotilla at least one-and-a-half miles from enemy ships, and allow it to use Prudence Island as a screen much of the way. By contrast, rowing south from Bristol down the middle channel would have placed Barton's party within a half-mile of two British frigates.

On the night of July 6, Barton's boats slid the roughly five miles across Narragansett Bay to Warwick Neck. There, Captain Ebenezer Adams of Westerly, an enterprising officer serving in Colonel Robert Elliott's Rhode Island State Artillery Regiment,[31] volunteered to join Barton's party as second-in-command.

Barton's raiding party spent the next two days on last-minute preparations. Rain and fog blanketed Narragansett Bay for most of July 9.[32] The ship's log for the 50-gun frigate HMS *Renown*, stationed to the south of Warwick Neck, described the evening's weather as "fresh gales and squally with rain."[33] Barton postponed the raid until the next night.

On July 10, the weather turned pleasant. A cooling breeze replaced the previous day's strong winds, and just enough clouds lingered to shroud the bay in darkness. Conditions for a nighttime raid were ideal.[34] That evening, Barton finally shared the details of his plan with his men, and issued a warning: "The enterprise will be attended with danger and it is probable some of us may pass the shades of death before it is accomplished.... I will not ask you to encounter any hazard but what I shall be exposed to equally with you. I pledge my honor that in every difficulty and danger I will take the lead." After a momentary pause, the soldiers "with one voice cried out we will go!" The lieutenant colonel then issued the following directives:

> Soldiers, you must be sensible how much the success of our enterprise depends on the strictest attention to orders. I entreat you not to have the least idea of plunder for if that has overthrown the greatest armies what will it do with us, who are but a handful. I charge you not to utter a syllable and when you come to the boats let each one place himself in his own boat and upon his own seat. If there is any one in the party who has been so imprudent as to furnish himself with spirituous liquors, I order him to leave it. I must entreat you as you regard your lives and honor that you keep yourselves cool and at the same time firmly resolved to face every danger that shall attend us in our present undertaking.

Concluding his remarks, Barton stated the underlying purpose of the mission and sought divine assistance:

> I doubt not if you succeed that your country will reward you; if not you will be rewarded in the eternal world for we are endeavoring to get him that is bound in prison, General Lee. As this may be the last time I ever shall have an opportunity of addressing you all, I offer up my sincere prayer to the Great Disposer of all events that he will be pleased to smile on our intended enterprise. If consistent with his will, may success attend us and each one be returned to his friends.

Barton's men had precious little time to consider the consequences of volunteering for this dangerous secret mission. The first and most obvious was being shot or caught in shell fire. Perhaps even worse, however, was the possibility of being captured and placed in the holds of a prison ship anchored in Newport Harbor. A single shot by an alert sentry in a guard boat or in a guard house could result in overwhelming force being arrayed against them, either in the form of a 32-gun warship or an entire regiment of British soldiers. In either case, Barton and his men would have no choice but to surrender. Indeed, had they been caught, these soldiers would have wound up in one of the floating jails during a humanitarian crisis that broke out shortly after the raid. On July 22, the

British agreed to exchange a group of American prisoners described as "chiefly sick"—some skeleton thin, others covered with vermin, and still others disfigured by infections or dying of fever. One of the men, a captain of a commercial vessel out of North Carolina, was released stark naked, and died a week later. Similarly diseased and dying prisoners were exchanged in early and mid-August.[35]

Having delivered his inspiring speech and taken every last precaution, Barton ordered his men into their whaleboats. Each wore his standard army uniform, which for most meant looking suspiciously unmilitary. Barton probably considered having his men wear British uniforms (if he had access to any) or civilian clothing, either of which would have added to the enemy's surprise. But being captured in such garb also meant being hanged as a spy—a powerful deterrent.

Before departing, Barton informed the commander of the guard at Warwick Neck that if he heard three musket shots echo across the bay from northern Prudence Island, he should send a rescue party to pick up his men. If his men were forced onto the island by pursuing British vessels or even marines, the Americans would need every possible advantage.

Barton chose his route so as to avoid the five British frigates stationed in Narragansett Bay. Four of the warships formed the corners of a large imaginary rectangle through which Barton's small flotilla would have to carefully, and quietly, slip. Barton planned to enter the imaginary rectangle in the middle of its top side and leave it in the middle of its right side, and land on Aquidneck Island shortly thereafter.[36]

The biggest risk Barton's party took on the water was being spotted by guard boats sent out by the frigates after dark. "Boats employed rowing guard at night" was a typical entry in the log book of HMS *Diamond*, which sat about one-and-a-half miles north of Barton's intended landing site.[37] For July 8, 9, and 10, the log of HMS *Lark*, stationed about two miles to the north of the *Diamond*, noted, "rowed guard" each night.[38] One sailor who served on the frigate HMS *Orpheus* as it engaged in blockade duty in March 1777 wrote that "the strictest attention was paid at all times" by guard boat crews.[39] Each boat was loaded with muskets and pistols that could be used to quickly alert nearby frigates of trouble.

Fortunately for Barton and his men, the night of July 10 was not only "pleasant weather," but also particularly dark.[40] At about 9:00

p.m., the raiders pushed off from Warwick Neck, about ten miles northwest of their planned landing spot on Aquidneck Island. Barton's boat led the way. To make his "flag ship" easily identifiable to his men, the lieutenant colonel had fitted it with a ten-foot pole with a white rag tied to its end. Each boat's oars had been muffled, and Barton's oarsmen drove the boats silently southeastward between Patience and Prudence Islands, then continued along the latter's western shoreline. At some point, their small craft passed within about two miles southwest of the 32-gun HMS *Greyhound*, with a crew of 220, then stationed in the bay between Calf Pasture Point on the western shores of the mainland and Prudence Island.

Below Prudence Island Barton's boats headed southeast, slicing between the 32-gun HMS *Diamond*, anchored to the north off of Coggeshall Point, and the 50-gun HMS *Chatham*, to the south. The latter was the flagship of newly promoted admiral Sir Peter Parker, the British navy commander in Newport.[41] Carrying a crew of 367, Parker's ship was stationed just north of Gould Island. As they rounded Prudence Island's southern tip, Barton's men heard the pronouncement, "All's well" from nearby British guard boats.[42]

The low-slung whaleboats proceeded through the black bay water undetected. As they neared Aquidneck Island, just south of Weaver's Cove, the unmistakable sound of galloping horses briefly unnerved them. Were British dragoons patrolling the shoreline? Shaking off such worries, Barton concluded that "it must be horses running as they often would do."[43]

At about 11:30 p.m., Barton's five boats landed on the sandy western edge of Aquidneck Island, just above the mouth of Redwood Creek, a small stream that passed by the Overing house.[44] Barton had planned well: coast-hugging sand bluffs and dense foliage muffled the noise of the landing, and would shield his raiders even during the daytime.[45] This part of the island was lightly populated, and consisted mostly of farms. Most of the area's homes, including the Overing house, were up near the West Road. The closest house to Barton's landing site was the Stoddard house, roughly a quarter-mile to the west. It was there that General Prescott had commanded the first invasion forces that splashed ashore on December 8, 1776. From where Barton and his men now stood, the HMS *Diamond* sat about one-and-a-half miles to the northwest; Admiral Parker's HMS *Chatham* awaited action the same distance to the southwest.[46]

To reach the Overing house, Barton's raiders needed to scale the lurking sand bluffs and then traverse roughly one mile of rising ground to the West Road. From there, the grand home stood atop a small hill, just 50 yards to the east. Barton's party desperately sought to avoid detection by British guards; a single shot fired by a guard could end the raid in disaster. Prescott's guard of a corporal and nine privates was quartered just west of West Road, a quarter mile to the northwest of the Overing house.[47] His four dragoons were quartered in the Coggeshall house, also on the west side of the West Road, about 150 yards southwest of the Overing house. Barton's party would have to sneak between the two houses to reach the West Road without being spotted.

Just one sentry (a member of Prescott's guard) stood outside the Overing house itself. He was Walter Graham, a private in the British 22nd Regiment of Foot. Barton was fortunate that Graham was on duty that night. The Scot had tried to desert the regiment in 1772 and again in 1774, and was apparently not a willing soldier.[48]

Barton left five soldiers behind to man the all-important whaleboats that would be used to carry his party back across the bay to the mainland. If Barton's party was detected, each of the five men would need to push his boat into the shallow water in preparation for a speedy departure.

Barton led the balance of his men up the bluffs, and along the deep gully through which Redwood Creek flowed. Continuing uphill, the group flanked swampy ground and bolted eastward through an open-tilled field toward the West Road. From this field, peering through the darkness, they could probably see the guard house to the north, filled with slumbering British soldiers, and the Potter house, fifty yards to the south.[49] A lone sentry watched over the guard house—completely unaware of the approaching threat. A few more steps took Barton's troops to the West Road, just thirty-odd yards from Overing's property line. They were relieved to see no traffic on this main artery to and from Newport.

At this point Barton divided his men into five groups. He directed one to approach the Overing house from its rear, the south door, and a second to close on the house from the west. Taking a separate route, Barton would lead a third group through the property's front yard to the house's east door. The raid commander detailed the fourth group to watch the West Road, and the fifth to stand by in reserve "to act on emergencies," as needed.[50]

At about 11:50 p.m., Barton's third division, creeping uphill single file, approached the property's front gate through a stand of trees. From twenty-five yards away, Private Graham suddenly hailed them with an urgent, "Who comes there?" Barton ignored him. Graham tried again: "Who comes there?"[51] This time Barton answered, "Friends." Graham responded, "Friends, advance and give the countersign"—a request for that evening's password. Still guiding his men forward, Barton sternly barked, "We have no countersign to give; have you seen any deserters tonight?" Graham allowed Barton to approach. Even had he chosen to, he could not have fired his weapon—amazingly, it was not loaded.[52] Barton repeated his query, this time with some vehemence: "Have you seen any deserters?" Before Graham could respond, Barton was upon him, seizing the trembling private's musket and threatening him with death if he made any noise. "I won't," Graham meekly offered.[53] Barton's trick had worked brilliantly. "We asked him if General Prescott was in the house; he was so frightened that at first he could not speak but at last with a faltering voice and waving his hand toward the house, said yes," Barton recalled later.[54] Meanwhile, the Americans' second division crept up to the rear of the Overing house, and the third division assumed its position at the house's west door.

At Barton's signal, his eager men "burst all the doors open in an instant."[55] Finding the main front door locked, one of Barton's party, an African-American—either Jack Sisson, Guy Watson, or Prince Goodwin—took a running start and used his head as a battering ram to break the barrier door.[56] Inside the house were General Prescott in one bedroom; his aide-de-camp, Lieutenant Barrington, in another; John Henry Overing and his twenty-year-year-old son, John Henry Overing, Jr., sleeping in separate bedrooms on the first floor; a lone dragoon sleeping in a garret above the kitchen; and three African-American slaves or servants, also sleeping in the garret. Mary Overing and her eldest daughter, Henrietta, were not present.

Barton initially had trouble finding Prescott. On the first floor, his men barged into the Overings' bedrooms but did not find him. In frustration Barton, at the head of the stairway, yelled "for the soldiers to set the house on fire, for we were determined to have the General dead or alive!" Some of the men began calling out for General Prescott. At this, a voice from a second-floor bedroom asked, "What is the matter?" Barton recalled, "I proceeded from

The Overing House Raid 135

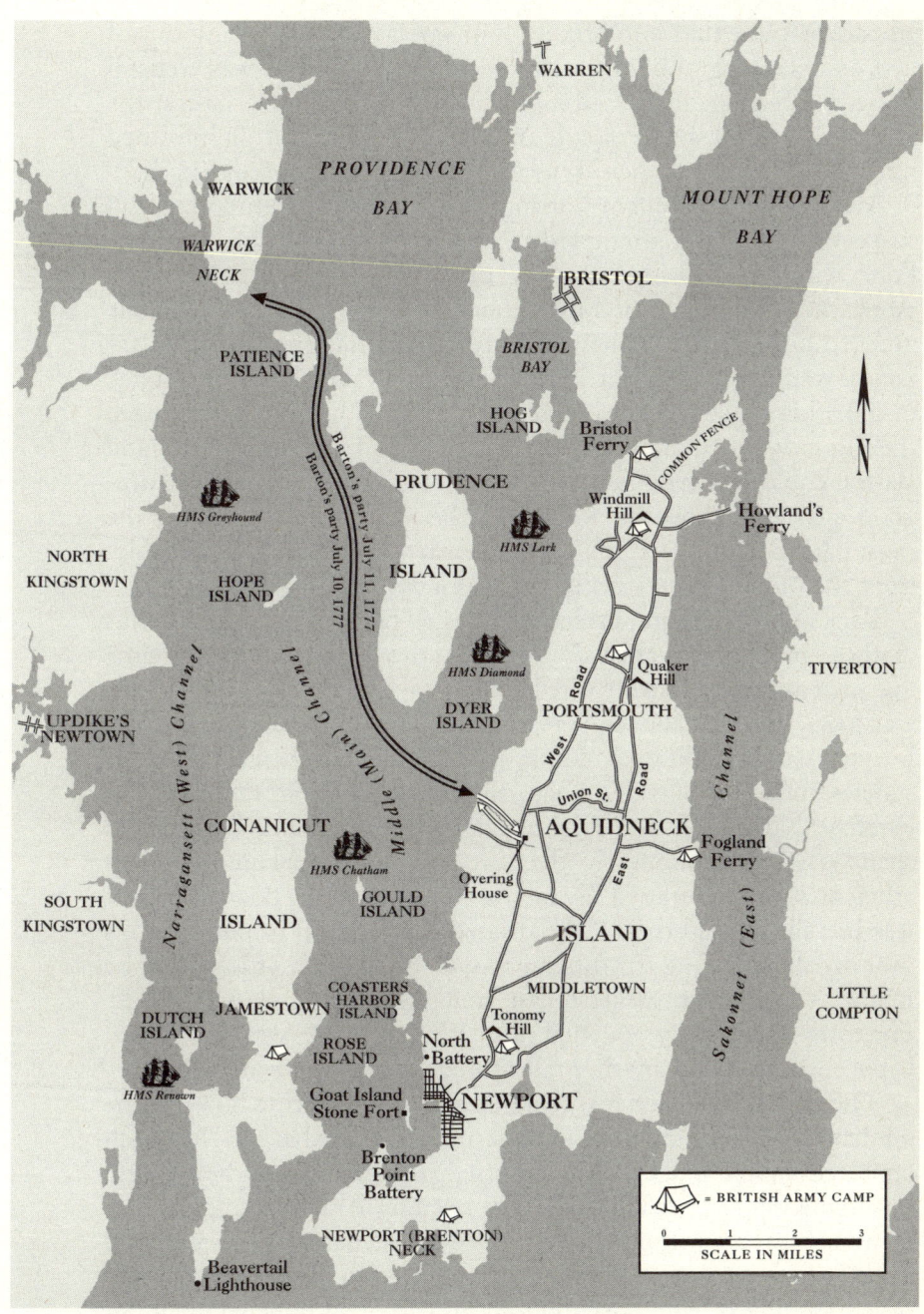

William Barton's raid to capture British general Richard Prescott.

whence it came and entering a room saw a man just rising out of bed, and clapping him on the shoulder, asked him if he was General Prescott." Sitting on the edge of his bed in his nightclothes, the groggy and astonished Prescott answered, "Yes sir." Barton informed him, "You are my prisoner." Prescott replied, "I acknowledge it, sir."[57]

Meanwhile, Lieutenant Barrington, hearing the commotion and suspecting its cause, attempted to escape by leaping out of a first-floor window, wearing just his night shirt and britches. The Americans waiting watchfully outside the house immediately grabbed him. As the nephew of Lord Barrington, the British secretary of war, Lieutenant Barrington was also a valuable prisoner. Back inside other raiders tried to snatch Overing and his son, but changed their minds when they put up a struggle. Time was short, and Barton could brook no delays. The raiders did not discover the dragoon quartered above the kitchen, as he wisely kept silent. For the most part, Barton's men followed his orders not to remove valuables from the home—even if its owner was a despised Loyalist.

Back in his bedroom, Prescott requested permission to "put on his clothes," probably his army uniform. But the Americans had no time for such niceties. Barton directed his captive to quickly don his waistcoat, britches, and slippers, provided him with a cloak, and had his men gather additional clothes in a bundle. He then escorted his shoeless prisoner outside, where the humbled Prescott joined the barefoot Barrington and frightened Private Graham. Barton had spent just seven minutes in the Overing house.[58] Maintaining his efficient pace, he ordered his men to return to their boats. Prescott was literally carried there. "We desired the General to put one arm over my shoulder and the other over one of the other officers that he might go with the greatest ease and dispatch,"[59] Barton wrote. Prescott's feet barely touched the ground as he was suspended between Barton and another tall, strong, and fast-moving officer.

The raiders had been fortunate to reach the Overing house without being spotted. And now, the one-mile distance back to the beach appeared much longer. But, rushing past the guard house and through a field of prickly barley the hustling Americans again covered the ground without being noticed. Just before he was placed into Barton's whaleboat, Prescott was allowed to put on his coat and other clothing.[60] He reportedly told his captor, "I hope you will not hurt me." Barton assured him that he would not.[61] Ensign Abel Potter guided the last of the group's boats into five feet of water, and

The Overing House Raid

"The Capture of Prescott." General Richard Prescott stands in his nightshirt, ready to be put on board a whaleboat and taken across Narragansett Bay following his capture. The hats worn by the American soldiers are like the ones worn in the 1830s, when the engraving by an unknown artist was made. (*Williams, Biography of Revolutionary Heroes*)

climbed aboard.[62] The flotilla began the long journey back across Narragansett Bay to Warwick Neck.

Along the way, Barton nearly had an entirely unexpected encounter. Cruising placidly through the bay at this time was a small boat containing John Knowles, wooing Henry John Overing's attractive, seventeen-year-old daughter Henrietta. Overing's wife Mary was also present, as her daughter's chaperone. Knowles later confessed to Lord Percy, "I was near taken the night the General was [taken prisoner]. When we had been frolicking, the two Miss Overings were in the boat with me and we passed their house. Major Barton who carried the General off says he saw our boat."[63]

At the Overing house, meanwhile, chaos reigned. Still in his bedclothes, the dragoon overlooked by Barton's men sprinted the quarter-mile to the guard house. Challenged by a sentry—who he suspected of being an American covering for the raiders—he quickly retraced his steps. One of Prescott's African-American servants then dashed out to alert the stubborn sentry, who followed him back to the house; the soldier, learning for the first time what had happened under his nose, said he had not seen anything. The dragoon then climbed onto his horse, rode a short way up the West Road, turned east onto Union Street, and raced the two miles to the British encampment at Fogland Ferry. The alarm had now been raised.

Assuming that the Americans had landed on Aquidneck Island's eastern coast, British rescue parties responded to that area. Prescott's ever-active dragoon, meanwhile, continued north another four miles to the British fort at Windmill Hill. There he broke the news of Prescott's seizure to Lieutenant Colonel John Campbell, who sent out detachments of his 22nd Regiment to scour the island's western shoreline.[64]

Back at Windmill Hill, at about 2:00 a.m. on July 11, British army officers finally deduced that the Americans might have come, and gone, by way of Narragansett Bay. And if they alerted the frigates off the coast, they might still be able to intercept the raiders. At 2:30 a.m. Royal artillerymen signaled their navy comrades with two cannon shots and three rockets. Off Arnold Point, Captain Richard Smith and other officers of the 32-gun *Lark* "heard the report of a gun and saw two sky rockets" on Aquidneck Island. Then, at 3:00 a.m., officers saw "saw two guns fired and several lights near ye camp" at Windmill Hill.[65] The "lights" were probably tar or other materials set ablaze in a kettle hung near the top of "beacon poles" to serve as an alarm.[66] But the signals drew no response. British navy officers did not believe the signals were intended for them. Because of the lack of wind, they correctly surmised that no American vessels would have dared venture into or out of the bay. Merely puzzled by the booming artillery pieces, sporadic rocket blasts, and light-throwing beacon poles, they "therefore did not send out any boats."[67] Captain Smith did send sailors to man the ship's barge and row ashore "to inquire ye cause of ye alarm."[68]

The Americans' good luck had continued. "It was fortunate for us then that the enemy on board the shipping could not know the cause of it [the firing], as they might with ease have cut off our return to the main," Barton wrote later.[69] At 4:00 a.m., the *Lark*'s barge, according to the keeper of the ship's log, "returned and informed us that the rebels had taken General Prescott and his aide-de-camp off ye island." Captain Smith then "sent an officer and the barge" to inform Admiral Parker on board HMS *Chatham*, which was anchored about five-and-a-half miles to the south (the sailors apparently did not have orders to stop at the *Diamond*, which was within two miles).[70]

Barton's raiding party again evaded British guard boats in the bay. Prescott remained quiet until the boat touched the shoreline at

Warwick Neck at about 3:30 a.m. He then turned to Barton and said, "Sir, you have made a damn'd bold push tonight." Barton replied stoically, "We have been fortunate."[71] That was an understatement.

The raid had lasted about six-and-a-half hours. After disembarking, Barton took his captives to the nearest house he could find. There, he asked Prescott and Barrington if they wanted to sleep for a few hours, and they agreed. In the meantime, he sent a rider to the town of Warwick, asking for a carriage and horses with which to transport the prisoners to David Arnold's Tavern in Warwick.[72] As Barton recalled later, he also "sent an express rider to Major General Joseph Spencer at Providence communicating the success of our enterprise" and requesting that a carriage be sent to carry the prisoners from Warwick to Providence. Captain Adams accompanied the messenger and personally met with the pleased and excited Spencer, to whom he described the evening's heady events.[73]

After sunrise, Barton brought his prisoners to Arnold's Tavern and gave them breakfast. Meanwhile, Thomas Sabin's carriage arrived from Providence, having been ordered there by Spencer. Along with it came a small detachment commanded by Colonel Robert Elliott of the Rhode Island State Artillery Regiment. With Barton joining the detachment, Prescott, and Barrington were then whisked into the waiting carriage and driven to Providence. They arrived at about noon, and Prescott was taken to the Providence home of privateer captain Samuel Chace.[74] Barton then met with Spencer, who lavished the enterprising lieutenant colonel with praise for his stunning feat.

Across the bay during the early morning of July 11, British soldiers searching along Aquidneck Island's western shore finally discovered the Americans' landing site. In the heavy dew that coated the ground, they "could trace their track up to the house and back again."[75] It was not difficult to deduce that Barton's party had come from, and returned to, a location somewhere across the bay.

7

An Officer of Equal Rank

Word of Prescott's capture spread across Rhode Island like wildfire. Those who did not immediately hear about it were able to read a business-like summary of the raid in the July 12 edition of the *Providence Gazette*. On that day, Barton's superior, Colonel Joseph Stanton, wrote to the state's governor, Nicholas Cooke:

> I most sincerely congratulate your honor on the success of Colonel Barton and at the same time feel a peculiar pleasure in being in the least degree accessory in the forming of the plan with Colonel Barton to take General Prescott. The officers for the expedition were well chosen and the plan of attack well executed. History scarcely affords such an instance, and it must be a most mortifying scene to General Prescott when he reflects that he was taken on an island in the midst of the British fleet and his army, and that without the discharge of a single gun. May Heaven be thanked for favoring the attempt.[1]

General Spencer rushed a note announcing Prescott's capture to Washington on July 11.[2] Washington received the news with great joy on July 16, at his camp at The Clove in New York (near Suffern).[3] In his reply to Spencer, Washington gushed: "The conduct of Colonel Barton in particular and the officers and men of his party in general cannot be too highly applauded. This is among the finest partisan exploits that has taken place in the course of the war on either side. It discovers so intrepid and enterprising a spirit as does the greatest honor to those who undertook and effected it."[4]

Washington eagerly forwarded to Philadelphia an extract of Spencer's letter, along with a second letter that Spencer had addressed to the Continental Congress's president, John Hancock, who was then presiding over Congress. The commander-in-chief ended his transmittal letter with, "Lieutenant Colonel Barton and the small handful under his command, who conducted the enterprise, have great merit."[5] Spencer's second letter was read in Congress on July 19. Delegates responded by enacting a resolution lauding Barton and his men.[6] On July 25, Congress passed a second resolution praising the "gallant behavior of Lieutenant Colonel Barton . . . and the brave officers and men of his party" and directing that "an elegant sword" be presented to the raid's leader.[7] It was a special honor. In the course of the war, Congress would award ceremonial swords for meritorious conduct to just fifteen patriot officers, including only three to state or militia officers.

News of Prescott's capture boosted American morale. From Philadelphia on July 20, John Adams wrote to his wife Abigail that "The little masterly expedition to Rhode Island has given us some spirits." Adams was impressed by "[t]he subtlety, the ingenuity, the activity, the bravery, and the prudence, with which" Barton's raid was conducted.[8] Rhode Islanders were relieved to be rid of Prescott, and quietly celebrated the apparent end of his tyrannical reign. In a letter to Benjamin Franklin, then posted as a diplomat in Paris, Benjamin Snowden wrote, "It gives me pleasure to hear that the military brute P_____ [Prescott] is for a time deprived of a power to exercise his natural insolence."[9]

The larger significance of Prescott's capture was clear to both officers and soldiers. Soldier-physician James Thacher, serving in Washington's main Continental army, wrote in his journal, "The event occasions great joy and exultation, as it puts in our possession an officer of equal rank with General Lee, by which means an exchange may be obtained."[10] Connecticut governor Jonathan Trumbull wrote to Washington, "I hope this capture of General Prescott may procure the releasement of General Lee."[11] In Rhode Island, Colonel Stanton ended his July 12 letter to Governor Cooke by observing, "We hope once more to hear that brave General Lee heads our troops."[12] On July 12, General Smith sent one of his aides, Captain Henry Barry, to meet with Rhode Island officials and inquire about Prescott's treatment as a prisoner. When Barry returned to Newport, he stated that Rhode Island officers told him that Barton and his party had "attempted the enterprise, entirely with a view to have a person in their hands as an equivalent for General Lee."[13]

In reply to Spencer, Washington wrote, "I shall immediately make a proposition for an exchange between him [Prescott] and General Lee, which if it succeeds will retrieve the latter from a disagreeable confinement, and will probably bring about the releasement of our officers in general . . . and if it fails, it will still answer a valuable end by showing General Howe's conduct and intentions in a point of view that will operate well for us, both in the minds of the public, and in those of his and our officers who are prisoners."[14]

Comparisons between Barton's capture of Prescott and Harcourt's capture of Lee immediately began to appear in American newspapers. On July 12 the *Providence Gazette* crowed that "A lieutenant-colonel of the horse, with at least seventy light dragoons, took Major-General Lee (betrayed by a Tory), five miles from his troops. A lieutenant-colonel of foot, with only thirty-eight privates and six officers, has taken a chief commander, when almost encircled by an army and navy." The *Gazette*'s editors gleefully credited Barton's men for demonstrating "infinite address and gallantry," quoting from "Howe's letter to the British ministry, relative to the capture of General Lee." Describing the British firing of rockets after realizing that Prescott had been seized, they giddily noted that the effort was *"too late—the Bird had fled."*

By July 29, Philadelphia's *Pennsylvania Evening Post* had reprinted the *Providence Gazette*'s entertaining commentary. On August 7, the *Post* offered its own opinion:

> In the planning and execution of this enterprise, Colonel Barton has given a noble proof of his zeal and ability to render the most important services to his country. In comparison to this action, how contemptible was that of Colonel Harcourt, for which the King, his master, was in raptures, and lavished upon him such extravagant encomiums—his surprise, with a large force, of General Lee, unguarded, several miles distant from his army, and betrayed by an ungrateful wretch, on whom he had just before been conferring great and unmerited favors.

The day after Barton's escape to Warwick Neck with General Prescott, lookouts on HMS *Lark* "saw several whaleboats from the northwest off Providence" at about 3:30 p.m. These were probably Barton's men, crossing to Bristol on their way back to Tiverton. The *Lark* slipped its anchor to chase them, but never had a chance. Barton's raiders safely returned to their stations on the east side of the Sakonnet Channel.[15] When Barton rejoined his regiment at Tiverton, so many of his fellow officers and men wanted to hear his story that Barton scrambled atop a woodpile to tell it. He gave "all the credit of the transaction to his trusty soldiers who accompanied him," according to his biographer, Catherine R. Williams.[16]

Official laurels for Barton and his raiders began to flow their way. The Rhode Island General Assembly voted to extend appreciation to Barton's party "for their brave execution" and awarded the men $1,120 in cash to be divided "in proportion to the wages of the said officers and soldiers."[17] The cash grant was consistent with rewards for capturing enemy soldiers offered by the General Assembly in March of 1777, which offer had expired—$1,000 for a general, $100 for a lieutenant, and $20 for a private.

Barton saw his new-found fame as an opportunity to improve his depressed finances. Never well-to-do to begin with, and forced to abandon his hat-making business when he joined the army, Barton found it difficult to support his growing family on a state officer's salary. Barton therefore submitted a memorial to the Continental Congress making the following request: "Sincerely lamenting that his private circumstances in life will not allow him to wear [the sword Congress had awarded him], and ardently wishing to do his country more essential benefits, your memorialist requests your honorable boards to give him such rank and pay in the Continental line as may enable him with reputation to wear and wield that sword in your service."[18] On Christmas Eve of 1777, a sympathetic Congress passed the following resolution: "That Lieutenant Colonel William Barton, on account of his enterprising spirit, and his merit in taking Major General Prescott prisoner, be promoted to the rank and pay of colonel in the service of the United States; and that he be recommended to General Washington, to be employed in such services as he may deem best adapted to his genius."[19] Barton thus became a colonel in the Continental army, with increased pay and prestige, though he remained in the Rhode Island theater.

Prescott's capture stunned the British. In Newport, a sensible British staff officer, Major Frederick Mackenzie, continued to keep a detailed diary in which he reflected the views of his fellow officers and soldiers. While commending the boldness of Barton's attempt and its "masterly" execution, Mackenzie expressed frustration. "It is certainly a most extraordinary circumstance," he wrote, "that a general commanding a body of 4,000 men, encamped on an island surrounded by a squadron of ships of war, should be carried off from his quarters in the night by a small party of the enemy... without a shot being fired."[20] Furthermore, he noted with incredulity, "a shot fired by the sentry would have given the alarm, and a single boat falling in with them, would in all probability have frustrated their design." He also complained that Barton's party must have had "the most perfect intelligence" of the locations of the sentries and guard houses from local inhabitants, "as they could not possibly have come a... better way to the [Overing] house."[21]

Mackenzie was further disappointed by the efforts of British navy officers to deflect blame for the affair. "The gentlemen of the navy, when talking of the surprise of General Prescott," he wrote, "said they had nothing to do with the defense of the Island, their business being to prevent the enemy's ships from getting out" of blockaded Narragansett Bay.[22] The Royal Navy officers may have been surprised by the judgment of General Spencer to the contrary. In his letter to Congress, he wrote that Barton's party "had the good fortune to escape discovery by the enemy's guard boats, although several ships of war lay around in those parts, which doubtless General Prescott chiefly depended upon for his protection."[23] A British officer in New York City complained that "the rebels" never would "have had the temerity to make such an attempt," except for "a bad lookout from the fleet."[24]

Several British officers in Newport mentioned the incident in letters to Lord Percy, the former commander of the Newport garrison. Lieutenant Colonel James Marsh of the British 43rd Regiment wrote defensively, "your Lordship is certain that our troops were not to blame, in the loss of our chieftain [Prescott] when the nearest camps were on Windmill Hill, Fogland Ferry and the town. His quarters were three miles from either of the encampments, but still... it appears wonderful that the General might be taken from amidst of fleet and army. Therefore I am afraid the enemy will censure him, and all his friends can say they were very sorry for him."[25]

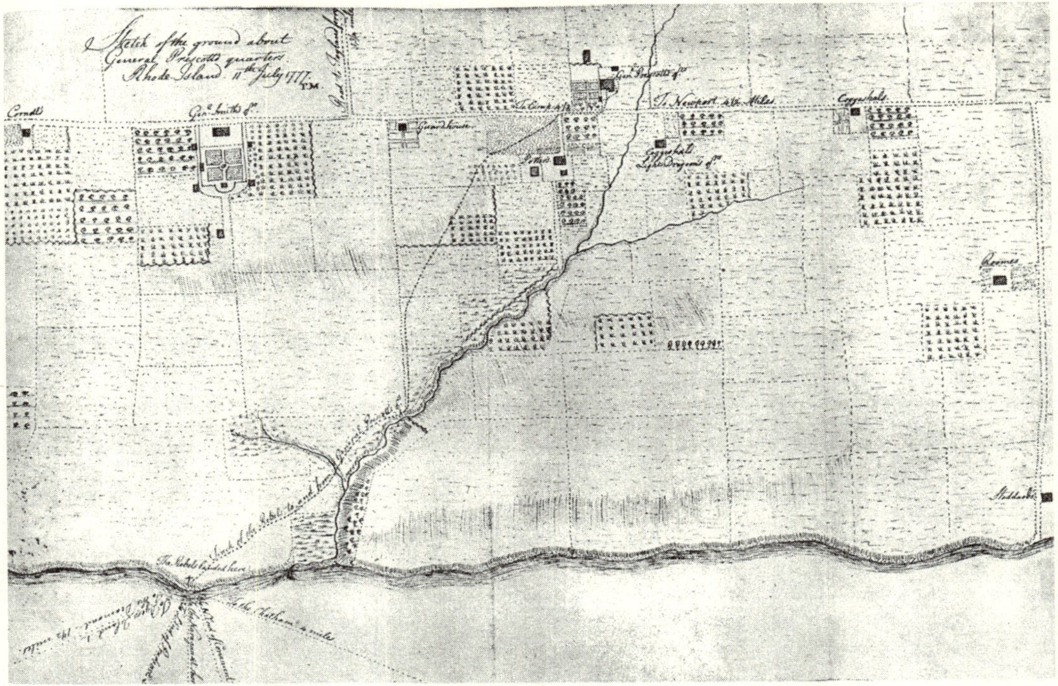

This hand-drawn British map was made shortly after Prescott's capture. "Gen'l Prescott's qtrs" is the Overing house. "To Camp 4 1/2 miles" and "To Newport 4 1/2 miles" show the West Road. "Road to Fogland Ferry" is Union Street. "General Smith's qtrs" is the William Redwood estate, formerly the headquarters of General Francis Smith. "Coggeshall's Light Dragoon's qtrs" and "Guardhouse" show locations of British dragoons and guards. "The Rebels landed here" is shown by a cross. "Track of the Rebels to and from General Prescott's qtrs" is shown by the dotted line. Redwood Creek, passing the Overing house and ending near the landing spot, is shown. The dotted lines at the bottom of the page show the distances to the various islands in the bay and two British frigates: "To the Chatham 4 miles" and "To the Diamond 1 1/2 miles." "Sketch of the grounds about General Prescott's quarters, Rhode Island, July 11, 1777," by Major Frederick Mackenzie. (*Mackenzie, Diary, vol. 1*)

Lieutenant Colonel John Campbell of the 22nd Regiment was nevertheless impressed by Barton's men. They had taken no money or other property from Overing's house, even though there was "good silver" to be had, and they had refrained from carrying off Overing family members or servants. "They had but one object in mind and accomplished it," he grudgingly conceded.[26]

British officers failed to admit that Prescott had made the same error in judgment that Lee had made: each had opted for quarters far from his troops. In Philadelphia, the Loyalist Dr. James Allen, harkening back to Prescott's earlier incarceration in the city, wrote "Poor old General Prescott is again taken prisoner by a coup-de-main on Rhode Island, having separated himself from his army with his aide-de-camp only."[27]

Brigadier General Francis Smith, who temporarily took over as commander of the British forces on Aquidneck Island, increased the guard at his house and ordered that sentries' muskets were "for the future to be loaded."[28] This suggests that the musket of Private Walter Graham, the lone sentry at the gate of the Overing house, was indeed not loaded. His firearm may not even have been primed with powder—rendering it useless as a signal gun. Major Mackenzie expressly stated that Graham's musket had not been loaded, but did not mention whether or not his gun had been primed.[29]

On July 12, General Smith dispatched Captain Thomas Welch of the 17th Dragoons, another of General Prescott's aides, to New York City on board a Royal Navy vessel to convey Smith's written message of Prescott's capture to General Howe.[30] Commanded by Lieutenant Robert Deans of Admiral Parker's flagship, HMS *Chatham*, the vessel also carried a letter from Parker for General Howe's brother, Admiral Richard Howe.[31] Deans and Welch arrived in New York during the afternoon of July 14, when General Howe and his staff "received the unpleasant but reliable news."[32]

Welch's report convinced Major General James Robertson that "The wideness of the channel, and the disposition of the men-of-war, made Prescott think his situation the more secure."[33] Captain Friedrich von Muenchhausen complained that "The sentry at [Prescott's] door must either have been asleep or was bribed, since not a single shot was fired."[34] A British army captain wrote from New York to Lord Percy, "I am sure [Prescott's capture] will make a good deal of noise at home. It is loudly [talked] of here."[35] And Captain John Bowater, still assigned by the navy to keep an eye on

Charles Lee, noted that in New York Prescott "is very much condemned for being at a lonely house four miles from his camp with only one sentinel and a corporal's guard at a great distance. ... He treated the inhabitants with great severity and I shall not be surprised to hear the rebels have hanged him."[36]

Amid questions about the circumstances surrounding Prescott's capture were telling references to his value as an officer. "News came that General Prescott was taken prisoner at Rhode Island in a very idle way. He is not much regretted," commented Ambrose Serle, a civilian aide to Howe.[37] As Prescott's replacement, Howe selected Major General Robert Pigot, whom the 32-gun warship *Niger* delivered to Newport's Long Wharf on July 21.[38]

Rumors that Prescott had been found in a compromising situation quickly spread through both the British and American armies. On July 17, on the *Niger*, transporting General Pigot to Newport, the story circulated that when Prescott was captured, he was found "in bed with a farmer's daughter near Newport."[39] Patriot minister Ezra Stiles wrote the same day that Barton had been "informed that the General was to lodge there that night with some of his whores. [True.]"[40]

Of course no one was more interested in the Prescott affair than Charles Lee, who remained cooped up on the *Centurion* in New York Harbor. In a July 27 letter to the Earl of Denbigh, Captain Bowater mentioned that the report of Prescott's capture had "put our prisoner Mr. Lee in high spirits, thinking he should be exchanged, but he has just now been told that he is in a very different predicament and that no such thing will happen."[41] Howe, it seemed, still considered Lee a deserter, and ineligible for exchange.

Meanwhile, in Providence, on the morning of July 11, Prescott and Barrington were handled as befitted their status as gentlemen. According to John Howland, who had just returned to Rhode Island after serving in Lee's division in New Jersey, it was decided that Prescott and Barrington needed "to be put in better trim" before being presented to General Spencer. Howland was asked to dress the men's hair and otherwise assist them. As he recalled many years later,

> [Prescott] was a small, feeble old man, but his aide, Barrington, was a handsome young man. ... The neck stocks then worn were composed of fine cambric, with a strap which buckled at the back of the neck. When the aide stood before

the glass [mirror] adjusting his shirt collar and stock, he asked me to pin the stock. As I was doing this, I said, "have you not stock buckle, sir?" He replied quickly, "no, and a gentleman of the house has just loaned me his stock, for by God, we came away in such a damn'd hurry."[42]

Prescott's clothing troubles had continued after leaving the Overing house in his slippers. He needed a pair of shoes to be presented to Spencer and other officers. The story of how he got them was told to Barton's biographer, Catherine R. Williams, by Samuel Cory, then eighty-six years old. After the raiding party had returned to and landed at Warwick Neck, Williams wrote:

> The prisoner [Prescott] made great complaint of having no shoes; his feet were much scratched and swollen, and Colonel Barton procured a pair of one of the officers at Warwick for him; and he told Samuel to take them up to him, and put them on. Sam took the shoes, and Prescott protested he could not wear them, his feet were so swelled, and they would not fit, etc. But then Sam very deliberately sat himself down, and went about putting them on, saying his orders were to put them on General Prescott, not to see whether they fitted, and that he must obey orders. It was in vain the captive General remonstrated, and writhed about with most hideous contortions of countenance, Sam kept at work with the gravest face, although ready to burst with laughter, until he had forced the shoes on.[43]

Eventually, Prescott and Barrington were delivered to Spencer's headquarters. Despite his fearsome reputation, Prescott impressed Spencer as merely acquiescent. "The General at present seems very submissive and well pleased with the treatment he has had, not only since he arrived at this place, but from Colonel Barton and his party," Spencer wrote to Connecticut governor John Trumbull.[44]

The next morning, General Smith dispatched Captain Henry Barry, then serving as the Town Major of Newport, north to Providence to meet with Prescott to review his health and accommodations, and deliver the general's servant, Isaac Carder, and clothes.[45] Barry's ship was permitted to go no further up the bay than Pawtuxet, some three miles south of Providence. With Governor Cooke temporarily absent, Barry negotiated terms, on board the 28-gun Continental frigate *Providence*, with Stephen Hopkins, Rhode Island's most famous politician and a signer of the

Declaration of Independence. Hopkins then served in his capacity as president of the Rhode Island Council of War. Captain Barry described his visit in a letter to Lord Percy:

> The day after this unfortunate accident [Prescott's capture] I was sent, in a flag of truce, up the River [Narragansett Bay], with orders from Brigadier General Smith, if possible, to see General Prescott and learn from him his situation and what he would wish should be done, but I was suffered to proceed no further than the Providence ship-of-war, about three miles from the town, where I remained for two days, and was very civilly treated and well entertained by the Rebel officers on board. . . . Then I was obliged to enter into a long correspondence with old Mr. Hopkins, who, your Lordship knows, is a member of the Congress. It was carried on by both sides with much civility and respect, and in the end I obtained leave for the General's servant with such things as he wanted to be sent him, and was assured that he as well as his aide-de-camp would be well treated, they having given their paroles.[46]

On July 13, Hopkins denied Barry's request to meet with Prescott. This decision was in retaliation for a recent British refusal to allow a Rhode Island representative on a flag-of-truce ship to visit Newport.[47] However, the following day, after receiving a note from Prescott that he was being treated well, the Americans permitted Barry's ship, before returning to Newport, to drop off Prescott's servant and some of his clothing for delivery to the general.[48]

Spencer, meanwhile, wanted Prescott moved inland to Lebanon, the wartime capital of Connecticut, to prevent British forces from attempting their own raid to retake their general. Immediately after hearing of Prescott's capture, Spencer had written to Washington: "General Prescott is now at Warwick—I have sent for him here . . . . For the present I shall send him to the immediate care of Governor Trumbull, as it is not thought best here to keep him in this more exposed state."[49] After Prescott's servant joined the general on July 14, the Americans prepared to transport the British general to Lebanon. First, Spencer had Prescott sign the following parole agreement:

> I, Richard Prescott Esq., major-general in the services of his Britannic Majesty, being made a prisoner of war by the army of the United States of America, do promise upon my

word and honor, and upon the faith and credit of a gentleman, to depart from here to the First Society in the town of Lebanon, in the State of Connecticut, being the place of my destination and residence, and there to remain until otherwise disposed of by Governor Trumbull (who is desired by General Spencer to take the particular charge of me) until the commander-in-chief of the United States shall manifest his pleasure with regard to my disposal, or until I shall be duly exchanged or discharged; and that I will not directly or indirectly give intelligence of any kind, or say or do anything to the prejudice of the United States of America, during the time of my restraint. Given under my hand, at Providence, this 14th day of July, A.D., 1777. Rd. Prescott.[50]

It galled Prescott to sign the parole, as it implied that the United States existed as a separate country. But he did so, hoping it would improve his situation. Later that same day, Colonel William Peck of Rhode Island, with a strong guard, moved Prescott, Carder (his servant), and Barrington (who also signed a parole agreement) by carriage to Lebanon.[51]

It must have depressed Prescott to leave Rhode Island, as it would place him far from his former command and out of reach of the British navy. Lieutenant Colonel John Campbell, commander of the 22nd Regiment, who had served under Prescott on Aquidneck Island, observed that Prescott would be "distressed" being a captive of the Americans for a second time, "for few like the confinement, the company, or the country less than he does."[52]

General Spencer intended to allow Prescott to reside in and freely circulate among the houses of Lebanon's "First Society." But Washington had other ideas. Prescott, he believed, should fare no better than Lee, who was living in a few rooms on the musty *Centurion*. In a July 17 letter to Governor Trumbull, Washington requested that Prescott be "genteelly accommodated, but strongly guarded" in order to prevent his escape, without the privilege of local parole (that is, Prescott would not be permitted to roam freely in Lebanon).[53] On July 23, Prescott, Carder, and Barrington were moved again "[i]n consequence of advice from General Washington," Governor Trumbull explained. "I have ordered General Prescott to be removed from this town [Lebanon] to East Windsor, where he is to remain under a guard commanded by Lieutenant Timothy Allen till further orders. . . . The General is to be treated with politeness, but strictly watched and guarded so as to give him not ye least opportunity for escape."[54] While in East Windsor, Prescott occupied the southeast, second story room in the house of Captain Ebenezer Grant, a successful merchant.[55] According to a local historian writing around 1857, Prescott, during his stay there, "was very haughty and aristocratic, looking upon his captors with the greatest contempt, especially despising the frugal meals of the farmers, on whom he was billeted. His guard . . . used to amuse themselves by annoying him and listening to his wholesale curses against the Americans."[56] In late August, Prescott received from Newport two trunks packed with more clothes, as well as some money.[57]

Prescott behaved very differently than his counterpart Charles Lee conducted himself as a prisoner. While Lee constantly mulled ways to help the British end the war, Prescott exercised little more than simple patience.

General Washington wasted no time attempting to exploit Prescott's capture. "His Excellency George Washington no sooner had intelligence of the matter than he sent a flag to General Howe demanding an exchange of General Lee, the event of which I have not heard,"[58] wrote Rhode Island native General James Varnum to Governor Nicholas Cooke. In a July 16 note to Howe, Washington wrote succinctly, "The fortune of war having thrown Major General Prescott into our hands, I beg leave to propose his exchange for Major General Lee."[59] Washington even offered to release Prescott from captivity as soon as Howe agreed to the exchange, without waiting for Lee to be released first. The American commander also expressed the hope that a way could be found to "effect the exchange of Lieutenant Colonel Campbell and the Hessian field officers for a like number of ours of equal rank in your possession."[60]

Howe did not deign to respond to the proposal. He was still waiting for London's decision on whether to treat Lee as a deserter, and, in any event, he did not want to be rushed by the upstart Washington. On July 28, Washington touched on Howe's silence in a letter to a congressional delegate. "Most probably, he [Howe] will take some time before he agrees to it, having declared him [Lee] unexchangeable in one instance, and only argumentatively to be in the same predicament of other officers, in another," he observed. "His objection, most likely arose from a supposition we should never have a major general in our possession."[61]

Washington made the exchange offer at a time when he and the British commander-in-chief were struggling to determine the protocol for prisoner exchanges in general. In correspondence with Lord Germain, Howe explained that he did not trust Washington to exchange Campbell and the Hessian field officers; he was "well convinced" of Washington's "intentions to proceed no further in this business" than exchanging Lee for Prescott.[62] Nor did Howe feel that Washington was fulfilling his obligations to exchange British and Hessian officers and soldiers who had been captured earlier in the war.[63] Both Lee and Prescott would have to languish as prisoners indefinitely.

In mid-August 1777, the troop transport *Lady Gage* docked at Portsmouth, England. It carried wounded and sick British soldiers, and the first news of Prescott's capture to reach England. In his formal report to the secretary of the American Colonies, Lord George Germain, General Howe described Prescott's capture as an "unlucky accident" that was "as distressing as it was unexpected."[64] In response, Germain expressed to Howe his "great uneasiness" about "so unexpected an event."[65]

British newspapers eagerly got to work tracking down details of the capture from the newly arrived transport's passengers. They focused on two salacious points: Prescott's shortage of clothing when he was spirited away, and rumors of his female companionship in the Overing house. The August 16–19 edition of London's *General Evening Post* reported that "rebel troops . . . took him naked out of his bed, not allowing him time to put on his clothes."[66] The *London Evening Post* stated that Prescott "had retired in the evening with his aide-de-camp, and a sergeant's guard, to sleep a mile from his post, with a *lady*, but was discovered, and taken by a party of Provincials at two o'clock in the morning."[67]

In little time, Prescott's capture became the subject of verse, song, and ribald jokes, attracting that talented breed, London's epigram writers. The following epigram published in two London newspapers around August 22 refers to Arnold offering a smaller reward for Prescott's capture than Prescott had first offered for him:

On a LATE Capture
'TWIXT PRESCOTT AND LEE,
What a Difference there be,
May be found by the Price of their Head;
But 'tis certain that Lee

Reconnoitering would be,
While PRESCOTT went only To-bed!⁶⁸

On August 30, the following epigram appeared in London's *Public Advertiser*:

On the Captures of General Lee and General Prescott;
the first while he was reconnoitering the Field of Mars
[the Roman god of war];
the second the Field of Venus [goddess of love].

The British transports ships that delivered word of Prescott's plight also brought news of General John Burgoyne's capture of Fort Ticonderoga in early July. This was a significant war development, but the Prescott story—one of a relatively minor military figure—continued to titillate readers.[69] The latitude given London writers and newspapers to lampoon a man who was both a gentleman and a general of the British army was remarkable.

The public ridicule of Prescott was apparently too much for King George III to stomach. "His Majesty (says a Morning Paper) complains of the injustice done to Prescott by the News-Writers," reported the *Public Advertiser* on September 1. This report of royal disfavor caused the humorists some pause for several weeks. But the cease-fire ended with the September 18–20 edition of the *London Evening Post*. "When General Prescott was taken prisoner," it declared, tongue-in-cheek, "all he was heard to say, when the Provincials were bearing him on their shoulders, out of the court-yard of the house was, '*give me my breeches—give me my breeches*.'"

With that, English wits returned to their favorite topic with relish. The following offering appeared in three London newspapers later that month:

"The Handerkerchief!"–Othello cries,
(The Handerkerchief, the Stage replies)
"I prize it more than Riches."
A diff'rent Note poor Prescott roars,
For nought resounds th' Atlantic Shores:
"But where? *Oh where's my Breeches?*"⁷⁰

Even the controversy surrounding the media's ridicule became a target of humor. The September 26, 1777, edition of London's *Morning Chronicle* attributed the following epigram to "Miles":

On the Capture of a certain General.

A General of late has been vilely abus'd,
And, without any reason, most falsely accused;
For how could a man be neglectful of duty,
Who was taken when storming the fortress of beauty?

The *London Chronicle*, too, capitalized on the fun, printing an especially humorous bit that incorporated every lurid claim:

On General PRESCOTT being carried off naked,
"unannointed, unannealed."
WHAT lures there are to ruin a man;
Woman, the first and foremost all bewitches!
A nymph thus spoil'd a General's mighty plan,
And gave him to the foe—without his breeches.[71]

Eventually, London's epigram writers became bored and moved on to their next topic.

In fact, no credible evidence exists indicating that Prescott was found with a woman in his bed or that he stayed at the Overing house in order to sleep with Mary Overing, Henrietta Overing, or any other local woman—despite the legend that persists to this day.[72] None of those who spread rumors on the subject were in a position to know the truth. It is also unlikely that Prescott would have slept with a local woman in a house that was still occupied by its owner (and the husband of Mary Overing and father of Henrietta Overing). Prescott's explanation that he stayed at the Overing house in order to be closer to the action is probably the truth. Still, knowing his fellow countrymen, Lieutenant Colonel John Campbell had anticipated the sordid speculation sure to be spawned by the unusual conditions surrounding Prescott's capture. Just two days after Barton's brilliant raid, he shared his thoughts in a letter to Lord Percy:

> General Prescott, in order to do the different duties of commandant in town [in Newport] and commanding in camp [in the northern part of Aquidneck Island] kept his former house in Newport and took two rooms at Miss Overing's. He dined and did business every day in town. He slept, received reports and gave out orders every morning at Overing's. This pretext and circumstantial account may be disgusting to others but not displeasing to your Lordship who is so perfectly acquainted to this Island.[73]

Major Frederick Mackenzie recorded simply that "General Prescott having a good deal of business to transact in Newport, and being desirous of being near the camp at night, in case anything should happen, had fixed his quarters at Mr. Overing's, to which house he always came at night, and from whence he returned to town in the morning."[74]

As described in a prior chapter, the Americans in the summer months in 1777 frequently sent small raiding parties against British outposts in the northern part of Aquidneck Island, and other British generals had also stayed in nearby houses at various times, including Francis Smith, Prescott's immediate replacement.[75] In addition, the story that Prescott was taken from the Overing house without his pants on was inaccurate: the versions of the capture written by both the American Barton and the Scot Mackenzie state that Prescott was permitted to put on his britches, and did so, before he left his bedroom.

Lord George Germain. As secretary of state for the Colonies from 1775 to 1782, he was the civilian official most responsible for the conduct of the British war effort. Print published in *The London Magazine*, April 1780, from a painting by Sir Joshua Reynolds. (*Library of Congress*)

Meanwhile, British newspapers also addressed the more serious issue of the fates of the two captured generals. They reported that the exchange of Lee for Prescott was held up for the time being, but gave different reasons for it. In mid-August the *London Evening Post* reported "from good authority" that when Howe "was informed of the taking of General Prescott, he could barely keep his temper; and said that that officer might continue a prisoner, he would not exchange him."[76] Along the same lines, the August 29 edition of the *Morning Post and Daily Advertiser* stated that "The commander in chief [Howe] is so much incensed at the misconduct of General Prescott, that he refused to exchange him till the King's pleasure is known, notwithstanding General Washington has made overtures for that purpose." By contrast, London's *Gazetteer and New Daily Advertiser* stated more soberly and accurately: "It is reported that General Lee will be given in exchange for General Prescott and Lieutenant Colonel Campbell; but before Sir William Howe makes the exchange, he intends to wait for instructions from England upon the head."⁷⁷ If Howe was angered by Prescott's choices, he nevertheless later conceded to Lord Germain that the captured general had been "more unfortunate than inattentive to his duty."⁷⁸

On September 2, British secretary of war Lord Barrington, whose nephew had been taken with Prescott, sent Howe a letter informing him that, at King George III's direction, Prescott's promotion to full major general was being postponed "until inquiry shall be made into the particular circumstances of that officer's capture, which inquiry it is His Majesty's pleasure that you cause to be made."⁷⁹ A London newspaper put the following spin on that decision:

> Colonel Prescott has already experienced the displeasure of his Majesty, for his unmilitary conduct on Rhode Island, in quartering near five miles from his command. He had not got his rank as a general officer in the late promotion of Colonels, according to his seniority. Some say this is not owing to any resentment against the Colonel for his indiscretion, but merely political, and done to avoid giving him equal rank with General Lee, as the Congress, it is apprehended, would directly order Washington to insist on an exchange, to which the King has determined never to give his consent on any terms.⁸⁰

It was true that Prescott held the army rank of full colonel in England, and was a major general in North America only. Thus, there may have been some doubt whether he was of equal rank with Lee, who was a major general without qualification. But this argument carried little weight. When Prescott was exchanged back in 1776 for Major General Sullivan, he was treated as a major general. Moreover, he had signed his July 14, 1777, parole identifying himself as a major general. In any event, until an army court-martial was held examining the circumstances of his capture, Prescott suffered the indignity of having his promotion to full major general postponed.

Meanwhile, as English writers had lampooned Prescott, American scribes celebrated Lieutenant Colonel Barton with a bevy of popular poems and songs, including the following:

> Go to your king and to him say—
> Call home your troops, call them away,
> Lest Prescott's fate you share,
> For Barton with his sling and stone,

Has brought your great Goliath down,
And caught him in a snare.[81]

Barton's feat did not directly help the Americans win the war; neither Lee nor Prescott played a pivotal role on the battlefield. However, Prescott's capture did boost American morale at a time when most of the news for patriots was discouraging.

Barton's famous raid also spurred a number of similar, if less significant, raids by other Rhode Island officers. One such man was Westerly's Ebenezer Adams. A captain in Colonel Robert Elliot's State Artillery Regiment, Adams had been Barton's second-in-command on the mission to nab Prescott. Captain Adams figured that due to increased British patrols on Aquidneck Island, it would be too dangerous to try to duplicate the July 10 raid. Instead, he focused on small parties of British seamen who frequently visited uninhabited Prudence Island to wash their clothes and pick up fresh water and wood. On July 25, Adams and a small party of Rhode Island militia hid on the island. When two seamen from the frigate HMS *Diamond* splashed ashore with their laundry, Adams and his men took them prisoner and rowed them to the mainland undetected.[82]

Captain Adams boldly repeated his deed the next day, figuring that news of the prior day's captures would be slow to make the rounds among the British ships. He learned from locals that two British seamen from the frigate HMS *Lark*—who turned out to be Lieutenant William Otway and Midshipman Francis Brooks—had gone ashore to hunt. Adams's party found them "regaling themselves at a certain house." The Americans took them (and a young boy who worked on the *Lark*) prisoner, and again rowed off undetected. General Spencer was so pleased by these successes that he mentioned them in a letter to Washington.[83] The Rhode Island General Assembly voted its thanks by allowing Adams and his men to divide among themselves the arms and accoutrements taken in the raids.[84]

Some raids were spur-of-the-moment affairs. Learning on the night of September 5 that two seamen from HMS *Kingsfisher* were spending that night in a tent on the opposite shore of Aquidneck Island, a party of New England militia quietly rowed across the Sakonnet Channel to the shore, captured the two sailors, and returned them to the mainland.[85]

The Rhode Island militia saw another opportunity on Prudence Island in September 1777. They became aware that each morning, HMS *Juno*, a 32-gun frigate with a crew of about 220, sent a detachment of sailors and marines onto the south end of Prudence Island to obtain fresh water. During the evening of September 3, some 200 Rhode Island militiamen, led by Colonel Ezekiel Cornell (called "Old Snarl" by his men), quietly snuck from the western mainland over to the island. There, they concealed themselves behind stone walls and in an orchard near a spring that the British sailors and marines used. In the morning, a *Juno* long boat filled with a midshipman, seven seamen, six marines, and the ship's cooper slid up onto the island. The men disembarked, and the marines proceeded toward the spring. Without warning, Cornell's militiamen rose from their hiding places and fired. Three British marines were immediately hit; as they returned fire, the Rhode Islanders finished off two of them off with bayonets. "I took the equipment from off of a British soldier, the blood still streaming from his wounds," one Rhode Island militiaman vividly recalled more than fifty years later. The twelve surviving Englishmen were made prisoners.[86]

With the noisy discharge of muskets, the *Juno*'s Captain, Hugh Dalrymple, sent additional boats packed with marines to Prudence Island. Other nearby British ships followed suit, driving away the Rhode Island militiamen, who were glad to depart the island with their prisoners.[87] A third wounded British man lived just long enough to share the details of the ambush with the late-arriving rescue party. That night, the *Juno*'s crew buried the three dead marines on Dyer's Island.[88] The British were incensed that such a large body of American troops had fired on their outnumbered quarry rather than simply giving them an opportunity to secure their surrender with a show of overwhelming force.[89] Major Mackenzie recorded that one of the marines had been "mangled in a most shocking manner, having several shot through him, particularly three through the head; he was also stabbed several places with a bayonet." And he added menacingly, "The crews of the ships vow vengeance against them for this act of barbarity."[90] The British-supported *Newport Gazette* fueled the controversy, reporting that one of the marines "had his brains very inhumanely knock'd out with the butt-end of a musket."[91] However, no other account of the skirmish mentions this.

The argument that the Americans acted with unnecessary aggression has merit. However, the fact that the wounded men continued to fire may have justified the use of bayonets against them. The September 6, 1777, edition of the *Providence Gazette* reported that after first laying down their arms in surrender, the three marines had picked them up and again started firing. If true, that would have naturally spurred a harsh response.

General Washington understood the value of American kidnapping attempts and other such raids in a war of nerves. They lifted the morale of American patriots and lowered the spirits of occupying British and Hessian troops. "The frequent captures you make with your little parties have a very good effect and ought to be encouraged," the commander-in-chief wrote to General Spencer in September 1777.[92] The enemy soldiers and sailors seized on these missions were equally valuable. Each British man taken potentially meant one American exchanged and freed from dangerously overcrowded and unhealthy Newport prison ships.

8

The Generals Are Exchanged

Barton's capture of Major General Richard Prescott on the night of July 10, 1777, did not immediately alter the conditions of Lee's captivity. For now, Lee remained confined on the *Centurion*. On August 6, Lord Germain wrote to Howe, "your motives for postponing General Lee's departure for Great Britain are approved by the King."[1] If that was welcome news to Howe, Germain's letter conveyed no word as to Lee's ultimate fate.

Meanwhile Congress maintained its firm stance with respect to Lee. On August 7 it passed a resolution insisting that "Major General Prescott be retained as a pledge for the good treatment and release of Major General Lee," and that Prescott "be treated as nearly as circumstances will admit, in the same manner as the enemy shall treat the officer last mentioned."[2] South Carolina delegate Henry Laurens wrote that if Lee were hanged, he would favor imposing the same punishment on Prescott.[3]

With Prescott now serving as an ample counterbalance to the imprisoned Lee, Congress authorized the release of Lieutenant Colonel Campbell and the five Hessian field officers from confinement. In August 1777 Campbell left the Concord tavern he so despised and moved to a house in Concord, where he was permitted to move freely around the town and employ his four personal servants.[4] In the American prison camp at Dumfries, Virginia, a captive Hessian officer wrote on August 25, 1777, that "the sentries guarding our staff officers were removed today and they were allowed the same freedom as the other captured officers."[5]

On September 5, Washington wrote to Howe, repeating his Prescott-for-Lee proposal and hinting that Campbell and the Hessian officers could be exchanged too.[6] Howe replied "when you fulfill your engagement by a general exchange of the officers in your possession, and have returned the soldiers now detained as prisoners, for those already sent by me, I shall consent to your proposition for the exchange of General Lee."[7] Howe's curt response was nevertheless significant. For the first time, he had agreed to exchange Lee if an overall prisoner exchange agreement could be reached—even as he continued to await definite word on Lee's military status from London. Howe may have made the offer simply because he did not expect Washington to comply. In an October 25 letter to Germain, in fact, Howe explained that he had not accepted Washington's offer in part because he feared that the American commander would delay releasing Campbell and his Hessian colleagues even after Lee was exchanged.[8]

In Connecticut, authorities made sure that Prescott remained confined to the southeast, front room of Captain Ebenezer Grant's house in East Windsor. Meanwhile, Lee continued to find his confinement aboard the *Centurion* trying, probably in part because it made it difficult for him to dine with his old British-officer friends. He was relieved to have the companionship of his servant, Giuseppe Minghini, and one of his dogs, but he yearned for the freedom to walk the streets of New York City.[9]

Lee's treatment improved after Gates's stunning victory over Lieutenant General John Burgoyne's army at Saratoga, New York, on October 17, 1777. The American triumph left Burgoyne and dozens of other British and German officers and more than 5,000 soldiers in patriot hands.[10] The increase in British army prisoners held by the Americans spurred negotiations for prisoner exchanges in general. With no reinforcements coming from England, Howe needed these troops, and also wanted to relieve the discomfort of captured British and Hessian gentlemen officers. In a November 26, 1777, letter to Washington from his headquarters at Philadelphia, Howe proposed the mutual parole of officers. Washington quickly agreed.[11] On November 27, Howe, in a gesture to Lee, wrote to

General Clinton: "As the continuance of General Lee onboard ship may be attended with some inconveniences, I would recommend that he be removed to his former situation on shore."[12] Lee returned to his two rooms at City Hall.

Finally, on December 12, 1777, Howe received word from Germain concerning Lee's fate. Satisfied that no arguments would induce "Mr. Washington" to forego his stated determination to retaliate against captive British army officers, and conceding that it was "necessary to put an immediate end to a fruitless negotiation," King George III had reluctantly decided "that Lee (having been struck off the half-pay list) shall, though deserving the most exemplary punishment, be deemed a prisoner of war, and may accordingly be exchanged as such when you shall think proper."[13] The king's instructions also included a request for Howe to prioritize an exchange for Campbell (who was apparently a favorite of both men).

Now inclined to treat Lee as he would any other Continental officer, Howe sent orders to permit Lee to be released from confinement. After more than a year of being restricted to one or two rooms, Lee signed a parole agreement on December 27 allowing him to move freely in the city.[14] He then moved in with a pair of British officers and longtime friends: Lieutenant Colonel William Butler and Major Daniel Disney, of the 38th Regiment. Generals Henry Clinton and James Robertson even offered him the use of horses. Lee's situation, as he described it to Washington in a December 30 letter, was suddenly "rendered as easy, comfortable and pleasant as possible, for a man who is any sort a prisoner."[15]

In late December, the American Commissary General of Prisoners, Elias Boudinot, issued orders for Major General Prescott to be released from confinement in East Windsor and sent to New York City on parole.[16] Prescott, along with aide Lieutenant William Barrington, reached New York in mid-January.[17] As a parolee, the British general could not participate in military affairs until his equivalent, Lee, was exchanged and allowed to enter American lines free of any restrictions. Prescott and a number of other officers subsequently passed through New Haven, causing a Connecticut newspaper to speculate that as the British had "no officer of the rank of Prescott, but General Lee, it is presumed that that gentleman will soon be released from his confinement."[18] General Washington even wrote Lee from Valley Forge on January 27, 1778, expressing the expectation "that you will return in a few days to your friends on parole."[19]

But an immediate exchange was not to be. While he agreed in principle to exchange officers of equal rank, Howe remained at odds with Washington over the trading of ordinary soldiers.[20] With increasing frustration, he further insisted that both Campbell and the Hessian officers be exchanged and released *before* Lee and Prescott.[21] Howe remained suspicious that after Lee and Prescott were exchanged, Washington would renege on a deal for Campbell. Then, on January 30, Washington sent his command counterpart resolutions enacted by the Continental Congress that based any new general exchange on Britain compensating the Americans (in hard currency or replacement provisions, and not the less valuable Continental currency) for food given to British prisoners. Congress further asserted that any payments received from the British should be forwarded to the Board of Treasury, "in order that the same may be applied as a fund for relieving the distresses of the prisoners in the power of the enemy."[22] Howe was furious. He did not believe that American prisoners suffered (despite the emaciated dead bodies that were carried out of New York prisons on a daily basis). Prisoner exchange negotiations ground to a halt.

Meanwhile, Lee happily roamed around New York City. Loyalist William Smith reported in his diary on January 24, 1778, that "Mrs. Watkins, who lately came from New York, saw Lee walking the streets."[23] In early February a British officer stationed in Newport heard that "Lee is at New York and rides all over the island."[24]

By this time, Lee's views on American chances of winning the war had again shifted. In September 1777, German chaplain Philipp Waldeck wrote of a visit with an officer of the *Centurion* (probably Captain John Bowater, who had previously watched over Lee during his stay on that ship): "He told us that General Lee, who is a prisoner aboard his ship, is very unhappy with the present state of the rebellion, and has openly stated during his captivity that Washington need only move [his main army] from one province to another until the English are exhausted. The land is so extensive that England cannot outlast the colonies."[25] His faith in American arms, it seems, had evolved over the previous nine months. But his thoughts on "the present state of the rebellion" probably reflected his displeasure with American troops being trained to fight the British army on its terms—that is, in classic European-style combat— which he did not believe they could do successfully.

Moreover, Lee continued to believe it was in America's best interests to end the conflict and return to the British empire. In January

1778, Elias Boudinot entered New York City with Howe's permission to examine American prisoners and try to arrange an exchange of Prescott for Lee. Boudinot met with Lee, who apparently disparaged Washington and in effect recommended that Congress switch from conventional to guerrilla warfare, fighting from a base in the western Pennsylvania mountains. Boudinot chose not to pass Lee's suggestion on to Congress.[26] Around this time (probably after his meeting with Boudinot), Lee again wrote to a British commander, this time Major General James Robertson, about serving as a moderator in an effort to end the war.[27] This letter is significant. Since Lee was on the verge of being exchanged, it cannot be said that he was motivated merely by a desire to avoid being hanged by the British.

Meanwhile, Howe continued to refuse to release Lee, despite having authorized Boudinot to arrange the general's exchange.[28] In exasperation, Boudinot considered insisting that Prescott be returned to confinement in Connecticut until Lee was released. But Lee advised him against it, fearing that ramping up the dispute might lengthen his own captivity.[29] And by early March, Howe had finally ordered the captain of the *Centurion* to transport Lee by sea from New York to Philadelphia. Howe wanted to have one last meeting with Lee to discuss how to end the war.

The drama surrounding Lee's exchange wore on. Howe's decisions to transport Lee by sea and meet with the controversial general only delayed Lee's release, much to Washington's exasperation.[30] But Lee did not mind travelling to meet with Howe; based on a letter to General Clinton, he relished the opportunity. "It is both my interest and inclination to be at Philadelphia as soon as possible," he wrote. He concluded his letter with the assurance, "I once more do assure you, sir, that I most ardently, both for public and private reasons, wish to be at Philadelphia as soon as possible."[31] The "public" reasons were probably to discuss how he could help reconcile the Americans with their British foes. Fearing that a frigid sea voyage in March would trigger "a fit of gout," Lee asked Clinton for permission to travel by the overland route to Philadelphia.[32] Howe granted Lee's request on March 8, but it took more time for Boudinot to arrange passes for the British entourage to travel through the American-controlled countryside.[33]

On March 24, Joshua Loring, the British commissary general of prisoners, and Major Griffith Williams of the Royal Artillery, escorted Lee through American lines in New Jersey, and on to Philadelphia, which they reached the following afternoon.[34] Yet Howe remained uneager to release his high-profile prisoner to the American army, which was encamped twenty-five miles to the west at Valley Forge. He still wanted Lieutenant Colonel Campbell and the five Hessian officers, the longest-held prisoners, released first.[35] Lee, meanwhile, waited in a popular Philadelphia coffee house.[36] Howe's delay caused a frustrated Congress on March 30 to pass a resolution instructing Washington that "it should be a preliminary in the proposed cartel for a general exchange of prisoners, that Major General Lee be absolutely exchanged for Major General Prescott, and if refused, that no exchange take place till the further order of Congress."[37] That very day a messenger arrived in Boston with orders to release Campbell and send him southward in anticipation of his exchange.[38]

In early April, Elias Boudinot was invited to Philadelphia to address prisoner exchange issues. "When I was setting off from camp," Boudinot later recalled, "General Washington called me into his room, and in the most earnest manner entreated of me, if I wished to gratify him, that I would obtain the exchange of General Lee, for he was never more wanted by him than at that moment, and desired that I would not suffer trifles to prevent it."[39] Washington was pleased to hear from Boudinot shortly thereafter that Lee would be released in two days.[40] Realizing that with the Americans having released Prescott on his parole, he could hardly deny Lee the same treatment, Howe informed Washington on April 3, 1778, of his orders to permit Lee "to pass my lines tomorrow morning, under a parole similar to the one given to Major General Prescott."[41] Further negotiations fixed the time for Lee's long-awaited release as the morning of Sunday, April 5.[42]

First, Howe had his meeting with Lee. "Contrary to the expectations of all of us, General Lee had another long conference with General Howe," noted Captain Muenchhausen on April 3.[43] Howe's officers were surprised that their leader would again lend the dignity of his office to Lee. Howe never revealed to his superiors what transpired at the meeting. In a June 4 letter to Benjamin Rush, Lee wrote that he told Howe that, in prosecuting King George III's war in America, he had been the unwitting "instrument of wickedness and folly." Howe, Lee claimed, "not only took patiently the observation, but indirectly assented to the truth of it," and then made an awkward "apology for his treatment of me."[44] Acknowledging that the British commander-in-chief was a good field commander, he suggested that Howe did so blindly. "He shut his eyes, fought his battles, drank his bottle, [and] had his little whore."[45]

Lee and Howe probably discussed his offer to broker a peaceful resolution to the war. If so, the American general kept that secret from Boudinot, Rush, and other American patriots. It may not have mattered. Unknown to Lee, Howe had by now been recalled for failing to win the war. Lieutenant General Sir Henry Clinton would soon replace him.

Finally, on the morning of April 5, Lee was escorted out of Philadelphia toward American lines.[46] Boudinot described the long-anticipated event:

> [T]he greatest preparations were made for his reception. All the principal officers of the [American] Army were drawn up in two lines, advanced of the camp about 2 miles towards the enemy. Then the troops with the inferior officers formed a line quite to headquarters. All the music of the army attended. The General [Washington] with a great number of principal officers, and their suites, rode about four miles on the road towards Philadelphia and waited till General Lee appeared. General Washington dismounted and received General Lee as if he had been his brother. He passed through the lines of officers and the Army, who all paid him the highest military honors to headquarters, where Mrs. Washington was and there he was entertained with an elegant dinner, and the music playing the whole time.[47]

The "elegant dinner" prepared to celebrate Lee's release was attended by Washington, his wife Martha, Nathanael Greene, and fifteen other Continental officers.[48]

It did not take long for Lee to remind his American colleagues of his less-genteel side. According to Boudinot, Lee stayed in bed late the next morning, forcing his fellow generals to delay their breakfast until he joined them. "When he came out, he looked as dirty as if he had been in the street all night," Boudinot recalled. "Soon after," Boudinot added, "I discovered that he had brought a miserable dirty hussy with him from Philadelphia (a British sergeant's wife) and had actually taken her into his room by a back door and she had slept with him that night."[49]

Technically, Lee remained on parole, unable to reenter American service. Howe refused to formalize his full exchange for Prescott until Lieutenant Colonel Campbell entered British lines.50 This put him at irritating odds with Congress, which, while willing to exchange Campbell for Colonel Ethan Allen, did not wish to do so until Prescott's and Lee's exchange was complete. Howe, meanwhile, continued to seethe over Congress's demand for hard-currency compensation for provisions given to British prisoners.51 Unable to participate in army affairs, Lee travelled to York, Pennsylvania, where Congress was sitting, arriving on April 9.52

Lee found Congress in an uproar over the matter of his exchange. After discovering that Washington and his prisoner exchange commissioners had agreed to trade Allen for Campbell before settling the Lee-Prescott exchange, a number of delegates accused the commander-in-chief of violating Congress's instructions to the contrary. These delegates, suspicious of Washington's rising power and eager to display the supremacy of civilian authority over the military, drafted a rebuke to the general: "Congress are concerned to find that an absolute exchange is agreed on for Lieutenant Colonel Campbell and Lieutenant Colonel Allen and that General Lee is only permitted to come out on parole. They will, however, suspend their judgment in this matter till they are informed of whether your commissioners were acquainted with the resolution of Congress of the 30th ultimo [March 30], previous to such agreement."53 Delegates sympathetic to Washington managed to have this and other harsher language intended to insult the commander deleted.54 Lee helped to defuse matters by not insisting on his full exchange before the Allen-Campbell exchange occurred.55

The dispute in Congress, Lee wrote, "almost frightened me from giving my opinion on any subject."56 But he did meet with the new president of Congress, Henry Laurens, and other delegates to discuss his controversial military views. According to Boudinot, Lee insisted on advising Congress on how to prosecute the war, since, according to the general, "nothing else could save" the patriot cause. Lee informed Boudinot that "he found the army in a worse situation than he expected" and that "General Washington was not fit to command a sergeant's guard."57 Boudinot also noted that after Laurens's meeting with Lee, the former was so "disgusted" by Lee's views that he did not even report them to Congress.

Lee also discussed with Laurens and other members of the Continental Congress his detailed "Plan for the Formation of the

American Army." It called for a complete reorganization of the army, despite his being absent from it for almost one-and-a-half years. Lee considered the idea that American officers and soldiers were the equal of their British counterparts "nonsense," and the notion that they could conduct an "offensive war" against the British army "insanity." Lee's plan, in the words of historian Thomas Fleming, "made a mockery of Washington's . . . attempts to professionalize the Continental Army," which Lee called the "European Plan." The Englishman wrote, "if the Americans are servilely kept to the European Plan, they will make an awkward figure" and "be laughed at as a bad army by their enemy." Lee concluded that "a plan of defense, harassing and impeding can alone succeed."[58] On April 13, a pleased Lee forwarded his plan to Washington, who fundamentally disagreed with its premises.[59]

Four days later, with no solution to his exchange status in sight, Lee asked Henry Laurens to exchange him and other officers for Lieutenant General John Burgoyne. He reasoned that while Burgoyne was of no further value to Britain, Washington, "to speak vainly . . . cannot do without me." Howe and other British leaders, Lee asserted, would not want to exchange Prescott because "they put not the least value upon him."[60] Laurens did not take Lee's idea seriously.

Meanwhile, Washington appointed four prisoner-of-war commissioners, including his aide-de-camp, Lieutenant Colonel Alexander Hamilton, to meet with a delegation assembled by Howe. In mid-April, the two parties hammered out a general agreement.[61] Co-authored by Boudinot and Hamilton, it would serve as a model for future prisoner exchanges. It included provisions requiring exchanges to be made every two months, the release of the longest-held prisoners first, and the prohibition of any officer or soldier from being "thrown into dungeons" or any other kind of "unnecessarily rigorous confinement." The treaty specifically banned the transportation of prisoners across the Atlantic for punishment.[62]

In Fredericksburg, Virginia, the five Hessian officers captured at Trenton on December 26, 1776, waited with ebbing hopes. Finally informed on February 10, 1778, that they would soon be exchanged, they endured two more months of delay and counter-orders, until they were allowed to pass into British-held Philadelphia on April 20, 1778.[63]

The next day, the long-delayed formalization of the Lee-Prescott exchange was finally agreed to.[64] Exhibiting a rare flash of humor, and indicating his giddiness at having Lee back in his military councils, Washington wrote to Lee that he looked forward to seeing the newly released general ride "his hobby horse, which I hope will not, on trial, be found quite so limping a jade as the one you set out to York on."65 Lee received the news at his Virginia farm, where he was addressing his private affairs. He would rejoin the army on May 20.66

In mid-April, the combatants also agreed to exchange Lieutenant Colonel Ethan Allen for Lieutenant Colonel Archibald Campbell outside New York City. It is not clear if the swap occurred before or after April 21. Allen's biographer, Willard Sterne Randall, wrote:

> For Allen, his exchange was a particular triumph. He had refused to try to escape, although all the men who had been captured with him had already escaped, except two French Canadians who had died. But Ethan Allen insisted that he be treated as an officer appointed by the Continental Congress and therefore held a legal commission from a legitimate government. That he was exchanged for a member of Parliament must have seemed an even greater personal victory for the man who had been considered a contemptible wretch by so many New York aristocrats, Loyalists, and British cabinet ministers.67

Taken to Staten Island on his way to American lines on May 3, Allen met with Lieutenant Colonel Archibald Campbell, who was travelling from Morristown to New York City. Allen recalled that Campbell "saluted me in a handsome manner, saying he was never more glad to see any gentleman in his life, and I gave him to understand that I was equally glad to see him. . . . The gentlemen present laughed . . . and conjectured that sweet liberty was the foundation of our gladness; so we took a glass of wine together."68 It appears that Allen and Campbell were formally exchanged on May 6.69

Allen, in a letter to Henry Laurens, stated that he could never forget his treatment as a prisoner—"the malevolent cruelty inflicted on me by the British in the course of my captivity is scarcely to be paralleled in history."70 The renowned leader of the Green Mountain Boys would later publish a narrative of his captivity that became a popular seller and helped Americans understand just how poorly the British had treated patriot prisoners. Campbell would go on to enjoy a fine military and political career, marked by highlights that included capturing Savannah, Georgia, with minimal casualties in early

1779; serving as governor of Jamaica from 1782 to 1784, and successfully defending that island colony from French threats; and again serving as governor, this time of Madras, India, from 1786 through 1789.[71]

Meanwhile, Richard Prescott tried to return to his military duties and preserve his rank, as they had existed prior to his July 10, 1777, capture. He persuaded Howe that his capture had not been due to his own neglect of duty. In a January 17, 1778, letter, Howe urged Germain to ask King George III to promote Prescott to the rank of full major general, as had been planned prior to his capture. Prescott, he explained, had simply been the victim of bad luck and that by limiting the general's command opportunities "the King will be deprived of the services of a very useful officer."[72] The king agreed. Prescott was appointed a major general in March.[73]

Word of Prescott's promotion, however, would not reach America for some time. In the interim, the general faced a court-martial, which was held in General James Robertson's New York City quarters on April 23. (The charge was not stated in the court-martial record, but it was probably related to neglect of duty.) The court's board members, Generals Robertson, Daniel Jones, and John Vaughn, probably did not expect an adverse result, but felt it appropriate to go through the proper motions. After explaining his defensive arrangements on Aquidneck Island and reasons for spending his nights at the Overing house in Middletown, Prescott pathetically stated for the record: "Yesterday completed the thirty-fourth year of my service. It is humiliating to be under the necessity of defending my conduct after such a length of service. The only consolation left me is a consciousness of having discharged my duty with zeal and to the best of my judgment."[74]

Prescott's colleagues sympathized with his plight, and concluded that "the quarters taken by the General were tediously chosen as being centrical to the several corps where his presence might be necessary and from whence his orders could be soonest conveyed, and that the west side of the island had always been considered as secure from the stations of the men-of-war and the distance of the enemy. They desire leave to add in the course of this inquiry, they had occasion to remark on the many instances of the General's care and attention to his duty."[75] On August 5, Secretary of War Lord Barrington informed Clinton, "The proceedings of the Board of General Officers appointed to examine into the conduct of Major-

General Prescott who was made prisoner at Rhode Island, have been approved by the King."⁷⁶

When Lee returned to Valley Forge in mid-May, after an absence of seventeen months, he rejoined a much-improved Continental army, and a more professional officer corps. At the time of his capture in December 1776, Lee and some others had believed that Washington was not long for his job, and that his army was close to disintegration. But much had since changed. For one, Washington had beaten back a serious challenge to his position, known as the "Conway Cabal," and emerged more respected than ever as the one man who could hold the disparate Continental forces together. In addition, his subordinates, such as the Marquis de Lafayette and Anthony Wayne, had gained valuable experience. Finally, during the previous, painful winter at Valley Forge, Major General Friedrich Wilhelm von Steuben had transformed an unsure Continental army into a truly capable fighting force. Then, shortly before Lee's return, Washington and his "new model" army received stunning news: the French had entered into an alliance with the United States and declared war on Great Britain.

Baron von Steuben, wearing his Prussian medal. (*Library of Congress*)

Lee appreciated neither Washington's new status nor the army's improvements. Rather than act with discretion and humility after his lengthy absence, he behaved as if it were still December 1776. Arriving at Valley Forge in late May, Lee "immediately began to quarrel with the Marquis Lafayette" and "assured himself that General Washington was ruining the whole cause."⁷⁷ Perhaps feeling threatened by the presence of the experienced Steuben, Lee led criticism of the Prussian.⁷⁸ He even spread a rumor that Steuben in effect was a fake—an obscure military man constantly wearing a decorative Prussian military medal that was regarded as worthless in his native country. As was often the case, Lee's criticism contained more than a kernel of truth, but he was being unnecessarily mean-spirited.⁷⁹

Soon after replacing Howe as commander of British forces in North America, Henry Clinton received word from the British cabinet of the French alliance, along with orders to evacuate Philadelphia and move to New York City. Clinton transported Loyalists, some German troops, and supplies by sea, but chose to march the bulk of his army across New Jersey. It was a risky move, as it exposed his twelve-mile-long column of 10,000 troops and 1,500 supply wagons to attack by opportunistic Americans.[80]

Suspecting that Clinton was about to move north, Washington held two councils of war, on June 17 and 24, to consider whether an attack on the British army was advisable. Dominated by Charles Lee, most Continental officers voted against it. They preferred to keep the 12,000-man Continental army together until a French fleet arrived with reinforcements, which would allow the allies to conduct a joint sea and land operation.[81] With typical color, Lee wrote the commander-in-chief that "to risk an action in our present circumstances would be to the last degree criminal."[82] The most that Washington's senior officers would recommend was to detach 1,500 men "to act as occasion may serve, on the enemy's left flank and rear."[83]

Acceding to his generals' wishes, Washington offered command of that 1,500-man detachment to Lee, who remained the senior major general. Lee was less than pleased by the assignment, which (probably with some justification) he suggested was "a more proper business of a young volunteering general than that of the second in command in the army."[84] Washington therefore offered the job to Lafayette, who eagerly accepted.[85]

Meanwhile, the commander-in-chief received new support for the bolder offensive he had envisioned. Like Washington, his young but brilliant aide, Lieutenant Colonel Alexander Hamilton, itched to demonstrate the army's improved capabilities. He complained that Washington's senior officers "would have done honor to the most honorable society of midwives, and to them only."[86] He scorned Lee as "a driveler in the business of soldiership or something much worse"—a strongly worded insinuation about Lee's loyalty. Nathanael Greene, too, backed Washington. "People expect something from us and our strength demands it," he declared.[87] Finally, in a note to his commander, Lafayette revealed that he and five other generals had favored a more aggressive response than that proposed by Lee and his supporters. The Frenchman suggested sending more troops to attack Clinton's rear guard or baggage train.[88]

Heartened, Washington reversed course, ordering a larger body of 4,240 soldiers, including some of the army's best units, to follow

Clinton's troops and "attack them as occasion may require."[89] He did not, however, change the commander. Seeing the increased size of Lafayette's command, Lee informed Washington that it seemed "undoubtedly the most honorable command next to the commander-in-chief." Lee now requested to lead the enlarged force in the field, warning that if he was not so appointed, he would consider himself "disgraced"—a hint that he would resign.[90] Lee, wrongheaded though he often was, had a point. On June 26 Washington replaced Lafayette with Lee. In a gesture to justify the replacement of his much younger and well-liked subordinate, Washington added two brigades—another 1,000 soldiers—to Lee's force. At more than 5,000 men, almost half the American army, it now unquestionably required the experienced managerial skills of a senior general.[91]

When Lee caught up with Lafayette at Englishtown on June 27, the British army was less than five miles to the southeast, near Monmouth Court House. Little time remained before Clinton reached higher, easily defended ground and a quick path to British navy ships waiting in Lower New York Bay to pick up his troops. Washington directed Lee to attack the next day, but he did not specify whether the action was intended to harass enemy forces or to bring on a general engagement. He did promise to bring the rest of the army within supporting range.

When Lee set out early the next morning to reconnoiter the terrain of the likely field of battle, he was chagrined to discover running west to east three deep ravines filled with thick brush and swampy marshes extending for one-and-a-half miles through the open fields between his army and those of the enemy. Lee would have to send his troops through the ravines in order to attack the British rear guard. But if the British army pinned his troops against a ravine before Washington and his main force could work through the ravines to aid him, Lee's detachment would be in serious trouble. Nevertheless, with his men already on the march on what would be a scorching hot summer day, Lee decided to continue to carry on and make contact with the enemy to the east.

Lee's troops marched through the West Ravine and then through a passage in the Middle Ravine. When they reached open ground, they fanned out and formed a long line. They made contact with Clinton's rear guard, and spent the next few hours in haphazard action. Lee finally decided to initiate an attack, ordering 600 men to "amuse" the British center, while he sent orders for a brigade of Virginians on his left to encircle and cut off Clinton's rear guard. At the same time, he ordered Lafayette to lead three regiments and some artillery forward to a position on Lee's right flank.[92]

Lee was confident in his plan, but Clinton did not cooperate. Seeing a rare opportunity to engage the American army on open ground, he recalled a large body of troops situated just east of his rear guard and ordered Lord Cornwallis, their commander, to attack Lee's right flank under Lafayette. Lee's regiments would now face 6,000 enemy troops, including the cream of the British army, some of the best troops in the world.[93] At about noon Clinton's army began advancing in earnest, causing widespread confusion in the ranks of Lee's regiments.

Suddenly outnumbered roughly three to two, Lee lost control of his force. On the Americans' left, both Brigadier General Charles Scott and Brigadier General William Maxwell decided, inexplicably, to pull their troops back.[94] Soon most of Lee's force was streaming to the west back through the Middle Ravine, to the bewilderment of Lee, who had issued no orders to retreat. He considered making a stand, but the numbers moving against him were quickly becoming overwhelming. Not wishing for his remaining disorganized forces to be pinned against the Middle Ravine and rereading the unauthorized retreat as a blessing in disguise, Lee ordered the rest of his men to withdraw.[95]

At this crucial moment, Washington approached the battlefield with the balance of the American army. Reaching Lee, he stated, with anger in his voice, "I desire to know, sir, what is the reason for this disorder and confusion."[96] The commander-in-chief's "severe" tone surprised Lee, who had been expecting "congratulation and applause" for avoiding a crushing defeat.[97] According to the most credible account, by Washington's aide-de-camp, Lieutenant Colonel Tench Tilghman, Lee stammered in return, "Sir. Sir." After recovering, he insisted that "from a variety of contradictory intelligence, and from his orders not being obeyed, matters were thrown into confusion, and he did not choose to beard the British army with troops in such a situation. He said besides, the thing was against his own opinion." Tilghman added, "General Washington answered, whatever his opinion might have been, he expected his orders would have been obeyed, and then rode on towards the rear of the retreating troops."[98]

Lee had no time to properly explain his force's predicament. Washington calmed down enough to order Lee to take over the army's new defensive line, posted just as British troops would emerge from the Middle Ravine. Lee had already ordered three New England regiments there.[99] Lee responded that he would obey the order and "would not be the first to leave the field."[100] His men fought courageously for an hour, which allowed his other troops to pass in good order through the West Ravine and gave Washington valuable time to establish his next defensive line facing the exit from the West Ravine.[101]

Lee was pleased that his division had retreated without the loss of any artillery pieces, colors, or large numbers of soldiers, despite facing Clinton's best troops. He rode over to Washington, expecting praise; instead, his commander peremptorily ordered him to the rear to reorganize his scattered division. Washington subsequently changed his mind and gave the job to Steuben.[102] Dr. James McHenry, an aide to Washington, recalled seeing Lee "on horseback, observing to a number of gentlemen who were standing around, that it was mere folly or madness . . . to make attempts against the enemy where they possessed so great a superiority in cavalry."[103]

General Clinton tried one last time to secure a decisive victory. He sent his overheated and fatigued troops tramping into the West Ravine after the Americans, hoping to turn Washington's left flank. But Continental artillery firing from nearby hills blunted the charge, and Clinton wisely decided to withdraw. Colonel John Laurens, who was himself nearly killed in the action, later declared that the American troops ended up "masters of the ground" where "the standards of liberty were planted in triumph."[104] The battle was over.

The Battle of Monmouth Court House was a tactical draw from which each side drew positives. Clinton was subsequently able to slip away to New York City with his huge baggage train intact. For the Americans, the result was more far-reaching. "In the wake of the combat at Monmouth Court House," historians Joseph Bilby and Katherine Bilby Jenkins wrote later, "the Americans who fought there realized they had accomplished something memorable, and that the course of the war had inalterably changed. . . . Monmouth provided solid evidence that the Americans had indeed finally created a regular army."[105]

For Charles Lee, what could have been a return to glory instead marked the beginning of a long ordeal that would lead to his disgrace.

He might have avoided that fate had he laid low after Washington's scolding, and then privately explained to the general what had transpired in one of the most confusing battles of the war. Indeed, Washington took no action against Lee either immediately after the engagement or on June 29. Without any additional information, however, many Continental officers were convinced that Lee's retreat had been unjustified. James McHenry complained that as a result of the retreat, "we lost the fairest opportunity this war has afforded to destroy the British army."[106]

In a June 30 letter to his commander, Lee complained that the "use of so very singular expressions as you did on my coming up to the ground where you had taken post" raised the question of whether Lee was "guilty either of disobedience of orders, of want of conduct, or want of courage." Lee defended his generalship, asserting that "had we remained on the first ground, or had we advanced, or had the retreat been conducted in a manner different from what it was, this whole army and the interests of America would have risked being sacrificed." Rather than explaining to Washington that the latter's subordinates had simply misunderstood the battlefield situation (which was largely the case), Lee accused these men—but not the commander-in-chief himself—of being "very stupid," misinformed "wicked persons," or "dirty earwigs."[107]

Washington responded to Lee the same day, stating that he found Lee's language "highly improper," and that his battlefield statements to Lee had been "warranted by the occasion." Lee, he declared, would have the opportunity to defend himself against any accusations that he had made "an unnecessary, disorderly, and shameful retreat," without explaining whether that would be by court-martial, by an army board of inquiry, or through a congressional investigation.[108] Lee was especially stung by Washington's use of the phrase "shameful retreat"—a phrase that he had not previously used in his letter. As he later recalled, he "read and read it over a dozen times and thought it still a delusion" before he "waked and was convinced of the reality."[109]

Rather than letting the matter stand and allowing his anger to evaporate, Lee immediately fired off another letter to his commander, including one particularly venomous line: "I trust the temporary power of office and the tinsel dignity attending it will not be able by all the mists they can raise to obfuscate the bright rays of truth."[110] By referring to Washington's position as commander-in-chief as "temporary" and having "tinsel dignity," and by insinuating that Washington and his staff would attempt to deceive the investigators, Lee insulted his superior. He added that he hoped to have the "opportunity of showing to America the sufficiency of her respective servants," thus raising the specter of a showdown between the Continental army's top two generals. Lee concluded that he would be "retiring from the army," presumably until the matter had been resolved in his favor.[111] He then quickly followed up with a third letter. Free of insults (probably because its author had realized—too late—that he had gone overboard in his prior missive), it requested that Washington arrange a court-martial by which he could clear his name.[112]

Washington responded quickly. In addition to Lee's own noxious letters, he had received a joint memorandum from Brigadier Generals Anthony Wayne and Charles Scott charging that the retreat was unfounded, "as we had the most pleasing prospect from our numbers and position of obtaining the most glorious and decisive victory."[113] On the evening of June 30, Washington informed Lee of the three charges against him. Lee already knew of two—"disobedience of orders, in not attacking the enemy on the 28th of June, agreeable to repeated instructions" and "misbehavior before the enemy on the same day, by making an unnecessary, disorderly, and shameful retreat." Now Washington added a third: "disrespect of the commander-in-chief," in Lee's first two letters of June 30. Coincidentally, the officer Washington sent to place Lee under arrest, Colonel Alexander Scammell, the adjutant general of the army, had been at Widow White's Tavern on the morning of Lee's capture.[114]

Lee's post-battle insolence toward the commander-in chief reflected shockingly poor judgment, and ignorance of Washington's now-unsurpassed stature in the patriot cause. North Carolina congressional delegate John Penn understood it very well, observing that Lee "has made it a quarrel with General Washington and of course you know he must fail."[115] Elias Boudinot agreed, crowing to Alexander Hamilton of Washington after the battle, "none dare to acknowledge themselves his enemies."[116] Only one man—Lee—was foolish enough to openly attack his commander-in-chief.

Lee's outrage soon extended to the press. After the battle, the *New Jersey Gazette* published an account of the action that omitted mention of the good work Lee had done, particularly in defending the entrance to the Middle Ravine. In a July 3 letter to Robert Morris, Lee wrote hysterically, "not content with robbing me and the brave men under my command of the honor due us, a most hellish plan has been formed (and I must say at least not discouraged by headquarters) to destroy forever my honor and reputation." The bitter general went as far as to state that although American troops had forced the enemy to flee the last field of battle, "by all that's sacred, General Washington had scarcely any more to do in it than to strip the dead."[117]

A court-martial presided over by twelve Continental officers convened at Brunswick on July 3 and lasted almost six weeks. The court found Lee guilty on all charges, although it dropped "shameful" from Washington's characterization of his subordinate's retreat. On August 12 it sentenced him "to be suspended from any command in the armies of the United States of North America for the term of twelve months."[118]

Regardless of whether Lee should have been convicted of making an unnecessary retreat, his battlefield performance was not stellar. He failed to obtain proper intelligence of the ground of what would be the battlefield and lacked a plan of attack. Lee, who had never before commanded a sizeable force in battle, lost control of his detachment.[119] Yet Joseph Bilby and Kathy Bilby Jenkins perceptively asked in their history of the Battle of Monmouth Court House whether Lee's mistakes in the battle were "greater than Wayne's allowing himself to be surprised" in the night-time rout of Wayne's command at Paoli, or "even Washington's failure to make a thorough reconnaissance" prior to his defeat at the Battle of Brandywine.[120]

Much evidence actually supported Lee's generalship. The general had been aggressive, seeking to bag Clinton's rear guard, until he realized he was facing a much larger enemy force. Moreover, it appears that Lee's orders had been discretionary, authorizing him to avoid a general engagement. Perhaps the best evidence was from the pen of Clinton himself, who, considering his advantage in numbers, had no doubt that Lee's withdrawal had saved Lee's force from annihilation. "Had Washington been blockhead enough to sustain Lee, I should have caught him [Lee] between two defiles [ravines]; and it is easy to see what must have happened," the British commander wrote later.[121]

Contemporary historians, both British and American, who interviewed battle participants and reviewed the court-martial record, largely agreed that Lee had acted properly. In 1860, the discovery of Lee's plan of March 1777 in the British archives, which revealed that he had submitted to British commanders a recommendation detailing how the Americans could be defeated, however, changed views of him. It convinced many historians that Lee's decision-making at Monmouth Court House was driven by a plot to undermine the patriot cause. Recently, however, historians such as John Alden, John Shy, and Theodore Thayer, have rejected that possibility.

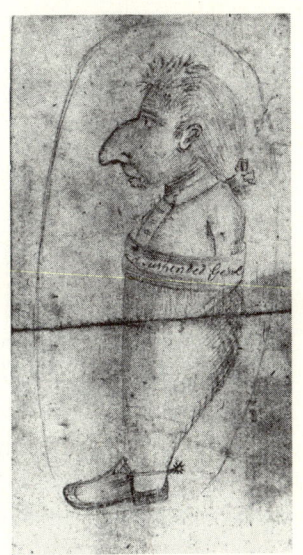

"Suspended General." Caricature of General Charles Lee in an officer's boot and with an oversized nose, by Colonel Thaddeus Kosciusko, probably in 1778. (*The Pennsylvania Magazine of History and Biography, 1891*)

Lee's foremost biographer, John Alden, and a student of the Battle of Monmouth Court House, Theodore Thayer, have persuasively argued that Lee should have been acquitted of the first two charges brought against him, but not the third.[122] "No one who carefully reads the record of the trial, examines the ground, and considers the British side of the battle would find Lee guilty of the first two charges," John Shy asserted. "But no one who reads his letters to Washington will believe him innocent of the third. Under the circumstances an acquittal on the first two charges would have been a vote of no-confidence in Washington."[123] As for Lee's sentence, Thayer wrote, "From the time of the verdict until now, it has been argued that Lee's sentence was too light if he was indeed guilty as charged."[124] It appears that the court found Lee guilty of all three charges in order to placate Washington, but levied a punishment ample enough for just one—disrespecting his commander-in-chief. Conviction on that charge alone merited a one-year suspension.

On October 23 Congress addressed the matter of Lee's court-martial. It was the delegates' duty to either confirm or reject the general's conviction and sentence. Lee's friend and booster, and leader of a faction in Congress that worried about Washington possessing too much power, the influential Richard Henry Lee, led the effort to nullify it. Such a result might, he thought, even produce an offer to resign from a shamed Washington. Gouverneur Morris, a New York delegate, on October 25 wrote to Washington, "General Lee's affair hangs by the eye lids."[125] In the end, Richard Henry Lee's efforts failed. Benjamin Rush complained that delegates had begun to "talk of *state* necessity and of making justice yield in some cases to policy"[126]—that supporting the commander-in-chief at this juncture of the war was more important than exonerating Lee.

Recognizing the hopelessness of Charles Lee's cause, Richard Henry Lee left for home before the final vote. Several other likely Lee supporters absented themselves as well. On December 5, 1778, Congress upheld Lee's sentence. But the vote was surprisingly divided, with six states confirming, two rejecting, two divided, and one without a quorum (this translated into sixteen delegates to confirm and seven to reject, with one abstaining).[127]

With his expectation of vindication crushed, a bitterly resentful Charles Lee lashed out at Washington and Congress in a lengthy, December 3, 1778, Philadelphia newspaper article. The commander-in-chief, Lee argued, had not won a single major battle on his own, and the victories for which he had taken credit had actually been secured by his subordinates.[128] Expecting such a reaction, Washington confided to Joseph Reed, now a Lee enemy, that Lee's "temper" had always been too "violent to attract my admiration." The Virginian considered it a wonder that he had "escaped the venom of his tongue and pen so long," since any commander under whom Lee served eventually became the target of his vitriol.[129]

Thanks to his angry and impolitic diatribes Lee's indignities did not end with his suspension. Insults to a gentleman were often resolved by the victim challenging his tormenter to a duel, typically with pistols or swords.[130] If Washington could at least publicly brush off his post-court-martial attacks, Lieutenant Colonel John Laurens—the general's aide and son of the president of the Continental Congress—would not. Charging that Lee "had spoken of General Washington in the grossest and most opprobrious terms of personal abuse," and acting out of "personal friendship and respect for [Washington's] character," the young Laurens challenged the major general to a duel.[131] Lee accepted, and the two met on the outskirts of Philadelphia on the afternoon of December 23. The men fired simultaneously. Lee missed his target; Laurens's shot scraped Lee's arm, leaving a bloody wound but no permanent damage. Negotiations between the duelists' seconds ended the matter.[132] Lee subsequently received challenges from Generals Baron von Steuben and Anthony Wayne, but managed to wrangle his way out of duels with each.

Taking the offensive, Lee then sought a duel with William Henry Drayton, a delegate to the Continental Congress and a respected judge from South Carolina. The problems between the two men stemmed from harsh words Lee had spoken about Drayton during the defense of Charleston in June of 1776. Lee had criticized a fort whose construction Drayton had overseen, complaining that Drayton "might be a very good chief justice, but he is a damned bad engineer."[133] Drayton harbored a grudge, and finally obtained a measure of revenge by offering his opinion of Lee's conduct in New Jersey in November 1776 to a Charleston grand jury. "The veteran [Lee], disobeying his [Washington's] orders . . . loitering when he should have bounded forward . . . he allowed himself to be surprised and made a prisoner, at a distance from his troops," he argued to the jury (which must have wondered what relevance it had to any local criminal matter). "Washington, in the abyss of distress, seemed to be abandoned by his officer next in command."[134]

Lee responded to Drayton's claims by sharing his opinion of his accuser with one of Drayton's South Carolina colleagues, who passed it on to Drayton himself. On February 3, 1779, Drayton wrote to Lee, reiterating his grand jury accusations and suggesting that Lee had deliberately allowed himself to be captured.[135] Lee's colorful response spared no insult. "Until very recently, I was taught to consider you only as a fantastic, pompous *dramatis persona*, a *mere malvolio*, never to be spoken or thought of but for the sake of laughter; and when the humor for laughter subsided, never to be spoken of or thought of more," he wrote. "But I find I was mistaken. I find that you are as malignant a scoundrel as you are universally allowed to be a ridiculous and disgusting coxcomb."[136] Lee ended his diatribe by offering to duel Drayton if he found his letter too harsh or impudent. But the South Carolina judge chose to ignore the challenge.[137]

By August 1779 Lee was back at his estate at Prato Rio in the Shenandoah Valley, where he languidly and unsuccessfully labored as a farmer. When his suspension expired, he heard a rumor that Congress intended to dismiss him from the Continental army, presumably to save money. Although it is doubtful that such an action was under serious contemplation, Lee, with characteristic passion and imprudence, fired off a letter to the current president of Congress, Samuel Huntington of Connecticut. "I understand that it is in contemplation of Congress, on the principle of economy, to strike me out of their service," he raged. "Congress must know very little of me, if they suppose that I would accept of their money, since the confirmation of the wicked and infamous sentence which was passed upon me."[138] Not surprisingly, Congress found this wrathful letter so offensive that on January 10, 1780, it did in fact dismiss him from the service.[139] Lee responded with a letter of apology, claiming that his letter was based on misinformation provided to him, but it was too late.[140] His military career was over.

In reality, Lee's dismissal had probably been inevitable, for three reasons. First, Lee held views that were fundamentally different from those of Washington. He believed that Continental army troops could not survive standing shoulder-to-shoulder and firing at close range, in the classic European style, against British grenadiers and light infantry. He therefore favored avoiding large-scale confrontations with the British army, fearing the effects of a significant defeat on the fragile patriot cause. His views were not necessarily wrong, but they were very much out of step with those of his commander-in-chief, and outdated after the French allied themselves with the Americans. Lee also advocated increased reliance on a civilian militia, rather than on well-trained, experienced Continental soldiers. This view was misplaced; as the war progressed, it became clear that the militia was not a serious, long-term military solution.

Second, a military organization can have only one leader. By continually sniping at a unit's head, a senior subordinate undermines him, and weakens the command from within. As a result, its performance suffers. Lee pushed his views aggressively, showing little restraint or discretion. It was only a matter of time before he and Washington had a serious confrontation.

Third, while Lee was highly competent and sometimes even brilliant, he was also highly critical of those in authority, and sarcastic and vindictive in army politics. He had exhibited these characteristics throughout his career, starting with his service in the French and Indian War. Lee's vitriol led to so much strife within the Continental army that it was better off without him.

Unwittingly, Congress, in dismissing Lee, got it right. What Congress did not know was that Lee, during his captivity, had persuaded himself that America could not win the war. What is more, he had actively offered to assist high-level British authorities in negotiating a peaceful end to the conflict, one that ended with the American colonies back under British rule. Had these facts been known upon Lee's release and visit to Congress in April of 1778, Congress would have relieved Lee of his command and possibly had him hung as a traitor.

Unable to return to England, and bitter about his treatment at the hands of Washington and Congress, Lee remained at his Prato Rio farm. There, according to his Georgia friend, Edward Langworthy, he lived "in a house more like a barn than a palace. Glass windows and plastering would have been luxurious extravagances; and his furniture consisted of a very few necessary articles."[141] To a visiting gentleman, who found a kitchen in one corner, a bed in another, books in the third, saddles and harness in a fourth, Lee said, "Sir, it is the most convenient and economical establishment in the world. The lines of chalk, which you see on the floor, mark the divisions of the apartments, and I can sit in any corner, and give orders, and overlook the whole, without moving from my chair."[142] Lee apparently had difficulty paying for improvements to his modest, one-story house.[143] He spent his time reading his books, raising dogs, living the life of a "wretched farmer," and dreaming of forming a "military republic" in the west.[144]

In August 1782, Lee reached out to Robert Morris, who had frequently advanced funds to him. "I have not a farthing in the world," he wrote.[145] Shortly thereafter he travelled to Philadelphia to sign the documents making official the sale of his farm for 6,100 pounds to John Vaughn, a buyer that Morris had found.[146] While in town Lee did not stay in the homes of any of his former friends, probably because he was still considered a pariah. While boarding in a second-floor room at the Sign of the Conestoga Wagon tavern on Market Street, he contracted a fever.[147] Attended by his loyal Italian servant, Guiseppe Minghini, and two of his dogs, Lee became seriously ill and, at the age of fifty-one, died on the evening of October 2. Before his death, John Bernard, an English actor and travel writer, was informed: "A friend calling to see him at the inn where he was lying in Philadelphia, found him, attended by a faithful Italian, sitting upright in bed, hands clinched on its frame, and his eyes glaring fiercely. At that moment he imagined himself once more amid the shock and shout of battle, and as the fire of life shot up its latest spark, he uttered his last words: 'Stand fast, my brave grenadiers!'"[148] One observer, probably a physician, noted that Lee's "two faithful dogs, who frequently attempted in vain to awaken their dead master" then "laid themselves down by his corpse for a considerable time, so long that it became necessary for new masters to remove them."[149]

The funeral of the former major general was held two days later, on October 4. The procession—a "large concourse of very respectable citizens"—started at the City Tavern and ended at Christ Church on Second Street.[150] Numerous luminaries attended, including the new president of Congress, John Hanson of Maryland; financier Robert Morris and delegate Gouverneur Morris; two prominent French officers, the Duc de Lauzun and Baron de Viomesnil; and Major General Benjamin Lincoln.[151] Afterward, Morris wrote of Lee that he had "formerly rendered considerable services to America, but who by an eccentricity of character had been later led into conduct unworthy of his talents and abilities and by means whereof he had lost the esteem even of those who wished to be his friends."[152]

In his will, Lee bequeathed property to his only true friends left in America, most of them his former aides-de-camp, in addition to his loyal servant Minghini, and Elizabeth Dunn, his housekeeper. (Minghini and Dunn would marry and remain in Berkeley County, where their descendants were found for several generations thereafter.)[153] Lee included a rather cheeky comment in his will, which created a sensation when it was published in 1784. "I desire most earnestly that I may not be buried in any church or churchyard or within a mile of any Presbyterian or Anabaptist meeting-house;" he quipped, "for, since I have resided in this country, I have kept so much bad company when living, that I do not choose to continue it when dead."[154] (His former aide, Jacob Morris, may not have had the will in hand when he had Lee buried at the Anglican Christ Church.) Four months after Lee's funeral, a Philadelphian described Lee's shockingly humble burial place: "He lies buried in Christ's Church yard. No stone marks his bed. Indeed, those who saw his open grave can scarcely mark the site, as it is continually trodden by persons going into and coming out of church. Behold the honor of the great!"[155] The Christ Church building, with its tall spire (the highest in North America until 1810) still stands today. In 1861, Lee's remains were disinterred and buried next to the church's exterior south wall.[156] A plaque now commemorates this spot.[157]

Just as being captured changed the life of Charles Lee, Richard Prescott's capture altered his. After his reinstatement to active command, on July 9, 1778, Prescott returned to Newport, where he served as second-in-command under Major General Robert Pigot. In the Rhode Island campaign that followed in late July and August 1778, Pigot successfully defended Aquidneck Island from an assault by French expeditionary forces under Charles Henri Théodat, Comte d'Estaing, and American forces under the command of Major General John Sullivan. But Prescott fumed over being assigned a secondary role in the Battle of Rhode Island. On September 28, Pigot departed for New York, and Prescott assumed command of Newport's British garrison.[158] During his subsequent time in the seaport city, military incidents were infrequent and insubstantial.

At the same time, conditions of American prisoners held at Newport improved. Records reveal no deaths of American prisoners during Prescott's tenure.[159] Yet Prescott could still be prickly about prisoner exchanges. By May 30, 1779, the Americans had returned eighty more soldiers and seventy more sailors to Prescott than he had sent to American authorities in Providence. The American officer handling such business sent two letters to Prescott, asking him to fulfill his obligations. Prescott returned the two letters unopened, claiming that he did not recognize the name "United States." The offended American then complained that Prescott had on at least two prior occasions acknowledged the fledgling nation's existence, when he had signed paroles after being captured in 1775 and again in 1777.[160]

Prescott brought with him to Rhode Island William Barrington, who had been exchanged shortly after the trade of John Campbell for Ethan Allen and who had been promoted to captain.[161] After his transport vessel was driven ashore on a southern Rhode Island beach on December 10, 1778, Barrington was captured a third time, a most notable wartime achievement. This time his captivity was short lived, as General John Sullivan generously agreed to send him and his fellow prisoners quickly back to Newport.[162]

In the fall of 1779, fearing the return of d'Estaing's squadron of warships from the Caribbean to Newport, Clinton ordered the evacuation of the city. Prescott supervised the withdrawal, destroying British fortifications but making sure that his troops did not damage Newport homes. Bound for New York City, Prescott and his flotilla of more than 100 vessels sailed out of Narragansett Bay on October 25.[163]

Upon his return to England on February 1, 1780, Prescott was assigned to command British troops on the Caribbean island of Antigua. In January of 1782 he arrived with reinforcements on St. Kitts Island and, with the British troops he joined, defeated a smaller French force, but then was prevented from capturing St. Kitts by another French force that remained on the island.[164] On November 26, 1782, he was promoted to lieutenant general, and later retired to his home in Middlesex County. His death in 1788 drew no interest from English newspaper editors, who declined to publish the news.[165]

London authorities dragged their feet in rewarding William Harcourt for his capture of General Lee and it created tension with Howe, who had pushed for it. Finally, the following announcement appeared in the September 2, 1777, edition of the *London Chronicle*: "Col. Harcourt, who took Gen. Lee prisoner, is appointed an aide-de-camp to the King."[166] Harcourt would return to London to serve in the court of King George III as his personal military aide, a prestigious position.

Shortly after hearing this welcome news, Harcourt received word of the death of his father, who had retired to his estate at Nuneham Park. Earl Harcourt accidentally drowned by falling headfirst into a well on his property trying to save his pet dog, which was found standing on top of his feet.[167] His death prompted one London newspaper editor, with less tact than the moment deserved, to observe that "the Great" should "read a political lesson of morality," in that "it should remind them, that a *moment* puts them on a level with their kindred dust, and that *titles* and *large possessions*, except accompanied by virtue, are no recommendations beyond the grave."[168] William Harcourt's older brother George Simon assumed the title of Earl Harcourt.

Harcourt's views of Great Britain's prospects in the Revolutionary War evolved more quickly than those of most of his fellow officers. A few days after capturing Lee in December 1776, Harcourt wrote that "it seems to be the universal opinion the rebels will no longer refuse treating upon the terms which have been offered them."[169] But after Washington's surprising victories at Trenton and Princeton, and the failure of the American army to disintegrate in the winter of 1776–1777, his confidence waned. In March 1777 he conceded that the American army "is now a formidable enemy," but still forecasted a prompt end to the war, provided the British were reinforced and the French did not intervene.[170] Just two months later, Harcourt lamented to his father that the Americans were so well supplied, so firmly committed to independence, and so difficult to defeat, that he despaired of a quick decision.[171] Following Lieutenant General John Burgoyne's defeat at Saratoga in October, he told his brother that if Burgoyne's army "had penetrated" from Canada to Albany, "America would not even then have been conquered." He wondered if Lord George Germain "will have strength enough" to continue "this business for another year."[172]

Harcourt did not hesitate to blame his commander for the twin disasters of Trenton and Saratoga. In letters to his father, Harcourt pointed out the "fault in the original arrangement of the winter quarters" after Howe's December 1776 campaign in New Jersey. These, he asserted, "were much too extensive for an army of our numbers, and the position of Trenton in itself was extremely faulty."[173] As for his friend, General Burgoyne, Harcourt wrote that "the loss of his army was unavoidable from the moment we sailed from New York."[174] In other words, a movement against Philadelphia should not have been attempted until Howe had moved northward from New York City, joined forces with Burgoyne descending from Canada, and brought both armies safely to Albany.[175]

William Harcourt began his service to King George III in early 1778, continuing what would become a long and successful, if not brilliant, career in the military and as a royal courtier.[176] Within a year of returning home he married Mary Lockhart; the couple had no children. After Burgoyne resigned from the army in October 1779, King George III appointed Harcourt colonel of the 16th Regiment of Light Dragoons (later called the Lancers), a post that he held for almost fifty years.[177] Harcourt served as aide-de-camp to the king until October 21, 1780, when he was replaced by Lieutenant Colonel Archibald Campbell, the officer who had been confined for some thirty days to the odious Concord, Massachusetts, common jail.[178] Prior to the war's end, in November of 1782, Harcourt was raised to the rank of major general.

During the Napoleonic Wars, Harcourt served with the British army in Holland, and was promoted to lieutenant general. In 1794 he succeeded the Duke of York in command of the British army in Holland. He eventually attained the rank of field marshal, and for nine years served as governor of the Royal Military College. Upon the death of his brother in 1809, Harcourt became the third Earl Harcourt of Stanton Harcourt and took his seat in the House of Lords. He and his wife were intimate friends with King George III and Queen Charlotte, and, for many years, Harcourt served as groom to the royal bedchamber.[179] Harcourt lived out his life as a strong and unimaginative supporter of royal rule during a time when the middling ranks of English society struggled for basics, such as voting rights.

Panel on William Harcourt's monument, depicting his capture of General Lee. From St. George's Chapel, Windsor, England. (*St. George's Chapel*)

For all his accomplishments, laurels, titles, and offices, Harcourt was proudest of the events of December 13, 1776. After his death on June 18, 1830, his surviving family members commissioned a white marble statue of him—one whose panels depicted his leading role in the capture of Charles Lee. Originally intended for Stanton Harcourt Church in Oxfordshire, King William IV took a liking to the "splendid statue" and had it placed in St. George's Chapel at Windsor Castle.[180]

9

The Ordeal of William Barton

William Barton, the man behind the unlikely capture of General Richard Prescott, went to prison late in his life and remained there for more than thirteen years. His downfall, like Lee's, was partly of his own making. The fame and glory he gained by his exploit created within him excessive pride that did not serve him well in this ignoble period of his life.

Barton's unforgettable raid of July 10–11, 1777—the most spectacular and successful special operation of the war—marked the pinnacle of his career. For the rest of the war he remained in the Rhode Island theater. Although Congress made him a colonel in the Continental army, Barton had no background commanding Continental troops, and Washington never invited him to join the main army. Meanwhile, Rhode Island's General Assembly, taking note of his Continental appointment and fearing that he could be called to serve in the Continental army "upon the shortest notice," withdrew Barton's appointment as commander of one of the state's two infantry regiments and removed him from the state's payroll.[1] Barton therefore fell into a sort of military limbo, commanding neither Continental nor state troops.

In April 1778, the Rhode Island Council of War asked Barton to sail to Newport in a flag-of-truce vessel to investigate prison conditions and supply captured Americans with food and clothing.² On April 28, Barton visited the Provost, the former Newport County jail now used as a prison by the British army. He was able to distribute some supplies and obtain a list of all of the ninety-eight prisoners then held in Newport. But the commander of the British navy in Newport refused Barton access to the two prison ships under his control. British officers suspected that Barton was in Newport only to gain intelligence for another special operation, and therefore required him to return to Providence after only a short time.³ The Rhode Island Council of War may have been better served had it selected for this role a civilian government official, and not someone as provocative as Barton.

Barton saw some military action shortly thereafter. Suspecting that the Americans were preparing for an invasion of Newport, General Robert Pigot, who had replaced Prescott in command in the Rhode Island theater, planned a preemptive raid on Warren and Bristol. It began in the early morning hours of May 25, 1778, when some 500 British and German regulars led by Lieutenant Colonel John Campbell of the British 22nd Regiment landed near Warren. They immediately seized and burned more than seventy flatboats that the Americans had collected in a creek to repair for future use in an invasion. After burning buildings storing American military supply caches, as well as homes and other buildings used to house American troops in the area, Campbell's men retreated south toward Bristol Neck, where British transport ships waited to take them back to Newport.⁴

Word of Campbell's raid did not reach Major General John Sullivan, then serving as the American commander of the Rhode Island theater, at his Providence headquarters until 8:00 a.m. Fearing that it was a feint designed to mask a major assault on Providence, Sullivan kept the few troops he had at his disposal at their stations. He did order Colonel Barton, with about twenty men, to do what he could. Mounting up, Barton and his men rushed from Providence down the "Great Road" towards Bristol, eager to see some action. South of town, Barton took command of about 200 state and militia troops who had gathered there and begun sniping at Campbell's rear guard. The Americans fired from a distance under cover of stone walls and trees. The British responded with musketry, supplemented by more robust fire from British warships off Bristol Neck. This kept the Americans at bay. The British navy transports arrived at the ferry landing just after noon, and Campbell's men managed to step into the flatboats and other small vessels and embarked for Aquidneck Island.

While Barton encouraged his troops from horseback, exposed to enemy fire, a musket ball struck him just above his right knee and careened upward into his hip. His men carried him to a house in Bristol where the bullet was extracted from his hip. For the next several months a lingering fever endangered his life.[5] On June 20, 1778, Barton received a letter from Henry Laurens congratulating him on "your late acquisition of glory" and requesting the colonel "under your own hand" to "describe the state of your wounds and health in general."[6] Unfortunately, Barton's wound was serious enough to keep him out of action for more than a year. He missed the entire Rhode Island campaign of July and August 1778, including the climactic Battle of Rhode Island. Then, reinforced by a powerful French fleet, units from Washington's main army, and thousands of New England state troops and militiamen, Sullivan landed on Aquidneck Island, hoping to recapture Newport. But a fierce storm damaged the French fleet, leaving Sullivan's army vulnerable. Sullivan did manage to defeat an attacking British army in the Battle of Rhode Island on August 29, which enabled him to transport his army safely back to the mainland the next day.[7]

On June 15, 1779, the recently appointed commander of the Rhode Island theater, Major General Horatio Gates, presented the recovering Barton with a new opportunity. He gave him command of a newly raised light infantry corps of about 200 men charged with better protecting the Rhode Island coast and annoying the enemy.[8] On June 30, Gates ordered the Rhode Island quartermaster general, Ephraim Bowen, to build and deliver to Colonel Barton "five cedar boats for the use of his light corps."[9] Once the whaleboats were completed, Gates sent Barton's light corps down Narragansett Bay toward Newport in search of prisoners, from whom Gates hoped to discover brewing British plans.[10] On August 16, Gates again ordered Barton's command down the bay, this time with provisions for six days and strict orders for quiet. They were "to attack, and make reprisals, upon the enemy, as your courage and experience shall dictate."[11] It is not known if Barton's light corps undertook either expedition. If they did, given that the serious wounds he suffered in May 1778 may still have hampered him, it is not clear if Barton accompanied his light corps on their missions. Later, however, his men did gather intelligence about the anticipated evacuation of Newport by the British army, in part by slipping onto enemy-held Conanicut Island and secretly meeting with patriot sympathizers. Barton's light troops also assisted in regaining the port city after the fleet of transports carrying Prescott's soldiers departed on October 25.[12] In February 1780, Barton's corps merged into the other state regiments, leaving him again with no command.[13]

As the war wound down, Barton began to ponder how he could make a living to support his large, still-growing family. Many American stalwarts of the Revolutionary War would fall back on their previous careers as merchants, lawyers, or successful farmers. Barton, by contrast, had been a hatter. And now that he was a war hero, he probably felt it beneath his station to return to that trade. Instead, he earned a few dollars renting out his old shop to other tradesmen.[14] He worked to find ways to transform his military reputation into a substantial career, in order to make more money and accumulate more property.

One approach Barton took was requesting relief from the Rhode Island and federal governments. In 1781, he asked the Rhode Island legislature to pay him the difference between the amount he was owed for his military service and the depreciated currency he had originally received for it. The General Assembly responded by transferring to him a Newport lot and a parcel of South Kingstown land that had been confiscated from Loyalist Thomas Banister of Newport, it "being the balance due to the said William Barton" for the "depreciation of his wages."[15]

In 1785, Barton submitted a memorial to the Continental Congress, then sitting in New York City, requesting compensation for the serious wound he had received while leading troops during the May 25, 1778, British raid on Bristol, which left him unable to find work that would suit him.[16] In May 1785, a congressional committee recommended to Congress the following:

> [T]he said Barton sometime in May 1778, while commanding a party of militia in the State of Rhode Island, received a wound, which hath hitherto been incurable and from which there is not at present any prospect of relief.
>
> That the said Barton hath rendered essential services to the United States in other instances and particularly in the capture of General Prescott, whereupon
>
> *Resolved*, that the Board of Treasury take order for the pay-

ment of $1,500 to the said William Barton in consideration of his services in the U.S. and the wound he hath received in an action during the late war.[17]

With Barton making the trip to New York City for the vote, Congress enacted a bill authorizing the payment of $1,500 on September 7, 1785.[18] To a friend in Providence Barton wrote that he expected "some will grumble like a bear with a sore head because Congress has done this for me," but he pointed out that he would gladly return the money "if I could be cured of the wound I received in the course of [fighting for] my country."[19] (While in New York City, Barton consulted several physicians about his injuries. The doctors advised him to have an operation to remove one of his testicles. Believing that such an operation would pose "the greatest danger of losing my life," Barton declined.)[20]

In 1782 Barton commenced a career as a politician and government civil servant. Between 1782 and 1789 he served several terms in the lower house of the Rhode Island General Assembly, representing Providence.[21] He was selected as adjutant general of the state militia in 1788 and was promoted to brigadier general in 1790, after which he was routinely called "General Barton."[22] After serving in this post for many years, Barton rose to the state militia's top command, serving as major general from 1802 to 1808.[23]

In 1786, to his great satisfaction, Barton finally received the presentation sword promised to him by the Continental Congress in 1777 for his capture of Prescott. Due to a lack of funds, Congress had had to delay awarding Barton's ceremonial sword (and those of fourteen other honorees) until long after the war. In June 1784, Robert Morris, then head of the Continental Office of Finance, determining that the "swords can be best executed in Europe," had authorized Lieutenant Colonel David Humphreys to purchase ten of them during his diplomatic trip to Europe.[24] Humphreys, a wartime aide to Washington, ordered the swords from master fourbisseurs (sword makers) at the Liger family workshop in Paris, France.[25]

Upon Humphreys's return to New York City, the June 1, 1786, edition of the *New York Journal* reported that he "brought with him a number of elegant swords made agreeably to different resolves of the honorable Congress to be presented to a number of gentlemen, who by acts of heroism and valor, distinguished themselves in the late Revolution."[26] Humphreys delivered the "ten elegantly mounted swords" to the War Department and by letter informed Henry Knox, secretary of war, "You will find the names of the officers, to whom these honorary presents were voted, engraved on the different swords."[27]

The swords, all French in style, were slim, silver hilted, and elegantly crafted. Each featured a blue-steel blade in a triangular shape that tapered evenly to a point. Each was heavily decorated with gold figures and designs. The grip of each sword displayed the coat of arms of the United States on one side and an inscription from Congress to the recipient, with the date of the congressional resolution granting the sword, on the other. While each weapon was based on the same general pattern, the talented workmen in Liger's shop made subtle differences in design. Each scabbard was made of lizard skin with a silver throat and middle band.

Knox had Barton's sword delivered to the Rhode Islander, accompanied by the following letter, dated August 1, 1786:

> In consequence of the resolve of Congress of the 25th of July, 1777, I have the honor to transmit to you the sword therein directed, as a permanent evidence of the just sense entertained by that illustrious Assembly, of your address and gallant behavior, and the party under your command, in making prisoners, on Rhode Island, Major General Prescott, and Major William Barrington, his aide-de-camp.
>
> To the expressive approbation of the Supreme National Authority was added the unanimous applause of the American army. The enterprise was justly regarded as one of those hazardous actions, whose success depends on the exact combination and execution of a variety of parts, and therefore the more glorious.
>
> The circumstances of the late war prevented the execution of the orders of Congress, as it respected the *sword*, until the present period.[28]

In an August 10 letter, Barton thanked Congress and expressed his appreciation that "my military conduct met the approbation of that band of heroic brothers, the late American army."[29] (Remarkably, Barton's sword, and each of the other nine swords brought back by Humphreys, was passed down to generations of family members and still exist today, a few of which are currently shown in museums.)

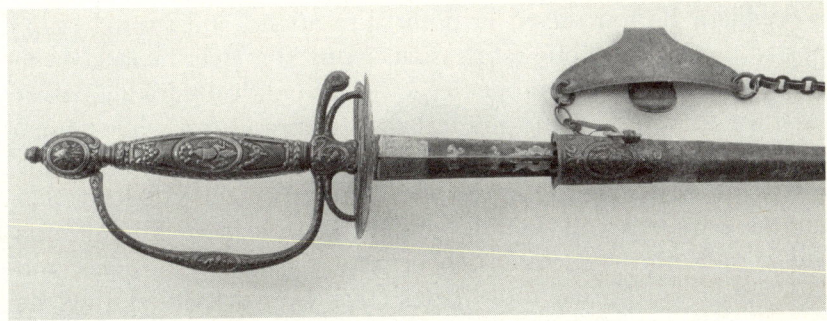

Sword and scabbard, awarded to William Barton by the Continental Congress on July 25, 1777, and presented to him in 1786. Made by the Liger family workshop in Paris, France, 1785 or 1786. (*Rhode Island Historical Society*)

In 1787, Barton acceded to a request by the French consulate in New York City to provide it with an account of Prescott's capture, sending not only his narrative, but also "a sketch of the river, islands, and part of the enemy's shipping."[30] According to an unidentified acquaintance of Barton's, this submission was forwarded to, and "read and admired" by King Louis XVI of France himself.[31] It was probably around this time that Barton posed for his portrait wearing a blue Continental army overcoat, and a red sash and sword (the artist, whose identity is not known, did not paint the colonel's new ceremonial sword).

Barton soon found himself in the center of Rhode Islanders' debate over whether or not to adopt the new United States Constitution. By late 1789 the state was the sole holdout of the original thirteen states, and sentiment against joining the federal union was widespread. Rhode Island's controversial decision to print its own paper money, which allowed debtors to pay creditors with depreciated currency, was slowly reviving the state's moribund economy. Many citizens preferred limited, and local, government control, and feared direct congressional taxation. Eventually, with threats by Congress to treat Rhode Island as a foreign country and to impose tariffs on its trade goods, pressure built to hold a state constitutional convention. It was held in South Kingstown in March 1790, but delegates opposing the Constitution managed to postpone a vote. By the time the convention reconvened in Newport on May 25, 1790, sentiment had shifted. On May 29 delegates voted to ratify the Constitution by the slim margin of thirty-four to thirty-two.[32]

William Barton served in both conventions, and strongly supported the constitution's ratification.³³ Unfortunately, he lacked the writing skills to leave a proper legacy of his political thinking. What little we know of Barton's political views indicates that while he was a member of the Federalist faction, which was dominated by the merchant class, he supported the ordinary man. He held that increased trade would improve employment prospects for common sailors and other workers in seaport towns such as Providence and Warren, his birthplace. From notes taken by a delegate during the state's first constitutional convention, we know that Barton expressed his concern about whether Congress had the power to impose a poll tax on individuals, as opposed to a tax based on the value of property. He described the prospect of a poll tax as "grievous," declaring that "There are many people in the seaports who have not a foot of land and will pay more than many large farmers." Barton further complained that "Congressmen of fortune do not feel for the common people."³⁴ Later in the session, he objected to an adjournment without adopting the Constitution, arguing that retaliatory congressional taxes imposed on the state's trade would harm his constituents. Barton reportedly took the following position: he "entreats and beseeches" delegates to vote to ratify the Constitution immediately, as "it is for the poor and needy that he is solicitous."³⁵

The politician's populist reputation was confirmed by New York merchant Royal Flint, who described Barton to Federalist leader Alexander Hamilton as "popular among the lower class of people," as well as having "much influence in Providence."³⁶ When the state's second convention ratified the United States Constitution on May 29, Barton received the signal honor of personally delivering the news to George Washington, by now serving as the country's first president in New York City.³⁷

As a staunch Federalist in an era destined to be dominated by that party, Barton seemed a good candidate for a federal government post. In September 1789, anticipating his state's ratification of the Constitution, Barton wrote to President Washington to request a federal appointment. "Reflecting that the wounds I received in the service of my country are such as injure me in pursuing my business on the profits of which a very large family depend for support," the Rhode Islander explained, "I am induced to present myself as a candidate for some office in the customs for the port of Providence."³⁸ After Rhode Island ratified the Constitution in May 1790, two

Maryland Federalists pushed Barton's candidacy with Washington. On June 14, 1790, the president responded by appointing Barton to Rhode Island's top customs post, Inspector of the Surveys and Ports for the port of Providence.[39]

While he obtained this post as revenue officer for the port of Providence, Barton complained in 1796 that the income he derived from it was insufficient to support his family.[40] He never managed the transition to successful merchant or real estate speculator, which could have brought him financial security. (By contrast, his youngest brother, Seth Barton, moved from Warren and became a prosperous shipping merchant in Baltimore.)[41] The still-struggling ex-soldier continued to seek assistance from the federal government. At a time when the government lacked a system of military pensions for wounded veterans, individual applications to the United States Congress were the norm. In 1809, Barton applied for a pension due to his wounds. After debating the matter for some time, Congress narrowly failed to approve it.[42]

In September 1812, Barton's narrative of his capture of Prescott was published for the first time in Philadelphia's prestigious *Port Folio* under the heading "American Gallantry."[43] The periodical's editors subsequently explained that "It was not thought proper, in the narrative of General Barton to alter a single word," because they "wished to present to the reader in its plain, artificial style, the picture of a warm and glowing heart, and of patriotism that would do honor to the most cultivated mind." Barton did not write this account himself (his handwriting was virtually illegible and his spelling was poor), but he did dictate and sign it.[44] *The Port Folio's* editors added that Barton had not wanted his narrative published until after his death, but that "he was prevailed upon to recede, by the earnest solicitations of private friendship" to agree to its publication.[45] Barton later claimed that he sent this narrative "in a confidential letter to a friend," and that it was published "without his knowledge or consent."[46] This may have been the same version he had submitted in 1787 to the French consulate in New York City. He might also have had it recorded around 1812.[47]

Like many other Rhode Island veterans, Barton eventually began exploring ways to earn a living outside the state. With Rhode Island's postwar economy in a funk, many of the state's citizens sought cheap land and new lives in Vermont, upstate New York, and the new Northwest Territory. Revolutionary War veterans sometimes sought free land grants; Barton led one group of mostly Providence veterans that petitioned for such a tract from the Vermont legislature. Other petitioners in his group included Vermont's Ira Allen, Ethan Allen's brother and an ex-soldier and politician, and naval hero John Paul Jones. Barton was fortunate to have obtained the support of the influential Allen brothers, who admired the Rhode Islander for nabbing the man who had treated Ethan so cruelly as a captive back in 1775.

On October 23, 1781, the Vermont General Assembly, after conferring with Ira Allen, granted Barton's group thirty-six square miles of land in the remote, northeastern part of the state.[48] The Assembly, "having the highest sense of the merit of Colonel William Barton as an active, brave and intrepid officer in the Army of the United States," voted to "grant him two of said rights in said township free of all expense."[49] Three years later, on October 16, 1784, "at the request of the Proprietors," the Assembly further agreed to change the name of the planned new town from Providence to Barton, in honor of the Revolutionary War hero.[50] Surrounded by sparkling lakes, ponds, and rivers, the town was still unsettled and mostly populated by old-growth trees.

On October 17, 1789, Vermont politicians authorized a charter for the town of Barton, and divided the six-square-mile tract of land it would occupy into seventy shares.[51] Barton received six shares of land, Ira Allen eighteen, Daniel Owen (lieutenant governor of Rhode Island) three, and John Paul Jones three. Most of the other grantees received one share. Vermont's legislature, however, imposed a difficult hurdle. In an effort to encourage settlement, it required each grantee to cultivate five acres and either build a house or settle a family on each share of land within three years, or else forfeit the land. After proper surveys of the land were obtained, some of the land was sold at auction in December 1791.[52]

As a result of the prestige he earned from his service during the Revolutionary War, and his current service as a general in the state militia, Barton was on the same social level as many of his peers in and near Providence. But unlike most of them, he lacked the money to support the lifestyle of a gentleman. The beleaguered former war hero saw his land in Vermont as a way to improve his lot and ensure his position in Rhode Island society. Barton was one of the few Rhode Island grantees to actually settle in Barton, arriving in 1794 at the age of forty-seven. He left his wife and children behind in Providence. After building a crude wooden hut with a dirt floor, he began clearing land and planting crops, and harvested between thirty and forty bushels of wheat in his first season. Next, he built (or at least oversaw the construction of) the town's first sawmill.[53]

Back in 1791, the proprietors of Barton had agreed to impose a tax on their shares of land in order to defray the costs of surveying, allotting parcels, and otherwise organizing the town. The rights to collect the tax—and, most importantly, to foreclose on the land if the tax remained unpaid—was sold off at auction, along with some of the land. After Ira Allen failed to pay his taxes, William Barton purchased the town's rights to collect them, which he thought gave him the rights to foreclose on Allen's land. Eyeing a badly needed financial boost, Barton had acted against the Vermont leader who had made the land grants possible in the first place. Barton's tax collector then deeded Allen's land to Barton, who in turn sold part of it. At the same time, Jabez G. Fitch of Vermont acquired rights to Allen's land from Allen and claimed ownership of all of his lots. With the title to land sold by Barton in dispute, Fitch commenced legal proceedings against four of the five parties who had bought land from Barton. Fitch sought a court order ejecting them from what he considered his property.

The history of the legal drama surrounding the town of Barton became as murky as the title to the disputed land. It appears that in 1802, the Vermont Supreme Court upheld a decision against Barton and his purchasers on the grounds that the tax collector had failed to give proper public notice of the tax transfer. This was certainly a decision that would be upheld in today's courts, although back then the rules were not as well known or developed. While the case was still pending, the parties agreed to submit it to a panel of three arbitrators, who ruled against Barton. But the monetary award imposed on Barton was so insignificant that Fitch refused to abide by it.[54]

Fitch then conveyed title to the disputed lands to Herman Allen, a nephew of Ira Allen, and Samuel Fitch, perhaps one of his sons. After three years of further wrangling, according to one summary of the proceedings, Barton finally "obtained a decree, awarding him large sums of money and the title of the lands litigated," but that "the money was not paid, nor were the deeds lodged."[55] Allen and Fitch filed a motion for a rehearing, but the judge rejected it, stating in 1810 that "the old gentleman [Barton] should be perplexed no longer."[56] Samuel Fitch escaped a summons, but Herman Allen was thrown in prison for eighteen days for failing to abide by the court's ruling.

In 1811, for unknown reasons, Chief Judge Royal Flynn of the Vermont Supreme Court reopened the case. After a new trial, the court ruled against Barton. Allen and Fitch then brought actions to enforce their judgments against Barton, as did one of the purchasers of Barton's lots. After failing to pay these debts, Barton was thrown into the debtor's prison in Danville, Vermont, in late September 1812.[57]

At this time throughout the United States, it was common for debtors to be incarcerated in the local jail for even minor debts until the debts were paid (often with the assistance of family or friends) or until the creditors agreed to cancel the debts. A debtor could languish in prison for years. There was, as yet, no ability for a debtor to declare bankruptcy, use his assets to pay what debts he could, and then be permitted a fresh start.

Debtors were not handled as harshly as criminals; for example, they were allowed to ply their trade in prison to help pay off their debts. In addition, some states permitted the limits of the debtor's "jail yard" to extend well beyond the prison itself. In Danville, the debtor's jail yard extended to the town limits. The two-square-mile town then housed about sixty families. Barton chose to reside at an inn where, according to John Howland, he enjoyed "good society, and appeared to enjoy life as usual."[58] Another man who visited Barton in Danville around 1813 wrote of him: "His aspect appeared quite military, and his manners prepossessing. He was still a little lame from the wound in his thigh; seemed fond of referring to the incidents of the 'Olden Time,' and of describing how battles were fought, and 'fields were won;' spent much time in reading and writing, endeavoring, though at a late period, to make amends for a limited education."[59]

Still, the "General" could not leave town to visit his family in Providence. He stubbornly refused to pay his debts or let family or friends pay them. Years passed. In 1814, unable to return home to perform his duties, Barton resigned his coveted federal position as Surveyor and Inspector of the port of Providence. He was replaced by one of his sons, John B. Barton.[60] In 1815, Congress finally enacted a law to provide pensions for "invalid" veterans of the Revolutionary War. Barton was personally named in the statute and began receiving a pension of $30 per month.[61] Even with that, it is not clear whether or not Barton had the financial means to pay his debts. According to one contemporary account, Barton "openly proclaims his ability to pay the debts in question."[62] Yet it is not clear that Barton could pay them without having to sell his Providence home. He claimed that the debt for which he was jailed was $600, and that he had judgments against him from Allen and Fitch of $2,330.[63] However, on the docket of the Orleans County Court, which had jurisdiction over the town of Barton, there were only two final judgments against him listing total damages and court costs of just $320.[64]

Since being jailed, Barton had insisted that either his creditors cancel his debts, or that the government or certain other parties—but not his family or friends—pay them. By 1819, his stubbornness was frustrating his friends. "I regret extremely that you persist in your resolution to remain in your present uncomfortable situation, until relieved from your embarrassments by the aid of Congress and aid afforded without your solicitations," Boston publisher Samuel Brown Barrel wrote to Barton.[65] Unmoved, Barton submitted assorted petitions requesting either the United States Congress or the Vermont legislature to pay his debts.

In October 1818, Barton wrote to Dudley Chase, the former U.S. Senator from Vermont, then serving as chief justice of the Vermont Supreme Court. Barton complained of the unjust legal decision that took away his lands and alluded to the powerful forces in Vermont arrayed against him: "Permit me to say that I fought for a government of equal rights. The poor should have the same justice as the rich." Barton requested that Chase intercede on his behalf with the Vermont General Assembly. Probably not expecting success, he requested that the legislature at least "change my imprisonment to Montpelier," the state's capital. He further informed Chase that he had asked a friend to pay for "a humble stone placed at the head of my grave giving the number of years of my imprisonment for lands that was decreed to him." He concluded his letter by asking Chase to visit his grave "and say 'what a pity this old man could not have been laid in his one burying place with his dear family.'"[66] Nothing came of this letter.

In 1820, Congressman Samuel C. Crafts of Vermont informed Barton that Congress would not pay his debts, and added, accurately, that "Congress has no power whatever to interfere with the decisions of the state courts." Crafts, also serving as an Orleans County judge, encouraged Barton in vain to allow his friends to clear his financial slate.[67] Later that year Barton tried something new: he had Congressman Crafts deliver a letter to President James Monroe. Describing himself as "an old officer of the first war with the mighty Britons," Barton wrote that "if the President can with perfect honor to himself devise any way that I can with honor return to my family, it will give me more satisfaction than is in my power to express."[68] In November 1821, a Committee on Insolvency of the Vermont General Assembly concluded that while "the Committee fully appreciates the services" of Barton in the Revolutionary War, it "regrets that he does not draw from his pocket that relief which he solicits from this Assembly."[69]

Meanwhile, Barton had asked his Boston friend Samuel Brown Barrell to publish his account of General Prescott's capture, followed by his explanation of what he perceived to be the legal injustices that had led him to debtor's prison in Danville. Barrell did so, sticking mainly to the version published by Philadelphia's *Port Folio* in 1812. He did make it more readable, and added a few interesting flourishes.[70] However, proceeds from the pamphlet's sale did not approach what Barton owed, and the timing of its release—while Barton's petition for financial redress was pending before the Vermont General Assembly—failed to have the desired effect.

In an 1821 letter to his father, Barton's devoted son, John B. Barton, expressed the family's frustration and sadness over his continued absence. "I would say something to you on the subject of your return to Providence but what can I say that I have not already said?" he wrote. "I pray you once more to return to the bosom of your family, sure and certain am I that your staying in Vermont will answer no good purpose and I pray you to consider what must be the feelings of your family were you to be called from this world while absent from them."[71] Like so many others, this appeal failed to move Barton. His son's letter suggests clearly that his father had chosen to remain in his predicament. Back in Rhode Island, Barton's wife, Rhoda, remained without a husband. While he lingered in financial purgatory, three of their sons would die.[72] Grandchildren would be born, and friends and old war comrades would pass away.

Why did Barton sacrifice so much for the sake of a few old debts? It was apparently due to pride and honor. One Danville newspaper reported that Barton "has made a solemn oath that he will never leave

Letter from William Barton, from the "Limits in Danville," to Dudley Chase, dated Oct. 10, 1818. Barton asked the former U.S. senator and current Vermont chief justice to intercede on his behalf to persuade the Vermont General Assembly to pay his debts. Barton's poor handwriting and spelling is indicated. (*Author's Collection*)

the place of confinement without, as he emphatically expresses himself, *some* satisfaction for the injustice which has been done him."[73] A Danville observer, William Matlock, wrote in 1824 that when Barton "last left his home and family at Providence, Rhode Island, to attend to this concern, he made a solemn vow, to use his own expression, never to return until he received remuneration from some source for his losses in Vermont."[74] Yet another Danville resident, Moses Hall, wrote in 1820 to Thomas B. Barton, one of the debtor's relatives, that Barton "submits with fortitude to the principle that honor is due to him who suffers for the equal administration of justice."[75] Barton himself informed Dudley Chase in 1818 that "I have made up my mind a long time since that the world shall never say that I was the first man who paid for lands that was [already paid for and] deeded to him."[76] Thus, Barton's sense of honor and pride outweighed his desire and obligation to return to Providence to be with his wife, family, and friends.

Beginning in 1821, sympathetic reports of Barton's plight began to circulate in northern newspapers. One of them, written in 1822 by the son of one of Barton's old war acquaintances, expressed horror that such an elderly and noble patriot was spending his last days in debtor's prison. Upon first meeting Barton in Danville, the son recorded the following:

> The old gentleman appeared out of health and soon informed me that he was a prisoner confined with the limits for debt. "A prisoner!," I exclaimed, "where is your family and friends, where is your country?" In a few moments he related the history of those transactions which led to his misfortune. The tears flowed down his manly cheeks—his sensibility had almost deprived him of utterance, when he exclaimed, "never will I leave this confinement, until my country redresses my wrongs. I will sooner die here, than become a victim of oppression and fraud."
>
> Recovering himself, he observed that his honor was dear to him, and that now, when age had almost ruined him for the grave to be forgotten by that country, whose cause he had so nobly defended, and whose liberties he had so conspicuously contributed to support, was the bitterest of all his troubles.... He was far removed from his affectionate family—oppressed by the iron grasp of judicial insensibility—a victim of fraud and caprice.[77]

However justified Barton's stance may have been, he clearly placed maintaining it above the happiness of his family. He refused to leave Danville until his honor had been restored.

It seems that that the awards and fame bestowed on Barton for his capture of General Prescott swelled his sense of pride and drove his unfortunate intransigence. His 1777 extraordinary achievement had propelled him from the obscurity of Rhode Island state service to the notoriety of a genuine national hero. Before the war, Barton had been a humble and hard-working hatter. Prescott's capture earned him a colonelcy in the Continental army. After the war he had risen to the rank of major general in the state's militia, and personally delivered word to President George Washington that Rhode Island had voted to become one of the United States. And when, in his view, he was victimized by Vermont's legal system, he saw it as an ugly blow to his honor. By then his pride would not allow him to bow before what he viewed as an unjust application of the laws.

Sympathy for Barton continued to grow as the years rolled by. The sentiments of the editor of a Salem, Massachusetts, newspaper were typical: "There seems to be a warm expression for the veteran General William Barton, of Providence, who performed one of the bravest deeds of the Revolution (the capture of the British General Prescott) and who has, for twelve years past, away from his family and friends, been deprived of that liberty which he nobly hazarded his life in achieving for his country, and remains immured in a *comfortless prison for the crime of poverty*."[78] John Greenleaf Whittier, the famous poet, wrote a poem on the tragedy of an American Revolutionary war hero stuck in debtor's prison—verse reportedly inspired by Barton's circumstances.[79]

The Marquis de Lafayette, during his triumphant 1824-25 tour of the United States. Enamel portrait by William Russell Birch, ca. 1824-34. (*Society of the Cincinnati*)

Still, a few held a different view of Barton's imprisonment. The following letter, penned by a "Massachusetts Yeoman," was published in the July 25, 1825, edition of the *Norwich Courier*:

> There has, we suspect, been much misplaced sympathy for Gen. Barton. His imprisonment, if it may be called such, is entirely voluntary on his part. He has the means of discharging the judgment under which he is imprisoned; but refuses on the ground that it was an unjust one. He boards, it is said, at a respectable hotel, out of sight of the jail, has ample limits to range in, and lives easily upon a pension which he receives from the [federal] government. Now whether the lawsuit which terminated in the judgment against him was rightly decided is one question; whether, under existing circumstances, he is entitled to any great commiseration is a very different question, and one not of difficult solution.

Finally, fate intervened in Barton's sad case. In 1824–1825, the Marquis de Lafayette undertook a triumphal tour of the United States. He no doubt heard of Barton's imprisonment for debt when he visited Providence on August 24–25, 1824, and met with

Lieutenant Colonel Stephen Olney and other Rhode Island veterans. Making Vermont his last stop in New England, the Frenchman learned more about his friend's plight during a June 1825 visit in Montpelier with Isaac Fletcher, adjutant general of Vermont's militia. Lafayette probably heard more about Barton's situation when he met with Revolutionary War veterans the next day in Burlington.

Barton had known Lafayette personally, and had probably first met him when the French general served in the Rhode Island campaign of August and September 1778. The two had almost certainly met when Lafayette visited Providence in October 1784.[80] Lafayette himself had been imprisoned for five years, from 1792 to 1797, at the behest of the emperor of Austria, who held Lafayette responsible for the fall of Louis XVI. Fletcher's meeting with Lafayette, in fact, was the result of Barton's request to the former to extend the Rhode Islander's "great affection and sympathy" for Lafayette, and apologize for his not being able to visit in person. In one of his last acts before returning to France, while on board the United States Navy frigate *Brandywine* that would carry him there, Lafayette wrote a draft, presumably on his New York bank, to pay the sums for which Barton was confined.

Upon receiving Lafayette's draft in early December 1825, Fletcher immediately travelled to Danville to inform Barton. "The scene was rendered more interesting by the peculiarly delicate manner in which the business was conducted," a Danville newspaper noted of their meeting. Indeed, the atmosphere must have been quite tense, with onlookers wondering how the obstinate Barton would respond. After all, he had long refused to let friends assist him with his financial troubles. But Barton accepted the Frenchman's generosity and, as the newspaper reported, "General Barton was at liberty to return to his family, after a separation of more than thirteen years."[81]

Some must have wondered if Barton had actually sent Fletcher to Lafayette with a direct request to pay his outstanding debts. There are, however, some indications that others may have planted the idea with the famous Frenchman before he met Fletcher. The first suggestion that Lafayette attempt to liberate his old friend appeared in a letter published in the *Hartford Times* on September 7, 1824. Others objected to the Revolutionary War hero spending his last days in a Vermont debtor's prison, while his countrymen were lavishing gifts on Lafayette at every stop on his nationwide tour.[82]

Perhaps the French nobleman heard and responded to this line of criticism by deciding on his own to pay Barton's debts. Lafayette had the financial resources to satisfy Barton's obligations. On December 22, 1824, Congress had voted to grant Lafayette an astounding $200,000 in cash and western lands that he quickly sold for another $100,000.[83]

Following his official release, Barton was, for unknown reasons, transported to Boston, where word of his liberation quickly reached the public. "Gen. Barton, who has been in prison many years for debt, has been liberated by a remittance from Gen. Lafayette!" boomed the *Boston Palladium* on December 9, 1825.[84] An unidentified gentleman travelling from Boston to Providence a week later found himself sharing a stagecoach with "General William Barton," who was finally bound for home. The gentleman noted that Barton "carried with him" the ceremonial sword that Congress had awarded him. He subsequently described his brief run-in with Barton in a letter to the *Boston Commercial Gazette*:

> It seemed to astonish the old General to see the great alterations on the road as we approached Providence; and when he spoke of the Marquis (as he always calls Lafayette), his eyes filled with tears of gratitude. He had been a very powerful man and retains now, in the 77th year of his age, much of the vigor of his younger days. He would often sing a few lines of an old revolutionary song, with a clear and strong voice.... But when the old General entered his ancient home, and embraced the wife of his youth, his children, and his children's children, and met his old black servant, it was a scene which I cannot attempt to describe—they were all overjoyed and melted into tears. It was a long time before he could believe it to be a reality.[85]

Barton was finally reunited in his South Main Street home with his wife Rhoda and son John B. Barton. Rhode Islanders were thrilled to have him back. As one of the last surviving Revolutionary War heroes, he would remain in demand on special occasions of all sorts. On July 10, 1826, he led a procession of notables through Providence, honoring the deaths of John Adams and Thomas Jefferson, both of whom had passed away six days earlier on July 4.[86] The next year, the city invited him to ride in a fashionable horse-drawn carriage as a special guest in Providence's Independence Day celebration.⁸⁷ Barton enjoyed the following July 4th in Newport, which he had not seen in twenty years. A few days later, accompanied by "ten or twelve" of Newport's "most respectable townsmen," Barton visited the now-famous Overing house, where he had captured General Prescott forty-nine years earlier. "His visit to the place awakened many old and delightful recollections, and he returned highly gratified with his excursion," noted one area newspaper.⁸⁸

As a result of a new pension plan for veterans approved by Congress in 1828, Barton was awarded a pension of $600 per year.⁸⁹ According to a *National Gazette* report, federal pension records showed that he was one of only twenty-six surviving officers from the Revolutionary War, and one of just five surviving colonels (no generals remained).⁹⁰ Despite his declining health, he could be seen walking the streets of Providence almost daily.⁹¹ Lauded as a hero for the remainder of his days, Barton died on October 22, 1831, at the age of eighty-three. Tributes to him filled Rhode Island newspapers, one of which asked that "history inscribe upon her page under his name: one of the bravest among the brave defenders of liberty."⁹² He was buried in Providence's North Burial Ground.⁹³

By the time of his death, Barton's daring capture of General Prescott had become a nationally honored event. Indeed, in 1832 a literary magazine mentioned the opening of a new play in Providence, "The Capture of Prescott, or the Heroism of Barton." Many collections of famous American stories produced through at least mid-century included a narrative of Barton's raid.⁹⁴ "Almost everyone is acquainted with the circumstances of the taking of General Prescott . . . by [Colonel] Barton of Providence," noted one newspaper in the introduction to a poem on the subject.⁹⁵ At some point, probably shortly after Barton's death, an American fort overlooking the bluffs at Howland's Ferry, in Tiverton, first built in June of 1777, was named Fort Barton. Today it is a town park that goes by the same name.⁹⁶ Only with the coming of the Civil War, and the countless incidents of bravery and horror associated with that national conflict, did Barton's legendary capture of Prescott begin to fade from public consciousness.

APPENDIX

Some Minor Participants in the Special Operations and What Became of Them

Francis Geary (1752-1776)

Cornet Francis Geary, educated at Balliol College in Oxford and the same rank as Banastre Tarleton when they served together at Widow White's Tavern, might have risen much higher in the British army. But as previously noted, the 24-year-old Geary was shot and killed in an ambush by local militia shortly after Lieutenant Colonel Harcourt's famous raid. In March 1777 a British magazine offered details of his death:

> Cornet Geary ... of Burgoyne's Light Dragoons, had been out with a small party to Flemington [New Jersey], and on his return, in pursuing through a hollow way by the side of a wood, he was told that a rebel was leveling at him on a rail; he leaned forward on his horse to escape the shot, then received that or some other (for a volley was fired) in his forehead, and fell dead from his horse. The dragoons fired ten rounds and attempted to bring off his body, but the villains kept within cover and being many in number, kept a constant fire, so that the dragoons were forced to return without the body of the young gentleman.[1]

The militiamen, led by Captain John Schenk, stripped Geary of his uniform, leather boots, leather high hat, scarf, spurs, and watch. Local farmers buried him near where he fell.[2]

Writing to Geary's father, Admiral Sir Francis Geary, Harcourt could not bring himself to state that his eldest son had been shot dead; instead he used the following stilted language: "Unfortunately, a ball took place, which in one moment deprived you of a son, and the regiment of an officer, whose loss cannot be sufficiently lamented."[3] The father carried on with his successful Royal Navy career.

Cornet Geary's story did not end there, thanks to some especially insensitive treatment of his gravesite. In 1891, a "committee" of several members of the Hunterdon County Historical Society learned the location of Geary's still-marked grave, and exhumed his remains. As reported in the society's newsletter:

> The grave was opened to the depth of 2 1/2 feet where the thigh and other bones were found and the silver buttons from his vest bearing the figure "16" and the letters "QLD" signifying the 16th Regiment, Queen's Light Dragoons. Other pieces of bones, a number of teeth, and some bits of cloth were found. He had been buried laying on his right side with his face to the south. No ball was found in the skull or the grave. Perhaps this is evidence to bear out the tradition which said the ball entered Geary's forehead and passed entirely through his head. The Committee removed from the grave the silver tops of four buttons.[4]

In 1907, a Geary family member had a memorial stone placed at the dragoon's gravesite. It remains there today.[5]

Walter Graham

Private Walter Graham, the 22nd Regiment soldier who stood guard at the front door of the Overing house on the night General Prescott was captured, was taken prisoner along with Prescott and Lieutenant Barrington. As with most ordinary soldiers of this era, little is known of his background. Don N. Hagist, a historian of the British army during the Revolutionary War, was able to identify Graham as the sentry and glean some personal information by reviewing muster rolls of the 22nd Regiment. Hagist recorded:

> Walter Graham first appears on the rolls of the regiment on 12 December 1772, meaning that he was probably enlisted by a recruiting party earlier that year. The regiment was serving in Scotland at the time, and most of the men who joined that year (whose nationalities we know) were Scottish, suggesting that Graham was probably Scottish. There is evidence that he deserted in 1772 before joining the regiment (that is, while still with a recruiting party), and was taken up and returned by the 15th Regiment. On 27 March 1774 when the regiment was in Dublin, Ireland, Graham deserted again. This time he returned on 17 June of the same year, but it is not known whether he returned voluntarily or was apprehended. The regiment seems to have been able to keep better control of Graham for the next few years as it moved from Ireland to

Boston, then to Halifax and New York, and finally to Rhode Island at the end of 1776.[6]

About two weeks after Graham's capture, the Rhode Island Council of War passed the following resolution:

> Resolved that the Sheriff of the County of Providence forthwith take into custody the soldier who was taken prisoner upon Rhode Island by Lt. Col. Barton and his party, and confine said soldier in close jail in the County of Providence. And the keeper of said jail is hereby directed to receive him and closely keep him until further orders.[7]

By "closely keep him," the Council meant affixing Graham with iron cuffs firmly attached to the jail. He was not allowed access to the jail yard, as some military prisoners were.

About this time, the commander of British troops in Newport, General Robert Pigot, allowed a recently paroled American soldier named Samuel Buffum to travel to Providence. There, Buffum went before the Council of War and asked to be formally exchanged, either for a locally-held sergeant of the 17th Light Dragoons or for Walter Graham. The Council approved an exchange for the equally low-ranked Private Graham.[8]

Neither Graham nor Buffum, however, ever returned to their respective armies. According to a May 21, 1778, letter from Governor Nicholas Cooke of Rhode Island to General Pigot, "Graham was put on board the cartel vessel, while under the care of our people, in order to be sent [to Newport], but made his escape."[9] This left Buffum in an obvious bind. Advised by the Council of War to return to a British jail in Newport until a proper exchange could be agreed upon, Buffum consented, following prisoner exchange protocol of the day. But he subsequently broke his parole and secretly left the state.[10]

Walter Graham was not listed as a deserter from the 22nd Regiment of Foot until June 8, 1778, probably because the regiment took that long to conclude that he was not in fact coming back. After his escape, he was not mentioned again in British army records.[11] American authorities, wanting to encourage deserters from the British army, also left Graham alone.

Graham thus became one of thousands of ordinary British and Hessian soldiers who deserted the British army to create new lives in America. Many of the British soldiers were from working-class

English, Scottish, and Irish families, and saw desertion as a way out of the sometimes suffocating, hierarchical world of Great Britain. Similarly, Hessian troops from small, dreary farms owned by German aristocrats saw economic opportunity in America. One Hessian stationed on Aquidneck Island observed that the poorest man in America, if only he busied himself, could live like the richest man in Germany.[12] Soldiers often also grew weary of strict, martial life in British and Hessian regiments, and from back-breaking chores such as digging trenches and building fortifications.

Military deserters faced with few immediate job opportunities sometimes simply joined what had been the opposing army. According to unit returns, a man named Walter Graham signed on for a brief stint with a Cranston militia outfit in June of 1778.[13] This was probably the Walter Graham in question, since there is no other record of a Walter Graham in Rhode Island census or military service records for the Revolutionary War. But Graham was not cut out for army life. The war was still in full-swing, but no record of his joining the Continental army or any other state regiment or other militia unit exists. The 1782 Rhode Island census lists no Graham; Walter, it seems, had left the state.[14] The federal census of 1790 lists a Walter Graham as head of a household in Adams, Massachusetts. Three young sons and two females (one likely his American wife) resided with him.[15] This man was probably the former British sentry. He had successfully created a new life as an American.

Lieutenant Abel Potter, one of Barton's officers during the Prescott mission, provided additional clues to Graham's whereabouts. Applying for a veteran's pension long after the war, Potter wrote of Graham: "This same sentinel afterwards taught school in Pownal, Vermont, and claimant sent a member of his family to school to him."[16] Graham, then, may have moved to Pownal, in the southwest corner of Vermont, or at least commuted there from Adams, which was only about eleven-and-a-half miles away. Census and other records that affirm Potter's presence in Pownal also list several Grahams—presumably Walter's sons—nearby.[17] And, interestingly, records of the American Civil War reveal that a Walter Graham from nearby Arlington enlisted as a private in Company E of Vermont's 10th Regiment in 1862, and eventually rose to the rank of second lieutenant.[18] Evidently of heartier martial stock than the Scot left to guard Richard Prescott's door, this Walter Graham may have been his direct descendant.

JACK SISSON (1756-1781), GUY WATSON (1757-1837), AND PRINCE GOODWIN (1743-1821)

Just as British wits mocked the peculiar circumstances surrounding General Prescott's capture, American humorists focused on reported oddities of Lee's. The most obvious was the story of a man battering down an Overing house door with his head. If such an event did occur, white storytellers may have embellished on its details over the years. Three different men of color have been credited for this remarkable act: Jack Sisson, Guy Watson, and Prince Goodwin.

Blacks, as well as Native Americans and other persons of color, were highly visible in Rhode Island, as they were in other parts of New England. Due to the active role of Providence and Newport merchants in the African slave trade, the state had the highest percentage of blacks in New England—6.1 percent in 1774.[19] The majority of those were slaves. During the war Rhode Island blacks and other men of color served in state infantry units. Although they could not be drafted, slaves were permitted to serve as substitutes for their white masters, and in doing so could earn their freedom. In fact, at the time of Barton's raid in July 1777, at least twenty black men were serving in the 1st Rhode Island Regiment of Continentals, in Washington's main army.[20] Of course, their loyalty did not protect them from the racial prejudice that dominated the times. The bizarre story of an African-American smashing through Overing's door with his head may have reflected such sentiment.

Nor did Barton mention such an incident in his narrative of the raid. And yet accounts of it having occurred do exist. One had the African-American breaking down the door to Prescott's bedroom, and not the main entry door to the house. Barnstable, Massachusetts, native James Thacher, who served as a physician in the Continental army for most of the war, in an August 3, 1777, diary entry touching on Barton's raid, noted that "A negro man named Prince, instantly thrust his beetle head through the panel-door, and seized his victim while in bed."[21] However, Thacher's diary was not published until 1823, and some of his writing around the August 3, 1777, entry suggests that it was actually written long after the war, perhaps for dramatic purposes. Thacher, it seems, added mention of Prince's door-smashing exploit only after reading or hearing about it years later. His source was probably the following obituary, which ran in the November 3, 1821, edition of the *Providence Gazette*:

In Plymouth (Mass.), Prince, a negro man, aged about 78 years. He was one of the forty brave volunteers, who with Lieut. Col. Barton, in 1777, captured Gen. Prescott, in his quarters on Rhode Island. Col. Barton, with his confidential Prince, came to the door of the General's chamber, which was fast closed. Prince, with a leap, plunged his head against the door, and knocked out the panel, through which the Colonel entered, surprised the General in his bed, and brought him and one of his aides safe to the main.

Prince's full name was probably Prince Goodwin, and he likely resided in Plymouth, Massachusetts.[22] The details of Thacher's journal entry closely resemble those in the obituary. Thacher went a step further by crediting Prince with first seizing Prescott in his bed, which also contradicts Barton's narrative.[23] It appears likely that wanting to add humor to his text, Thacher, sometime in the early 1820s, added Prince's exploit to his original diary entry.

The first written account of Prince's unlikely heroics may have appeared in 1818, thanks to Joseph Dennis, another surviving member of Barton's party. Dennis informed Barton's Boston publisher, Samuel Brown Barrell, that "the door" to the Overing house "being fast, a negro . . . broke in the door with his head."[24] Barrell asked Barton to expand on this and other parts of his original draft before he published the narrative, but he never did. The author believes this version is the most credible, as it came from a participant in the raid, and it would make sense that the main front entry door would have been locked and needed to have been forced open. In his narrative, Barton mentions all the doors of the Overing house being "burst" open at once. The author believes that over the years oral histories of the raid altered the story to the African American bursting open Prescott's bedroom door, perhaps to make the story more exciting. However, the author concedes that it is very possible that the African American forced open Prescott's bedroom door and not the house's main entry door.

In 1835, a ballad or poem describing the capture of Prescott by Barton and his party was published in several newspapers. Its introduction states that the song was "written by a sailor of Newport" and "is often related by an aged gentleman living in Newport." While its origins may harken as far back as 1777, it was probably written sometime between 1821 and 1824, when stories of Barton's plight were often in the news. In any event, the author referred to "Cuffee," a traditional African-American name that signified to readers that this participant was a slave. With the name change, the author used alleged slave dialogue, which was designed to identify him as an uneducated, ignorant slave. The poem has "A tawny son of Africa's race" leading Barton's party "through the ravine" and up to the Overing house. This portion of the poem picks up when Barton's party arrived at Prescott's bedroom door.

> But to get in they had no means
> Except poor Cuffee's head,
> Who beat the door down then rush'd in
> And seized him in his bed.

The poem or song then goes on to narrate the widely repeated story that the awakened general was not even given time to dress, but gives the slave an additional role in order to provide the opportunity of recording his alleged slave dialogue:

> "Stop! Let me put my breeches on"
> The general then did pray:
> "Your breeches, massa, I will take
> For dress we cannot stay."[25]

In the 1820s, Guy Watson was credited as the hard-headed man who battered down Prescott's door. Of mixed (African American and Narragansett Indian) heritage, Watson was a former slave from South Kingstown, Rhode Island. He joined the 1st Rhode Island Regiment of Continentals on February 19, 1778. His enlistment records reveal that he was then twenty-three years old, and five feet seven-and-a-half-inches tall.[26] The 1st Rhode Island Regiment was formed at this time specifically to be stocked by slaves, free blacks, Narragansett Indians, and other men of color. It was the only such segregated unit in the American army, albeit with white officers. To help fill it, the state's General Assembly agreed to free any slave that joined, and to pay his owner up to $400.[27] Guy Watson enlisted and earned his freedom. He served for five grueling years, fought in several battles (including the Battle of Rhode Island), and in 1786 earned a pension as a result of his wartime injuries.[28]

Watson's service earned him wide respect after the war. In the early 1800s he was often seen "attending elections, courts and the General Assembly in his Continental regimental coat."[29] In 1818, white men working at the South Kingstown court house helped the illiterate Watson prepare and submit his federal pension application on the grounds that he was destitute and disabled. His application made no mention of a role in Barton's raid. But at some point in the 1820s—again, as Barton's plight as a debtor kept interest in his story alive—Watson's presence at the Overing house came to be accepted. In 1828, more than fifty years after the raid, a Rhode Island newspaper directly credited Watson as a raid participant.[30]

After that, Watson's presumed role as the soldier whose head perforated Prescott's front door was celebrated on stage. At the end of 1831, a Rhode Island weekly literary magazine mentioned the performance of a new play, "The Capture of Prescott, or the Heroism of Barton." In the magazine's squib, the play's writer extended his thanks "to a brace of colored ladies and gentlemen in the gallery, who recorded their testimonials of applause in favor of Guy Watson, as acted by Mr. McGuire."[31] The black audience, although consigned to the upstairs gallery and forced to watch a white Irishman, probably in black face, play Guy Watson, was thrilled to see a man of color honored as a Revolutionary War hero.

Finally, on March 2, 1837, the old soldier passed away. His obituary, which ran in several Rhode Island newspapers, offered some interesting details:

> Guy Watson, a colored man, and a relic of the revolutionary army, died a few days since at South Kingstown, R. I. . . . Guy Watson was servant to General Barton. He accompanied his commander on the expedition to Rhode Island for the capture of General Prescott. He seized and disarmed the sentinel on duty before General's quarters, led the way to Prescott's bedroom, and burst open the door with his head. Old Guy has constantly visited Providence in his military uniform, on the 4th of July, and has ever been an object of interest to our citizens.[32]

Barton's authoritative narrative, however, does not mention Watson. Moreover, the raid leader claimed that he disarmed Private Graham outside the Overing house, which raises serious doubt about Watson's role. Watson's obituary also lists him as Barton's servant, which is unlikely, since Barton was never wealthy enough to have his own servant or slave. African Americans did sometimes serve in a military capacity as "waiters," or servants, for officers, and Watson could have served Barton in this capacity. In 1839, Barton biographer Catherine R. Williams identified Watson as the man who battered down Prescott's door. But the sources she used to reach that conclusion are unknown.[33] And she, like other writers of that era, may have been influenced by still-circulating stories based on less-than-solid evidence.

If a man of color did batter down a door to the Overing house, the author believes it is unlikely Watson was the man. First, prior to his enlistment in the 1st Rhode Island Regiment, he had been a slave. While a few slaves served in Rhode Island military units, it was rare up to February 1778. Moreover, the fact that Watson's role in the operation was not mentioned in his 1818 pension application undermines the claim that he was a member of Barton's party.

In his 1851 history of the American Revolution, historian Benson Lossing credited boat steerer Jack Sisson for doing in the door to Prescott's bedroom. "With four strong men, and Sisson, a powerful negro who accompanied him, Barton ascended the stairs and gently tried the door," he wrote. "It was locked; no time was to be lost in parleying; the negro drew back a couple of paces, and using his head for a battering-ram, burst open the door at the first effort. . . . Barton placed his hand gently upon the general's shoulder, told him he was his prisoner, and that perfect silence was now his only safety."[34] Sisson's name was not on the list of raid participants originally made public by New England newspapers in 1824.[35] But this may have been because Sisson was a boat steerer; published lists excluded the name of another boat steerer named Howe. Historian Catherine R. Williams, after speaking with some of the surviving participants, did include Sisson in her list of raiders.[36] If a man of color did batter down a door in the Overing house, then it probably was Jack Sisson. Sisson later joined the 1st Rhode Island Regiment, and died while serving in that unit on December 26, 1781.[37] Thus, he did not have a chance to defend his claim to fame after the war. On the other hand, even Williams's list is known not to be a complete list of all the participants, and it is possible the man was Watson (less credible evidence supports Prince as the identity of this man).

Two other claims were made in print that different African American men participated in Barton's raid. In his recollections, published in 1857, John Howland recalled that Barton's party had been "guided by a negro who had been a servant in the family"—a reference to Quako Honeyman, Prescott's former groom.[38]

However, it is unlikely that Barton would have allowed Honeyman to participate in the raid. He was not a soldier, and if the British had caught him they likely would have executed him as a spy. Honeyman did his part by confirming Prescott's presence at the Overing house and his daily routine. Barton did not need him as a guide. (In 1782, the Rhode Island General Assembly, citing Honeyman's "great and essential service," halted efforts by the Honeyman family to re-enslave Quako and declared him a free man.[39])

One other supposed participant died tragically in 1821 and drew press attention. "On Thursday morning the body of Richard Rhodes, a man of color, was found in Warwick, a little south of the village of Pawtuxet, lifeless and frozen," reported the *Providence Gazette* on January 27, 1821. "This black man was in the revolutionary army, and . . . rendered signal services to this country. He was . . . one of the few brave followers of [Col.] Barton, who succeeded in taking Prescott from the midst of the enemy on Rhode Island [*i.e.*, Aquidneck Island]." Rhodes, who was born in Africa, indeed was a veteran of the Continental army, having joined the 1st Rhode Island Regiment as a seventeen-year-old slave in early 1778. He served for the balance of the war, despite being severely wounded in the arm during the Battle of Monmouth Court House. After the war he hired himself out as a sailor, and worked on board commercial vessels.[40] But there is no evidence that Rhodes was with Barton on the fateful night. And like Watson's pension application, his 1818 request for federal assistance made no mention of a role in the raid.[41]

If Rhodes and Watson sought prestige late in their lives by claiming to have participated in Barton's raid to capture Prescott, or by giving themselves a much more important role than they actually had, they were in good company. When making claims for Revolutionary War pensions, several white veterans either falsely claimed they participated in the raid to capture Prescott, or embellished their roles. For example, in his 1832 pension application, Elisha Baker of the 2nd Rhode Island State Regiment claimed that he and "Col. Barton, with one other, the guide, entered the bedroom of General Prescott by window and took him out naked and hurried him to the boats and brought him safe past the British ships lying in the channel."[42] No other evidence has been found indicating Baker's involvement in the raid or that Barton entered the Overing house through a window. Furthermore, when removed from the house, Prescott was not "naked"—he had on his waistcoat, breeches, and slippers. As a further examples of false claims, in the 1832 pension application submitted by Abel Potter, and the 1837 pension application submitted by John Hunt, while both men participated in the raid, each man claimed that he had captured the sentry at the front door of the Overing house and was the first to enter Prescott's bedroom.[43]

Orin Fowler, a Fall River historian, wrote in 1841 that Daniel Page, a Native American who had served as a boatman with Barton's party, "was one of the first to seize the sentinel at the door, and was one of two who led Prescott by the arm, a captive, from the Overing house, at which he was taken." "After leaving the house," Fowler claimed, "the Indian, recollecting that Prescott's sword was left behind, returned to the chamber, found the sword, and overtook the company before they reached their boats."[44] The author does not believe any of these accounts is credible. The statement that Page went back to get Prescott's sword is inconsistent with his alleged role as one of two men who led Prescott away to the boats; it is unlikely that he would have risked going by himself back to the Overing house; and if Prescott's sword had been seized, it likely would have been mentioned by Barton, Spencer, and others, and in newspaper accounts. It seems that some veterans of the Revolutionary War could not resist gaining attention by embellishing their roles.

The African Americans and other men of color who joined the 1st Regiment of Rhode Island Continentals or other outfits had no need to exaggerate their wartime service. They fought and sometimes died alongside their white comrades—they battled not only for their country's freedom, but for their own liberty. The courageous role of the "Black Regiment" in repelling three charges by Hessian troops during the Battle of Rhode Island, for example, was used as an argument in 1842 for the abolition of slavery in the South.[45]

NOTES

CHAPTER I: THE AMBITIOUS CHARLES LEE
1. Boatner, *Encyclopedia of the American Revolution*, 381 and 388.
2. Quoted in Commager and Morris (eds.), *Spirit of 'Seventy-Six*, 276.
3. Alden, *General Charles Lee*, 5-7.
4. Lamb, *Journal of Occurrences During the Late War*, 101. Lieutenant Thomas Hughes of the British 53rd Regiment, when he was a prisoner, met Lee in January of 1779, and described him in his journal as "a short little man with an aquiline nose. . . ." Diary Entry, Jan. 8, 1779, in Benians (ed.), *Hughes Journal*, 60.
5. Bunbury, *Correspondence of Sir Thomas Hanmer*, 454.
6. Diary Entry, Oct. 4. 1777, in Burgoyne (ed.), *Waldeck Diary*, 44.
7. S. Moylan to R. Morris, Jan. 7, 1777, in Griffin, *Stephen Moylan*, 48. Lee's best biographer, John R. Alden, believed that Stephen Moylan, an American officer in the Revolutionary War, invented the term, and stated that he did not find the term used by anyone else. Alden, *General Charles Lee*, 334, n. 47.
8. It does not appear that Lee joined his regiment in marching to Fort Duquesne, near present-day Pittsburgh, under the command of General Edward Braddock, whose force was ambushed and crushed on July 9, 1755, by French-led Native American warriors. Lee never mentioned his role in the ill-fated expedition in his known writings, including with Washington, who served as a colonel of American troops under Braddock and barely escaped with his own life. One report had Lee assigned to a supply camp far from the front lines. Patterson, *Knight Errant of Liberty*, 25; see also Alden, *General Charles Lee*, 8. In the best history of Braddock's expedition, the author states that Lee participated in it, but "played no noteworthy role." Crocker, *Braddock's March*, 265. Washington once mentioned Braddock's retreat in a letter to Lee, but the language used does not indicate that Lee was necessarily in the battle. G. Washington to C. Lee, May 9, 1776, in Twohig et al. (eds.), *Washington Papers* 4:244. One year after the battle, Lee mentioned the disaster in a letter to his sister, Sidney, but, again, not in a way that necessarily indicated he fought in the battle. C. Lee to S. Lee, June 15, 1756, *Lee Papers* 1:3. The author does not believe Lee fought in the battle; if Lee had done so, he very likely would have mentioned it in his writings.
9. Alden, *General Charles Lee*, 9-13.
10. Ibid., 10-11; C. Lee to S. Lee, Sept. 16, 1758, and the "Narrative" enclosed with the same letter, *Lee Papers* 1:8 and 11-15.
11. Quoted in Alden, *General Charles Lee*, 14.
12. Alden, *General Charles Lee*, 19-22; Hargrove, *General John Burgoyne*, 38.
13. Alden, *General Charles Lee*, 27-37.
14. C. Lee to S. Lee, March 1, 1766, in *Lee Papers* 1:42-43.
15. Alden, *General Charles Lee*, 47.
16. Ibid.
17. Quoted in Patterson, *Knight Errant of Liberty*, 61 (told to Thomas Rodney of Delaware).
18. Lee, "Strictures on a Pamphlet . . . Addressed to the People of America" (Philadelphia, 1774), in *Lee Papers* 1:151, 161-62.
19. Quoted in Alden, *General Charles Lee*, 59 (citing Aug. 22, 1774, editions of the *Boston Gazette* and the *Boston Evening-Post*).
20. John Bernard Recollections, in Bernard, *Recollections of America*, 97.
21. See Resolution, June 17, 1775, in Ford (ed.), *Journals of the Continental Congress* 2:97; Alden, *General Charles Lee*, 75.
22. Quoted in Bunbury, "Memoir of General Lee," *Lee Papers* 4:177-78.

23. Alden, *General Charles Lee*, 79. Before accepting his position, Lee met with a congressional delegation and requested that he be indemnified against loss of his English property. When Congress agreed, on condition that his property actually be seized, Lee accepted his appointment. Id., 76-77; Resolution, June 17, 1775, in Ford (ed.), *Journals of the Continental Congress* 2:98-99; Alden, *General Charles Lee*, 75. Lee was criticized in some quarters for this indemnification arrangement, but he was one of the few American leaders who risked losing virtually all of his property in England. In giving up his lieutenant colonelcy alone, Lee forfeited the ability to sell it for a substantial sum.
24. G. Washington to J. A. Washington, March 31, 1776, in Twohig et al. (ed.), *Washington Papers* 7:570.
25. A. Adams to J. Adams, Dec. 10, 1775, in Butterfield et al. (eds.), *Adams Family Correspondence*, Series 2, 1:335. Abigail wrote that Lee "was determined that I should not only be acquainted with him, but with his companions too, and therefore placed a chair before me into which he ordered Mr. Spada to mount and present his paw to me for a better acquaintance."
26. J. Adams to J. Warren, July 24, 1775, in "Warren-Adams Letters," *Mass. Hist. Soc. Coll.* 1:72, 89 (1917).
27. C. Lee to R. Morris, Jan. 3, 1776, in *Lee Papers* 1:233.
28. C. Lee to R. Lee, April 5, 1776, in ibid., 380. Charles Lee impressed Richard Henry Lee, who wrote that the general's "military talents are considerable; and his zeal for the American cause equal to his martial accomplishments." R. H. Lee to R. C. Nicholas, April 30, 1776, in Ballagh (ed.), *Richard H. Lee Letters* 1:183-84.
29. Quoted in Lengel, *General George Washington*, 131.
30. Alden, *General Charles Lee*, 119-30.
31. Congressional Resolution, July 20, 1776, in Ford (ed.), *Journals of Continental Congress* 5:593; B. Rush to C. Lee, July 23, 1776, in Smith (ed.), *Letters of Delegates* 4:527.
32. J. Adams to A. Adams, Oct. 7, 1776, in Smith (ed.), *Letters of Delegates* 5:311.
33. Diary Entries, Oct. 14, 1776, in "Journal of Sergeant Young," *Penn. Mag. of History and Biography* 8:258 (1884) (Lee arrives at headquarters) and Bushnell (ed.), *Journal of Solomon Nash*, 37 (same).
34. Alden, *General Charles Lee*, 141. Tench Tilghman, one of Washington's aides, wrote on October 17, "You ask if General Lee is in health and our people feel bold? I answer both in the affirmative. His appearance among us had not contributed a little to the latter." Quoted in Shy, "Charles Lee: The Soldier as Radical," in Billias (ed.), *George Washington's Generals and Opponents*, 32.
35. Alden, *General Charles Lee*, 144; Lengel, *General George Washington*, 161; see also Gordon, *History of the Independence of the U.S.* 2:338 (Lee convinced generals to retreat from Manhattan Island).
36. Quoted in Irving, *Life of Washington* 2:381.
37. Lefkowitz, *The Long Retreat*, 20.
38. G. Washington Instructions to Major General Heath, Nov. 12, 1776, in Twohig et al. (eds.), *Washington Papers* 7:147; Lefkowitz, *The Long Retreat*, 22-23.
39. G. Washington Instructions to Major General Lee, Nov. 10, 1776, in Twohig et al. (eds.), *Washington Papers* 7:135.
40. In a letter to artillery general Henry Knox, Washington advised, "It is unnecessary to add, that if the army of the enemy should wholly or pretty generally throw themselves across the North [Hudson] River, that General Lee is to follow." G. Washington Instructions to H. Knox, Nov. 10, 1776, in ibid., 135; see also Lefkowitz, *The Long Retreat*, 24.
41. C. Lee to J. Bowdoin, Nov. 21, 1776, in *Lee Papers* 2:291.
42. See Morgan, "A Merchandise of Small Wares: Nathanael Greene's Northern Apprenticeship, 1775-1780," in Massey and Piecuch (eds.), *General Nathanael Greene and the American Revolution in the South*, 39.

43. C. Lee to J. Reed, Nov. 16, 1776, in *Lee Papers* 2:283.
44. S. Shaw to J. Eliot, Nov. 18, 1776, in Quincy (ed.), *Journals of Major Shaw*, 27; see also Diary Entries, Nov. 17, 1776, in Rau (ed.), "Sergeant Smith's Diary," *Mississippi Valley Hist. Review* 20:1, 261 (1933) (news of loss of Fort Washington arrived this day) and Dawson (ed.), *How Diary*, 36 (same). Private David How, an eighteen-year-old veteran of Bunker Hill, served in Colonel Paul Dudley Sargent's 16th Regiment of Massachusetts Continentals.
45. B. Rush to J. Adams, Sept. 21, 1805, in Butterfield (ed.), *Rush Letters* 2:906.
46. C. Lee to G. Washington, Nov. 19, 1776, in Twohig et al. (eds.), *Washington Papers* 7:187.
47. Quoted in Scheer and Rankin, *Rebels and Redcoats*, 197.
48. James Wilkinson Recollections, in Wilkinson 1:103.
49. G. Washington to C. Lee, Nov. 21, 1776, in Twohig et al. (eds.), *Washington Papers* 7:194. On November 23, Washington wrote to John Hancock, "I have written to General Lee to come with the Continental regiments immediately under his command; those with General Heath, I have ordered to secure the passes through the Highlands." G. Washington to J. Hancock, Nov. 23, 1776, in id., 196. In the first draft, Washington's secretary had written, "I have written to General Lee and ordered him to come over," but then he struck out the word "ordered." Id., 197, n. 3. By contrast, Washington described Heath's instructions as orders. Lee probably received word of Cornwallis's advance on Fort Lee on November 20 or early the next day. Heath stated in his memoirs that Reed, upon learning of the threat to Fort Lee on November 20, began writing Lee on "a rough piece of wrapping paper" with a pencil, and had written, "Dear General, we are flying before the British, I pray" when the pencil broke. Reed instructed the express rider, who carried the incomplete letter to Lee, to inform Lee to add after "I pray" the words "you to push and join us." Heath, *Memoirs*, 98-99.
50. J. Reed to C. Lee, Nov. 21, 1776, in *Lee Papers* 2:293-94.
51. Ibid.
52. C. Lee to President of the Massachusetts Council, Nov. 22, 1776, in ibid., 303.
53. Massachusetts Assembly to C. Lee, Dec. 8, 1776, in ibid., 339.
54. C. Lee to G. Washington, Nov. 24, 1776, in Twohig et al. (eds.), *Washington Papers* 7:210-11.
55. C. Lee to J. Reed, Nov. 24, 1776, in *Lee Papers* 2:305-6.
56. G. Washington to C. Lee, Nov. 24, 1776, in Twohig et al. (eds.), *Washington Papers* 7:208.
57. American Army Returns for November 1776, in Lesser, *Sinews of Independence*, 40-42.
58. C. Lee to G. Washington, Nov. 26, 1776, in Twohig et al. (eds.), *Washington Papers* 7:217. It is not clear if Washington received this letter. On November 28, it was reported to General Heath that "Cooper whom he [Lee] sent with dispatches to General Washington, has with the dispatches fallen into the hands of the enemy and is now confined at Hackensack." J. Morin Scott to W. Heath, Nov. 28, 1776, in "Heath Papers," *Mass. Hist. Soc. Coll.*, 7th Series, 4:31 (1904).
59. C. Lee to W. Heath, Nov. 26, in *Lee Papers* 2:314.
60. Diary Entries, Nov. 27-Dec. 3, in Rau (ed.), "Sergeant Smith's Diary," *Mississippi Valley Hist. Review* 20:1, 262 (1933); J. Hodgkins to S. Hodgkins, Dec. 3, 1776, in Wade and Lively, *This Glorious Cause*, 227. Colonel Paul Dudley Sargent's 16th Massachusetts Regiment marched at noon on November 28 and crossed at King's Ferry on December 2, but then waited until the other regiments arrived, with all of Lee's division marching south at noon on December 4. Diary Entries, Nov. 28-Dec. 4, 1776, in Dawson (ed.), *How Diary*, 37-38. Rain likely delayed somewhat the marching and crossing at King's Ferry. See Diary Entries, Nov. 30, 1776, in id., 38 ("It's been rainy")

and Dec. 3, 1776, in id. ("It's been very rainy this day and we have been pitching our tents"); Diary Entry, Nov. 30, 1776, in "Bamford's Diary," *Maryland Hist. Magazine* 28:19 (1933) ("Rained all last night and most part of this day").

61. Heath, *Memoirs*, 87-88. Prescott's and Wyllys's regiments are not referred to in the Returns of December 22, 1776, in Lesser, *Sinews of Independence*, 43, but they are mentioned in a letter Heath wrote to Washington. W. Heath to G. Washington, Nov. 18, 1776, in Twohig et al. (eds.), *Washington Papers* 7:176.

62. C. Lee to J. Spencer, Dec. 2, 1776, in *Lee Papers* 2:328.

63. G. Washington to C. Lee, Nov. 27, 1776, in Twohig et al. (eds.), *Washington Papers* 7:224.

64. C. Lee to G. Washington, Nov. 30, 1776, in ibid., 235.

65. Heath, *Memoirs*, 88.

66. G. Washington to W. Heath, Dec. 7, 1776, in Twohig et al. (eds.), *Washington Papers* 7:270.

67. Returns of December 22, 1776, in Lesser, *Sinews of Independence*, 43. This return of Washington's army includes the following regiments that marched under Lee: Thomas Nixon's 4th Continental (Mass.); James Mitchell Varnum's 9th Continental (R.I.); Daniel Hitchcock's 11th Continental (R.I.); Moses Little's 12th Continental (Mass.); Christopher Lippitt's 2nd Rhode Island militia; William Shepard's 3rd Continental (Mass.); Charles Webb's 19th Continental (Conn.); John Glover's 14th Continental (Mass.); John Bailey's 23rd Continental (Mass.); Loammi Baldwin's 26th Continental (Mass.); Paul Dudley Sergeant's 16th Continental (Mass.); Andrew Ward's Connecticut militia; John Chester's 6th Connecticut State; Joseph Read's 13th Continental (Mass.); Alexander McDougall's 1st New York State; Rudolph Ritzema's 3rd New York State. The total number of present and fit for duty and on duty in these regiments was 2,681. At the time, the number of present and fit for duty and on duty in the rest of Washington's army was 3,423, and several of those regiments were from Gates's original command. For the "lame and ragged left by General Lee," see W. Heath to G. Washington, Dec. 6, 1776, in Twohig et al. (eds.), *Washington Papers* 7:267 and Heath, *Memoirs*, 88. For disaffection among New England troops, see Edgar, *Road to Trenton*, 293-94.

68. Heath, *Memoirs*, 88.

69. W. Heath to G. Washington, Dec. 2, 1776, in Twohig et al. (eds.), *Washington Papers* 7:252; Diary Entries, Dec. 3-4, 1776, in Rau (ed.), "Sergeant Smith's Diary," *Mississippi Valley Hist. Review* 20:1, 262 (1933); Diary Entry, Dec. 4, 1776, in Dawson (ed.), *How Diary*, 38; Extract of a Letter from Peekskill, New York, Dec. 4, 1776, in *Freeman's Journal* (New Hampshire), Dec. 31, 1776 ("I am preparing to set off for the Jerseys, to which place General Lee with his division is now bending his course").

70. See Diary Entry, Dec. 3, 1776, in Dawson (ed.), *How Diary*, 38; Diary Entries, Dec. 2-3, 1776, in "Bamford's Diary," *Maryland Hist. Magazine* 28:18 (1933) and Mackenzie, *Diary* 1:118.

71. Lefkowitz, *The Long Retreat*, 62-63.

72. W. Howe to G. Germain, Dec. 20, 1776, in Davies (ed.), *Documents of the A.R.* 12:266; see also Lefkowitz, *The Long Retreat*, 81-82 and 94-97.

73. N. Greene to N. Cooke, Dec. 4, 1776, in Showman (ed.), *Greene Papers* 1:362.

74. W. Howe to G. Germain, Dec. 20, 1776, in Davies (ed.), *Documents of the A.R.* 12:266.

75. Quoted in Freeman, *George Washington* 3:282, n. 77.

76. McBurney, *Rhode Island Campaign*, 1-4.

77. Diary Entries, Dec. 5, 1776, in Muenchhausen, *At General Howe's Side*, 6, and Kemble, "Journal," *N. Y. Hist. Soc. Coll.* 102 (1883) ("General Howe went to Jersey").

78. G. Washington to C. Lee, Dec. 1, 1776, in Twohig et al. (eds.), *Washington Papers* 7:249.

79. Congressional Resolution, Dec. 2, 1776, in Ford (ed.), *Journals of the Continental Congress* 6:1000.
80. G. Washington to J. Hancock, Dec. 3, 1776, in Twohig et al. (eds.), *Washington Papers* 7:255.
81. G. Washington to C. Lee, Dec. 3, 1776, in ibid., 257.
82. C. Lee to G. Washington, Dec. 4, 1776, in ibid., 259. Despite Washington's desperate circumstances, Lee took time to address some of his personal business, adding to the letter, "it is paltry to think of our personal affairs when the whole is at stake, but I entreat you to order some of your suite to take out of the way of danger my favorite mare which is at Hunt Wilson's three miles the other side of Princeton." Id.
83. J. Hodgkins to S. Hodgkins, Dec. 3 and 20, 1776, in Wade and Lively, *This Glorious Cause*, 227-28.
84. Diary Entry, Dec. 7, 1776, in Rau (ed.), "Sergeant Smith's Diary," *Mississippi Valley Hist. Review* 20:1, 262-63 (1933).
85. See Diary Entries, Dec. 5-10, 1776, in ibid., 262-64 (Dec. 6 [should be 5]—"about noon we went forward 7 or 8 miles"; Dec. 7 [should be 6]—"We went away by sunrise and travelled until sunset"; Dec. 8 [should be 7]—marched from Ramapo to Pompton Plains, probably taking only part of the day; Dec. 9 [should be 8]—marched all day, arriving south of Parsippany; Dec. 10 [should be 9]—marched probably only part of the day, to Chatham; Dec. 11 [should be 10]—started marching in afternoon, reached Morristown; Dec. 12 [should be 11]—rested at Morristown, no marching). See also Diary Entries, Dec. 4-10, in Dawson (ed.), *How Diary*, 38 (Dec. 4—"At 12 noon we marched 10 miles to New Hampstead and stayed at night"; Dec. 5—"This day we marched to Clove and stayed at night"; Dec. 6—"This morning we set off very early and marched about 5 miles to Ringwood and drew three days provisions and cooked it. Then we marched to Pompton and stayed at night"; Dec. 7-9—David How was selected as a member of a party sent to Hackensack and Paramus for provisions; Dec. 10—"This morning we drew two days provisions and cooked it all. Then we marched to Morristown. Stopped there at night"; Dec. 11—"This day we pitched our tents in the woods here. This night it's been snowy and cold.")
86. W. Howe to G. Germain, Dec. 20, 1776, in Davies (ed.), *Documents of the A.R.* 12:266.
87. Diary Entry, Dec. 8, 1776, in Muenchhausen, *At General Howe's Side*, 7; see also W. Howe to G. Germain, Dec. 20, 1776, in Davies (ed.), *Documents of the A.R.* 12:266-67; Lefkowitz, *The Long Retreat*, 121-22.
88. G. Washington to L. Washington, Dec. 10-17, 1776, in Twohig et al. (eds.), *Washington Papers* 7:289.
89. G. Washington to R. Humpton, Dec. 1, 1776, in ibid., 248.
90. See Diary Entries, Dec. 9-10, 1776, in Lydenberg (ed.), *Robertson Diaries*, 115-16; W. Howe to G. Germain, Dec. 20, 1776, in Davies (ed.), *Documents of the A.R.* 12:266-67.
91. Historian Thomas Fleming wrote of this matter: "This stripping the Delaware of boats is usually described as a great American coup—a stroke of guerilla genius that stopped the British advance. But Washington knew this was a silly idea on December 9, 1776. If the British wanted to cross the river, he told Congress, there was nothing he could do to stop them. For one thing, they could easily bring their attack flatboats overland by wagon from New York. In fact, intelligence reports had led him to think they were doing just that. With a well-trained army engineering corps, and hundreds of carpenters in the British fleet, it would have been a simple matter for Howe to build boats or rafts in or around Trenton. The town had a hardware store and three blacksmith shops to give him all the nails and iron he needed. His chief engineer, with the help of some loyalists, found 48,000 feet of already cut boards only a few yards away from the house Howe was using as headquarters." Fleming, *1776, Year of Illusions*, 425.

92. G. Washington to J. Hancock, Dec. 8, 1776, in Twohig et al. (eds.), *Washington Papers* 7:273.
93. G. Washington Memorandum for Colonel Richard Humpton, Dec. 5, 1776, in ibid., 265.
94. C. Lee to G. Washington, Dec. 8, 1776, in ibid., 7:276. Cadwalader's Associators, with artillery, arrived at Trenton on December 7 and then moved to join Washington's main army at Bristol, Pennsylvania. See Seymour, *Pennsylvania Associators,* 164-65.
95. C. Lee to Committee of Congress, Dec. 8, 1776, in *Lee Papers* 2:338-39.
96. The author assumes Lee spent the night of December 8 at Chatham, since he wrote two letters from Morristown on December 8, one letter from Chatham on December 8, and another from Chatham on December 9. C. Lee to G. Washington, Dec. 8, 1776, in Twohig et al. (eds.), *Washington Papers* 7:276 (dateline Morristown); C. Lee to Committee of Congress, Dec. 8, 1776, in *Lee Papers* 2:338-39 (dateline Morristown); C. Lee to G. Washington, Dec. 8, 1776, in Twohig et al. (eds.), *Washington Papers* 7:277 (dateline Chatham); C. Lee to W. Heath, Dec. 9, 1776, in *Lee Papers* 2:340 (dateline Chatham). For Day's Tavern being the best in the village and where Lee likely stayed, see White, *A Village at War,* 73-74; Vanderpoel, *History of Chatham,* 143.
97. G. Washington to J. Hancock, Dec. 10, 1776, in Twohig et al. (eds.), *Washington Papers* 7:286.
98. C. Lee to G. Washington, Dec. 8, 1776, in ibid., 277. The letter delivered by Hoops has not been found. However, its contents can be gleaned from this letter of Lee's and the letter from G. Washington to J. Hancock, Dec. 8, 1776, in id., 273. For Washington sending out Hoops to find Lee, see G. Washington to J. Hancock, Dec. 8, 1776, in id., 273.
99. N. Greene to G. Washington, Dec. 7, 1776, in Showman (ed.), *Greene Papers* 1:366. After receiving intelligence that "General Lee is at the heels of the enemy," Greene wrote in the same letter, "I should think he had better keep upon the flanks than the rear of the enemy, unless it were possible to concert an attack at the same instant of time in front and rear." Id. Historian Theodore Thayer interpreted this statement as Greene believing that "Lee might do more good by hanging on to the rear of the enemy than by joining Washington." Thayer, *Colonial and Revolutionary Morris County,* 162. The author disagrees. In the same December 7 letter, as noted in the main text, Greene warned Washington that Lee needed more direction or he would go off and act on his own.
100. W. Heath to C. Lee, Dec. 8, 1776, in *Lee Papers* 2:336. The three regiments that had arrived at Peekskill were Greaton's, Bond's, and Porter's Regiments. Gates had with him Patterson's, Stark's, Read's, and Poor's Regiments. Id.
101. See Lefkowitz, *The Long Retreat,* 74 and n. 2.
102. C. Lee to W. Heath, Dec. 9, 1776, in *Lee Papers* 2:340.
103. G. Washington to C. Lee, Dec. 10, 1776, in Twohig et al. (eds.), *Washington Papers* 7:288.
104. G. Washington to C. Lee, Dec. 11, 1776, in ibid., 301. Lee probably never received this letter. Douglas Freeman thought that Moylan left Washington's headquarters on December 12. Freeman, *George Washington* 3:283, n. 82. While this may have been the case, the author believes it is more likely that Moylan left the day Washington penned his December 11 letter. See also S. Moylan to W. Heath, Dec. 15, 1776, in Force (ed.), *American Archives,* 5th Series, 3:1233.
105. It is not clear where Lee stayed at Morristown. He may have stayed at one of the taverns in the village. Mellick wrote that Lee camped "on the night of the eleventh on a little plain southwest of the Ford mansion" outside of Morristown. Mellick, *Story of an Old Farm,* 340. Lee could have used different quarters at Morristown the nights of December 9, 10, and 11.

106. See General Sullivan's Orders, Dec. 11, 1776, in Force (ed.), *American Archives*, 5th Series, 3:1167 (refers to troops marching on December 10 and orders marching for December 12); Diary Entries, Dec. 10-11 [should be 9-10], 1776, in Rau (ed.), "Sergeant Smith's Diary," *Mississippi Valley Hist. Review* 20:1, 263 (1933); Diary Entries, Dec. 10-11, 1776, in Dawson (ed.), *How Diary*, 38; see also Diary Entries, Dec. 9-10, 1776, in "Bamford's Diary," *Maryland Hist. Magazine* 28:21 (1933) (Dec. 9—"Very fine day") ("Dec. 10—"Sharp frost this morning, fine day").
107. C. Lee to G. Washington, Dec. 8, 1776, in Twohig et al. (eds.), *Washington Papers* 7:301.
108. Jacob Ford, et al. to A. McDougall, Dec. 19, 1776, in Force (ed.), *American Archives*, 5th Series, 3:1297.
109. G. Washington to C. Lee, Dec. 14, 1776, in Twohig et al. (eds.), *Washington Papers* 7:335. Lee never received this letter.
110. Diary Entries, Dec. 11-12, 1776, in Muenchhausen, *At General Howe's Side*, 7.
111. Resolution, Dec. 12, 1776, in Ford (ed.), *Journals of the Continental Congress* 6:1027.
112. R. Morris to S. Deane, Dec. 6, 1776, in "Deane Papers," *N.Y. Hist. Soc. Coll.* 408 (1886); see also R. H. Lee to P. Henry, Dec. 3, 1776, in Ballagh (ed.), *Richard H. Lee Letters* 1:227 ("We hear that Gen. Lee has crossed North River and is following quickly after the enemy, but we are not sure that his numbers are sufficient for anything decisive").
113. Diary Entry, Dec. 16, 1776, in Rodney (ed.), *Rodney Diary*, 13.
114. W. Gordon to G. Washington, Jan. 8, 1778, in Twohig et al. (eds.), *Washington Papers* 13:175. William Gordon wrote to the commander-in-chief, "I have been told that it was in contemplation among some of the delegates a little before General Lee was taken, to exalt him to the supreme command of the army, and that it was first projected by a Virginian. You most probably know if there was any foundation for the report." Id. Washington, however, denied any knowledge of this matter. G. Washington to W. Gordon, Jan. 23, 1778, in id., 322.
115. W. Stirling to G. Washington, Dec. 12, 1776, in ibid., 319-20.
116. G. Washington to H. Gates, Dec. 14, 1776, in ibid., 7:333.
117. G. Washington to W. Heath, Dec. 14, 1776, in ibid, 334.

CHAPTER TWO: WIDOW WHITE'S TAVERN
1. J. Sullivan to G. Washington, Dec. 13, 1776, in Twohig et al. (eds.), *Washington Papers* 7:328.
2. General Sullivan's Orders, Dec. 11, 1776, in Force (ed.), *American Archives*, 5th Series, 3:1167. Lee had apparently by this time relinquished his idea of remaining to protect the last area in northern New Jersey, the Watchung Mountains, under patriot control. To give some assurances to Ford's New Jersey militia, Lee gave an "express promise" that three Continental regiments then marching to the area from northern New York "would be detained here [Morristown] for the protection of this State." Jacob Ford, et al. to A. McDougall, Dec. 19, 1776, in id., 3:1297. The three regiments were commanded by Colonels Greaton, Bond, and Porter. Id. Washington, however, on December 12 wrote General Heath that he still wanted those three regiments to join him with "all imaginable haste" for the "preservation of Philadelphia." G. Washington to W. Heath, Dec. 12, 1776, in Twohig et al. (eds.), *Washington Papers* 7:312. Nine days later, at the urging of Heath and Major General Alexander McDougall, and with Lee's and Gates's divisions having crossed over the Delaware River into Pennsylvania, Washington changed his mind and agreed that these three regiments should remain at Morristown. G. Washington to A. McDougall, Dec. 21, 1776, in id., 401; see also A. McDougall to G. Washington, Dec. 19, 1776, in id., 377-78; J. Ford, et al. to A. McDougall, Dec. 19, 1776, in Force (ed.), *American Archives*, 5th Series, 3:1297.

3. Diary Entry, Dec. 12 [should be 11], 1776, in Rau (ed.), "Sergeant Smith's Diary," *Mississippi Valley Hist. Review* 20:1, 264 (1933).
4. See Diary Entries, Dec. 12-13 [should be 11-12], 1776, in ibid., 20:264 (1933) (Dec. 11—"As soon as we lay down it began to snow very fast and continued most all night. We were ordered to turn out by the light and strike our tents, but were prevented by the storm.") (Dec. 12—"about 11 o'clock we marched forward. The snow melting made the travelling exceedingly bad, the roads being of a kind of clay was becoming mortar"); see also Diary Entries, Dec. 11-12, 1776, in Dawson (ed.), *How Diary*, 39 (Dec. 11—"This day we pitched our tents in the woods here [Morristown]. This night it's been snowy and cold"; Dec. 12—"We struck our tents this morning"). This weather pattern is confirmed by the diary of a British officer stationed in New York City. Diary Entries, Dec. 11-12, 1776, in "Bamford's Diary," *Maryland Hist. Magazine* 28:21 (1933) (Dec. 11—"p.m. some snow") and (Dec. 12—"A little snow on the ground this morning cold. The snow soon disappeared and the weather grew very warm."). The snow would have been deeper in the Watchung Mountains, where Lee's men were marching, than in New York City. North of Lee's division in the New Jersey mountains, the snowstorm on the evening of December 11 had halted the progress of Gates's regiments. H. Gates to G. Washington, Dec. 12, 1776, in Twohig et al. (eds.), *Washington Papers* 7:308; James Wilkinson's Recollections, in Wilkinson, *Memoirs* 1:100.
5. Diary Entry, Dec. 13 [should be 12], 1776, in Rau (ed.), "Sergeant John Smith's Diary," *Miss. Valley Hist. Review* 20:264 (1933).
6. Sullivan wrote to Washington on December 13, "I received your Excellency's letters to him [Lee] of the 10th and 11th instant, and shall endeavor to join the Army as soon as possible." J. Sullivan to G. Washington, Dec. 13, 1776, in Twohig et al. (eds.), *Washington Papers* 7:328.
7. Diary Entry, Dec. 11, 1776, in Dawson (ed.), *How Diary*, 39 ("We struck our tents this morning and marched to Benards Township and stayed at night in the woods").
8. Diary Entry, Dec. 13 [should be 12], 1776, in Rau (ed.), "Sergeant John Smith's Diary," *Miss. Valley Hist. Review* 20:264 (1933).
9. Congressional Resolution, Sept. 19, 1776, in Ford (ed.), *Journals of the Continental Congress* 5:784; see also Congressional Resolution Sept. 23, 1776, in id., 809 (advancing de Virnejoux two months' pay); J. Sullivan to G. Washington, Dec. 13, 1776, in Twohig (ed.), *Washington Papers* 7:328 and n. 3.
10. René-Etienne Henry Vic Gaiault de Boisbertrand, Memorandum for the American Commissioners, Sept. 5, 1778, in Stevens (ed.), *Facsimiles* 23:1948; Resolution, Jan. 8, 1777, in Ford (ed.), *Journals of the Continental Congress* 7:18-19; R. E. de Gaiault to President of Congress, Dec. 10, 1776, in Force (ed.), *American Archives*, 5th Series, 3:1162; see also William Bradford's Recollection of Lee's Capture, Diary Entry, Jan. 1, 1777, in Dexter (ed.), *Stiles Diary* 2:106; quote from a letter from an English officer, in Scull, *The Evelyns in America*, 215 ("Mr. Gayault [Gaiault] informed me, that he was only two days with Gen. Lee as aide-de-camp"). Prior to his capture on December 13, Boisbertrand had sent a Mr. Couleaux, who was a partner of Pierre Penet and who had accompanied Boisbertrand to America, on to Congress with the secret dispatches. See René-Etienne Henry Vic Gaiault de Boisbertrand, Memorandum for the American Commissioners, Sept. 5, 1778, in Stevens (ed.), *Facsimiles* 23:1948; R. E. de Gaiault to President of Congress, Dec. 10, 1776, in Force (ed.), *American Archives*, 5th Series, 3:1162.
11. William Bradford's Recollections of Lee's Capture, Diary Entry, Jan. 1, 1777, in Dexter (ed.), *Stiles Diary* 2:106 (in addition to Bradford and the two French officers, Lee had with him "perhaps a dozen guards"); Extract of a Letter from Verplanck's Point, Dec. 21, 1776, in *New England Chronicle*, Jan. 9, 1777 ("There were but 13 men with the General"); *Providence Gazette*, Dec. 28, 1776 (Lee had with him "8 or 10 of his guards").

12. See Return of Colonel Hitchcock's Regiment, Nov. 1, 1776, in Force (ed.), *American Archives*, 5th Series, 3:506 ("October 29—William Bradford, Esquire, Adjutant, appointed aide-de-camp to General Lee").

13. Quoted in William Bradford's Recollections of Lee's Capture, Diary Entry, Jan. 1, 1777, in Dexter (ed.), *Stiles Diary* 2:106. Bradford did not identify the sick aide whom he replaced. Nourse had written a letter in his capacity as "private secretary" to Lee as late as December 6, 1776. See J. Nourse to W. Heath, Dec. 6, 1776, in *Lee Papers* 2:331. Major James Wilkinson reported seeing Nourse in a tavern several miles from Basking Ridge the night of December 12. James Wilkinson's Recollections, in Wilkinson, *Memoirs* 1:102. Thus, the author surmises that Nourse left Lee's entourage on or about December 10.

14. For Widow White's Tavern being three miles from the main body of Sullivan's troops, see J. Sullivan to G. Washington, Dec. 13, 1776, in Twohig (ed.), *Washington Papers* 7:328; see also Diary Entry, Dec. 13, 1776, in Dawson (ed.), *How Diary*, 39 ("This morning the light horse took General Lee as he was 3 miles from our army"). For the fork in the road being two miles north of Basking Ridge, see Diary Entry, Aug. 28, 1781, in Acomb (ed.), *Journal of von Closen*, 114.

15. For the fork in the road, see A Map Containing Part of the Provinces of New York and New Jersey, by Andrew Skinner, ca. 1781, Geography & Map Reading Room, Library of Congress and A Sketch of the Northern Parts of New Jersey, by John Hills, 1781, id.

16. Voorhees, "The Whitaker Family of Somerset County," *Somerset County Historical Quarterly* 2:99-104 (1913); Littell, *Family Records of the First Settlers of Passaic Valley*, 468 (stating that Mary moved to Long Island after her marriage to Ebenezer White and then returned to Basking Ridge after Ebenezer's death, which must have occurred prior to 1776). For more information on Mary White, see the useful online article, Widow White's Tavern at www.t3.consortium.com/drafts/widowwhites.php. Dartmouth College records indicate Mary was born in 1719, which would make her fifty-seven years old in 1776.

17. E. Hazard Diary Entry, Aug. 12, 1777, in ibid., 301. The tavern building was located at the corner of South Finley Avenue and Colonial Drive just south of Basking Ridge. Di Ionno, *A Guide to New Jersey's Revolutionary War Trail*, 145-46. It was on the west side of South Finley Avenue, about a half-mile south of the village. A historic maker at this corner commemorates Lee's capture at the tavern. The fate of the tavern's structure after the Revolutionary War is uncertain. Di Ionno wrote that it was demolished just before World War II. One source indicates that the tavern was torn down prior to 1878 and that a new building had been constructed at the site. See Messler, *Centennial History of Somerset County*, 135 (writing in 1878, Widow White's Tavern "is the last house on the south end of the village, and since destroyed"). The April 16, 1905, edition of the *Bernardsville Times* reported that "About twenty-five years ago an addition was added to the front part of the tavern. None of the old building was disturbed, but remains today the same as 125 years ago." It noted that "[s]ome of the bullets," meaning bullet hoes, caused by Harcourt's troopers "may still be seen at the rear of the old building." A June 30, 1993, article in *The Bernardsville News*, which summarized the tavern's ownership and alterations over the years, quoted a Basking Ridge man saying that there was "no sign at all" of the building in May 1950. The article quoted from J. H. Horn's *Historic Somerset*, which was published in 1965 and stated that the "last vestige of the original building (a fireplace) was destroyed a few years ago." The newspaper articles cited in this note and other information can be found in the online article, Widow White's Tavern at www.t3.consortium.com/drafts/widowwhites.php. The formal name of the location today is Basking Ridge, Bernards Township, Somerset County, New Jersey.

18. This can be gleaned from a letter sent by James Caldwell later on December 12 and delivered to Lee at Basking Ridge, in which Caldwell confirmed receiving Lee's letter and stated that it was considered advisable to move the local militia back to Chatham, as it was thought the militia could better serve the cause by staying at that place "till the expected army approaches for their support." J. Caldwell to C. Lee, Dec. 12, 1776, in *Lee Papers* 2:347.
19. H. Gates to G. Washington, Dec. 12, 1776, in Twohig et al. (eds.), *Washington Papers* 7:308; James Wilkinson's Recollections, in Wilkinson, *Memoirs* 1:100; see also J. Wilkinson to H. Gates, Dec. 12, 1776, in Force (ed.), *American Archives*, 5th Series, 3:1190 (at Sussex Court House on Dec. 12; Wilkinson had heard that Washington's army had already crossed over the Delaware River and was uncertain of the location of Lee's division; "[p]ursuant to your orders, I shall proceed to General Washington with all possible speed"). While the credibility of Wilkinson's autobiography has been questioned due to his traitorous connections to the Spanish in the West in his later years, the author believes his account of Lee's capture is as credible as other eyewitness reports.
20. James Wilkinson's Recollections, in Wilkinson, *Memoirs* 1:102-3.
21. Ibid., 99.
22. Ibid., 105, n.
23. Elisha Bostwick Recollections, in Powell, "A Connecticut Soldier Under Washington," *William and Mary Quarterly Review*, 3rd Series, 6:97 (1949).
24. See Coffin, *Life of Scammell*, 78-80. It is not clear if Scammell spent the night of December 12 at Widow White's Tavern or arrived the next morning from Sullivan's headquarters. Wilkinson intimates it was the latter, and the author has adopted that view in the narrative. See James Wilkinson's Recollections, in Wilkinson, *Memoirs* 1:109-10. However, Scammell was at this time Lee's aide, and he wrote a letter on Lee's behalf from Morristown on December 11. A. Scammell to W. Heath, Dec. 11, 1776, in *Lee Papers* 2:344-45. Therefore, it is possible that Scammell did accompany Lee to Widow White's Tavern on December 12 and spent the night there. Scammell's writings on this topic are unfortunately not available. He was killed in a charge at Yorktown in 1781, and his correspondence was lost after his biographer passed away before completing the project. Allen, *American Biographical Dictionary*, 723.
25. James Wilkinson's Recollections, in Wilkinson, *Memoirs* 1:109-10. General John Armstrong later asserted that Lee was planning on December 13 to attack Brunswick. Alden, *General Charles Lee*, 332, n. 20.
26. The use of a second messenger is surmised from Tarleton's December 19 letter to his mother, in which he stated that he captured a "Yankee Light Horseman" who admitted that "he had just left General Lee from whom he had an express to carry to General Sullivan at Pluckemin." B. Tarleton to J. Tarleton, Dec. 18, 1776, in Bass, *Green Dragoon*, 21. This statement by Tarleton, made only a few days after the raid, supports Wilkinson's claim that Lee gave orders for Sullivan to march his troops to Pluckemin. The messenger was probably one of the "two or three light horsemen, in whom you can depend" sent to Lee by James Caldwell the prior day. J. Caldwell to C. Lee, Dec. 12, 1776, in *Lee Papers* 2:348.
27. C. Lee to H. Gates, Dec. 12/13, 1776, in ibid.
28. Diary Entry, Dec. 5, 1776, in Muenchhausen, *At General Howe's Side*, 6.
29. Journal Entry, Dec. 6-7, 1776, in Kemble, "Journal," *New York Hist. Soc. Coll.* 102 (1884); see also Diary Entry, Dec. 9, 1776, in id., 102 ("Lee at this time in Jersey with a corps of about 3 thousand men"); Diary Entry, Dec. 10, 1776 in id., 103 ("From what I hear of General Howe's situation, he will not be able to pass the Delaware; in that case, he must return, and I hope will find Mr. Lee out").
30. Diary Entry, Dec. 10, 1776, in Muenchhausen, *At General Howe's Side*, 6-7.
31. Diary Entry, Dec. 11, 1776, in ibid., 7.

32. J. Caldwell to C. Lee, Dec. 12, 1776, in *Lee Papers* 2:347 (discussing how to dispose of supplies taken from the British by local militia under Colonel Ford); Thayer, *Colonial and Revolutionary Morris County,* 162 ("By Lee's order, Colonel Ford with a body of Morris County militia, raided Woodbridge one night and drove off four hundred cattle, two hundred sheep, and many horses"). The author has not found evidence that Lee ordered this raid, but it could well have been the case.

33. L. Stirling to G. Washington, Dec. 12, 1776, in Twohig et al. (eds.), *Washington Papers* 7:319.

34. W. Harcourt to Earl Harcourt, Dec. 19, 1776, in Scull, *The Evelyns in America,* 227 and Harcourt (ed.), *Harcourt Papers* 11:182; see also W. Howe to H. Clinton, Dec. 21, 1776, Henry Clinton Papers 19:16, William L. Clements Library ("Lieutenant Colonel Harcourt offering to go with the party, Lord Cornwallis consented"). General Howe reported the following to his civilian superior in London, Lord George Germain: "During Lord Cornwallis's stay at Pennington, a patrol of thirty dragoons from the 16th Regiment was sent out to gain intelligence of a corps under the command of General Lee, reported to be in Morris County, on their way to cross the Delaware at Alexandria." W. Howe to G. Germain, December 20, 1776, New York, in Davies (ed.), *Documents of the A.R.* 12:266; see also R. Mackenzie to E. Percy, Dec. 20, 1776, Hugh Percy Papers, British Manuscript Project, microfilm reel Aln 25, Library of Congress ("To know his [Lee's] real situation, Colonel Harcourt was detached on the 12th or 13th from the Delaware to reconnoiter the country towards Morristown, where the body of the rebels then were") (Captain Robert Mackenzie served as an aide to Howe); Diary Entry, Dec. 12, 1776, in Lydenberg (ed.), *Robertson Diary,* 116 (Captain Archibald Robertson wrote in his diary for December 12, "Lieutenant Colonel Harcourt with 30 dragoons was sent on a patrol from Pennington today towards Morristown to get intelligence of General Lee's Army"); Ensign Glyn's Diary Entry, Dec. 13, 1776, quoted in Bass, *Green Dragoons,* 19 ("Lt. Col. Harcourt with a party of light dragoons having the Cornets Geary and Tarleton with him, was detached from Trenton beyond Pennington, to gain intelligence of the rebel General Lee's corps, which was supposed to be about Rocky Hill").

35. *New York Gazette,* Dec. 15, 1777; Sept. 18-20, 1777; *London Chronicle,* Sept. 18-20, 1777. Simon Harcourt "was the 27th in paternal descent from Bernard, a nobleman of the blood royal of Saxony, who being born in Denmark, was surnamed the Dane, and from whom so many noble and illustrious families, besides his Lordship's are descended." His grandfather, Simon, Baron and Viscount Harcourt, had been declared Lord High Chancellor of Great Britain in 1712. Simon Harcourt married Rebecca le Bass, daughter and heiress of Charles le Bass of Pipwell Abbey in Northamptonshire. *New York Gazette,* Dec. 15, 1777.

36. Hargrove, *General John Burgoyne,* 29; *Dictionary of National Biography* 8:1211; Scull, *The Evelyns in America,* 209. The *Dictionary of National Biography* states that the 16th Regiment was funded "entirely" by Harcourt's father. This claim cannot be confirmed, but it is undermined to some extent by the fact that Secretary of War William Barrington issued the warrant to raise the regiment to Burgoyne, and that Harcourt joined the regiment as a captain, not as its colonel or lieutenant colonel. Hargrove, *General John Burgoyne,* 29; *Dictionary of National Biography* 8:1211. The confusion may be clarified by the following excerpt from the *Harcourt Papers* about William Harcourt: "He entered the army at an early age; his first command was that of a troop in a cavalry regiment, raised at the sole expense of his father. The troop went by the name of Captain Harcourt's Black Horse." Harcourt (ed.), *Harcourt Papers* 11:145. This outfit was likely a small county unit and not the 16th Regiment of Light Dragoons.

37. *Royal Military Calendar* 1:280-81.

38. Letter from an Officer of the 6th Regiment, in *St. James's Chronicle or the British Evening Post,* March 1-4, 1777 (London) ("Col. Harcourt of Burgoyne's Light

Dragoons"); *New York Gazette,* Dec. 23, 1776 ("Colonel Harcourt of Burgoyne's Light Horse"); Diary Entry, Dec. 14, 1776, in Uhlendorf (ed.), *Baurmeister Letters,* 75 ("Burgoyne's Dragoons").

39. *Dictionary of National Biography* 8:1211.
40. Hargrove, *General John Burgoyne,* 36-38 (Burgoyne ordered Lee to make the raid); Fonblanque, *Political and Military Episodes,* 50-51 and n. 1; Alden, *General Charles Lee,* 156. While it is sometimes said that Harcourt accompanied Lee in this raid with troopers from the 16th Regiment, there is no record of it. Hargrove, *General John Burgoyne,* 36-38. At this time, Harcourt was a captain in the 3rd Dragoons and would not become lieutenant colonel of the 16th Regiment until 1770. *Royal Military Calendar* 1:281.
41. Quoted in Riddle, "Raid on Flemington," *Brigade Dispatch* 23:4, 18 (Autumn 1992) (citing WO 4/94, PRO, 321-22).
42. *General Evening Post* (London), Feb. 27-March 1, 1777.
43. W. Harcourt to Earl Harcourt, June 29, 1778, in Harcourt (ed.), *Harcourt Papers* 11:175; see also W. Harcourt to Earl Harcourt, July 19, 1776, in Harcourt (ed.), *Harcourt Papers* 11:176 (bad weather prevented Harcourt's convoy from clearing the English Channel and forced it to stay over at St. Helens); see also W. Barrington to G. Germain, Jan. 16, 1776, WO 4/95, British National Archives (322 horses needed for regiment consisting of 490 officers and men; not all horses for officers included); Muster Rolls, 16th Light Dragoons, April 22, 1777, WO 12/1246, British National Archives (listing number of horses in each company).
44. Muster Rolls, 16th Light Dragoons, April 22, 1777, WO 12/1246, British National Archives.
45. W. Howe to G. Germain, Nov. 30, 1776, New York, in Davies (ed.), *Documents of the A.R.* 12:259; Diary Entry, Oct. 3, 1776, in Kemble, "Journal," *N.Y. Hist. Soc. Coll.* 91 (1884) ("Colonel Harcourt arrived with the 16th Light Horse, one transport excepted"); Diary Entry, Oct. 3, 1776, in Tatum (ed.), *Serle Journal,* 118-19 ("The *Daphne* . . . with 12 sail of transports having on the 16th or Burgoyne's Regiment of Light Horse, came up this morning. They . . . lost about 40 horses"); Diary Entry, Dec. 14, 1776, in Uhlendorf (ed.), *Baurmeister Letters,* 75; W. Harcourt to Earl Harcourt, Oct. 7, 1776, in Harcourt (ed.), *Harcourt Papers* 11:175; Muster Rolls, 16th Light Dragoons, April 22, 1777, WO 12/1246, British National Archives (horses and soldiers dying during sea passage). Ambrose Serle stated that one of the transport ships "was missing, which (as we afterwards learned) was taken by the Rebels." Diary Entry, Oct. 3, 1776, in Tatum (ed.), *Serle Journal,* 119. This capture was confirmed in the October 7, 1776, edition of the *Boston Gazette.* The newspaper reported that Richard Derby of Salem had arrived in Boston on October 2 on board the brigantine *Massachusetts,* and that Derby had spoken with Captain Daniel Souther, who informed him that "a few days after he sailed he fell in with and took a brigantine of about 250 tons from Falmouth in England, mounting six three-pound cannon and having on board a captain and about 20 privates of the 16th Regiment of Dragoons, with their horse accoutrements." In total, Souther took thirty-five prisoners, both sailors and soldiers. The captured vessel was separated from Souther's privateer in another storm, but must have eventually been brought into a safe American port. The muster rolls for the 16th Regiment of Light Dragoons, dated April 22, 1777, indicate that 48 of its men were "prisoners with the rebels." Muster Rolls, 16th Light Dragoons, April 22, 1777, WO 12/1246, British National Archives. These captives must have included those taken on board the separated transport. This capture was not reported in the *Naval Documents of the American Revolution.* For an image of the exterior and interior of a British horse transport vessel, see Morgan, Crawford et al. (eds.), *Naval Docs. of the A.R.* 9:12. Coincidentally, ten of the captive dragoons were brought to Morristown on December 11. Diary Entry, Dec. 12 [should be 11], 1776, in Rau (ed.), "Sergeant John Smith's Diary," *Miss. Valley Hist. Review* 20:264 (1933) ("This day some

prisoners were brought in town," including "Ten of the Light Horsemen who were taken off the coast of New England by one of our cruisers").

46. Ketchum, "New War Letters of Banastre Tarleton," *N.Y. Hist. Soc. Quarterly* 51:1, 62-63 (1967).

47. Bass, *Green Dragoon*, 15-16.

48. See the link titled Arms in the 16th Queen's Light Dragoons website, which is for the American re-enactors of the regiment. See www.16thqueenslightdragoons.blogspot.com.

49. W. Howe to G. Germain, Nov. 30, 1776, New York, in Davies (ed.), *Documents of the A.R.* 12:259; W. Howe's Orders, Oct. 6, 21, 24, and 27, 1776, in "British Army Orders," *N.Y. Hist. Soc. Coll.*, 384, 393, 396, and 398 (1884).

50. C. Lee to W. Howe, Nov. 26, 1776, in *Lee Papers* 2:316; see also Diary Entries, Oct. 23, 25, and 27, 1776, in "Sergeant John Smith's Diary of 1776," *Mississippi Valley Hist. Review* 20:257-58 (1933). In his letter, Lee sensibly proposed "that every hospital should be sacred from insults" and that "the surgeons and attendants should not be considered as lawful prisoners." C. Lee to W. Howe, Nov. 26, 1776, in *Lee Papers* 2:316-17. Howe never responded to the letter.

51. W. Howe to G. Germain, Nov. 30, 1776, New York, in Davies (ed.), *Documents of the A.R.* 12:260; Diary Entries, Nov. 21, 1776, in Boyle (ed.), *Sullivan Journal*, 86 and Stirke, "A British Officer's Revolutionary War Journal," *Maryland Hist. Magazine* 56:2, 165 (June 1961).

52. B. Tarleton to unknown, Nov. 23, 1776, in Ketchum, "New War Letters of Banastre Tarleton," *N.Y. Hist. Soc. Quarterly* 51:1, 62-63 (1967).

53. Captain Henry Knight Orderly Book, Aide-de-Camp to General Howe, Dec. 1, 1776, New York, in British Orderly Books, New York Historical Society.

54. W. Harcourt to Earl Harcourt, Dec. 5, 1776, in Harcourt (ed.), *Harcourt Papers* 11:178.

55. T. Stanley to unidentified British officer serving in Europe, Feb. 11, 1777, Ms. Am. 228, Rare Books and Manuscripts, Boston Public Library. Prior to this quotation, Stanley wrote, "We had a bitter brush with them the other day near Brunswick. They attacked a foraging party of ours and were beat off with considerable loss. We had only a Captain Cunningham of the Light Infantry killed and about ten men killed or wounded." Stanley was originally with the 16th Regiment of Light Dragoons, but transferred to the 17th Light Dragoons as a captain on February 25, 1776. Baule and Gilbert (eds.), *British Officers*, 168. A return of British soldiers through November 16 showed that the 16th Regiment had suffered the following losses since October 3: "One sergeant, one rank and file, and one horse—wounded; one rank and file— missing." Return of ... Officers and Rank-and-File Killed, Wounded, and Missing, Belonging to the Army under the Command of His Excellency, the Honourable General Howe ... from the 17th of September to the 16th of November, Dec. 1, 1776, in Force (ed.), *American Archives*, 5th Series, 3:1055.

56. Captain Henry Knight Orderly Book, Aide-de-Camp to General Howe, Trenton, Dec. 12, 1776, in British Orderly Books, New York Historical Society.

57. Harcourt stated that his party consisted of "three officers and thirty men," for a total of thirty-three. W. Harcourt to Earl Harcourt, Dec. 19, 1776, in Scull, *The Evelyns in America*, 227 and Harcourt (ed.), *Harcourt Papers* 11:182. This would have included Colonel Harcourt, Captains Eustace and Nash, Lieutenant Leigh, Cornets Geary and Tarleton, and another twenty-seven men. The total number of thirty-three is supported by General Howe's letter to Lord Germain and the account of Captain Friedrich von Muenchhausen, who stated that Harcourt "took thirty dragoons with him yesterday to make a patrol in the rear." W. Howe to G. Germain, December 20, 1776, New York, in Davies (ed.), *Documents of the A.R.* 12:266; Diary Entry, Dec. 13, 1776, in

Muenchhausen, *At General Howe's Side*, 7. In addition, Captain Archibald Robertson wrote in his diary for December 12, "Lieutenant Colonel Harcourt with 30 dragoons was sent on a patrol from Pennington today towards Morristown to get intelligence of General Lee's Army." Diary Entry, Dec. 12, 1776, in Lydenberg (ed.), *Robertson Diary*, 116. An unidentified officer of the 6th Regiment contemporaneously wrote that Harcourt "took 30 men with him." Letter from an Officer of the 6th Regiment, in *St. James's Chronicle or the British Evening Post*, March 1-4, 1777 (London). Another British officer similarly wrote, "Colonel Harcourt was out with thirty men." Extract of an Authentic Letter from an Officer at New York, Dec. 21, 1776, in *Morning Chronicle and London Advertiser*, Feb. 27, 1777. Neither von Muenchhausen, Robertson, the officer of the 6th Regiment, nor the other British officer likely would have included in this count of thirty men Colonel Harcourt or the two captains who accompanied him. Tarleton, by contrast, wrote that Harcourt's party, in addition to Harcourt and Eustace, consisted of a captain, two cornets, and twenty-five privates, for a total of thirty men. However, Tarleton wrote that Harcourt "detached Lieutenant Leigh with dragoons to cut up all the men in my rear." B. Tarleton to Jane Tarleton, Dec. 18, 1776, in Bass, *Green Dragoon*, 20-22. The author believes that the total of thirty-three regular officers and soldiers is credible. Most descriptions of the raid, strangely, do not mention Leigh. One other report that does, by Captain Thomas Stanley of the 17th Dragoons, is set forth in note 95 of the next chapter.

58. Extract of an Authentic Letter from an Officer at New York, Dec. 21, 1776, in *Morning Chronicle and London Advertiser*, Feb. 27, 1777. While the author of the letter does not identify himself, it can be gleaned from its contents that he was an officer under the rank of lieutenant and was present at Brunswick when Lee was held there while a prisoner. The historian G. D. Scull also states that the guide was a Yorkshire man, probably relying on that newspaper report. Scull, *The Evelyns in America*, 215.

59. Apart from the reports of the Yorkshire man described in the note immediately above, the author has found only two British or Loyalist third-person contemporary references to the participation of a guide. See Jones, *History of New York* 1:128 (Harcourt's party was "guided by an honest Loyalist"); Diary Entry, Dec. 1776, in Boyle (ed.), *Sullivan Journal*, 87 (Harcourt "having with him a guide"). Two reports written in March 1777 indicate that the guide was Major Richard Witham Stockton. Lee's biographer, John Alden, does not believe Stockton was the guide, writing persuasively, "If it were true, other references to Stockton's services to Harcourt would doubtless be available." Alden, *General Charles Lee*, 332-33, n. 21. Stockton filed a claim for compensation with the British government in 1783, but did not claim in it that he served as a guide for Harcourt's party. Richard William Stockton Loyalist Rev. War Claim, summarized in Coldham (ed.), *American Migrations*, 434. In a claim for compensation from the British government after the war, William Robins, born in 1759 and at the outbreak of the war residing in Quibbletown (now New Market) in Somerset County, New Jersey, stated that he joined British forces in 1776 and that initially "he served as a guide under Lord Cornwallis and performed a variety of confidential services, including that of a principal guide at the capture of General Lee." Quoted in Jones, *Loyalists of New Jersey in the Revolution*, 179-80 (summarizing official British records). After serving in Tarleton's British Legion in the south and surrendering at Yorktown, Robins in 1784 returned to New Jersey to see his mother and under the treaty of peace to reclaim some part of his father's property, which had been seized by his two half-brothers. Robins's compensation claim provided that "instead of meeting with any protection he was seized, tied to a tree and severely flogged." Quoted in id., 180; see also Dornfest, *Military Loyalists of the A.R.*, 262. In another claim for compensation from the British government following the war, Asher Dunham of New Jersey stated that "in November 1776 he joined the Royal Army at New Brunswick in New Jersey, and gave them every

intelligence and rendered them every other service he was capable of." He added that he "was at the time frequently employed by General Skinner and others to procure information for the Royal Army, that he was in the country on that service at the time Colonel Harcourt took the rebel Major General Lee, and did actually join him on that occasion." Asher Dunham Loyalist Claim, quoted from The On-Line Institute for Advanced Loyalist Studies, at www.royalprovincial.com (citing British Public Records Office, Audit Office, Class 13, Volume 21, folios 154-55); Jones, *Loyalists of New Jersey in the Revolution*, 67. See also discussion on Dunham in next chapter in the main text accompanying notes 46 to 47.

60. Extract of a Letter from New York, Dec. 17, 1776, in *London Chronicle*, March 1-4, 1777.

61. B. Tarleton to J. Tarleton, Dec. 18, 1776, in Bass, *Green Dragoon*, 20.

62. Harcourt's route is based on a map, dated February 11, 1777, made by Major John Clark of Pennsylvania, when he served as an aide to General Nathanael Greene. See "A Map of the Rariton & Adjacent Country, with a Plan of the Roads," Feb. 11, 1777, Mansucript Maps Collection, Box 3, Folder MS Map 4, Manuscripts Division, Department of Rare Books and Special Collections, Princeton University Library. Clark wrote on the map, "The dotted lines from White's Tavern to Millstone Court House is the route of the enemy's light horse when they took Maj. General Lee near Basking Ridge." Clark submitted the map to Greene when the two were stationed for the winter at Morristown. General Howe wrote that Harcourt's party "went by way of Hillsborough near the Millstone River, from thence across the Rariton [River] to Pluckemin and Morristown." W. Howe to H. Clinton, Dec. 21, 1776, Henry Clinton Papers 19:16, William L. Clements Library. The author doubts that Harcourt's party travelled through Pluckemin or reached Morristown.

63. Diary Entry, Dec. 13, 1776, in "Bamford's Diary," *Maryland Hist. Magazine* 28:21.

64. B. Tarleton to J. Tarleton, Dec. 18, 1776, in Bass, *Green Dragoon*, 21.

65. Diary Entry, Dec. 13, 1776, in Muenchhausen, *At General Howe's Side*, 7 ("Early this morning he [Harcourt] chanced upon a light dragoon of the rebels who was on sentry duty. The sentry was about to shoot but was cut down before he could fire"); Letter from an Officer of the 6th Regiment, in *St. James's Chronicle or the British Evening Post*, March 1-4, 1777 (London) ("in the morning he [Harcourt] fell in with one of their advanced sentinels, and dispatched a dragoon, who cut him down"); Diary Entry, Dec. 13, 1776, in Laughton (ed.), "Journals of Henry Duncan," *Naval Miscellany*, 137 ("falling in near Lee's army, [Harcourt] killed or took the sentinel, who refused to say where Lee was"). The author believes this American sentry was killed, as there is no other reference to him being a prisoner in any other account of the raid.

66. See discussion of James Compton in main text in next chapter accompanying note 52. One of these civilians could also have been a Mr. Macklewraith, an elder of the Presbyterian church at Mendham. See end of note 70 below.

67. B. Tarleton to J. Tarleton, Dec. 18, 1776, in Bass, *Green Dragoon*, 21. Captain Friedrich von Muenchhausen, Howe's aide-de-camp, was told the details of the raid by an unknown member of Harcourt's detachment. Muenchhausen wrote that: "Early this morning he [Harcourt] chanced upon a light dragoon of the rebels who was on sentry duty. The sentry was about to shoot but was cut down before he could fire. Colonel Harcourt reasoned that, judging from the presence of the mounted guard, the enemy could not be far away. He thereupon carefully pushed ahead and seized a second light dragoon on sentry duty before he could sound the alarm. Under emphatic threats of being hanged, the prisoner confessed that General Lee with a corps of 900 men was not far behind. Colonel Harcourt was about to force this fellow to lead him and his party to the house where General Lee was staying, but the sentry said he did not know the exact location of the house." Diary Entry, Dec. 13, 1776, in Muenchhausen, *At General Howe's Side*, 7.

68. B. Tarleton to J. Tarleton, Dec. 18, 1776, in Bass, *Green Dragoon*, 21. Captain Henry Duncan of the Royal Navy, then stationed in New York City, was told this version, which he wrote down in his diary: "Harcourt, falling in near Lee's army, killed or took the sentinel, who refused to say where Lee was. At this time one of the rebels' horsemen rode up to our party and told them that they were all prisoners, for that there was the army close by them. The colonel asked him where Lee was, and that if he hesitated to tell he would instantly put him to death. The fellow was frightened, and showed the house, about quarter of a mile from the main army." Diary Entry, Dec. 13, 1776, in Laughton (ed.), "Journals of Henry Duncan," *Naval Miscellany*, 137. Captain Robert Mackenzie, an aide-de camp to General Howe, wrote that "By taking a messenger from Lee, he [Harcourt] found out his quarters."

69. B. Tarleton to J. Tarleton, Dec. 18, 1776, in Bass, *Green Dragoon*, 21. For Widow White's Tavern being about a mile off the main road, see Extract of a Letter from Verplanck's Point, Dec. 21, 1776, in *New England Chronicle*, Jan. 9, 1777.

70. Diary Entry, Dec. 13, 1776, in Muenchhausen, *At General Howe's Side*, 7. In an account that otherwise was credible, and consistent with von Muenchhausen's, an officer of the 6th Regiment wrote that "in the morning he [Harcourt] fell in with one of their advanced sentinels, and dispatched a dragoon, who cut him down; he had not gone far when he perceived another, who he caused to be secured; while this was doing a horseman galloped up to the party before he perceived them. He was stopped and questioned by Col. Harcourt; he had a letter from [illegible] some rebel officers, yet denied knowing where Lee was quartered; but the Colonel ordered the rope to be got ready to tie him up; he, without further hesitation, pointed out the house." Letter from an Officer of the 6th Regiment, in *St. James's Chronicle or the British Evening Post*, March 1-4, 1777 (London). Charles Stedman, who served as a British officer in America in the Revolutionary War and wrote a history of it, in part based on his interviews of fellow British officers, said of Harcourt: "Collecting information, as he advanced into the country, the colonel was induced to proceed farther. In his progress he intercepted a countryman [i.e., an American], charged with a letter from General Lee, by which he understood where he was, and how lightly he was guarded." Stedman, *History of the American War* 1:226-27. Lieutenant Johann Heinrich von Bardeleben of the Hessian von Donop Regiment wrote in his diary that Harcourt had "captured an enemy captain, from whom he extracted various reports, among others that General Lee was staying at a house about seven miles farther away and had only a guard with him." Diary Entry, Dec. 27-31, 1776, in Burgoyne (ed.), *Diary of von Bardeleben*, 83. An entirely different version was provided to the authors of a history of New Jersey in about 1842. They wrote: "Col. J. W. Drake of Mendham, in conversation with one of the compilers of this volume, stated that the individual who acted as a guide to Col. Harcourt's party was a Mr. Macklewraith, an elder of the Presbyterian church at Mendham. While walking in the road, he was suddenly surrounded by a party of British cavalry, who pressed him into their service." Barber and Howe, *Historical Collections of New Jersey*, 445, n. This version differs from the British version in that Macklewraith was neither a military man nor a messenger, and nor was he on horseback. Macklewraith could have been one of the civilians who either first informed Harcourt's party that Lee was nearby at Basking Ridge or provided directions to the village.

71. William Bradford's Recollections of Lee's Capture, Diary Entry, Jan. 1, 1777, in Dexter (ed.), *Stiles Diary* 2:106 (woods and orchard); James Wilkinson's Recollections, in Wilkinson, *Memoirs* 1:105 (lane).

72. James Wilkinson's Recollections, in Wilkinson, *Memoirs* 1:105. Another report stated that "The lady of the house took him [Lee] upstairs in order to hide him between the chimney and the breast work, over the fireplace, but could not, the place being too small." Extract of a Letter from Verplanck's Point, Dec. 21, 1776, in *New England Chronicle*, Jan. 9, 1777.

73. James Wilkinson's Recollections, in Wilkinson, *Memoirs* 1:105 and 107, n. Captain von Muenchhausen was informed by a British raid participant that "an 18-man guard detail of General Lee, which had been in the nearest barn, came out, and they and the dragoons began shooting at one another." Diary Entry, Dec. 13, 1776, in Muenchhausen, *At General Howe's Side*, 7. While it may have been the case that Lee's guard consisted of eighteen men and that most of them had been in the barn at the time Harcourt's dragoons charged the tavern, the author believes that the American versions of Bradford recalling that the guard was of about a dozen men, and of Wilkinson recalling that most of the guard was caught away from the barn and their guns, are more credible. The version told by the editors of the *Lee Papers* was more consistent with von Muenchhausen's account: "The General's guard had been carelessly disposed at an outbuilding, and the sentry at the door of the house, when he saw the dragoons coming, at first mistook by their swords, which were different from those used by the Americans. The guard rallied as the alarm was given, and attempted to join in the defense, but they were immediately overpowered with merciless severity. Some of them were wounded, two were killed while attempting to escape, and the remainder probably owed their safety to Harcourt's haste and anxiety to make a sure of his prize." *Lee Papers* 2:388-89. According to a British officer, then posted either in New Jersey or New York City, Harcourt's dragoons "received some fire of a guard posted in an out-house, and, without loss, killed two sentinels at the [illegible] and took them prisoner, after killing those who resisted." Letter from an Officer of the 6th Regiment, in *St. James's Chronicle or the British Evening Post*, March 1-4, 1777 (London). This version is consistent with both the version told in the main text and von Muenchhausen's account.

74. Diary Entry, Dec. 14, 1776, in Uhlendorf (ed.), *Baurmeister Letters*, 75 ("A rebel of the General's watch . . . seized his musket and fired. A dragoon cut him down. This discouraged the others from coming out of the barn.")

75. Extract of a Letter from Verplanck's Point, Dec. 21, 1776, in *New England Chronicle*, Jan. 9, 1777 (also in *Connecticut Journal*, Jan. 15, 1777, and *Connecticut Gazette*, Jan. 17, 1777).

76. William Bradford's Recollections of Lee's Capture, Diary Entry, Jan. 1, 1777, in Dexter (ed.), *Stiles Diary* 2:106.

77. As well as being confirmed in the main accounts by Tarleton, Wilkinson, and Bradford, British general James Robertson wrote General Henry Clinton on December 19 from New York City, "Lee's guard fired to no effect and ran away." J. Robertson to H. Clinton, Dec. 19, 1776, Henry Clinton Papers 19:13, William L. Clements Library.

78. B. Tarleton to J. Tarleton, Dec. 18, 1776, in Bass, *Green Dragoon*, 22.

79. While Bradford in his recollections did not state who fired from the tavern, Tarleton stated that it was Bradford and the two Fench officers. B. Tarleton to J. Tarleton, Dec. 19, 1776, in Bass, *Green Dragoon*, 22. Robertson wrote to General Henry Clinton on December 19 from New York City that "Lee discharged a pistol" before surrendering. Ibid. Captain Thomas Harris, later Lord Harris, of the 28th Regiment, made the same claim. Thomas Harris Recollections, quoted in Moore, "The Treason of Charles Lee," in *Lee Papers* 4:389-90. These are the only reports of Lee firing a pistol, and do not seem credible.

80. W. Howe to H. Clinton, Dec. 21, 1776, Henry Clinton Papers 19:16, William L. Clements Library. This report confirms that Colonel Harcourt, at least, was wearing his regiment's traditional tasseled helmet during the raid.

81. *Connecticut Courant*, Dec. 23, 1776.

82. B. Tarleton to J. Tarleton, Dec. 18, 1776, in Bass, *Green Dragoon*, 21; see also W. Howe to H. Clinton, Dec. 21, 1776, Henry Clinton Papers 19:16, William L. Clements Library ("upon threats of setting fire to" Widow White's Tavern, "General Lee made his appearance at the door"); Extract of a Letter from Verplanck's Point, Dec. 21, 1776,

in *New England Chronicle,* Jan. 9, 1777 ("the captain gave orders to set fire to the house").
83. B. Tarleton to J. Tarleton, Dec. 18, 1776, in Bass, *Green Dragon,* 21; quote from a letter from an English officer, in Scull, *The Evelyns in America,* 215 ("Mr. Gayault informed me that . . . . when he heard the firing of the Light Dragoons, he ran out hastily, and was taken prisoner").
84. René-Etienne Henry Vic Gaiault (or Gayault) de Boisbertrand Memorandum for the American Commissioners, Sept. 5, 1778, in Stevens (ed.), *Facsimiles* 23:1948.
85. William Bradford's Recollections of Lee's Capture, Diary Entry, Jan. 1, 1777, in Dexter (ed.), *Stiles Diary* 2:106; see also Extract of a Letter from Verplanck's Point, Dec. 21, 1776, in *New England Chronicle,* Jan. 9, 1777 ("They [the British] fired three times at the messenger, but missed him").
86. William Bradford's Recollections of Lee's Capture, Diary Entry, Jan. 1, 1777, in Dexter (ed.), *Stiles Diary* 2:106.
87. Ibid.
88. Alden, *General Charles Lee,* 158.
89. James Wilkinson's Recollections, in Wilkinson, *Memoirs* 1:106.
90. B. Tarleton to J. Tarleton, Dec. 18, 1776, in Bass, *Green Dragoon,* 22.
91. Diary Entry, Dec. 13, 1776, in Muenchhausen, *At General Howe's Side,* 7. Another account of this episode is as follows: "Colonel Harcourt met a Yorkshireman, who was acquainted with the country, and had him for a guide. He ordered the Frenchman to get up behind him, but he being not so alert as the Yorkshireman wished, he struck him on the head with his pistol, which so offended him, that he has not been in temper since; the indignity of being struck by a peasant is too mortifying for him, yet this fellow in his own country had not the rank of a gentleman." Extract of an Authentic Letter from an Officer at New York, Dec. 21, 1776, in *Morning Chronicle and London Advertiser,* Feb. 27, 1777. The historian G. D. Scull quotes this report word for word; he likely obtained it from the prior newspaper report. Scull, *The Evelyns in America,* 215. The British officer's statement that Boisbertrand was not a gentleman in France was not accurate.
92. *Providence Gazette,* Dec. 28, 1776.
93. Eliza Quincy Recollections, in Quincy, *Memoir,* 25. Eliza's father was John Morton.
94. British sources stated that at least two and as many as five American soldiers were killed in the raid. W. Howe to H. Clinton, Dec. 21, 1776, Henry Clinton Papers 19:16, William L. Clements Library (patriot losses were a French officer "much wounded, and three or four more killed or wounded"); Diary Entry, Dec. 13, 1776, in Lydenberg (ed.), *Robertson Diary,* 116 ("four or five were killed"); Diary Entry, Dec. 17, 1776, in Kemble, "Journal," *N.Y. Hist. Soc. Coll.* 103 (1884) (two killed); Letter from an Officer of the 6th Regiment, in *St. James's Chronicle or the British Evening Post,* March 1-4, 1777 (London) ("killed two sentinels"); Extract of an Authentic Letter from an Officer at New York, Dec. 21, 1776, in *Morning Chronicle and London Advertiser,* Feb. 27, 1777 ("the two sentinels were killed, with several others"); Diary Entry, Dec. 13, 1776, in Laughton (ed.), "Journals of Henry Duncan," *Naval Miscellany,* 137 ("killed two or three"). The best American source on the number of killed was from the 1842 recollections of an elderly lady who had resided in Basking Ridge at the time of the raid. She recalled that two American guardsmen were mangled horribly and died by British swords. See her quote in the next note. Several of the contemporary reports indicated that one of Lee's aides was wounded, but do not name him. See, e.g., Extract of a Letter from Verplanck's Point, Dec. 21, 1776, in *New England Chronicle,* Jan. 9, 1777. The wounded aide was William Bradford, but the wound must not have been too serious. After Harcourt's party departed, Bradford jumped on a horse and rode to tell Sullivan the news, and afterwards joined his old Rhode Island regiment. A sergeant of that regiment wrote in

his diary the same day that "Mr. William Bradford came to us wounded and informed that General Lee and a French colonel were taken prisoner by about 60 or 70 of the Light Dragoons and carried off." Diary Entry, Dec. 14 [should be 13], 1776, in Rau (ed.), "Sergeant John Smith's Diary," *Mississippi Valley Hist. Review* 20:1, 264-64 (1933). For Boisbertrand's wounds, see text accompanying note 84 above.

95. Quoted in Barber and Howe, *Historical Collections of New Jersey*, 444, n. The authors Barber and Howe stated that the villager who made the recollection was "A respectable elderly lady, now a resident of Basking Ridge, (July, 1842)." According to Barber and Howe, she wrote that "two of the guard retreated about 40 rods in a northwesterly direction. They were pursued, overtaken, and refusing to surrender, were killed. The cavalry, from fear of alarming the American troops in the vicinity, by the report of the their fire-arms, used their sabers only, and hacked them so terribly that it was found very difficult to remove their bodies to the graveyard, and they were put in boxes and interred in the field where they lay."

96. B. Tarleton to J. Tarleton, Dec. 18, 1776, in Bass, *Green Dragoon*, 22.

97. Ibid.

98. *Freeman's Journal* (Portsmouth, New Hampshire), Jan. 7, 1777 (with a dateline of Providence, December 28). The author of this account went on to state that one of the British dragoons was killed and another was wounded. Neither claim is credible. This account may have derived from a second-hand source who had heard reports from William Bradford, who was visiting Rhode Island around this time.

99. See *Morning Post* (London), June 4, 1776.

100. B. Tarleton to J. Tarleton, Dec. 18, 1776, in Bass, *Green Dragoon*, 22.

101. This story was told to Captain Thomas Rodney of Delaware by a doctor, when Rodney was travelling in the area near Hillsborough shortly after Lee's capture. Diary Entry, Jan. 18, 1777, in Rodney (ed.), *Rodney Diary*, 46-47. It is supported by a December 17 letter, written by Captain Sir James Baird and published in Britain, which stated that Harcourt on his return stopped at a village where two companies of the British 71st Regiment were stationed and dined with his fellow officers. Extract of a Letter from New York, Dec. 17, 1776, in *London Chronicle*, March 1-4, 1777, and *Scots Magazine* 39:80 (1777) (identifying the author as Baird); see also Diary Entry, Dec. 11, 1776, in Lydenberg (ed.), *Robertson Diary*, 116 ("71st Regiment at Brunswick and Hillsborough"). Major Moyney has not been identified.

102. B. Tarleton to J. Tarleton, Dec. 18, 1776, in Bass, *Green Dragoon*, 22; see also Diary Entry, Dec. 13, 1776, in Lydenberg (ed.), *Robertson Diary*, 116 (Harcourt's party "returned this evening to Pennington afer a march [ride] of near 60 miles").

103. Ibid.

104. J. Galloway to G. Galloway, Dec. 14, 1776, MSS L1999F527, Society of the Cincinnati.

105. W. Harcourt to Earl Harcourt, Dec. 19, 1776, in Scull, *Evelyns in America*, 227 and Harcourt (ed.), *Harcourt Papers* 11:182.

106. W. Harcourt to F. Geary, Dec. 18, 1776, in Force (ed.), *American Archives*, 5th Series, 3:1277. See also Diary Entry, Dec. 13, 1776, in Lydenberg (ed.), *Robertson Diary*, 116 ("Another patrol of an officer and eight [dragoons] this day went towards Flemington, the officer was killed"); Baule and Gilbert (eds.), *British Officers*, 72 (Geary killed in action at Flemington on December 14, 1776); Extract of a letter from New York, Jan. 8, 1777, in *St. James's Chronicle* (London), March 4, 1777. Geary's death and background are expanded upon under the subheading "Francis Geary (1752-1777)" in the Appendix.

107. Muster Rolls, 16th Light Dragoons, April 22, 1777, WO 12/1246, British National Archives. It is not known if Evans was killed in the same ambush that took Geary's life.

108. Quoted in Barber and Howe, *Historical Collections of New Jersey*, 444, n. (see note 95 above).
109. Eliza (Morton) Quincy Recollections, in Quincy, *Memoir*, 25.

CHAPTER THREE: A SEVERE BLOW TO THE CAUSE
1. John Howland Recollections, in Stone, *Life of Howland*, 64-65.
2. Diary Entry, Dec. 13, 1776, in Dawson (ed.), *How Diary*, 39. How continued, "We returned back after our army and overtook it in the evening at Germantown and encamped there." Id. See also J. Sullivan to G. Washington, Dec. 13, 1776, in Twohig (ed.), *Washington Papers* 7:328 ("I have taken every step to regain him, but almost despair of it"). Catherine Mundy, then five years old, recalled many years later that General Sullivan (as family tradition had it) and other officers quartered the night of December 12 in Bedminster at the home of her grandfather, Aaron Malick, called the "Old Stone House." Mundy remembered, "There was a great fuss made in the morning, because a big officer had been captured or killed, or something of that sort." Continuing, she stated, "quite a number of big officers stayed at Grandfather's, and an officer came in the forenoon and told of this officer being captured or killed." She further recalled that "Grandfather Malick had to go to Germantown with soldiers on horseback, and did not get home again until in the afternoon." Catherine Mundy Recollections, in Mellick, *Story of an Old Farm*, 337. Presumably, Aaron Malick guided the soldiers on horseback to Sullivan's camp; or he might have been the guide for the small party that chased after Harcourt's party.
3. James Wilkinson's Recollections, in Wilkinson, *Memoirs* 1:111.
4. Diary Entry, Dec. 14 [should be 13], 1776, in Rau (ed.), "Sergeant Smith's Diary," *Mississippi Valley Hist. Review* 20:1, 264-65 (1933).
5. Stephen Olney Recollections, in Williams, *Life of Barton*, 186.
6. S. Moylan to W. Heath, Dec. 15, 1776, in Force (ed.), *American Archives*, 5th Series, 3:1233.
7. J. Sullivan to W. Heath, undated [probably Dec. 15, 1776], in Hammond (ed.), *Sullivan Letters* 1:300-1. The author believes this letter was written on the 15th because Sullivan refers to receiving intelligence of a nearby British force "yesterday," which would have been the 14th.
8. Stephen Olney Recollections, in Williams, *Life of Barton*, 186; see also Diary Entries, Dec. 14-17 [should be 13-16], 1776, in Rau (ed.), "Sergeant Smith's Diary," *Mississippi Valley Hist. Review* 20:1, 264-65 (1933).
9. J. Sullivan to W. Heath, Dec. 14, 1776, in Hammond (ed.), *Sullivan Letters* 1:304.
10. John Howland Recollections, in Stone, *Life of Howland*, 66.
11. Diary Entry, Dec. 14 [should be 13], 1776, in Rau (ed.), "Sergeant John Smith's Diary," *Mississippi Valley Hist. Review* 20:1, 264-65 (1933).
12. Ibid.
13. James Wilkinson's Recollections, in Wilkinson, *Memoirs* 1:111-12.
14. J. Sullivan to G. Washington, Dec. 13, 1776, in Twohig (ed.), *Washington Papers* 7:328.
15. G. Washington to L. Washington, Dec. 10-17, 1776, in ibid., 290.
16. G. Washington to J. Hancock, Dec. 15, 1776, in ibid., 344. This letter was read before Congress in Baltimore on December 20. Ford (ed.), *Journals of the Cont. Congress* 6:1028-29.
17. J. Hancock to G. Washington, Dec. 23, 1776, in Smith (ed.), *Letters of Delegates* 5:643.
18. J. Hancock to R. Morris, Dec. 23, 1776, in ibid., 642.
19. N. Greene to Ca. Greene, Dec. 16, 1776, in Showman (ed.), *Greene Papers* 1:368 and N. Greene to Ch. Greene, Jan. 20, 1777, in id., 2:8.

20. John Trumbull, Jr., to Jon. Trumbull, Dec. 16, 1776, in Force (ed.), *American Archives*, 5th Series, 3:1247. Naturally, Widow White's Tavern became a place of comment for passers-by. Shortly after Lee's capture, Major Joseph Bloomfield of the New Jersey Continentals wrote in his journal, "lodged at Mrs. White's in Basking Ridge, the house where General Lee was lately taken prisoner by a party of light horse." Diary Entry, Jan. 11, 1777, in Lender and Martin (eds.), *Bloomfield Journal*, 121. In August 1777, the surveyor general of the Continental Post Office, Ebenezer Hazard, during a tour of New Jersey, recorded in his journal, "I forgot to mention the 7th instant that I saw the house in which General Lee was taken. I should never have expected to find a General there." E. Hazard Diary Entry, Aug. 12, 1777, in Gerlach (ed.), *New Jersey in the A.R.*, 301.
21. Diary Entry, Dec. 20, 1776, in Thacher, *Journal*, 66-67.
22. *New England Chronicle*, March 13, 1777.
23. W. Whipple to J. Bartlett, Dec. 23, 1776, in Mervers (ed.), *Bartlett Papers*, 140.
24. John Howland Recollections, in Stone, *Life of Howland*, 65.
25. Diary Entry, Dec. 22, 1776, in Rodney (ed.), *Rodney Diary*, 19.
26. N. Greene to C. Greene, Jan. 20, 1777, in Showman (ed.), *Greene Papers* 2:8.
27. S. Webb to Jos. Trumbull, Dec. 16, 1776, in Ford (ed.), *Webb Correspondence* 1:174.
28. Ramsay, *History of the Am. Rev.* 2:294.
29. E. Gerry to J. Warren, Dec. 23, 1776, in Smith (ed.), *Letters of Delegates* 5:641. Historian Jared Sparks wrote in 1846, "How was it possible, it was asked, for a man of his experience and ability to place himself in a situation, where he could be seized by a handful of British dragoons, without even a show of resistance, unless he had previously resolved to become a voluntary captive and had secretly concerted measures to this end with the enemy? In the vexation of a bitter disappointment, this suspicion, perhaps, was natural; but it was utterly unfounded. All the testimony confirms that, up to the time of his capture, he was faithfully and assiduously devoted to the cause he had espoused." Sparks, *Life of Charles Lee*, 149. For the record, the author does not believe any argument that Lee wanted to be captured is credible.
30. J. Sullivan to G. Washington, Dec. 13, 1776, in Twohig (ed.), *Washington Papers* 7:328.
31. H. Lee to G. Washington, Jan. 20, 1778, in ibid., 13:292.
32. Bass, *Green Dragoon*, 38.
33. George Hanger Recollections, in Hanger, *An Address to the Army*, 88, n.
34. For a detailed description of this incident, see Hartmann, *American Partisan*, 57-59; for other secondary sources, see Bass, *Green Dragoon*, 38 and Cecere, *Wedded to My Sword*, 68-71. For contemporary sources, see J. Ewald Diary Entry, Jan. 23, 1778, in Tustin (ed.), *Diary of the American War*, 121 (Crewe's party was eighty men); Diary Entries, Jan. 19-20, 1778, in Muenchhausen, *At General Howe's Side*, 47 (Crewe's party was forty men); H. Lee to G. Washington, Jan. 20, 1778 (two letters), in Twohig (ed.), *Washington Papers* 13:292 and 293-94; Washington's General Orders, Jan. 20, 1778, quoted in id., n., 293; G. Washington to H. Lee, Jan. 20, 1778, in id., 294; *New Jersey Gazette*, Jan. 28, 1778, quoted in Moore (ed.), *Diary of the A.R.* 2:10; and Hanger, *An Address to the Army*, 88, n. The author thanks Dr. Dennis Conrad for bringing this incident to his attention. Henry Lee mistakenly thought the attackers numbered 200 men. H. Lee to G. Washington, Jan. 20, 1778, in Twohig (ed.), *Washington Papers* 13:292. Crew's detachment did capture four of Lee's men who were on patrol. Id. It should be pointed out that the stone house occupied by Henry Lee offered a better defense against carbine fire and the threat of burning than the wooden Widow White's Tavern. For a discussion of the current location of the stone house and the failure to find authority that it was ever named the Spread Eagle Tavern, as some secondary sources state, see Baskin, "Banecdotes: the Tarleton Nursery School . . . and Tavern?," www.home.golden.net/marg/bansite/banecdotes.77nursery school.

35. Jos. Trumbull to Jon. Trumbull, Dec. 17, 1776, in Force (ed.), *American Archives*, 5th Series, 3:1265.
36. *Connecticut Courant* (Hartford), Dec. 23, 1776; also quoted in Force (ed.), *American Archives*, 5th Series, 3:1202 and Moore, *Diary of the Revolution* 1:361.
37. William Bradford's Recollections, in Diary Entry, Jan. 1, 1777, in Dexter (ed.), *Stiles Diary* 2:105-7.
38. A. Stephen to T. Jefferson, Dec. [about 20], 1776, in Boyd (ed.), *Papers of Jefferson* 1:659. Along a similar vein, Lieutenant Joseph Hodgkins of the 12th Continental Regiment from Massachusetts, who marched in Lee's division, informed his wife, "I will tell you that General Lee was invited by a gentleman to put up with him that night and whether that man or another informed the enemy, I can't say." J. Hodgkins to S. Hodgkins, Dec. 20, 1776, in Wade and Lively (eds.), *This Glorious Cause*, 228.
39. See Griffin, *Stephen Moylan*, 79; Bernard, *Retrospections of America*, 60-61.
40. Stockton was appointed captain of the New Jersey Volunteers in August of 1776, and became major on December 3 or 10, 1776. Dornfest, *Military Loyalists of the A.R.*, 326. Stockton was not released from his imprisonment until about September 1, 1779. In 1780, he was convicted of murder on British-held Long Island and sentenced to death, but was not executed. He later moved to Canada and died in St. John, New Brunswick. Id.; Sabine, *Biographical Sketches of Loyalists*, 334-35. Stockton is sometimes misidentified as Richard V. Stockton. Sabine, *Biographical Sketches of Loyalists*, 334-35.
41. H. Hughes to Joshua Huntington, March 2, 1777, in "Huntington Papers," *Connecticut Hist. Soc. Coll.* 20:53 (1923).
42. Extract of a Letter from an Officer at Morristown, Feb. 21, 1777, in *New England Chronicle*, March 6, 1777.
43. Extract of a Letter from Unidentified Writer, March 24, 1777, Philadelphia, in *Scots Magazine* 39:248 (1777). Washington disapproved of Stockton's treatment since he was a military officer. See Sabine, *Biographical Sketches of Loyalists*, 335.
44. Jones, *Loyalists of New Jersey*, 212.
45. Lee's biographer, John Alden, did not believe Stockton was a guide for Harcourt's party. Alden, *General Charles Lee*, 332-33, n. 21.
46. Asher Dunham Loyalist Claim, quoted from The On-Line Institute for Advanced Loyalist Studies, at www.royalprovincial.com (citing AO 13/21, folios 154-55, PRO, British National Archives).
47. Ibid. Stockton, Dunham, and six other captive officers of the New Jersey Volunteers were eventually brought to Carlisle, Pennsylvania, and placed in the jail there. Stockton, Dunham, and the other six officers signed a letter submitted to the Continental Congress asking to be relieved of the dreadful conditions in the Carlisle jail. It read, in part: "We crave leave to observe to your honors that this prison is perhaps the worst on the continent, being rather a ruin than a gaol. Every part of it distributes air as through the holes of a colander, affecting the body with strange sensations and destroying our health. While at the same time we have to glass in the windows, seven of us are obliged to sleep in one room without anything but one blanket each." R. Stockton, A. Dunham, et al., to Continental Congress, Oct. 1777, in Papers of the Continental Congress, m247, r100, i78, vol. 18, p. 117, National Archives Building. Dunham was finally exchanged on August 26, 1778. J. Loring certification, in Asher Dunham Loyalist Claim, quoted from The On-Line Institute for Advanced Loyalist Studies, at www.royalprovincial.com (citing AO 13/21, folio 151, PRO, British National Archives). He was, with other Morris County men, declared to have "joined the enemy against their country" and had his property in Morris County confiscated by local authorities. *New Jersey Gazette*, Dec. 16, 1778. See also Dornfest, *Military Loyalists of the A.R.*, 108-9.
48. Diary Entry, Jan. 18, 1777, in Rodney (ed.), *Rodney Diary*, 46-47.
49. G. Washington to L. Washington, Dec. 10-17, 1776, in Twohig (ed.), *Washington Papers* 7:290.

50. Diary Entry, Dec. 20, 1776, in Thacher, *Journal*, 66.
51. W. Shippen to R. H. Lee, Dec. 17, 1776, in Force (ed.), *American Archives*, 5th Series, 3:1258.
52. Council of Safety Minutes, Aug. 29, 1777, in *Minutes of the Council of Safety of NJ*, 126. Compton and two other accused Tories were given the choice of "entering on board the vessels of war of the United States of America" or being tried "for their lives agreeably to the law." Id. The men chose the latter course, the results of which the author is not aware. Council of Safety Minutes, Aug. 30, 1777, in id., 127. A James Compton, born in 1750 in Somerset County, New Jersey, whose father of the same name died in Basking Ridge in 1783, is reported to have died on July 28, 1813, in Bernards Township, Somerset County, New Jersey. See Davis Family Genealogy at www.davistree.info (search for James Compton). This man was probably the same James Compton discussed in this note.
53. S. Webb to Jos. Trumbull, Dec. 16, 1776, in Ford (ed.), *Webb Correspondence* 1:174.
54. Elias Boudinot Recollections, in Boudinot, *Journal*, 73.
55. Diary Entry, Aug. 28, 1781, in Acomb (ed.), *Journal of von Closen*, 114. Closen called Widow White's Tavern "Bullion Tavern" and its proprietor "Mademoiselle Bullion," and complained about "a rather mediocre dish" he ate there. Id. Bullion's Tavern was located south of Basking Ridge at Liberty Corner. Accordingly, Closen possibly never made it to Basking Ridge and Widow White's Tavern. Alternatively, he may have visited Widow White's Tavern but misidentified it as Bullion's Tavern.
56. W. Ellery to N. Cooke, Dec. 25, 1776, in Smith (ed.), *Letters of Delegates* 5:653-54.
57. Extract of a letter from unidentified source, Dec. 24, 1776, Lower-Makefield, Pennsylvania, quoted in *Connecticut Gazette*, Jan. 24, 1777; also quoted in Moore, *Diary of the Revolution* 1:360-61 (stating that the story was first printed in Philadelphia and later copied in many American newspapers).
58. Warren, *History . . . of the Am. Rev.* 1:183. Many who wrote of Lee's capture mentioned his being carried off without his hat or coat. See, e.g., Diary Entry, Dec. 20, 1776, in Thacher, *Journal*, 66-67; Jos. Trumbull to Jon. Trumbull, Dec. 17, 1776, in Force (ed.), *American Archives*, 5th Series, 3:1265.
59. G. Washington to L. Washington, Dec. 10-17, 1776, in Twohig (ed.), *Washington Papers* 7:290.
60. John Trumbull, Jr., to Jon. Trumbull, Dec. 16, 1776, in Force (ed.), *American Archives*, 5th Series, 3:1247.
61. James Wilkinson Recollections, in Wilkinson, *Memoirs* 1:106.
62. William Bradford's Recollections, in Diary Entry, Jan. 1, 1777, in Dexter (ed.), *Stiles Diary* 2:106.
63. Diary Entry, Dec. 13, 1776, in Laughton (ed.), "Journals of Henry Duncan," *Naval Miscellany*, 137.
64. Extract of a letter from Verplanck's Point, Dec. 21, 1776, in *New England Chronicle*, Jan. 9, 1777.
65. J. Robertson to H. Clinton, Dec. 19, 1776, Henry Clinton Papers 19:13, William L. Clements Library.
66. Diary Entry, Jan. 1777, in "Martin Hunter's Journal," *Valley Forge Journal* 4:1, 19 (June 1988).
67. See, e.g., J. Sullivan to G. Washington, Dec. 13, 1776, in Twohig (ed.), *Washington Papers* 7:328; R. H. Lee to Commissioners in France, Dec. 21, 1776, in Ballagh (ed.), *Richard H. Lee Letters* 1:231; W. Ellery to N. Cooke, Dec. 25, 1776, in Smith (ed.), *Letters of Delegates* 5:653.
68. Diary Entry, Dec. 14 [should be 13], 1776, in Rau (ed.), "Sergeant John Smith's Diary," *Mississippi Valley Hist. Review* 20:1, 264-65 (1933) ("Mr. William Bradford came to us wounded and informed that General Lee and a French colonel were taken

prisoner by about 60 or 70 of the Light Dragoons"); J. Sullivan to G. Washington, Dec. 13, 1776, in Twohig (ed.), *Washington Papers* 7:328 (informed Washington that a party of seventy dragoons surrounded Widow White's Tavern).
69. William Bradford Recollections, in Diary Entry, Jan. 1, 1777, in Dexter (ed.), *Stiles Diary* 2:106.
70. Diary Entry, Dec. 13, 1776, in Muenchhausen, *At General Howe's Side*, 7.
71. Letter from New York, from the Lady of a Captain of the 71st Regiment, Dec. 18, 1776, in *Scots Magazine* 39:80 (1777).
72. Extract of a Letter from New York, Dec. 27, 1776, in *London Chronicle*, March 1-4, 1777.
73. W. Harcourt to L. Nuneham, Dec. 17, 1776, in Scull, *The Evelyns in America*, 226 and Harcourt (ed.), *Harcourt Papers* 11:180. A short biography of then-General Harcourt, in 1820, stated that his capture of Lee "occasioned such consternation in the army of the enemy, and such exultation in that of the British, that for some time it was believed it would have decided the fate of the war." *Royal Military Calendar* 1:281.
74. Willcox, *Portrait of a General*, 126 (citing Clinton's personal notebook).
75. Extract of a Letter from on Board the *Diamond*, Capt. Fielding, dated Rhode Island, Jan. 8, 1777, in *London Chronicle*, Feb. 20, 1777, and *St. James's Chronicle or the British Evening Post* (London), Feb. 22, 1777.
76. General William Howe's General Orders, quoted in Harcourt (ed.), *Harcourt Papers* 11:183.
77. Extract of a Letter from New York, Dec. 27, 1776, in *London Chronicle*, March 1-4, 1777.
78. Quoted in Burrows, *Forgotten Patriots*, 71.
79. Extract of a Letter from New York, Dec. 27, 1776, in *London Chronicle*, March 1-4, 1777.
80. Extract of a Letter from an Officer of the 64th Regiment, in York Island, to his Friend in London, Dec. 30, 1776, New York, in Force (ed.), *American Archives*, 5th Series, 3:1294.
81. Extract of a letter from an Officer to his Friend at Edinburgh, dated Newport, Rhode Island, Jan. 5, 1777, in *Edinburgh Advertiser*, Feb. 22, 1777, and *St. James Chronicle or the British Evening Post* (London), Feb. 22, 1777.
82. Letter from "E. B.," an unnamed volunteer officer of the 6th Regiment, undated (probably around mid-January 1777), in *St. James's Chronicle or the British Evening Post* (London), March 4, 1777.
83. W. Howe to H. Clinton, Dec. 21, 1776, Henry Clinton Papers 19:16, William L. Clements Library.
84. Diary Entry, Dec. 13, 1776, in Muenchhausen, *At General Howe's Side*, 7; Diary Entry, Dec. 17, 1776, in Kemble, "Journal," *N.Y. Hist. Soc. Coll.* 103 (1883).
85. Thomas Harris Recollections, quoted in Moore, "The Treason of Charles Lee," in *Lee Papers* 4:389-90; see also Extract of an Authentic Letter from an Officer at New York, Dec. 21, 1776, in *Morning Chronicle and London Advertiser*, Feb. 27, 1777 ("Lee's behavior was dastardly to the last; he begged for quarter, and hoped his life would be spared; Col. Harcourt told him he should be well used").
86. Extract of a letter from an Officer to his Friend at Edinburgh, dated Newport, Rhode Island, Jan. 5, 1777, *Edinburgh Advertiser* and *St. James Chronicle or the British Evening Post* (London), Feb. 22, 1777; see also Extract of a Letter from New York, Dec. 27, in *London Chronicle*, March 1-4, 1777; Letter from "E. B.," an unnamed volunteer officer of the 6th Regiment, undated (probably around mid-January 1777), in *St. James's Chronicle or the British Evening Post* (London), March 4, 1777.
87. *New York Gazette*, Dec. 23, 1776, quoted in Force (ed.), *American Archives*, 5th Series, 3:1377.

88. William Bradford's Recollections, in Diary Entry, Jan. 1, 1777, in Dexter (ed.), *Stiles Diary* 2:106.
89. Ibid.
90. J. Galloway to G. Galloway, Dec. 14, 1776, MSS L1999F527, Library of The Society of the Cincinnati.
91. *General Evening Post* (London), Feb. 11-13, 1777; *Morning Post and Daily Advertiser* (London), Feb. 13, 1777.
92. Unidentified London newspaper, with dateline of Feb. 26, 1777, quoted in *Pennsylvania Evening Post,* July 10, 1777. General Richard Montgomery had been killed leading the assault on Quebec in December 1775.
93. *Annual Register . . . for the Year 1777,* 7.
94. *Morning Chronicle and London Advertiser,* Feb. 21, 1777.
95. Extract of a letter from on board the *Diamond,* Capt. Fielding, dated Rhode Island, Jan. 8, 1777, in *London Chronicle,* Feb. 20, 1777, and *St. James's Chronicle or the British Evening Post* (London), Feb. 22, 1777. As the prior letter indicates, British newspapers sometimes received letters written by British officers from America that contained inaccurate information. The following letter was written by Captain Thomas Stanley of the 17th Dragoons on December 23, 1776, from Spanktown, New Jersey. Despite the fact that Stanley was writing from New Jersey, that the letter was close to the date of Lee's capture, and that Stanley and Harcourt served in the only two cavalry regiments in the British army in North America, Stanley got almost every relevant fact wrong: "He [Lieutenant Colonel Harcourt] was sent out about eight days ago towards Morristown in Morris County. On the road at a turning he met a man on horseback, who when he saw the dragoons, wished to avoid them. Harcourt seeing his confusion, galloped up to him, knew he was a Rebel, and that he would recognize him. The man in his fright acknowledged himself to be one of their light horse and that he was sent with dispatches by General Lee to General Sullivan. Harcourt asked him where General Lee was and told him he would give him fifty guineas if he would conduct him to the place. The man refused the money but said that if Colonel Harcourt would give him his pardon, he would conduct him so that he might take Lee. The bargain was soon made, and the man immediately conducted him to a tavern at Baskenridge, where he said he believed Lee was there at dinner. The dragoons immediately surrounded the house. By this time Lee's guard, which consisted of about twenty-eight men, took the alarm and began to fire upon the dragoons from the house, but luckily the first shot that was fired by the dragoons took place and killed the man who seemed to be their head, which disheartened them so much, that they fired only at random afterwards. Harcourt dismounted with Lt. [Thomas] Leigh of the regiment and his dragoons and rushed into the room where Lee was at dinner with two French officers, one of them his aide [Virnejoux] and the other called himself Lt. [Boisbertrand], and seized him by the collar. The aide [Virnejoux] attempted to assist, and raised his pistol, upon which Lt. Leigh of the regiment very coolly stepped up and shot him through the head. They then obliged Lee to run on foot aside of Harcourt's horse, who held him by the collar for the ride, till they were safe and could provide him with a horse, and so they brought him off to the army. About a [quarter?] mile from the house where he was taken, the whole army consisting of about eight thousand men and 15 pieces of cannon were encamped. Colonel Harcourt had but forty men with him. What a fine feather it will be in his cap." T. Stanley to unidentified British officer serving in Europe, Dec. 23, 1777, Ms. Am. 228, Rare Books and Manuscripts, Boston Public Library.
96. *Morning Post and Daily Advertiser* (London), Feb. 13, 1777.
97. Ibid., Feb. 17, 1777. According to one report, when General Lee was brought into the British camp, "he demanded to be received under the proclamation; but on being refused the benefit thereof, and told that he would be tried as a deserter, he flew into a

most unbounded rage, and exclaimed against the repeated acts of false faith and treachery which had reduced him to his present situation." Quoted in Scull, *The Evelyns in America,* 215-16. Lee's most accurate biographer, John Alden, gave no credence to this report, calling it "preposterous." Alden, *General Charles Lee,* 333, n.23. The author agrees.

98. *Morning Post and Daily Advertiser* (London), Feb. 17, 1777.

99. *Morning Chronicle and London Advertiser,* Feb. 21, 1777.

100. On December 19, 1776, from British headquarters in New York City, Major General James Robertson wrote Lieutenant General Henry Clinton a letter discussing Lee's recent capture and imprisonment. J. Robertson to H. Clinton, Dec. 19, 1776, Henry Clinton Papers 19:13, William L. Clements Library. In this letter Robertson reported that Lee "is now at Brunswick" under guard, and added the following: "I have read his letter to Primrose Kennedy. I cannot give you verbatim, but the sense is: The amazing alertness of Col. Harcourt and the poltroonery of my guard . . . ." Robertson then provided the rest of the quote. Thus, it appears that Lee did write a letter to his friend Captain Kennedy, who was ill in England, and that General Robertson, based in New York City, had the opportunity to review this letter prior to its delivery. Given that Robertson said he could only provide the "sense" of Lee's letter, and that his "sense" was quoted almost verbatim by the *Morning Chronicle and London Advertiser,* it appears that this London newspaper received the copy of Lee's letter from Robertson's letter. The author believes this story is credible and, furthermore, that the language used in Lee's letter is consistent with his writing style. As to the letter imitating a speech by Caractacus, Lee was well schooled in Roman antiquity. The original of the letter has not survived. The author believes that a copy of Robertson's letter was passed on by a passenger on board the HMS *Experiment,* which arrived in England on February 12, to a London newspaper editor. The *Experiment* participated in the capture of Newport, Rhode Island, on December 8, anchored in Narragansett Bay for a few weeks, left for Lower New York Bay, and from there, in mid-January, departed for England. Log of HMS *Experiment,* Nov. 29, 1776-Jan. 20, 1777, ADM 51/331, British National Archives. Thus, there was ample opportunity for Robertson to have mail delivered to the *Experiment* at Narragansett Bay or Lower New York Bay prior to its departure for England. It could not have been Clinton who carried the letter. At the time, after commanding the expeditionary force that captured Newport on December 8, 1776, Clinton departed for London on a British frigate on January 12. General H. Clinton Orders, Jan. 12, 1777, in Hagist, *General Orders, Rhode Island,* 22. He arrived in England on February 28, more than a week after Lee's letter to Kennedy had been published in the *Morning Chronicle and London Advertiser* newspaper. For Kennedy being in England sick in December of 1776, see W. Howe to P. Kennedy, Dec. 3, 1776, cited in Conway, "British Army Officers and the American War for Independence," *William and Mary Quarterly,* 3rd Series, 41:2, 270 (April 1984).

101. J. Robertson to H. Clinton, Dec. 19, 1776, Henry Clinton Papers 19:13, William L. Clements Library (Lee "is now at Brunswick and the Judge Advocate tells me he is ordered thither").

102. Alden, *General Charles Lee,* 165.

103. W. Howe to G. Germain, Dec. 20, 1776, New York, in Davies (ed.), *Documents of the A.R.* 12:269. In a letter to General Clinton, Howe was even more direct: "As I look upon him [Lee] in the light of a deserter from the service [the British army], he is kept a close prisoner at Brunswick, where Major General Grant now commands." W. Howe to H. Clinton, Dec. 21, 1776, Henry Clinton Papers 19:16, William L. Clements Library.

104. Minutes of Cabinet, Feb. 25, 1777, in Barnes and Owen (eds.), *The Private Papers of John Montagu, Earl of Sandwich* 1:285.

105. G. Germain to W. Howe, March 3, 1777, Davies (ed.), *Documents of the A.R.* 14:48.
106. W. Howe to G. Germain, Dec. 20, 1776, in ibid., 12:267.
107. *Morning Post and Daily Advertiser* (London), Feb. 13, 1777.
108. The English historian G. D. Scull wrote about a similar exchange. See *The Evelyns in America*, 218. Scull most likely obtained the quote from the March 1, 1777, edition of the *London Evening Post.*
109. G. Germain to W. Lee, March 3, 1777, CO 5/94, British National Archives.
110. W. Howe to G. Germain, Dec. 20, 1776, in Davies (ed.), *Documents of the A.R.* 12:268; Diary Entry, Dec. 14, 1776, in Muenchhausen, *At General Howe's Side*, 7; see also J. Robertson to H. Clinton, Dec. 19, 1776, Henry Clinton Papers 19:13, William L. Clements Library ("Lord Cornwallis and afterwards General Howe have marched through Jersey to the banks of the Delaware, which they have no means of passing").
111. W. Howe to H. Clinton, Dec. 21, 1776, Henry Clinton Papers 19:16, William L. Clements Library.
112. W. Howe to G. Germain, Dec. 20, 1776, in Davies (ed.), *Documents of the A.R.* 12:269.
113. Diary Entries, Dec. 14-16, 1776, in Dawson (ed.), *How Diary*, 39-40 ("crossed at Philipsburg to Easton on October 15 and spent next day helping baggage be ferried across the river"); Rau, "Sergeant Smith's Diary," *Mississippi Valley Hist. Review* 20:1, 264-67 (1933) (crossed to Easton on Dec. 16); John Howland Recollections, in Stone, *Life of Howland*, 66-68 (same); Jacob Francis Revolutionary War Pension Application, in Dann (ed.), *The Revolution Remembered*, 394 (with Sullivan's division; after Lee's capture, marched "to the Delaware and crossed over to Easton"); see also sources in next footnote. For the Delaware River being 500 yards wide at this point and swift moving, see Diary Entry, Jan. 15, 1779, in Benians (ed.), *Hughes Journal*, 62.
114. W. Shippen to R. H. Lee, Dec. 17, 1776, in Force (ed.), *American Archives*, 5th Series, 3:1248 ("in good spirits" quote); Bethlehem Moravian Church Diary, Dec. 17, 1776, quoted in Dwyer, *The Day is Ours!*, 205 ("towards evening some three or four thousand men [under General Sullivan] arrived and went into camp"); Diary Entry, Dec. 17, 1776, in Dawson (ed.), *How Diary*, 40 ("This morning we set out and marched 12 miles to Bethlehem and stayed in the woods there"). Dwyer's *The Day is Ours!* provides many details from the journals and letters of ordinary soldiers participating in the New Jersey and Pennsylvania campaign of 1776.
115. See David Avery Diary, Dec. 15-17, 1776, quoted in Dwyer, *The Day is Ours!*, 203 (Avery crossed with the main body of Gates's troops on the 15th, spending the night at Mount Bethel, in Northampton County; on the 16th, "marched to Nazareth, about 13 miles, a town of Moravians"; and on the 17th, "proceeded and came to Bethlehem, about nine miles"); Nazareth Moravian Church Diary, Dec. 16, 1776, quoted in id. ("In the afternoon, the New England troops arrived and were distributed in the town. . . . They were quiet and orderly, having received strict orders to that effect"); John Trumbull, Jr. to Jon. Trumbull, Dec. 16, 1776, in Force (ed.), *American Archives*, 5th Series, 3:1246 ("I arrived at this place [Bethlehem, Pennsylvania] last evening, with General Gates. A part of our troops will come in today, and the others tomorrow"); H. Gates to G. Washington, Dec. 17, 1776 in Twohig (ed.), *Washington Papers* 7:361 (Gates and Arnold still in Bethlehem).
116. W. Stirling to W. Heath, Dec. 16, 1776, William Heath Papers, microfilm reel 8, Mass. Historical Soc.
117. See G. Washington to R. Morris, Dec. 22, 1776, in Twohig (ed.), *Washington Papers* 7:412 ("General Gates is here, and a small division under him of about 600 is expected today"); J. Sullivan to J. Hancock, Dec. 22, 1776, in Hammond (ed.), *Sullivan Letters* 1:305 (Sullivan writing from Buck's County); Diary Entries, Dec. 17-21, 1776,

in Rau (ed.), "Sergeant Smith's Diary," *Mississippi Valley Hist. Review* 20:1, 265-67 (1933); Diary Entries, Dec. 17-23, in Dawson (ed.), *How Diary*, 40; John Howland Recollections, in Stone, *Life of Howland*, 66-68 (crossed the Lehigh River using a "rope ferry"). Lieutenant Joseph Hodgkins of the 12th Continental Regiment wrote to his wife Sarah on December 20 from Buckingham Township, Pennsylvania, "we have been on the march ever since ye 29th of last month and we are now within 10 or 12 miles of General Washington's army. We expect to be there tonight." J. Hodgkins to S. Hodgkins, Dec. 20, 1776, in Wade and Lively, *This Glorious Cause*, 227.

118. Of course, a number of excellent books have focused on Washington's victories at Trenton and Princeton and their importance, such as David Hackett Fischer's *Washington's Crossing* (Oxford University Press, 2004); Richard M. Ketchum's *The Winter Soldiers: The Battles for Trenton and Princeton* (Holt, 1973 and 1999); Thomas Fleming's *1776: Year of Illusions* (W. W. Norton, 1975); and David McCullough's *1776* (Simon and Schuster, 2005). For casualties at Trenton, see Fischer, *Washington's Crossing*, Appendix N, 405-6.

119. Reed, "General Joseph Reed's Narrative," *Penn. Mag. of History and Biography*, 8:393 (1884). Cadwalader's force at this juncture probably consisted of his entire division (the 11th Continental Regiment and 9th Continental Regiment from Rhode Island, the 4th Continental Regiment from Massachusetts, and Rhode Island state troops under Colonel Lippitt, with an aggregate effective strength of about 880 men), and Philadelphia Associators and other militia (with an effective strength of about 1,000 men). See Stryker, *Battles of Trenton and Princeton*, 345-46.

120. Diary Entry, Dec. 31, 1776, in Rodney (ed.), *Rodney Diary*, 28-29; see also Reed, "General Joseph Reed's Narrative," *Penn. Mag. of History and Biography* 8:400 (1884) ("taking the enemy in an unguarded and unexpected point, capturing their whole baggage, and releasing General Lee then a prisoner at Brunswick were offered as reasons for the march" to Brunswick, but that the "opinion failed and orders were sent to General Cadwalader on the last day of December to join the main body at Trenton as soon as possible").

121. L. Cliffe to B. Cliffe, Jan. 2, 1777, Loftus Cliffe Papers, folder 5, William L. Clements Library. For some unknown reason, Cliffe and other officers then at Brunswick blamed Lee for the loss of the Hessian troops at Trenton. Id.

122. Diary Entries, Jan. 1-4, 1777, Glyn Journal, Rare Books and Special Collections, Princeton University Library; see also Diary Entry, Jan. 3, 1777, in Lydenberg (ed.), *Robertson Diaries*, 120; Diary Entry, Jan. 1777, in "Martin Hunter's Journal," *Valley Forge Journal* 4:1, 20 (June 1988); James Wilkinson Recollections, in Wilkinson, *Memoirs* 1:149 (Colonel John Fitzgerald, visiting Brunswick around January 5, 1777, under a flag of truce, met with British officers, who spoke of their "forced march from Trenton to Brunswick—such was the alarm for the safety of their magazine").

123. Stedman, *History of the American War* 1:238; Stryker, *The Battles of Trenton and Princeton*, 299-303.

124. H. Knox to L. Knox, Jan. 7, 1777, quoted in Twohig et al. (eds.), *Washington Papers* 7:529-30, n. 10; see also James Wilkinson Recollections, in Wilkinson, *Memoirs* 1:148 ("[I]t was the desire of the commander-in-chief, and the inclination of every officer, to make a stroke at Brunswick, which had been left with a small garrison... but our physical force could not bear us out; the men had been under arms eighteen hours, and had suffered much from cold and hunger. The commander and several general officers halted at the forks of the road in Kingston, while our troops were filing off to Rocky Hill, when the exclamation was general, 'Oh! That we had 500 fresh men to beat up their quarters at Brunswick.' But the measure was found to be impracticable and we proceeded down the Millstone River, and halted at Somerset Court House."); John Howland Recollections, in Stone, *Life of Howland*, 76. ("We left Princeton about noon, and we

afterwards understood that the advanced guard of Cornwallis from Trenton, arrived at Princeton about half an hour after our rear left it. Our course was eastward, and Cornwallis naturally supposing we were bound to Brunswick, where was General Howe's headquarters, pushed on the same road after us till we arrived at a cross road bearing north towards Somerset, which we pursued. He did not choose to follow us, but kept on his way to Brunswick.")

125. For Washington's route after the Battle of Princeton, see map in Fischer, *Washington's Crossing*, 342; see also John Howland Recollections, in Stone, *Life of Howland*, 77; James Wilkinson Recollections, in Wilkinson, *Memoirs* 1:148-49.

126. Diary Entries, Jan. 3-4, 1777, in Lydenberg (ed.), *Robertson Diaries*, 120; Twohig et al. (eds.), *Washington Papers* 7:529-30, n. 10. Ensign Martin Hunter of the British 52nd Regiment wrote in his journal, "I never experienced such a disagreeable night's march in my life. It was as dark as possible, and a very cold hard frost, and the horses being tired, the guns got on so slowly that we did not arrive at Brunswick before ten the next morning." Diary Entry, Jan. 1777, in "Martin Hunter's Journal," *Valley Forge Journal* 4:1, 20 (June 1988).

127. Same sources as in note 124.

128. S. Moylan to R. Morris, Jan. 7, 1777, in Griffin, *Stephen Moylan*, 48.

129. Diary Entry, Jan. 7, in Macveagh (ed.), *Cresswell Journal*, 179-80.

130. W. Harcourt to Earl Harcourt, Jan. 13, 1777, in Scull, *The Evelyns in America*, 228-29 and Harcourt (ed.), *Harcourt Papers* 11:203.

131. John Howland Recollections, in Stone, *Life of Howland*, 69.

132. James Wilkinson Recollections, in Wilkinson, *Memoirs* 1:126-27.

133. Letter from a British officer to a London friend, in *London Packet*, March 3-5, 1777.

134. Extract of a Letter from Nantz, March 10, 1777, in *Pennsylvania Evening Post*, May 17, 1777.

135. Quoted in Moore, "The Treason of Charles Lee," in *Lee Papers* 4:402. For more on how lucky the Americans were that Lee was captured when he was, see Fleming, *1776, Year of Illusions*, 427-28.

136. Ibid., 402-3.

137. H. Winthrop to M. Warren, Jan. 14, 1777, in "Warren-Adams Letters," *Mass. Hist. Soc. Coll.* 72:1, 283 (1917).

138. W. Gordon to G. Washington, Jan. 6, 1777, in Twohig et al. (eds.), *Washington Papers* 8:1.

CHAPTER FOUR: A PRISONER OF HIGH VALUE

1. Scull, *The Evelyns in America*, 213 (defiant); Diary Entry, Dec. 14, 1776, in Muenchhausen, *At General Howe's Side*, 7 (impudent).

2. Extract of an Authentic Letter from an Officer at New York, Dec. 21, 1776, in *Morning Chronicle and London Advertiser*, Feb. 27, 1777.

3. Quoted in Wilkin, *Some British Soldiers in America*, 218.

4. J. Hancock to G. Washington, Jan. 6-7, 1777, in Twohig et al. (eds.), *Washington Papers* 8:3-4 (Hancock cited Lee's aide, Major Eustace, as the source for this exchange); see also Diary Entry, Dec. 14, 1776, in Muenchhausen, *At General Howe's Side*, 7; Scull, *The Evelyns in America*, 213-14 (Scull's version is consistent with the prior two contemporary reports).

5. Extract of an Authentic Letter from an Officer at New York, Dec. 21, 1776, in *Morning Chronicle and London Advertiser*, Feb. 27, 1777.

6. W. Harcourt to Lord Nuneham, March 18, 1777, in Harcourt (ed.), *Harcourt Papers* 11:211.

7. Diary Entry, Dec. 14, 1776, in Muenchhausen, *At General Howe's Side*, 7-8.

8. W. Howe to G. Germain, Dec. 20, 1776 (from New York), in Davies (ed.), *Documents of the A.R.* 12:269.
9. Ibid.
10. W. Howe to H. Clinton, Dec. 21, 1776, Henry Clinton Papers 19:16, William L. Clements Library.
11. J. Grant to P. Harvey, Dec. 26, 1776, quoted in Nelson, *James Grant*, 109 ("civil"); Extract of an Authentic Letter from an Officer at New York, Dec. 21, 1777, in *Morning Chronicle and London Advertiser*, Feb. 27, 1777 (request for money). See also Diary Entry, Feb. 16, 1777, in Uhlendorf (ed.), *Baurmeister Letters*, 83-84 ("Several days ago he [Washington] sent in a bank note, in the name of Congress, for the maintenance of General Lee, which, however, was promptly returned.")
12. Extract of an Authentic Letter from an Officer at New York, Dec. 21, 1777, in *Morning Chronicle and London Advertiser*, Feb. 27, 1777. The information in this paragraph, other than the quotes from Grant, was also quoted in Scull, *The Evelyns in America*, 213; Scull likely obtained the information from the letter cited in this note.
13. Diary Entry, Jan. 13, 1777, in Tatum (ed.), *Serle Journal*, 174; *New York Gazette*, Jan. 20, 1777 ("strong guard"). One other source says Lee arrived in New York City from Perth Amboy on January 14. Diary Entry, Jan. 14, 1777, in Montresor, "Journals," *N.Y. Hist. Soc. Coll.* 420 (1881). A New London newspaper reported that Lee was brought to New York City on January 16 and placed under guard in a small house "at the bottom of King Street." *Connecticut Gazette*, March 7, 1777.
14. Burrows, *Forgotten Patriots*, 57.
15. Quoted in ibid., 58.
16. Depositions of Samuel Young and William Houston, Dec. 15, 1776, in Force (ed.), *American Archives*, 5th Series, 3:1233-34.
17. Burrows, *Forgotten Patriots*, xi and 247. One historian who closely studied the matter argued that the British were "not guilty of excessive disregard of the welfare of prisoners." Bowman, *Captive Americans*, 126. He further argued that while prisoners suffered through neglect, the motivations behind the failure to provide for the captives "were not evil or vindictive in nature," but rather "stemmed from the complicated issues surrounding what was then a unique war. The limitations of the eighteenth century also contributed to the lack of care of the captives." Id., 132-33. While Bowman makes some decent points, the author believes that Burrows has the stronger argument.
18. Burrows, *Forgotten Patriots*, x-xi and 200-1.
19. Diary Entry, Sept. 5, 1776, in Mackenzie, *Diary* 1:39; see also Burrows, *Forgotten Patriots*, 36-38.
20. Quoted in Burrows, *Forgotten Patriots*, 274, n. 33.
21. Cox, *A Proper Sense of Honor*, 211-13. For a detailed discussion of the code of gentlemanly conduct as applied to the treatment of imprisoned Revolutionary War officers, see also Schaefer, "The Whole Duty of Man: Charles Lee and the Politics of Reputation, Masculinity, and Identity during the Revolutionary Era, 1755-1783," doctoral dissertation, University of Toledo (May 2006), 146-57.
22. Minutes, May 18, 1776, in Ford (ed.), *Journals of the Continental Congress* 4:361-62, n. 4.
23. Wheater, *Historical Record of the Seventh Royal Regiment of Fusiliers*, 67-68, 70-71, and 230.
24. Thomas Walker Statement, April 24, 1776, in Force (ed.), *American Archives*, 4th Series, 4:1177-79; see also Letter from Quebec, Oct. 25, 1775, in id., 3:1185.
25. Ethan Allen Recollections, in Allen, *Narrative*, 24; see also Randall, *Ethan Allen*, 378-80.
26. Quoted in Abbass, "Ethan Allen and Rhode Island in the Revolution," *R.I. in the Rev.* 4:456. D.K. "Kathy" Abbass has an excellent summary of Allen's treatment as a prisoner of the British navy in this article.

27. E. Allen to R. Prescott, Sept. 25, 1775, in Duffy (ed.), *Ethan Allen Correspondence* 1:52-53 and n. 2, 54.
28. Quoted in Burrows, *Forgotten Patriots*, 39; see also Randall, *Ethan Allen*, 370-85; Duffy (ed.), *Ethan Allen Correspondence* 1:54.
29. *Pennsylvania Packet*, Dec. 25, 1775; Richard Smith's Diary, Dec. 18, 1775, in Smith (ed.), *Letters of Delegates* 2:494; Wheater, *Historical Record of the Seventh Royal Regiment of Fusiliers*, 67-68 and 70-71.
30. R. Livingston to J. Jay, Dec. 6, 1775, in Smith (ed.), *Letters of Delegates* 2:450; see also Virginia Delegate to Unknown, Dec. 29, 1775, in id., 536 ("Montgomery, hearing of the treatment of our people, refused to see General Prescott when he was taken, which was showing a soldier-like spirit").
31. P. Schuyler to R. Montgomery, Nov. 30, 1775, in Ford (ed.), "Some Papers of Aaron Burr," *Proceedings of the American Antiquarian Society* 29:1, 63 (1920).
32. P. Schuyler to G. Washington, Nov. 28, 1775, in Twohig et al. (eds.), *Washington Papers* 2:453; G. Washington to J. Hancock, Dec. 18, 1775, in id., 576; Congressional Resolution, Dec. 2, 1775, in Ford (ed.), *Journals of the Continental Congress* 3:402 ("The Congress being informed that Mr. Ethan Allen, who was taken prisoner near Montreal, is confined in irons on board a vessel in the river St. Lawrence, *Ordered*, that General Washington be directed to apply to General Howe on this matter, and desire he may be exchanged"); J. Hancock to G. Washington, Dec. 2, 1775, in Twohig et al. (eds.), *Washington Papers* 2:470 (transmitting Dec. 2 resolution).
33. G. Washington to W. Howe, Dec. 18, 1775, in Twohig et al. (eds.), *Washington Papers* 2:575-76. Washington informed Hancock that "my reason for pointing out Brigadier General Prescott as the object who is to suffer Mr. Allen's fate is that by letters from General Schuyler and copies of letters from General Montgomery to Schuyler, I am given to understand that Prescott is the cause of Allen's sufferings. I thought it best to be decisive on the occasion, as did the generals whom I consulted thereupon." G. Washington to J. Hancock, Dec. 18, 1775, in id., 576.
34. W. Howe to Earl of Dartmouth, Dec. 19, 1775, in Davies (ed.), *Documents of the A.R.* 11:213.
35. Resolution, Jan. 2, 1776, in Ford (ed.), *Journals of the Continental Congress* 4:16; Richard Smith's Diary, Jan. 2, 1776, in Smith (ed.), *Letters of Delegates* 2:20-21; J. Hancock to G. Washington, Jan. 6, 1776, in id., 42.
36. Richard Smith's Diary, Jan. 24-25, 1776, in Smith (ed.), *Letters of Delegates* 2:148 (arrival) and 154 ("cruelty"); W. Livingston to S. Tucker, Jan. 27, 1776, in id., 158 ("modestly"). Robert R. Livingston, a fellow patrician with Schuyler in upstate New York, also heard in Albany that Prescott was "a man so demented so low as to break the windows of the barracks with his own cane." R. Livingston to J. Jay, Dec. 6, 1775, in id., 1:450. It appears that before retreating, Prescott personally broke the windows of the Montreal barracks, in order not to permit American invaders to benefit from the windows keeping out the cold weather.
37. Richard Smith's Diary, Jan. 25, 1776, in ibid., 154. Prescott later, meeting with Samuel Adams, Richard Smith, and another Continental Congress delegate, again defended his treatment of Allen on the grounds that he was acting under orders from General Carleton. Richard Smith's Diary, March 19, 1776, in id., 412.
38. Richard Smith's Diary, Jan. 25, 1776, in ibid., 154. Congress also heard testimony from another captive, Captain Chase, who had commanded the schooner *Gaspée* and had ordered Allen to be placed in irons. Id.
39. Resolution, Jan. 29, 1776, in Ford (ed.), *Journals of the Continental Congress* 4:101.
40. Quoted in Randall, *Ethan Allen*, 391.
41. *Morning Post and Daily Advertiser*, Jan. 16, 1777 (London); see also *Pennsylvania Evening Post*, Feb. 1, 1776 ("Last Monday Brigadier Gen. Prescott was removed from his apartments in the City Tavern to the new jail, by order of the Hon. Continental

Congress. It is said he was guilty of cruelly treating the prisoners taken from the Continental army in Canada, particularly Col. Allen, lately sent home to England, in irons").

42. Richard Smith's Diary, Feb. 5, 1776, in Smith (ed.), *Letters of Delegates* 3:204; see also Resolution, Feb. 1, 1776, in Ford (ed.), *Journals of the Continental Congress* 4:107 (allowing Prescott's servant to attend him and "in case his health requires it, that he be allowed the attendance of a physician"). Colonel James Paterson, Howe's adjutant general, met with Washington to discuss a variety of matters, including the treatment of prisoners, on June 20, 1776. At the end of the meeting, according to a summary of the discussions, the following exchange occurred: "Col. Patterson then proceeded to say he had it in his charge to mention the case of Gen. Prescott, who they were informed was treated with such rigor that, under his age and infirmities, fatal consequences might be apprehended. General Washington replied that Gen. Prescott's treatment had not fallen under his notice; that all persons under his particular direction he had treated with kindness, and made their situation as easy and comfortable as possible; that he did not know where Gen. Prescott was, but believed his treatment very different from their information. Gen. Washington then mentioned the case of Col. Allen and the officers who had been confined in Boston jail." Quoted in *Pennsylvania Packet*, July 29, 1777.

43. Richard Smith's Diary, March 19, 1776, in Smith (ed.), *Letters of Delegates* 3:412.

44. *Constitutional Gazette*, March 23, 1776 (dateline of Philadelphia). This excerpt was republished in the *Connecticut Courant* (Hartford), April 1, 1776 (quoting a report from Philadelphia, dated March 16, 1776) and *New England Chronicle*, April 4, 1776 (quoting a report from Philadelphia, dated March 23, 1776). It was also quoted in Moore (ed.), *Diary of the Revolution*, 226.

45. Thomas Walker Statement, April 24, 1776, in Force (ed.), *American Archives*, 4th Series, 4:1178, n.

46. Diary Entry, Sept. 24, 1776, in Tatum (ed.), *Serle Journal*, 113; see also Diary Entry, Sept. 25, 1776, in Kemble, "Journal," *N.Y. Hist. Soc. Coll.* 90 (1883) ("General Prescott came to Headquarters, having been exchanged for General Sullivan"); *Connecticut Courant*, Oct. 7, 1776 ("Sullivan and Prescott exchanged on September 25"). British Captain Frederick Mackenzie recorded the event in his journal: "General Prescott has been 16 weeks in close confinement in three different jails, and very ill-treated. He was last confined in Reading Jail with common malefactors, and the most notorious villains." Diary Entry, Sept. 25, 1776, in Mackenzie, *Diary* 1:64. It is not clear if any of these assertions are accurate. For Prescott's promotion to major general in North America only, see *London Gazette*, March 23-26, 1777 (War Office promotions announced.)

47. Abbass, "Ethan Allen and Rhode Island in the Revolution," *R.I. in the Rev.* 4:458; see also Ethan Allen Recollections, in Allen, *Narrative*, 37.

48. Quoted in Randall, *Ethan Allen*, 406. For a good discussion of the debate in England over Allen's fate, see Randall, *Ethan Allen*, 398-406; see also Burrows, *Forgotten Patriots*, 40; Duffy (ed.), *Ethan Allen Correspondence* 1:54, n. 1.

49. Quoted in Burrows, *Forgotten Patriots*, 60; see also Randall, *Ethan Allen*, 407-419.

50. Abbass, "Ethan Allen and Rhode Island in the Revolution," *R.I. in the Rev.* 4:459.

51. Quoted in ibid., 61.

52. Ibid.

53. *Annual Register . . . for the Year 1777*, 8 (1778). An unidentified British officer wrote on April 20, 1777: "I find that General Lee is confined in the guard house, contiguous to which is a small room in which he sleeps." Quoted in Scull, *The Evelyns in America*, 216-17. This quote is evidence that Lee was kept in two rooms.

54. Burrows, *Forgotten Patriots*, 71; Jones, *History of New York* 1:175; see also *Gazetteer and New Daily Advertiser* (London), June 12, 1777 (Lee "has been treated in a very gen-

teel manner during his confinement, the two officers on guard always dined with him, and he had leave to invite any person else he pleased").
55. W. Franklin to G. Germain, Nov. 10, 1778, in Davies, *Documents of the A.R.* 15:245.
56. Extract from a Letter from New York to General F. Haldimand in England, January 20, 1777, quoted in Scull, *The Evelyns in America*, 216, n. i.
57. Resolution, Dec. 20, 1776, in Ford (ed.), *Journals of the Continental Congress* 6:1029.
58. J. Hancock to G. Washington, Jan. 6-7, 1777, in Twohig et al. (eds.), *Washington Papers* 8:3.
59. R. H. Lee to P. Henry, Jan. 9, 1777, in Ballagh (ed.), *Richard H. Lee Letters* 1:249.
60. Preamble to Resolution, Jan. 6, 1777, in Ford (ed.), *Journals of the Continental Congress* 7:16.
61. Resolution, Jan. 6, 1777, in ibid. At the Battle of Trenton on the morning of December 25, 1776, Hessian commander Colonel Johann Gottlieb Rall and Major Friedrich Ludwig von Dechow of von Kynphausen's regiment were wounded, and both died on December 27. The unharmed captive Hessian officers included Lieutenant Colonel Balthasar Bretthauer, Major Johann Justus Matthaus, Lieutenant Colonel Franziscus Scheffer, and Major Ludwig von Hanstein. See Twohig et al. (eds.), *Washington Papers* 8:3, n. 5 and 47, n. 1. The author does not know the identity of the fifth Hessian officer who was to be pledged for the good treatment of Charles Lee. Richard Henry Lee called the offer of Campbell and the five Hessian officers for Lee "the European plan"—meaning it was a practice adopted in Europe to exchange a high-ranking officer for more than one lower-ranking officer. R. H. Lee to A. Stephen, Jan. 5, 1777, in Smith (ed.), *Letters of Delegates* 6:36. For Richard Henry Lee drafting the resolution, see ibid., 41, n.4.
62. G. Washington to W. Howe, Jan. 13, in Twohig et al. (eds.), *Washington Papers* 8:59-60.
63. W. Howe to G. Washington, Jan. 23, 1777, in ibid., 137.
64. Resolution, Feb. 20, 1777, in Ford (ed.), *Journals of the Continental Congress* 7:135.
65. Notes on Debates in Congress, Feb. 20, 1777, in ibid., 134, n.1 (citing *Burke's Abstract of Debates in Congress, North Carolina Colonial Records*, XI, 381). Congress also ordered the following: "That the Board of War transmit to each of the Hessian officers and Colonel Campbell copies of the resolve of Congress of the 6th of January, of such part of General Washington's letter of the 13th, and of General Howe's answer thereto, of the 23 of January, as relates to General Lee; and inform those officers that the conduct of General Howe alone induces Congress to treat them in a manner so very different from that which has ever been shown to all other prisoners of war of these States; and that, if any of them think proper to write on this subject to the British or Hessian general, that the letter shall be transmitted by a flag." Resolution, Feb. 20, 1777, in Ford (ed.), *Journals of the Continental Congress* 7:135.
66. Lt. Jakob Piel Diary Entry, March 1777, in Burgoyne (ed.), *Diaries of Hessian Officers*, 25; see also Alden, *General Charles Lee*, 181.
67. For the background on Archibald Campbell, see Campbell, "Introduction," *Journal of an Expedition against the Rebels of Georgia*, ix; *Dictionary of National Biography* 8:794; Campbell, J. L., "Campbell, Sir Archibald," *Oxford Dictionary of National Biography*, online edition, Jan. 2008; Baule, *British Army Officers*, 28; Ryan, "Hidden Concord: Concord Gaol," at www.concordma/magazine/dec98/campbell; A. Campbell to W. Howe, Feb. 14, 1776, in *Scots Magazine*, Aug. 1776, 427-29 and *Continental Journal* (Boston), June 19, 1776 (June 17 captures). The author of the "Introduction," Colin Campbell, wrote that "Campbell is the subject of an article, very incorrect in its earlier part, in the *Dictionary of National Biography* (VIII, 794); later commentators have repeated the *DNB*'s mistakes to the extent that one almost despairs of getting the record straight." Campbell, "Introduction," *Journal of an Expedition against the Rebels of Georgia*, ix. Campbell did not give up in Boston harbor without a fight. Only after his

vessel had run aground, its five light cannon had run out of ammunition, and its crew and his battalion had suffered eight killed and twelve wounded from the fire of five armed schooners and a 16-gun brig nearby did Campbell consider it honorable to surrender. Three of the regiment's other transports were also captured in Boston harbor or off the New England coast, resulting in the Americans gaining more than 400 captives. A. Campbell to W. Howe, June 19, 1776, in *Scots Magazine,* Aug. 1776, 427-29 and Walcott, *Campbell,* 15-17. For the most complete description of Campbell's capture in Boston Harbor and incarceration at Concord, see Walcott, *Campbell,* 10-51.

68. Resolutions, May 21, 1776, in Ford (ed.), *Journals of the Continental Congress* 4:370-72.

69. A. Campbell to W. Howe, June 19, 1776, in *Scots Magazine,* Aug. 1776, 427-29 and Walcott, *Campbell,* 15-17.

70. A. Campbell to W. Heath, April 13 and May 16, 1777, in "Heath Papers," *Mass. Hist. Soc. Coll.,* 7th Series, 4:74-75 and 97 (1904); Ryan, "Hidden Concord: Concord Gaol," at www.concordma/magazine/dec98/campbell; Walcott, *Campbell,* 21-22.

71. Resolution, Jan. 6, 1777, in Ford (ed.), *Journals of the Continental Congress* 7:16.

72. Resolution, Massachusetts Council, undated (probably Jan. 31, 1777), in Force (ed.), Massachusetts Council Records, Peter Force Transcripts, Series 7.E, Entry 82, reel 20, Library of Congress.

73. Extract of a Letter from Boston, Jan. 5, 1777, *The Remembrancer for the Year 1777,* 139. From the contents of the letter, the author believes it was penned by a member of the Massachusetts Council.

74. Ibid; see also A. Campbell to Mass. Council, March 31, 1777, in Massachusetts Council Records, Peter Force Transcripts, Series 7.E, Entry 82, reel 21, Library of Congress ("I was happy to find from General Howe a possible contradiction to those reports which of late have gained so much credit in the Province." This was undoubtedly a reference to information that Lee was being comfortably confined to two rooms in New York City, and was not being held in a military jail cell [as rumored in Massachusetts]).

75. Diary Entry, Feb. 1777, in Thacher, *Journal,* 73.

76. A. Campbell to Mass. Council, Jan. 31, 1777, in Massachusetts Council Records, Peter Force Transcripts, Series 7.E, Entry 82, reel 20, Library of Congress.

77. Walcott, *Campbell,* 26.

78. Excerpt of letter from A. Campbell to G. Washington, Feb. 4, 1777, in Twohig et al. (eds.), *Washington Papers* 8:454, n.1.

79. A. Campbell to W. Howe, Feb. 14, 1777, in *Scots Magazine* 39:249 (May 1777), *Continental Journal* (Boston), May 19, 1777.

80. Jones, *History of New York* 1:175.

81. W. Howe to G. Washington, Feb. 27, 1777, in Twohig et al. (eds.), *Washington Papers* 8:453.

82. G. Washington to J. Bowdoin, Feb. 28, 1777, in ibid., 461. Washington also informed Campbell that he had written Bowdoin to request that the conditions of his confinement be eased. G. Washington to A. Campbell, March 1, 1777, in id., 468-69.

83. G. Washington to J. Hancock, March 1, 1777, in ibid., 472-73; see also G. Washington to J. Hancock, March 6, 1777, in id., 522-23 (reiterating same argument). In his March 1 letter, the commander-in-chief also took the opportunity of adding that he opposed the doctrine of retaliation in this instance, on the grounds that the enemy held many more officers as prisoners and that harsh treatment of German officers might alienate regular German soldiers, whom the Americans were typically trying to entice to desert.

84. A. Campbell to Mass. Council, March 19, 1777, Massachusetts Council Records, Peter Force Transcripts, Series 7.E, Entry 82, reel 21, Library of Congress. Campbell also protested to the Council that his pair of pistols and sword had been seized from

him, as well as from his fellow captive officers. Seeing that the pistols and swords were getting "rusty," Continental agent John Bradford had them sold at public auction, with the proceeds added to the Continental treasury. Colonel John Glover purchased a sword, and Connecticut navy captain Seth Harding acquired Campbell's sword. J. Bradford to the Mass. Council, undated [probably March 1777] in id.
85. *Independent Chronicle* (Boston), April 17, 1777.
86. A. Campbell to W. Heath, April 13, 1777, in "Heath Papers," *Mass. Hist. Soc. Coll.*, 7th Series, 4:75 (1904).
87. A. Campbell to Mass. Council, March 31, 1777, Massachusetts Council Records, Peter Force Transcripts, Series 7.E, Entry 82, reel 21, Library of Congress.
88. W. Howe to G. Washington, May 22, 1777, in Twohig et al. (eds.), *Washington Papers* 8:289.
89. A. Campbell to W. Heath, May 16, 1777, in "Heath Papers," *Mass. Hist. Soc. Coll.*, 7th Series, 4:97 (1904).
90. W. Harcourt to Lord Nuneham, March 18, 1777, in Harcourt (ed.), *Harcourt Papers* 11:211.
91. A. Adams to J. Adams, May 18, 1777, in Adams (ed.), *Familiar Letters of John Adams and His Wife Abigail Adams* 274-75.
92. J. Adams to A. Adams, June 2, 1777, in Smith (ed.), *Letters of Delegates* 7:161-62.
93. W. Howe to G. Washington, April 21, 1777, in Twohig et al. (eds.), *Washington Papers* 8:230.
94. W. Howe to G. Washington, May 22 and June 5, 1777, in ibid., 496 and 611.
95. Diary Entry, June 8, 1777, in Muenchhausen, *At General Howe's Side*, 13.
96. G. Washington to W. Howe, June 10, 1777, in Twohig et al. (eds.), *Washington Papers* 8:665.
97. W. Howe to G. Germain, June 3, 1777, in Davies (ed.), *Documents of the A.R.* 14:102.
98. Quoted in Scull, *The Evelyns in America*, 215.
99. René-Etienne Henry Vic Gaiault (or Gayault) de Boisbertrand Memorandum for the American Commissioners, Sept. 5, 1778, in Stevens (ed.), *Facsimiles* 23:1948. Boisbertrand's aide-de-camp and two other companions who had accompanied him from France were captured on board an American vessel off Bedford by a British ship and taken to Newport, Rhode Island. They were then taken to New York, where they joined Boisbertrand in prison. Id.
100. Ibid.; see also extract of letter from a British officer, dated April 20, 1777, quoted in Scull, *The Evelyns in America*, 217 (Boisbertrand, "his aide-de-camp, an engineer and two sergeants, all Frenchmen, who were taken at the same time with Lee, were prisoners on board the *Inflexible* man-of-war, at the Nore"); List of the American Prisoners Confined in Forton Prison, Dec. 29, 1777, in Morgan, Crawford et al. (eds.), *Naval Docs. of the A.R.* 11:891 (Boisbertrand listed).
101. C. de Vergennes to Archbishop of Bourges, Sept. 5, 1778, in Stevens (ed.), *Facsimiles* 23:1949; A. de Sartine to the American Commissioners, Sept. 6, 1778, in Willcox et al. (eds.), *Franklin Papers* 27:364-65 and n. 9. Boisbertrand made two requests for reinstatement into the French army, but both were denied, possibly due to his poor physical condition stemming from his lengthy imprisonment. Nonetheless, in 1788, he was made Chevalier de Saint Louis. On March 1, 1791, when only forty-four years old, he retired as maréchal de camp and two years later he was awarded a pension. On June 20, 1820, he was admitted to the Invalides hospital because of "incurable infirmities." *Dictionnaire de Biographie Française* 15:908. He died in 1823.
102. C. Lee to G. Minghini, April 4, 1777, in *Lee Papers* 2:367-68.
103. State of the Supernumeraries Borne Onboard the Ships and Vessels of the Squadron under the Command of the Vice Admiral, the Viscount Howe, Off New

York, the 7th day of July 1777, in Morgan, Crawford et al. (eds.), *Naval Documents of the A.R.* 9:234 ("Mr. Lee & Servant" on board HMS *Centurion*).

104. C. Lee Circular Letter, May 7, 1777, Schoff Revolutionary War Collection 2:25, William L. Clements Library and quoted in Walcott, *Campbell,* 43-44. This letter was not published in the *Lee Papers* or any other publication (other than Walcott's book), and was not cited in Alden's or any other biography of Lee.

105. C. Lee to R. Morris, May 19, 1777, in *Lee Papers* 2:371.

106. Resolution, June 2, 1777, in Ford (ed.), *Journals of the Continental Congress* 8:411-12. Congress had reacted to a May 30, 1777, report from the Board of War, which recommended that "the Council of the Massachusetts Bay be informed that a letter from General Lee of the 19th instant to Robert Morris, Esq., having been laid before Congress, wherein, it is set forth, that, 'General Lee's table is very handsomely kept by the General (Howe) who has indeed treated him in all respects with kindness, generosity and tenderness,' the Council of the said State be requested to treat Lieutenant Colonel Campbell with every kindness and civility, consistent with the confinement of his person." Quoted in Ford (ed.), *Journals of the Continental Congress* 8:412, n.1.

107. A. Campbell to Mass. Council, May 26, 1777, in Walcott, *Campbell,* 48; see also A. Campbell to Mass. Council, May 11, 1777, in id., 45-47; A. Campbell to W. Heath, May 16, 1777, in "Heath Papers," *Mass. Hist. Soc. Coll.,* 7th Series, 4:97-98 (1904); Walcott, *Sir Archibald Campbell,* 43-44.

108. J. Bowater to Earl Denbigh, June 5 and 11, 1777, in Syrett and Balderston (eds.), *Lost Letters,* 130-31; see also Diary Entries, June 4, 1777, in Muenchhausen, *At General Howe's Side,* 13 and Ford (ed.), *Journals of Hugh Gaine* 2:35; Log of HMS *Centurion,* June 4, 1777, ADM 51/177, British National Archives ("1/2 past 5 received on board Mr. Lee as a prisoner"). The *Centurion* had a crew of 350 and was commanded by Captain Richard Braithwaite. See Disposition of H.M.'s Ships and Vessels in North America, 28 August 1777, in Davies (ed.), *Documents of the A.R.* 14:177.

109. Extract of a letter from an officer on board the *Eagle,* off New York, June 9, 1777, in Morgan, Crawford et al. (eds.), *Naval Documents of the A.R.* 9:78.

110. Diary Entry, June 4, 1777, in Muenchhausen, *At General Howe's Side,* 13 ("for security reasons"); Extract of a letter from an officer on board the *Eagle,* off New York, June 9, 1777, in Morgan, Crawford et al. (eds.), *Naval Documents of the A.R.* 9:78 ("for greater security").

111. State of the Supernumeraries Borne Onboard the Ships and Vessels of the Squadron under the Command of the Vice Admiral, the Viscount Howe, Off New York, the 7th day of July 1777, in Morgan, Crawford et al. (eds.), *Naval Documents of the A.R.* 9:234 ("General Clinton & Suite (21 persons) and Protection (8 persons)" on board HMS *Liverpool* and HMS *Otter*).

112. *New York Gazette,* June 9, 1777, and quoted in Ford (ed.), *Journals of Hugh Gaine* 2:35, n. 2.

113. Log of HMS *Centurion,* June 5, 1777, British National Archives, ADM 51/177.

114. J. Bowater to Earl Denbigh, June 5 and 11, 1777, in Syrett and Balderston (eds.), *Lost Letters,* 130-31. Describing Lee as an "atrocious monster," Bowater wrote to the Earl of Denbigh in England in June, "He is as perfect in treachery as if he had been an American born." Id.

115. C. Lee to H. Clinton, Aug. 22, 1777, Henry Clinton Papers 23:13, William L. Clements Library. One insult may have been that Commodore William Hotham refused Lee's request to meet, in his quarters on board the *Centurion,* with one of his aides, John Eustace. In making the request, Lee pointed out that "I cannot propose holding the least conversation with him but in the presence of the [navy] officers." C. Lee to W. Hotham, Aug. 24, 1777, Henry Clinton Papers 23:16, William L. Clements Library.

116. H. Clinton to C. Lee [undated, probably late Aug. 1777], quoted in Alden, *General Charles Lee,* 185; see also Willcox, *Portrait of a General,* 23 and n. 6 (in 1763 Clinton provided Lee with a letter of introduction to a German prince). Lee later expressed appreciation for Clinton's treatment of him as a prisoner in New York. Henry Clinton Memorandum, March 22, 1778, Henry Clinton Papers 32:26, William L. Clements Library.
117. Resolution, June 10, 1777, in Ford (ed.), *Journals of the Continental Congress* 8:449-50.
118. G. Washington to W. Howe, June 10, 1777, in Twohig et al. (eds.), *Washington Papers* 8:664-65.
119. W. Howe to G. Germain, July 6, 1777, CO 5/94, British National Archives.
120. *Annual Register . . . for the Year 1777,* 8 (1778).
121. G. Washington to W. Howe, June 10, 1777, in Twohig et al. (eds.), *Washington Papers* 8:665.

CHAPTER FIVE: RICHARD PRESCOTT COMMANDS
1. King George III to Earl of Sandwich, Jan. 22, 1777, in Barnes and Owen (eds.), *Papers of the Earl of Sandwich* 1:172.
2. Memorandum Concerning the Country Around Rhode Island, Anonymous to H. Percy, undated (probably late 1776 or early 1777), Hugh Percy Papers, British Manuscript Project, microfilm reel Aln 26, Library of Congress.
3. Proclamation of Governor Nicholas Cooke, Dec. 7, 1776, in Morgan, Crawford et al. (eds.), *Naval Documents of the A.R.* 7:395; *Boston Gazette,* Dec. 9, 1776.
4. B. Arnold to G. Washington, Jan. 13, 1777, in Twohig et al. (eds.), *Washington Papers* 8:55-56. Washington had requested that Arnold depart for Rhode Island in a letter of December 14, which Gates did not deliver to Arnold until December 17 when the two were in Bethlehem. Arnold, who apparently did not want to go and desired to remain to see action with Washington's main army, accurately advised that he did not think the British would invade the interior of New England that winter and recommended that he remain with Gates. H. Gates to G. Washington, Dec. 17, 1776, in id., 7:361. Washington finally sent Arnold to Rhode Island on December 22, so Arnold just missed the action at Trenton on December 25-26. G. Washington to N. Cooke, Dec. 21, 1776, in id., 392.
5. General Assembly Resolutions, March 1, 1777, Session, in Bartlett (ed.), *Records of R.I.* 8:155; Diary Entry, March 9, 1777, in Dexter (ed.), *Stiles Diary* 2:140-41; Broadside, March 1777, microfilm no. 43352, Brown University Library (original in Rhode Island Historical Society).
6. B. Arnold to G. Washington, March 11, 1777, in ibid., 8:552.
7. W. Howe to G. Germain, Nov. 30, 1776, in Davies (ed.), *Documents of the A.R.* 12:264-65; see also McBurney, *Rhode Island Campaign,* 2-3.
8. McBurney, *Rhode Island Campaign,* 20-21.
9. Ibid., 32.
10. For Barton's early life, see John Howland Recollections, in Stone, *Life of Howland,* 55; Williams, *Life of Barton,* 27-28 and Appendix, 120.
11. Swan, *General William Barton,* 3-4.
12. General Assembly Resolutions, August 1775 (third week), October 31, 1775, and March 1776, in Bartlett (ed.), *Records of R.I.* 7:359, 366, 403, 491, and 500.
13. Swan, *General William Barton,* 39.
14. *Providence Gazette,* Feb. 10, 1776.
15. Diary Entry, Jan. 8, 1776, in Dexter (ed.), *Stiles Diary* 1:653; *New England Chronicle,* Jan. 11-18, 1776, in Morgan, Crawford et al. (eds.), *Naval Documents of the A.R.* 3:844. On December 16, 1775, Barton and other colony troops had driven off a

party of Wallace's marines and sailors, who had landed on Brenton Point in an attempt to carry off hay for cattle on board their ships. Diary Entry, Dec. 16, 1775, in Dexter (ed.), *Stiles Diary* 1:644.

16. General Assembly Resolution, March 1776 session, in Bartlett (ed.), *Records of R.I.* 7:491 (Barton resigns and is discharged with honor); General Assembly Resolutions, May 1, 1776, in id., 519 and 538. Barton was reappointed major of the state's brigade in August of 1776. General Assembly Resolution, Aug. 1776 session, in id., 600.

17. General Assembly Resolutions, Dec. 10, 1776, session, in ibid., 8:56-72.

18. Ibid., 8:64. Barton was reappointed to his post in June of 1777. General Assembly Resolutions, June 1777 session, 8:263.

19. Barton, "Narrative of the Capture of Major General Prescott," Undated (probably around 1812), MSS 9003, vol. III, folder 13, R.I. Hist. Soc. There is circumstantial evidence that as early as March of 1777, Barton attempted to lead a party to capture on Aquidneck Island a German general of equal rank to Lee: Major General Friedrich Wilhelm von Lossberg, the commander of the Hessian troops stationed on the island. After the war, a Boston publisher of Barton's war exploits, seeking further elaboration from Barton on certain topics, wrote him that an acquaintance of Barton "tells me that in the month of March preceding (he thinks) you made a bold attempt to surprise and capture in his quarters a German general, who was on the east side of the Island, but that the attempt proved unsuccessful in consequence of intelligence conveyed to the enemy by . . . a deserter from your party. I wish you to draft the particulars of this enterprise also." S. B. Barrell to W. Barton, Sept. 24, 1818, Manuscripts, MSS 9006, v. 8, p.82, R.I. Hist. Soc. (Barrell named the supposed deserter, "one Sam Buffam," but the man who told Barrell this name probably became confused over another incident. See the discussion about Samuel Buffam in the Appendix to this book under the subheading of Walter Graham.) Barton failed to provide his publisher with any further details. Indeed, this reference is the only one known to exist of this attempt.

20. In the Rhode Island 1774 census, there were no Coffins in Portsmouth or Middletown, but there was a Paul Coffin in Newport, with six persons in his household. Bartlett (ed.), *R.I. Census 1774*, 10. The author assumes the man Barton met with was this Paul Coffin. Coffin was also a common name on Nantucket Island; the man instead could have been a Nantucket sailor who found himself stuck in Newport after the British invasion.

21. Barton, "Narrative of the Capture of Major General Prescott," Undated (probably around 1812), MSS 9003, vol. III, folder 13, R.I. Hist. Soc.

22. Diary Entry, Dec. 26, 1775, in Dexter (ed.), *Stiles Diary* 1:646.

23. Diary Entries, Dec. 25-27, 1777, in ibid., 645-47; N. Greene to S. Ward, Sr., Dec. 31, 1775, in Showman (ed.), *Greene Papers* 1:174; Patterson, *Knight Errant of Liberty*, 113-14.

24. C. Lee to N. Cooke, Dec. 7, 1776, in *Lee Papers* 2:331-32; see also C. Lee to G. Washington, Dec. 8, 1776, in Twohig et al. (eds.), *Washington Papers* 7:277.

25. General Assembly Resolutions, Dec. 10, 1776, Session, in Bartlett (ed.), *Records of R.I.* 8:64. The General Assembly dismissed Varnum and Malmedy after the first effort to organize an army to capture Newport ended in March 1777, deciding that it could rely solely on Spencer (who was paid by the Continental army). Bartlett (ed.), *Records of R.I.* 8:173-74 and 186; see also J. Varnum to G. Washington, April 1-4, 1777, in Twohig et al. (eds.), *Washington Papers* 9:43.

26. N. Greene to N. Cooke, Jan. 23, 1777, in Showman (ed.), *Greene Papers* 2:12.

27. Prescott's tyrannical attitude toward Newport residents was commented on by two British historians. George Trevelyan wrote that "Prescott is remembered as a tyrannical, violent-tempered man—a terror to the revolted colonists everywhere except in battle." Trevelyan continued, "Prescott, early in the war, when attacked by Richard

Montgomery on the river St. Lawrence, had tamely surrendered himself, a detachment of British soldiers, and eleven armed vessels for the safety of which he was responsible. He was exchanged for [American General John] Sullivan...." Trevelyan, *American Rev.* 4:335, n.1. Trevelyan also colorfully added that "Americans . . . came to regard [Prescott] as a convenient circulating medium for buying back their own captured generals." Id., 335. Another British historian wrote, "Prescott . . . made himself especially odious to the inhabitants by many acts of petty tyranny and oppression." Scull (ed.), *The Evelyns of America*, 279.

28. Griffith, *War for American Independence*, 393.

29. Wheater, *Historical Record of the Seventh Royal Regiment of Fusiliers*, 67-68, 70-71, and 230; Muster Rolls, 7th Regiment of Foot, W/O 12/2474, British National Archives (the seventy-five men had been stationed in Quebec).

30. Preble, *Culloden*, 120-37, 246, and 269-79.

31. Quoted in Burrows, *Forgotten Patriots*, 36.

32. Quoted in Conway, "British Army Officers and the American War for Independence," *William and Mary Quarterly*, 3rd Series, 41:2, 271 (April 1984). One particularly bloodthirsty British officer of the 71st Regiment, gloating over Howe's smashing victory in the Battle of Brooklyn, reportedly wrote of retreating American soldiers struggling in swamps to evade capture, "multitudes were drowned and suffocated in the morasses—a proper punishment for all rebels." The officer then bragged, "We took care to tell the Hessians that the rebels had resolved to give no quarter to them, which made them fight desperately and put all to death who fell into their hands." Extract of a letter from an officer in General Frasier's battalion, Sept. 3, 1776, in Commager and Morris (eds.), *Spirit of Seventy-Six*, 443. The letter is said to have been recovered from the Battle of Brooklyn battlefield and was then published in the *Massachusetts Spy*. Historian David McCullough stated that the letter was "very likely a fake, fabricated as propaganda" (McCullough, *1776*, 181), but the author believes it uses the language of an authentic letter and other sources corroborate this particular claim. Hessian colonel Heinrich von Heeringen wrote of the battle, "The English did not give much quarter, and constantly urged our people to do the like." Quoted in Lowell, *The Hessians*, 68. After Pennsylvanian rifleman Thomas Foster was captured and nearly hanged to death by his Hessian captors, a British officer informed him of his good fortune as Hessians had hanged a number of Americans this way after they had thrown down their weapons. Burrows, *Forgotten Patriots*, 6. That being said, the number of Americans captured in the battle far exceeded their killed, so this kind of treatment was the exception, even in the Battle of Brooklyn. See Schecter, *Battle for New York*, 148 and 153.

33. H. Mowatt to the People of Falmouth, Oct. 16, 1775, in Morgan, Crawford et al. (eds.), *Naval Docs. of the A.R.* 2:471. Mowatt was ordered to devastate Falmouth by Admiral Samuel Graves. S. Graves to H. Mowatt, Oct. 6, 1775, in id., 324-26. Graves had previously written that "burning and laying waste the whole country" was appropriate if needed to crush the American rebellion. Quoted in Burrows, *Forgotten Patriots*, 36.

34. *Annual Register . . . for the Year 1777*, 125.

35. *General Evening Post* (London), Aug. 16-19, 1777.

36. Depositions of Thomas Durfee, Henry Goddard, and Leonard Hill, in Burrington Anthony Rev. War Pension Application, National Archives Building; see also Benjamin Cowell, *Spirit of '76*, 253-54.

37. *Independent Chronicle* (Boston), Feb. 6, 1777. The article was repeated in *Boston Gazette*, Feb. 10, 1777 and *Pennsylvania Journal*, Feb. 19, 1777 (quoted in Moore (ed.), *Diary of the Rev.* 1:390).

38. P. Parker to the Secretary of the Admiralty, Dec. 11, 1776, in Force (ed.), *American Archives*, 5th Ser., 3:1175-76.

39. *Providence Gazette,* March 7, 1777; see also McBurney, "British Treatment of Prisoners During the Occupation of Newport, 1776-1778: Disease, Starvation and Death Stalk the Prison Ships," *Newport History* 79:263, 1-41 (Fall 2010).
40. John Howland Recollections, in Stone, *Life of John Howland,* 45.
41. Williams, *Life of Barton,* Appendix, 131-32; see also Peterson, *History of R.I.,* 215.
42. Ross, *Civil and Religious History of R.I.,* 44-45.
43. Williams, *Life of Barton,* 131-32; Lossing, *Pictorial Field-Book of the Rev.* 1:642, n.1; Ross, *Civil and Religious History of R.I.,* 44-45. Prescott also took out his anger on Solomon Southwick, the fiercely patriotic editor of the *Newport Mercury,* who had fled Newport, by ordering the building which housed the newspaper to be demolished. Williams, *Life of Barton,* 42-43, n.
44. Lossing, *Pictorial Field-Book of the Rev.* 1:642-43, n. 1. Captain Henry Savage, of the 37th Regiment, served as deputy quartermaster general for the British army during its occupation of Newport. Baule and Gilbert, *British Army Officers,* 158. Lossing also discusses a less-weighty annoyance: "I was informed that when Prescott took possession of his town quarters, he had a fine sidewalk made for his accommodation some distance along Pelham and up Spring Street, for which purpose he took the door-steps belonging to other dwellings. The morning after the evacuation [of Newport in October 1779], the owners of the steps hastened to Prescott's quarters, each to claim his doorstone. It was an exciting scene, for sometimes two or three persons, not positive in their identification, claimed the same stone. Prescott's fine promenade soon disappeared . . . and the worthy citizens of Newport bore off their long-abused door-steps." Lossing, *Pictorial Field-Book of the Rev.* 1:643, n. 1.
45. Williams, *Life of Barton,* 56 and Appendix, 133.
46. V. Asteroth Diary Entry, July 10, 1777, in Burgoyne (ed.), *Diaries of a Hessian Chaplain,* 28.
47. H. Kuemmel Diary Entry, Feb. 20, 1777, in ibid., 10.
48. J. Bowater to B. Fielding, July 27, 1777, in Balderston and Syrett (eds.), *Lost Letters,* 141.
49. After the departure of approximately 1,300 soldiers from Newport in mid-May 1777, the Newport garrison consisted of 129 officers and 2,935 rank-and-file soldiers, for a total of 3,064. Garrison of Rhode Island, Maj.-Gen. Prescott, State of the Garrison, May 8, 1777, in Atkinson, "British Forces in North America, 1774-1781," *Journal of the Society for Army Historical Research* 16:11 (1937). On June 19, 1777, Major Mackenzie wrote in his journal, "The *Niger* frigate arrived yesterday from New York, with several transports under convoy, having on board near 500 drafts and recruits, and the camp equipage for the regiments on this island." Diary Entry, June 19, 1777, in Mackenzie, *Diary* 1:142. The newly arrived 500 soldiers increased the total number of his officers and soldiers to approximately 3,500.
50. V. Asteroth Diary Entry, Dec. 13, 1776, in Burgoyne (ed.), *Diaries of a Hessian Chaplain,* 26.
51. Unknown Hessian officer to his Brother, June 24, 1777, in Stone (ed.), *Letters of Brunswick and Hessian Officers,* 209.
52. Quoted in Schroder, *Hessians in Newport,* 79-80.
53. Diary Entry, July 31, 1777, in Mackenzie, *Diary* 1:159 (carrying two 18-pound cannon in her bow, two 12-pound cannon in her stern, and four-to-six 4-pounders along her sides, as well as sixteen swivel guns on her deck); *Newport Gazette,* March 20, 1777.
54. Diary Entries, Feb. 22 and March 5, 1777, in Dexter (ed.), *Stiles Diary* 2:129 and 139 (map at 140); J. Goodwin Diary Entry, Feb. 22, 1777, in "Military Journal," *Essex Institute Hist. Coll.* 45:209 (July 1909); *Newport Gazette,* March 13, 1777; Diary Entry, Feb. 22, 1777, Lord Percy's Diary When He Commanded the Newport Garrison, British Manuscript Project, microfilm reel Aln 26, Library of Congress. A British sol-

dier wrote to a friend in England, "Last Saturday, the rebels came over from Providence in two row galleys with about 4 or 500 men, but got a severe drubbing and glad to get back again." J. Rowe to his Agent, Feb. 24, 1777, excerpt quoted in Andrews (ed.), *Guide to the Materials for American History* 2:324.

55. *Providence Gazette,* March 1, 1777. The *Newport Gazette* reported in its March 13, 1777, edition that "six men were taken out of her that night about 12 o'clock and buried, and three more have since died of their wounds." But those casualty figures are not supported by other evidence. One sailor from Rehoboth later recalled that the *Spitfire* received forty-four shots in her hull, mast, and rigging, and had four men wounded and one killed. This sailor, while commanding an 18-pounder cannon during the fight, had a British cannon ball fly so close to his face that it blinded him in one eye. Joseph Wheaton Recollections, undated, quoted in Snape, *Mighty Liberty Men,* 93. A Massachusetts militiaman serving in Tiverton, John Goodwin, recorded in his diary that the galley was "torn all to pieces, with one of the guns dismounted" and that the Royal artillery had "fired right into the muzzle of the eighteen pounder on board the galley." Goodwin also reported that two men had been mortally wounded, with one of them dying in the evening and the other dying the next day. J. Goodwin Diary Entries, Feb. 22-23, 1777, in "Military Journal," *Essex Institute Hist. Coll.* 45:208-9 (July 1909). One survivor, who lost the use of his left arm, later received a small pension from the Rhode Island General Assembly. Petition of Uriah Stone, June 1779, Petitions to the R.I. General Assembly, XVII, No. 84, R.I. State Archives. Then matters turned even worse for the Americans. In the evening, after the fighting had ended, a New England soldier fired a cannon from the Howland's Ferry fort in order to clear the gun. Unfortunately, it misfired and exploded, killing one man immediately and wounding six other soldiers "very bad." J. Goodwin Diary Entry, Feb. 22, 1777, in "Military Journal," *Essex Institute Hist. Coll.* 45:209 (July 1909); see also Diary Entry, March 5, 1777, in Dexter (ed.), *Stiles Diary* 2:139 (reporting that one of the guns at Howland's Ferry burst, killing a man); *Newport Gazette,* March 13, 1777 (reporting that a lieutenant of the *Spitfire* galley discharged the cannon at Howland's Ferry fort and was killed from the misfire, and that eight other men were wounded). The next day, one of the wounded men died. J. Goodwin Diary Entries, Feb. 22-23, 1777, in "Military Journal," *Essex Institute Hist. Coll.* 45:208-9 (July 1909); see also Diary Entry, March 5, 1777, in Dexter (ed.), *Stiles Diary* 2: 139. A Tory from Nantucket reported to Percy that the misfire occurred aboard the *Spitfire* during the action itself and that the lieutenant and five other sailors had been killed. James Tupper Military Intelligence Report, Mar. 8, 1777, Hugh Percy Papers, British Manuscript Project, microfilm reel Aln 26, Library of Congress. The author believes that the reports by Goodwin and Stiles are more reliable, as they were on the American side and likely had better access to more accurate information. They do not mention an officer being killed.

56. Diary Entry, Mar. 18, 1777, in Dexter (ed.), *Stiles Diary* 2:148-49.

57. J. Spencer to J. Hancock, July 11, 1777, Papers of the Continental Congress, Miscellaneous Letters Addressed to Congress 1775-1789, M247, microfilm reel 102, item 78, XX, folio 129.

58. *Providence Gazette,* May 3, 1777; J. Spencer to G. Washington, April 30 and Aug. 15, 1777, in Twohig et al. (eds.), *Washington Papers* 9:313 and 10:629.

59. The British, perhaps in early 1778, enlarged the redoubt with earthen-raised walls, and constructed inside of it two barracks, one to hold 300 men and the other 54. See McBurney, *Rhode Island Campaign,* 171 and 354, n. 2. The remnants of the steep earthen walls can still be seen today.

60. Brigadier General Francis Smith Orders, May 19 and 24, 1777, in Hagist (ed.), *General Orders, R.I.,* 47-51; see also Proceedings of a Board of General Officers held at New York, April 24, 1778, in id., Appendix II, 132; J. Campbell to E. Percy, July 13,

1777, Hugh Percy Papers, British Manuscript Project, microfilm reel Aln 27, Library of Congress.
61. Brigadier General Francis Smith Orders, June 17, 1777, in Hagist (ed.), *General Orders, R.I.,* 57; see also Proceedings of a Board of General Officers held at New York, April 24, 1778, in id., Appendix II, 132.
62. Brigadier General Francis Smith Orders, May 24, 1777, in ibid., 51; see also Proceedings of a Board of General Officers held at New York, April 24, 1778, in id., Appendix II, 132; J. Campbell to E. Percy, July 13, 1777, Hugh Percy Papers, British Manuscript Project, microfilm reel Aln 27, Library of Congress.
63. Proceedings of a Board of General Officers held at New York, April 24, 1778, in ibid., Appendix II, 132.
64. Brigadier General Francis Smith Orders, May 26, 1777, in ibid., 51.
65. Brigadier General Francis Smith Orders, May 24, 1777, in ibid., 49-50. At his court-martial, Prescott stated that at the time of his capture, the von Huyn and von Bunau regiments were stationed on heights above Newport. Proceedings of a Board of General Officers held at New York, April 24, 1778, in ibid., Appendix II, 132. Soldiers at this location could have easily been taken from the camp to serve as guards in Newport. See also J. Campbell to E. Percy, July 13, 1777, Hugh Percy Papers, British Manuscript Project, microfilm reel Aln 27, Library of Congress ("And the Huyne and Bunau Regiments on the heights near Newport did duty in town").
66. Brigadier General Francis Smith Orders, May 29 and June 1, 1777, in ibid., 52-53. At his court-martial, Prescott stated that at the time of his capture, the chasseurs were stationed on the east coast of Aquidneck Island south of Fogland Ferry near Black Point along the Sakonnet Channel. Proceedings of a Board of General Officers held at New York, April 24, 1778, in ibid., Appendix II, 132.
67. Diary Entry, July 11, 1777, in Mackenzie, *Diary* 1:149.
68. Brigadier General Francis Smith Orders, May 26, 1777, in Hagist (ed.), *General Orders, R.I.,* 51.
69. Baule and Gilbert, *British Army Officers,* 10; *London Evening Post,* Aug. 23-26, 1777 (nephew of Lord Barrington); *Morning Post and Daily Advertiser* (London), Aug. 27, 1777 (same). On May 4, 1777, a few days before Prescott assumed the top command of the Newport garrison, the following general order was issued: "All orders coming from Lieutenant Barrington of the 7th Reg. or Royal Fusiliers are to be observed as if coming from an aide-de-camp of General Prescott." Hagist, *General Orders, Rhode Island,* 42. For Barrington's previous captivity, see G. Washington to B. Franklin, Aug. 18, 1776, in Twohig et al. (eds.), *Washington Papers* 6:60 and n. 3.
70. Proceedings of a Board of General Officers held at New York, April 24, 1778, in Hagist (ed.), *General Orders, R.I.,* Appendix II, 133.
71. J. Bowater to B. Fielding, July 27, 1777, in Balderston and Syrett (eds.), *Lost Letters,* 141; see also Diary Entry, July 11, 1777, in Mackenzie, *Diary* 1:150. Lieutenant Colonel James Marsh of the British 43rd Regiment, in writing of the risk to Prescott of sleeping at the Overing house, thought that the angry "feeling the inhabitants of the island in general have for him made his safety precarious." J. Marsh to E. Percy, July 21, 1777, Hugh Percy Papers, British Manuscript Project, microfilm reel Aln 27, Library of Congress.
72. Diary Entry, July 11, 1777, and Map of the Grounds about General Prescott's Quarters, in Mackenzie, *Diary* 1:148-50; Proceedings of a Board of General Officers held at New York, April 24, 1778, in Hagist (ed.), *General Orders, R.I.,* Appendix II, 134; Williams, *Life of Barton,* 51. Mackenzie reported that Smith's house stood 856 yards from the gate to the Overing's property. Diary Entry, July 11, 1777, in Mackenzie, *Diary* 1:150. This converts to .486 miles. For the site of the former Redwood estate, see also Abbass, *R.I. in the Rev.* 1:308-9 (map indicating estimated location of Redwood

estate) and 3:542 (describing site). Prescott, after assuming command, had ordered General Smith to reside near the British fortifications at Windmill Hill, which was about three-and-a-half miles north of the Redwood estate. Proceedings of a Board of General Officers held at New York, April 24, 1778, in Hagist (ed.), *General Orders, R.I.*, Appendix II, 134. In December 1776, Smith slept at another house on the West Road. Diary Entry, Dec. 18, 1776, in Mackenzie, *Diary* 1:128 (General Smith's "quarters at Mr. Collins' house on the West Road, about 5 miles from Newport").

73. J. Campbell to E. Percy, July 13, 1777, Hugh Percy Papers, British Manuscript Project, microfilm reel Aln 27, Library of Congress.

74. Diary Entries, June 10, 1777, in Mackenzie, *Diary* 1:138 and Greene, "Diary," *Historical Magazine* 4:1 (1860) (four British troops killed, one wounded); *Providence Gazette*, June 14, 1777 (four or five of the enemy killed). In a letter to the Continental Congress, General Spencer wrote the following about this raid: "Another party of about fifty attacked one of the enemy's guards of thirty—dispersed them, killed three, wounded one, and came near taking the whole." J. Spencer to J. Hancock, July 11, 1777, Papers of the Continental Congress, Miscellaneous Letters Addressed to Congress 1775-1789, M247, microfilm reel 102, item 78, XX, folio 129.

75. Diary Entries, June 12, 13, and 20, 1777, in Mackenzie, *Diary* 1:139 and 142.

76. List of Works Erected by the British, in Particulars of the Attack of Rhode Island in August 1778, by an anonymous British artillery officer, The Royal Artillery Institution ("June 1777. A redoubt made round the Guard House at the entrance upon the Common Fence after the attack made upon the guard").

CHAPTER SIX: THE OVERING HOUSE RAID

1. General Assembly Resolution, Jan. 1782 Session, in Bartlett (ed.), *Records of R.I.* 11:510.

2. Williams, *Life of Barton*, 41, n.; see also David P. Hall Recollections, in Peterson, *History of R.I.*, 216; John Howland Recollections, in Stone, *Life of Howland*, 87. Quako Honeyman's role has not been confirmed by any of Barton's writings, the writings of other members of Barton's party, or any official government correspondence, so there is some question of whether he in fact ever worked for Prescott and gave information about the British general to Barton or other Rhode Island authorities. There are a few clues to Quako's role in Prescott's capture from his successful attempt to avoid being reenslaved by the estate of the Honeyman family in 1781, following the British evacuation of Newport in October of 1779. After Honeyman's estate sought to reenslave him, Quako petitioned the General Assembly requesting to be declared a free man. Quako explained that he had been a slave of Newport attorney James Honeyman, that during the British occupation of Newport he had been leased by him to an unidentified British regiment, that "James Honeyman had agreed to sell and dispose of him to Col. Campbell, a British officer" (Colonel John Campbell commanded the British 22nd Regiment, then stationed at Windmill Hill), and that "the service in a British regiment being extremely disagreeable to him, he fled the island of Rhode Island [Aquidneck Island]." General Assembly Resolution, Dec. 1781 Session, in Bartlett (ed.), *Records of R.I.* 11:493-94. The Rhode Island Council of War, Quako further explained, after interrogating him in Providence "permitted him to go at large, and have his liberty." Id., 494. Sympathetic to Quako's petition, the General Assembly voted "that the said Quako remain in the same situation he is at present" and that it further investigate the matter and reconsider it at its next session. Id. In its January 1782 session, the General Assembly dealt with Quako as follows: "Whereas Quako, a black man, formerly a person whom James Honeyman, Esq., late of Newport, in the county of Newport, deceased, held in the bonds of slavery, did, during the time that the British troops were in possession of said Newport, and at the time that said Honeyman was living, leave

said island, and flee from the said British troops, and place himself under the protection of this government; and did, by the information he then gave, render great and essential service to this state and the public in general; and the council of war having given unto the said Quako a permit to pass and repass freely, without molestation, and thereby the said Quako did consider himself as a freeman. . . . It is voted and resolved that the said Quako be, and he is hereby declared to be manumitted and absolved from all ties of bondage and slavery which he heretofore owed and was held to by said James Honeyman, Esq, deceased, or any of his representatives, and he is hereby declared to be a freeman accordingly." General Assembly Resolution, Jan. 1782 session, in id., 509-10.

The above information indicates that Quako was leased to a British regiment. He was probably leased to a high-ranking British officer who could afford it, perhaps Colonel Campbell himself. Most British regiments in the first half of 1777 were based north of Newport on Aquidneck Island, including at Windmill Hill and at Fogland Ferry. Thus, once Prescott had moved his quarters to the Overing house, it would have been a courtesy for Campbell or another officer to permit Quako to perform personal services for Prescott at the Overing house. It is also possible that, not wanting to interfere with the work of Henry John Overing's slaves, Prescott had Quako permanently assigned to perform services for him and his aide-de-camp, Lieutenant William Barrington, who also had a room at the Overing house. In addition, the above information indicates that Quako escaped to the mainland prior to James Honeyman's death. James Honeyman died on February 15, 1778, so Quako's escape could well have been prior to Barton's capture of Prescott the night of July 10-11, 1777. The above information does not state that Quako worked for Prescott or provided information on Prescott for Barton's raid. This omission may have been because Rhode Island authorities did not want to risk retaliation against Quako by the British or by Tories, as in January 1782, the war was not yet officially over.

Catherine R. Williams, in her 1839 biography of William Barton, wrote that "Quaim, the negro who had been employed in the kitchen of Mr. Overing, had carried a very perfect account of the situation of the General in the house." Williams, *Life of Barton*, 41, n. This account has the most credibility, even if she did not get Quako's name exactly right. Williams gained her knowledge of the raid in part from meeting with a former member of Barton's party, Samuel Cory, then still residing on Aquidneck Island in Portsmouth. Id., 56. David P. Hall of New York informed Edward Peterson, who published his history of Rhode Island in 1853, that "Quako Honeyman, formerly servant of the Rev. James Honeyman, who was at this time a waiter of General Prescott, communicated to Col. Barton his exact position, and accompanied him on the enterprise." David P. Hall Recollections, in Peterson, *History of R.I.*, 216. (The father of James Honeyman [the lawyer] was James Honeyman, rector of Trinity Church in Newport.) At this time, in both armies, it was not uncommon for African-Americans to be employed as "waiters"—personal servants for a regiment's officers or for a particular officer. Similarly, John Howland, a private in a Rhode Island regiment who later became the first president of the Rhode Island Historical Society, recalled in his 1857 memoir that Barton's party, "guided by a negro who had been a servant in the [Overing] family, proceeded to the chamber in which the general slept." John Howland Recollections, in Stone (ed.), *Life of Howland*, 87. Both Hall and Howland confirm Quako's role in formerly serving for Prescott and providing information regarding Prescott to Barton, but both also conflate Quako's role with that of another African American member of Barton's party the night of July 10-11. The author believes that these sources are sufficiently credible to include Quako in the main text of the story of Prescott's capture. For more on Quako Honeyman, see the Appendix.

3. General Assembly Resolution, Dec. 1781 Session, in Bartlett (ed.), *Records of R.I.* 11:493-94.

4. Barton, "Narrative of the Capture of Major General Prescott," undated (probably around 1812), MSS 9003, vol. III, folder 13, R.I. Hist. Soc.
5. F. Smith to W. Howe, July 21, 1777, in Hagist (ed.), *General Orders, R.I.,* Appendix II, 129 ("The man who commanded the Rebels was a Major Barton, having been some time on this island before we came here, the people of the [Overing] house knew him"); Diary Entry, July 11, 1777, in Mackenzie, *Diary* 1:150 (Barton "had been quartered at the house opposite [of Overing's house] for some time").
6. Curfman, "Captain George Whitehorne and Some of his Descendants," *New England Hist. and Genealogical Reg.* 146:16 (1992); Cummings, "Portrait of a Loyalist," Newport Restoration Foundation Report, 3. Father-in-law John Whitehorne's house was at 416 Thames Street and is currently owned by the Newport Restoration Foundation. Cummings, "Portrait of a Loyalist," Newport Restoration Foundation Report, 5.
7. Cummings, "Portrait of a Loyalist," Newport Restoration Foundation Report, 5. In 1794, there were only seventeen sugar bakers in the United States. Id. For a list of the items in John Henry Overing's inventory relating to the sugar refining operations at the time of his death in 1783, and a short description of the sugar house and its equipment sold by son Henry Overing in 1803, see id., 14. See also *Newport Mercury,* April 24, 1759 (Overing advertising sugar loaves for sale); id., May 29, 1798 (John Henry Overing's son-in-law, Thomas Handy, advertising for sale sugar and molasses "At the sugar house lately improved by Messieurs Overing and Auchmuty").
8. "A Plan of the Town of Newport in Rhode Island," by Charles Blaskowitz, 1777, Geography and Map Division, Library of Congress. In this map, "Overing's Wharf" is the southernmost one off Thames Street. Its location was south of Young Street.
9. Cummings, "Portrait of a Loyalist," Newport Restoration Foundation Report, 5; *Newport Mercury,* Oct. 13, 1810 (up for auction, "the distillery, sugar house, wharf and appurtenances, formerly the property of John Overing, deceased"); id., July 11, 1818 (up for public auction, "the Overing estate, No. 9 Thames Street, consisting of a lot of land with a dwelling house thereon"); id., Aug. 1, 1818 (up for public auction, "real estate of Henry John Overing, situated at the south end of Thames Street," including a "lot of land, with a dwelling house thereon standing"); List of Quarters Occupied in the Town of Newport, by the Army under Command of the Comte de Rochambeau, during the Winter Quarters of 1780-81, in Simpson and Simpson, "A New Look at How Rochambeau Quartered his Army in Newport (1780-1781)," *Newport History* 72-73; 249-50 (Fall 2003-Spring 2004); 116 (colonel of French artillery assigned to John Overing's house at 10 Thames Street).
10. Bartlett (ed.), *R.I. Census 1774,* 24 and 176.
11. Cummings, "Portrait of a Loyalist," Newport Restoration Foundation Report, 12-13 (citing Newport City Hall Probate Records 3:122). Because Cato, Toney, Robin, and Pomp were listed in the inventory, they were likely the only Overing slaves at this time. A Rhode Island 1782 census indicated that the Overing family was residing in the Middletown house with five African-Americans, likely including Cato, Toney, Robin, and Pomp. Holbrook, *Rhode Island 1782 Census,* 90. With respect to the eleven blacks living in the two Overing households in 1774, either the others were free servants or had been slaves who had been freed prior to 1783. Some may have run away and joined the British army, leaving Newport with it in 1779. With the coming of the American Revolution and the British occupation of Newport, trade by Newport merchants declined dramatically, which would have decreased the need for slaves as well. According to April Cummings, "Cato died in 1821 at the age of 100. He was free by the time he died, and is listed as being interred at the Common Burial Ground. Robin died in October 1803 and was buried at the Common Burial Ground." Id., 13. After leaving Newport in 1782, John Henry Overing, Sr., died in Bermuda in March of 1783;

as a result, an inventory of his Newport property was needed to probate his will. Id., 10. His wife, Mary, died in Newport in 1816 and was buried at Trinity Church. Id., 14. For more information on the Overing children and the subsequent ownership of the Prescott Farm, see id., 10-17; see also *Providence Gazette,* May 31, 1783 ("Henry John Overing, Sr. died in Bermuda"); *Providence Patriot,* Sept. 30, 1820 ("one colored man, a slave to the Overing estate, is over 100 years old"). Henry John Overing, Jr., died around May 1782. *Providence Gazette,* May 11, 1782.

12. Henry John Overing Loyalist Rev. War Claim, in Coldham (ed.), *American Migrations,* 145; see also Cummings, "Portrait of a Loyalist," Newport Restoration Foundation Report, 5 (house purchased in 1771, along with fifty-five acres).

13. Bartlett (ed.), *R.I. Census 1774,* 24 and 176.

14. "A Topographical Chart of the Bay of Narragansett," by Charles Blaskowitz, London, 1777, Geography and Map Division, Library of Congress.

15. Cummings, "Portrait of a Loyalist," Newport Restoration Foundation Report, 2-3. The Overing house, now known as the Nichols-Overing House, is and has been beautifully maintained for many years by the Newport Restoration Foundation, but it is not open to the public. The former Overing farm has been called the Prescott Farm since the nineteenth century. The Newport Restoration Foundation calls the Overing house the Nichols-Overing house (Jonathan Nichols was its original owner). Its exterior retains its original appearance, and it still sits on a hill on several acres of unimproved, nicely landscaped land, with a creek running through the southern part of the property. On the south side of the creek is a park with several buildings that can be viewed by the public, including what the Newport Restoration Foundation calls The Guard House. Estimated to have been constructed in the mid-1700s, it was once attached to the Overing house. The building's original purpose is not certain, but the Newport Restoration Foundation believes the first floor was likely used as a kitchen (particularly in summer months) and that the second floor was likely used as extra storage space and as sleeping quarters for farm and house slaves or servants, or for soldiers during the British occupation of Aquidneck Island. It is possible that the second floor of The Guard House is what Major Mackenzie called the garret—where the British dragoon slept. The Newport Restoration Foundation also moved other historic buildings to the park at Prescott Farm, including the Robert Sherman Windmill (originally built in Warren in 1812), the Hicks House (c. 1715, believed to have housed the Bristol ferryman and his family), and the Sweet-Anthony House (c. 1730, a good example of an ordinary eighteenth-century Aquidneck Island farm house). On the north side of the creek, in addition to the Overing house, are the Potter House (c. 1790, moved from Connecticut), the Almy-Cory House (c. 1800), and Goudy Cottage (1960). Each of these properties on the northern side, including the Overing house, has been restored and is rented to a tenant steward. For more on the Newport Restoration Foundation, see www.newportrestoration.org. The Prescott Farm is on land that straddles both sides of the border between Middletown and Portsmouth. Abbass, *R.I. in the Rev.* 3:329 and 541.

16. Curfman, "Captain George Whitehorne and Some of his Descendants," *New England Hist. and Genealogical Reg.* 146:17 (1992). Henry John Overing was on a list of sixteen Tories the Rhode Island Council of War ordered to be confined in the Newport jail after patriot forces regained Newport in October 1779. R.I. Council of War Records, Nov. 12, 1779, R.I. State Archives. While Overing was a Tory, that treatment may have been a bit harsh. The Reverend Ezra Stiles prepared a list of Tories from Newport and gave each from one to four stars, with one star indicating a mild Tory and four stars indicating an active, strong Tory. Stiles gave Overing only one star. Diary Entry, March 1, 1777, in Dexter (ed.), *Stiles Diary* 2:131-34. After the war, Overing's widow, Mary, and son, Henry John, Jr., applied for reimbursement of losses by filing a

Loyalist war claim with the British government. They stated that their "large mansion house" had been used as a hospital and barracks during the British occupation and had been left in a "ruinous condition." Rhode Island Loyalist Colonel George Wightman added a note to the file that he was not aware that Henry John Overing had taken an active part in favor of British occupation forces and that Overing had remained in Newport after its evacuation in October 1779 (rather than take refuge on British ships headed for New York). He added that he was not aware of any damage to the Overing house. Overing's claim was rejected. Henry John Overing Loyalist Rev. War Claim, in Coldham (ed.), *American Migrations*, 145.

17. Cummings, "Portrait of a Loyalist," Newport Restoration Foundation Report, 4; Curfman, "Captain George Whitehorne and Some of his Descendants," *New England Hist. and Genealogical Reg.* 146:17 (1992). The Overing family occupied a pew in the front of the church on the outer side of the inner-right row, a prominent position in the church seating hierarchy. Cummings, "Portrait of a Loyalist," Newport Restoration Foundation Report, 4. Some descriptions of Prescott's raid claim the Overings were Quakers (see, for example, Lossing, *Pictorial Field-Book of the Rev.* 1:643), but there is no reference to them in Quaker records.

18. Henry John Overing Loyalist Rev. War Claim, in Coldham (ed.), *American Migrations*, 145; Baule and Gilbert, *British Army Officers*, 139. Henry Overing joined the 54th Regiment as an ensign in 1779 and was promoted to lieutenant in 1781. Id.

19. J. Stanton to W. Barton, July 5, 1777, MSS 9003, vol. III, folder 17, R.I. Hist. Soc.

20. J. Stanton to N. Cooke, July 12, 1777, in Jones (ed.), "Rev. Corr.," *Proceedings of the American Antiquarian Soc.* 36:346 (Oct. 1926).

21. The description of Barton's raid to capture Prescott relies mainly on the description of the raid by William Barton himself. See Barton, "Narrative of the Capture of Major General Prescott," undated (probably around 1812), MSS 9003, vol. III, folder 13, R.I. Hist. Soc. This existing version was not handwritten by Barton, but was signed by him. It is likely that this version was transcribed from a draft by Barton himself or from an oral report. This version has neat, readable, and graceful handwriting, while Barton's handwriting was virtually illegible and his spelling was poor. Moreover, this version was the basis of the first published account of the raid in 1812. See "American Gallantry," in *The Port Folio*, 2nd Ser., 8:3, 245-51 (Sept. 1812). This published version in turn was used in summaries of the narrative that circulated in the early-to-mid 1800s. See, e.g., Farmer and Moore (eds.), *Collections, Historical and Miscellaneous; and Monthly Literary Journal* 3:371-78 (Concord, NH: J. B. Moore, 1824); *American Anecdotes, Original and Select*, 121-33 (Boston, MA: Putnam and Hunt, 1830); Henry C. Watson (ed.), *The Old Bell of Independence; or, Philadelphia in 1776*, 156-69 (Philadelphia, PA: Lindsay and Blakiston, 1852). Barton's account was also published in 1888 in Bayles, *History of Newport County*, 646-52. Other useful original sources for the raid are: Diary Entry, July 11, 1777, in Mackenzie, *Diary* 1:148-51; *Providence Gazette*, July 12 and 19, 1777; Article in *Pennsylvania Evening Post*, July 29, 1777, quoted in Moore (ed.), *Diary of the Rev.* 1:467-70; Diary Entry, Aug. 3, 1777, in Thacher, *Journal*, 86-87; Abel Potter Rev. War Pension Application, 1832, in Dann (ed.), *Revolution Remembered*, 22-26 and National Archives Building; John Hunt Rev. War Pension Application, 1837, National Archives Building; Diary Entries, July 10-11, 1777, Journals of Christopher French, MMC-1869, Library of Congress. In addition, Ross's *Civil and Religious History of R.I.* (1838), 45-47, Williams's *Life of Barton* (1839), 40-60, Cowell's *Spirit of '76* (1850), 147-50, Peterson's *History of R.I.* (1853), 215-18, and Lossing's *Pictorial Field-Book of the Rev.* (1859), 643-45, are relatively contemporary histories, and the authors were able to interview some of the participants. Ensign Abel Potter's pension application was discovered more recently. Some of its details differ in respects to the other original sources, and in particular give Potter and his brother, Captain James Potter, a greater role than reported elsewhere. Given that the pension application was written fifty-five years after

the event, the more contemporary sources are given more credence here. For more on the credibility of Abel Potter's and John Hunt's pension applications, see text accompanying note 43 in the Appendix. Brian Kelly's recent *Best Little Stories from the American Rev.*, 219-21, relies on Potter's narrative. For the ranks of Barton's officers, see also Smith (ed.), *Civil and Military List of R.I.* 1:354 (May 1777).
22. Barton, "Narrative of the Capture of Major General Prescott," undated (probably around 1812), MSS 9003, vol. III, folder 13, R.I. Hist. Soc.
23. See Williams, *Life of Barton*, Appendix, 128 ("John Hunt, James Weaver, and Samuel Cory belonged to the neighborhood where Prescott was encamped"); Samuel Cory Rev. War Pension Application, National Archives Building (Cory fought at the battles of White Plans and Princeton); discussion of Thomas Austin whipping story in in main text of prior chapter accompanying note 45.
24. Paul, *The Part Borne by Sergeant John White Paul*, 11. One volunteer, Samuel Cory, had been stationed at Howland's Ferry in Major Munroe's boat company, serving on a small armed boat in company with Rhode Island's two row-galleys. Samuel Cory Rev. War Pension Application, National Archives Building. Isaac Brown from Stonington, Connecticut, another volunteer, a private in the 1st Rhode Island State Regiment, had experience rowing whaleboats. During the Rhode Island Campaign in August 1778, he helped row whaleboats carrying provisions to the French fleet in Narragansett Bay and he helped transport by whaleboat two hundred troops from Aquidneck Island to Warwick Neck. Isaac Brown Rev. War Pension Application, National Archives Building.
25. The best estimates of the total number of men in Barton's party range from forty-five to forty-eight. For a thorough discussion of the identities of the men who participated in the raid, see Paul, *The Part Borne by Sergeant John White Paul*, passim. Paul noted that the standard list of the participants was made not by William Barton, but after the war by Barton's son, John B. Barton, who listed a total of forty officers and soldiers, not including Barton himself. Around 1850 John B. Barton handed this list to historian Benson J. Lossing, who published it in his history of the Revolutionary War. See Lossing, *Pictorial Field-Book of the Rev.* 1:644, n.1 (the list is also set forth in Bayles, *History of Newport County*, 652-53). Paul pointed out that this list is virtually identical to the one in Catherine R. Williams's biography of Barton, who had published her book earlier in 1839 and who must have collected the names from various surviving participants in the raid. Paul logically concluded that John B. Barton must have copied Williams's list and handed it to Lossing. Paul further persuasively argued that the list is incomplete and that there were forty-eight participants. (Paul was upset that John B. Barton had inadvertently excluded from the list his relative, John White Paul.) The author has discovered that the first attempt to publish the names of the participants in Barton's raid was apparently made in 1824, when Barton's narrative was published in several newspapers. See *Spooner's Vermont Journal* (Windsor, Vermont), Oct. 11, 1824; *Hallowell Gazette* (Hallowell, Maine), Nov. 10, 1824. This list contains thirty-seven names and was probably made with the assistance of William Barton. The publisher misspelled several names; he may have had difficulty reading Barton's poor handwriting. Catherine R. Williams apparently started with this list, as parts of her list are in the same order as the 1824 list. However, she corrected the spelling of a number of the names and added to the list the following persons: John Hunt, Thomas Austin, Jack Sisson ("the Black, and boat steerer"), and Howe or Whiting ("boat steerer"). See Williams, *Life of Barton*, Appendix, 127-28. She was able to speak with several surviving participants of the raid, including Samuel Cory, who could have provided the additional names. It was this list that John B. Barton then handed to Lossing.

A contemporary account based on a letter from "a writer in Providence, Rhode Island" indicated that there were thirty-eight privates and six officers. Article in *Pennsylvania Evening Post*, July 29, 1777, quoted in Moore (ed.), *Diary of the Rev.*

1:470, n.1. The *Providence Gazette* reported that the party consisted of thirty-eight men plus officers Barton, Adams, Phillips, Potter, Babcock, and Wielcocks, for a total of forty-five men. *Providence Gazette,* July 12, 1777. The Reverend Ezra Stiles repeated this estimate, but he may have been relying solely on the newspaper article. Diary Entry, July 17, 1777, in Dexter (ed.), *Stiles Diary* 2:192. General Spencer, on July 11, wrote that Barton and "the number of forty, including Captains Adams and Philips" in "four whaleboats" captured Prescott, but both the number of men and whaleboats seems too low. J. Spencer to J. Hancock, July 11, 1777, Papers of the Continental Congress, Miscellaneous Letters Addressed to Congress 1775-1789, M247, microfilm reel 102, item 78, XX, folio 129. Williams, in her biography of Barton, wrote that the party consisted of a total of forty-eight men: forty-one privates, five officers, Barton and his military servant (Jack Sisson, Guy Watson, or Prince Goodwin). Williams, *Life of Barton,* 47-48. Barton in his own narrative stated that he had forty volunteers and five officers, plus himself. If Barton was not including his military servant, then including the servant made forty-seven persons. (At a later point in the narrative, immediately prior to the raid, Barton said that he had forty-one men, officers included; this is likely an error and it is likely this figure does not include him and the five officers.) In his pension application in 1837, John Hunt said that forty-seven men volunteered to go with Barton. John Hunt Rev. War Pension Application, National Archives Building. The author believes forty-eight is the best estimate, based in part on the number of men to man the boats—forty-five—plus the additions of Barton, his military servant (Guy Watson or Prince Goodwin), and the last-minute addition, Captain Ebenezer Adams. With forty-five men, each of the five whaleboats would have had six oarsmen (three on each side), one man in reserve to help tired men, one boat steerer and one officer. It is also possible that each officer in a boat (other than Barton) and the extra man served as oarsmen, making four oarsmen on each side.

26. Cowell, *Spirit of '76,* 150; Williams, *Life of Barton,* 127.

27. Barton, "Narrative of the Capture of Major General Prescott," undated (probably around 1812), MSS 9003, vol. III, folder 13, R.I. Hist. Soc.; Williams, *Life of Barton,* Appendix, 127-28; Cowell, *Spirit of '76,* 150; Fowler, *History of Fall River,* 26. Catherine R. Williams, in her biography of Barton, states that Page was a member of the Narragansett tribe and that after the war he moved to Freetown, Massachusetts. In his history of Fall River, Orin Fowler described Page as from Freetown and that he was the last male member of the Pocasset tribe in Massachusetts. (Fowler was wrong on two counts. First, the Pocassets are a band within the Wampanoag tribe. Second, the Pocasset are still a distinct Native-American race within the Wampanoag tribe (centered in and around Fall River, Massachusetts) that is formally recognized by the U.S. federal government. See "Wampanoag people," in Wikipedia, at www.wikipedia.org/wiki/Wampanoag_people.) While not certain, the author believes Williams's account is the more credible based on the following: Page served in a Rhode Island regiment; there were other persons of color from the Narragansett tribe serving in Rhode Island regiments; and authors Williams and Fowler agree that Page moved to Freetown after the war. According to Rhode Island historian J. Lewis Diman: "To test their [the volunteers'] skill [at rowing], he [Barton] placed a stake in the river above Stone Bridge, near what used to be called the "Old Stills," where the present railroad bridge now stands, and exercised them in pulling round it. An Indian named Daniel Page, who years ago lived beyond the Fall River ponds, loved to tell the story that, in these trials, Barton's boat regularly came in last. Page proposed to make up another crew. His offer was accepted, and after that Barton always led the little flotilla." Diman, *The Capture of General Prescott,* 24. For the story of Page seizing Prescott's sword from his room, see the text accompanying note 44 in the Appendix. Page enlisted in Stanton's Rhode Island State Regiment on January 3, 1777, and remained in the regiment through 1780.

Index of Military Service Records, 1775-1783, R.I. State Archives. In the 1790 federal census, Daniel Page is listed as residing in Freetown, in Bristol County, Massachusetts, heading a household of seven persons of color. *Heads of Families at the First Census 1790, Massachusetts*, 46. He is not listed in the Massachusetts or Rhode Island census records for 1800, 1810, or 1820.

28. For a discussion of Jack Sisson, Guy Watson, and Prince Goodwin and their roles in the capture of General Prescott and how it affected their lives, see the Appendix.

29. Diary Entry, July 4, 1777, in Mackenzie, *Diary* 1:145-46.

30. Barton, "Narrative of the Capture of Major General Prescott," undated (probably around 1812), MSS 9003, vol. III, folder 13, R.I. Hist. Soc.

31. Smith (ed.), *Civil and Military List of R.I.* 1:355 and 357 (June and Dec. 1777).

32. Diary Entry, July 9, 1777, in Mackenzie, *Diary* 1:148 (weather).

33. Log of HMS *Renown*, July 9, 1777, ADM 51/776, British National Archives; see also Log of HMS *Greyhound*, July 9, 1777, ADM 51/420, British National Archives ("fresh gales and thick weather with rain"); Log of HMS *Diamond*, July 9, 1777, in Abbass, *R.I. in the Rev.* 4:116 ("First part moderate with some rain, middle and latter parts fresh breezes and squally with rain").

34. Log of HMS *Renown*, July 10, 1777, ADM 51/776, British National Archives (morning was "moderate and foggy with rain at times;" middle of the day's weather was "light airs and cloudy;" and evening was "moderate and cloudy"); Log of HMS *Greyhound*, July 10, 1777, ADM 51/420 British National Archives ("fresh breezes and cloudy"); Log of HMS *Diamond*, July 9, 1777, in Abbass, *R.I. in the Rev.* 4:116 ("Moderate and cloudy"); Diary Entry, July 10, 1777, in Mackenzie, *Diary* 1:148.

35. McBurney, "British Treatment of Prisoners During the Occupation of Newport, 1776-1779: Disease, Starvation and Death Stalk the Prisons Ships," *Newport History* 79:263, 5-9 (Fall 2010).

36. For the probable positions of the British frigates, see Disposition of Vice Admiral Richard Lord Howe's Fleet in North America, June 1777 and August 1777, with Rhode Island ships by disposition dated May 18, 1777, in Morgan, Crawford et al. (eds.), *Naval Docs. of the A.R.* 9:32 and 9:841. See the map at page 135 of this book for the stations of the ships. HMS *Orpheus* (32 guns and 220-man crew) was stationed in between Calf Pasture Point on the western shore of Narragansett Bay in between Updike's Newtown (now Wickford) and East Greenwich, and the midpoint of Prudence Island. HMS *Renown* (50 guns and 350-man crew) was stationed between South Ferry on the western Narragansett shore and Conanicut Island. HMS *Amazon* (32 guns and 220-man crew) was stationed in the waters between the northeast part of Prudence Island and Arnold's Point, Aquidneck Island. HMS *Juno* (32 guns and a 220-man crew) was stationed north of Dyer's Island between Coggeshall Point and Prudence Island, to the south of *Amazon*. HMS *Chatham* (50 guns and a 367-man crew) was stationed south of the *Amazon* and to the north of Gould Island. While since May 18 almost two months had passed, it appears that the stations had not changed by July 10. However, some of the ships at the stations had changed. By that date, HMS *Lark* (32 guns and 220-man crew) had replaced the *Amazon*; HMS *Diamond* (32 guns and 220-man crew) had taken the place of *Juno* above Dyer's Island; and HMS *Greyhound* (32 guns and 220-man crew) had taken the place of *Orpheus*. Diary Entry, July 11, 1777, in Mackenzie, *Diary* 1:149. For confirmation of the stations of these ships, see also Diary Entry, June 21, 1777, in id., 143 (*Greyhound* off East Greenwich); Diary Entry, June 4, 1777, in id., 135 (*Diamond* stationed north of Dyer's Island; *Lark* is stationed north of *Diamond*); Diary Entry, June 19, 1777, in id., 141 (*Lark* and *Diamond* fire guns to alert other ships to American vessel attempting to pass through channel); Diary Entries, June 20 and 22, and July 19, 1777, in id., 142-43 and 155 (*Lark* stationed south of Papasquash Point); Diary Entry, June 19, 1777, in id., 141 ("galley

went down to the *Chatham* this evening"); Diary Entry, Aug. 3, 1777, in id., 160 (Americans fire cannon from the Narragansett Shore at the *Renown*, which lay in the Narragansett (West) Channel between South Ferry and Conanicut Island); Log of HMS *Diamond*, June 7, 1777 and July 9-12, 1777, in Abbass, *R.I. in the Rev.* 4:112 (June 7—"At a single anchor in Rhode Island Harbor; Dyer's Island south by west about 1 mile") (July 9-12—"Anchored in Rhode Island Harbor").

37. Log of HMS *Diamond*, Nov. 17, 25, and 28, 1777, in Abbass, *R.I. in the Rev.* 4:123-25; see also Log of HMS *Diamond*, Feb. 6, 1778, in id., 4:131 ("boats as usual rowing guard").

38. Log of *HMS Lark*, July 8, 9, and 10, 1777, ADM 52/1826, British National Archives.

39. Diary Entry, March 30, 1777, in Laughton (ed.), "Journal of Bartholomew James," *Pubs. of the Navy Records Soc.* 6:40 (1896). General Joseph Spencer, in his letter to the Continental Congress, reported that Barton's party while rowing their whaleboats "had the good fortune to escape discovery by the enemy's guard boats." J. Spencer to J. Hancock, July 11, 1777, Papers of the Continental Congress, Miscellaneous Letters Addressed to Congress 1775-1789, M247, microfilm reel 102, item 78, XX, folio 129 and excerpted in *The Remembrancer for the Year 1777*, 271. The July 12, 1777, edition of the *Providence Gazette* noted that Barton's boats passed the enemy's ships "and guard boats." The historian Benson Lossing, who spoke with some of the participants in Barton's raid, also mentioned guard boats. Lossing, *Pictorial Field-Book of the Rev.* 1:643-44. None of the logs of the warships in Narragansett Bay mentioned sending out guard boats the night of July 10. The author believes this omission was because doing so was such an ordinary measure that it was not always remarked upon in ship logs. On the other hand, the weather was calm and the wind light, thus making it very unlikely that any American vessel would try to break out of the British navy's blockade of Narragansett Bay. Accordingly, the captains of the five British warships may not have all sent out guard ships that night. See also text accompanying note 42 below.

40. F. Smith to W. Howe, July 12, 1777, in Hagist (ed.), *General Orders, R.I.*, Appendix II, 129 (dark); Diary Entry, July 10, 1777, in Mackenzie, *Diary* 1:148 ("fair pleasant weather").

41. Same sources as in note 36 above.

42. Barton, "Narrative of the Capture of Major General Prescott," undated (probably around 1812), MSS 9003, vol. III, folder 13, R.I. Hist. Soc.; see also Williams, *Life of Barton*, Appendix, 142; Ross, *Civil and Religious History of R.I.*, 45. Williams accurately named three of the British warships on station that night, which gives her account credibility.

43. Barton, "Narrative of the Capture of Major General Prescott," undated (probably around 1812), MSS 9003, vol. III, folder 13, R.I. Hist. Soc.

44. F. Smith to W. Howe, July 12, 1777, in Hagist (ed.), *General Orders, R.I.*, Appendix II, 129; J. Campbell to H. Percy, July 13, 1777, Hugh Percy Papers, British Manuscript Project, microfilm reel Aln 27, Library of Congress.

45. For the term "sand bluffs," see Abbass, *R.I. in the Rev.* 1:306. Abbass noted that Barton's "landing spot is near where" HMS *Cerberus*, a 28-gun frigate "was later lost" during the Rhode Island Campaign in August of 1778, "and the 'sand bluff' is the same as the 'brow of the hill' described in the *Cerberus's* log." Id. Abbass later writes that the landing spot was "possibly at Carr's Point but [was] more likely nearer the creek mouth." Id. (map between pages 308 and 309). Major Frederick Mackenzie's Map of the Grounds about General Prescott's Quarters is the most reliable source for the landing spot, as he and other British army officers could tell from the beaten-down grass, brush, and bushes the route Barton's party had taken. He had the landing spot pinpointed as a small point just north of the mouth of Redwood Creek. See Mackenzie, *Diary* 1:148-49.

46. See map at page 135 of this book. Major Mackenzie's estimate that the *Chatham* was four miles from the landing spot of Barton's party does not seem accurate based on the assigned station of the ship. See Diary Entry, July 11, 1777, and Frederick Mackenzie Map of the Grounds about General Prescott's Quarters, in Mackenzie, *Diary* 1:148-49.

47. Mackenzie reported that from Overing's door to where Barton's party landed, tracing the tracks taken by Barton's party, the distance was 1,733 yards. Diary Entry, July 11, 1777, in Mackenzie, *Diary* 1:150. This converts to .985 miles. Mackenzie also reported that from Overing's gate to the guard house was 466 yards. Id. This converts to .265 miles.

48. Hagist, "Deserter Walter Graham, 22nd Regiment of Foot," July 19, 2009, in www.redcoat76.blogspot.com. An avid historian of the British army in North America (see, e.g., Hagist, Don N., *British Soldiers, American War, Voices of the American Revolution*, Yardley, PA: Westholme Publishing, 2012), Hagist discovered that the sentry's name was Walter Graham by reviewing muster rolls of the 22nd Regiment. For more on Graham's captivity and later life, see the Appendix.

49. This description is based on Frederick Mackenzie Map of the Grounds about General Prescott's Quarters, in Mackenzie, *Diary* 1:148-49 and the author walking the same ground. Mackenzie based his map of the route taken by Barton's party on the vegetation that was worn down by his men. A more colorful, and nearly as accurate description, is provided by Catherine R. Williams, the early biographer of William Barton. See Williams, *Life of Barton*, 55-56. Today, the land west of the Overing house and west of the West Road is in a similar state to the way it was on the night of July 10-11, except that there would have been more tilled farmland back then. The creek and sand bluff remain, and the area near the landing is overgrown with brush and much of it is swampy. The area near the landing is apparently owned by the United States Navy, as there are two abandoned navy buildings on the site; the area up near the West Road is owned by a recent housing development (fortunately there are not many houses in this tract, at least not yet). The creek and gully surrounding it are still in their natural states. Middletown Historical Cemetery No. 1, a plot used by the Coggeshall family, is near the path that Barton's party used.

50. Barton, "Narrative of the Capture of Major General Prescott," undated (probably around 1812), MSS 9003, vol. III, folder 13, R.I. Hist. Soc. Lossing's description states that "the main portion of the expedition passed about midway between a British guardhouse and the encampment of a company of light horse, while the remainder was to make a circuitous route to approach Prescott's quarters from the rear, and secure the doors." Lossing, *Pictorial Field-Book of the Rev.* 1:644. While the division of Barton's party may have occurred prior to Barton's party reaching the West Road, the author has assumed that the division of the parties did not occur until they reached the West Road. In part, the author reached this conclusion on the basis of Barton's description and the British finding only one path to the West Road. In 1818, a surviving member of Barton's party, Joseph Dennis, informed Samuel Brown Barrell, Barton's Boston publisher, about some of the raid's details. Barrell wrote to Barton, "Joseph Dennis says that you stopped your little party in the front yard of a house near that . . . in which Prescott was, that you watched there until the guard was relieved, and that you then proceeded Indian file to Prescott's quarters." S. B. Barrell to W. Barton, Sept. 24, 1818, MSS 9006, Shepley Papers, vol. 8, p. 82, R.I. Historical Soc. Barrell requested that Barton include these and other details in his narrative, but Barton never provided an expanded written version of the narrative to Barrell or anyone else. Because Barton did not include these details in his narrative, the author has not included them in the main text.

51. General Smith wrote to General Howe in New York that the sentry "was heard to challenge twice." F. Smith to W. Howe, July 12, 1777, in Hagist (ed.), *General Orders,*

R.I., Appendix II, 129. This is confirmed by two American sources. Barton, "Narrative of the Capture of Major General Prescott," undated (probably around 1812), MSS 9003, vol. III, folder 13, R.I. Hist. Soc.; article in *Pennsylvania Evening Post,* July 29, 1777, quoted in Moore (ed.), *Diary of the Rev.* 1:467-70.

52. Diary Entry, July 11, 1777, in Mackenzie, *Diary* 1:148. The day after the raid, General Smith increased the guard at his house and ordered that all sentries have their muskets loaded. Smith's General Orders, July 11, 1777, in Hagist (ed.), *General Orders, R.I.,* 59-60. This order supports Mackenzie's statement that the night before, the sentry at the Overing house did not have his musket loaded.

53. Abel Potter Rev. War Pension Application, in Dann (ed.), *Revolution Remembered,* 23 and National Archives Building (for "I won't" quote). Potter claimed that he first spoke to the sentry, rather than Barton, but the author does not find that claim credible.

54. Barton, "Narrative of the Capture of Major General Prescott," undated (probably around 1812), MSS 9003, vol. III, folder 13, R.I. Hist. Soc.

55. F. Smith to W. Howe, July 21, 1777, in Hagist (ed.), *General Orders, R.I.,* Appendix II, 129. Barton's and Mackenzie's accounts both refer to all of the doors being forced open at the same time. Barton, "Narrative of the Capture of Major General Prescott," undated (probably around 1812), MSS 9003, vol. III, folder 13, R.I. Hist. Soc.; Diary Entry, July 11, 1777, in Mackenzie, *Diary* 1:148.

56. Joseph Dennis Recollections, 1818, in S. B. Barrell to W. Barton, Sept. 24, 1818, MSS 9006, Shepley Papers, vol. 8., p. 82. This incident, and the different versions of it, are discussed at length in the main text accompanying notes 19 to 37 in the Appendix.

57. Barton, "Narrative of the Capture of Major General Prescott," undated (probably around 1812), MSS 9003, vol. III, folder 13, R.I. Hist. Soc. Historian Benson J. Lossing visited the Overing house around 1850 and wrote the following: "The present occupant kindly showed me the room in which Prescott was lying at the time of his capture. It is on the second floor, at the southwest corner of the house, or on the right as seen in the engraving." Lossing, *Pictorial Field-Book of the Rev.* 1:644-45, n. 2.

58. Diary Entry, July 11, 1777, in Mackenzie, *Diary* 1:149.

59. Barton, "Narrative of the Capture of Major General Prescott," undated (probably around 1812), MSS 9003, vol. III, folder 13, R.I. Hist. Soc.

60. John Howland Recollections, in Stone, *Life of Howland,* 87.

61. Barton, "Narrative of the Capture of Major General Prescott," undated (probably around 1812), MSS 9003, vol. III, folder 13, R.I. Hist. Soc.

62. Abel Potter Rev. War Pension Application, 1832, in Dann (ed.), *Revolution Remembered,* 22-26 and National Archives Building

63. J. Knowles to H. Percy, April 12, 1778, Hugh Percy Papers, British Manuscript Project, microfilm reel Aln 27, Library of Congress. Lieutenant John Knowles wrote the letter on board the *Grand Duke* transport vessel, which was then moored off Newport. While Knowles mentioned the "two Miss Overings," he must have meant Henrietta and her mother, Mary, serving as chaperone. Mary had a second daughter, but she was just two years old at the time. Curfman, "Captain George Whitehorne and Some of his Descendants," *New England Historical and Genealogical Reg.* 146:17 (1992). This book publicizes this incident for the first time. For Henrietta's unfortunate marriage to a disingenuous British officer at Trinity Church in 1778, see an article on the topic by Don N. Hagist in the Spring 2014 edition of *Newport History Journal.* She later married a distant relative, Robert Nicholas Auchmuty, at Trinity Church in 1785 and is buried in Greenwood Cemetery in Brooklyn, New York. Id. Her portrait, painted by Gilbert Stuart in 1816 when she was fifty-six years-old, hangs in the Brooklyn Museum. Lieutenant Knowles was an Agent of Transports for the Royal Navy but still held a rank in it. During the Revolutionary War, he was promoted to commander on

September 28, 1778, and to captain on July 1, 1780. He died in 1801, shortly after being made rear admiral of the White. See Syrett and DiNardo, *Commissioned Sea Officers of the Royal Navy*, 262.

64. Diary Entry, July 11, 1777, in Mackenzie, *Diary* 1:149.

65. Log of *HMS Lark*, July 10, 1777, ADM 52/1826, British National Archives.

66. A journal kept by a Hessian officer of the von Huyn regiment describes the use of "alarm poles" by the British army at the northern part of Aquidneck Island in the winter of 1777: "They [the rebels] frequently attacked our detachments and made several attempts to land, so that several times, especially during the night, signals were given by firing guns and setting alarm poles on fire for the regiments to turn out immediately." Quoted in Schroder, *Hessians in Newport*, 79-80. For the use of "beacon poles" around Providence and other coastal locations by Rhode Island authorities to provide an alarm in the event of a British invasion of the mainland, see Field, *Revolutionary Defences*, 49-55.

67. Diary Entry, July 11, 1777, in Mackenzie, *Diary* 1:149; see also *Providence Gazette*, July 12, 1777 ("sometime after [Barton's party left Aquidneck Island], the enemy fired rockets from their several posts, as signals for an alarm; but too late"); Diary Entry, July 10, 1777, Journals of Christopher French, MMC-1869, Library of Congress ("Signals were then made and guns fired but all to no purpose").

68. Log of *HMS Lark*, July 10, 1777, ADM 52/1826, British National Archives.

69. Barton, "Narrative of the Capture of Major General Prescott," undated (probably around 1812), MSS 9003, vol. III, folder 13, R.I. Hist. Soc.

70. Log of *HMS Lark*, July 10, 1777, ADM 52/1826, British National Archives.

71. Ibid.

72. The David Arnold Tavern was located on the "Main road in Old Warwick, a few rods south from the road to Warwick Neck." Geake, *Historic Taverns of R.I.*, 76.

73. J. Spencer to J. Trumbull, July 11, 1777, in "The Trumbull Papers," *Mass. Hist. Soc. Coll.*, 7th Ser., 3:16-17 (1902).

74. John Howland Recollections, in Stone, *Life of Howland*, 87.

75. Diary Entry, July 11, 1777, in Mackenzie, *Diary* 1:149.

CHAPTER SEVEN: AN OFFICER OF EQUAL RANK

1. J. Stanton to N. Cooke, July 12, 1777, in Jones (ed.), "Rev. Corr.," *Proceedings of the American Antiquarian Soc.* 36:346 (Oct. 1926).

2. J. Spencer to J. Trumbull, July 11, 1777, in "The Trumbull Papers," *Mass. Hist. Soc. Coll.*, 7th Ser., 3:16-17 (1902) (sending Captain John Wylie of Connecticut as the messenger). For the letter, see J. Spencer to G. Washington, July 11, 1777, microfilm reel 42, George Washington Papers, Manuscript Reading Room, Library of Congress.

3. Twohig et al. (eds.), *Washington Papers* 10:297, n.1.

4. G. Washington to J. Spencer, July 17, 1777, in ibid., 313.

5. G. Washington to J. Hancock, July 16, 1777, in ibid., 294. For Spencer's letter to Congress, see J. Spencer to J. Hancock, July 11, 1777, Papers of the Continental Congress, Miscellaneous Letters Addressed to Congress 1775-1789, M247, microfilm reel 102, item 78, XX, folio 129 and excerpted in *The Remembrancer for the Year 1777*, 271.

6. Resolution, July 19, 1777, session, in Ford (ed.), *Journals of the Continental Congress* 8:565.

7. Resolution, July 25, 1777, session, in ibid., 8:580; see also J. Hancock to W. Barton, July 26, 1777, in Smith (ed.), *Letters of Delegates* 7:377-78; J. Hancock to G. Washington, July 26, 1777, in Twohig et al. (eds.), *Washington Papers* 10:427.

8. J. Adams to A. Adams, July 20, 1777, in Smith (ed.), *Letters of Delegates* 7:354.

9. B. Snowden to B. Franklin, Oct. 16, 1777, in Willcox et al. (eds.), *Franklin Papers* 25:77.
10. Diary Entry, Aug. 3, 1777, in Thacher, *Journal*, 86-87.
11. J. Trumbull to G. Washington, July 25, 1777, in Twohig et al. (eds.), *Washington Papers* 10:422.
12. J. Stanton to N. Cooke, July 12, 1777, in Jones (ed.), "Rev. Corr.," *Proceedings of the American Antiquarian Soc.* 36:346 (Oct. 1926).
13. Diary Entry, July 13, 1777, in Mackenzie, *Diary* 1:153.
14. G. Washington to J. Spencer, July 17, 1777, in Twohig et al. (eds.), *Washington Papers* 10:313. Actually, the day before he wrote to Spencer, Washington had already written a letter to Howe proposing to exchange Prescott for Lee. G. Washington to W. Howe, July 16, 1777, in id., 296-97.
15. Log of HMS *Lark*, July 12, 1777, ADM 52/924, British National Archives; see also Log of HMS *Diamond*, July 12, 1777, in Abbass, *R.I. in the Rev.* 4:116. ("PM at 1/2 past 3 the *Lark* made the signal for an armed vessel coming down from Providence, which we repeated to the Commodore [Admiral Parker on HMS *Chatham* to the south]. The *Lark* got under way and gave chase. Hove short. At 5 p.m. the *Lark* came to.")
16. Williams, *Life of Barton*, Appendix, 126.
17. General Assembly Resolutions, Aug. 1777 session, in Bartlett (ed.), *Records of R.I.* 8:290.
18. Memorial of Lt. Colonel William Barton to the Continental Congress, undated (about Nov. 1777), Papers of the Continental Congress, Memorials Addressed to Congress 1775-1789, M247, microfilm reel 48, item 41, I, folio 148.
19. Resolution, Dec. 24, 1777, in Ford (ed.), *Journals of the Continental Congress* 8:1051.
20. Ibid., 150.
21. Ibid., 150-51.
22. Diary Entry, Dec. 14, 1777, in ibid., 223.
23. J. Spencer to J. Hancock, July 11, 1777, Papers of the Continental Congress, Miscellaneous Letters Addressed to Congress 1775-1789, M247, microfilm reel 102, item 78, XX, folio 129 and excerpted in *The Remembrancer for the Year 1777*, 271.
24. Captain John [illegible last name] to H. Percy, July 15, 1777, Hugh Percy Papers, British Manuscript Project, microfilm reel Aln 27, Library of Congress.
25. J. Marsh to H. Percy, July 21, 1777 in ibid.
26. J. Campbell to H. Percy, July 13, 1777, in ibid. Major Mackenzie wrote that some of Barton's party "took with them two small silver cups, a great coat, a book, and some other trifles, and broke to pieces a large looking glass in the parlor. . . . they did not take some money which was in the General's room, nor a pair of pistols which hung up in Mr. Barrington's." Diary Entry, July 12, 1777, in Mackenzie, *Diary* 1:151.
27. Diary Entry, July 30, 1777, in Allen, "Diary of James Allen," *Penn. Mag. of History and Biography* 9:287 (1885).
28. Smith's General Orders, July 11, 1777, in Hagist (ed.), *General Orders*, 59-60.
29. Diary Entry, July 11, 1777, in Mackenzie, *Diary* 1:148.
30. F. Smith to W. Howe, July 12, 1777, in Hagist (ed.), *General Orders, R.I.*, Appendix II, 129; see also W. Howe's Orders, Oct. 8, 1776, in "Gen. Sir William Howe's Orders, 1776," *N.Y. Hist. Soc. Coll.* 385 (1884) ("Capt.-Lieut. Welch of the 17th Regiment is appointed aide-de-camp to Major General Prescott"); Diary Entry, July 12, 1777, in Mackenzie, *Diary* 1:151.
31. Diary Entry, July 12, 1777, in Mackenzie, *Diary* 1:151; see also Log of HMS *Chatham*, July 12, 1777, ADM 51/192, British National Archives ("a.m. sent the first lieutenant, mate and 27 men to take command of the *Unicorn* prize, an armed sloop"). According to Major Mackenzie, the vessel departed Newport at 6:00 p.m. on July 12. Diary Entry, July 12, 1777, in Mackenzie, *Diary* 1:151. The ship's log for HMS

Chatham stated that the vessel left Newport at 7:00 a.m. on July 13, 1777. Log of HMS *Chatham,* July 13, 1777, ADM 51/177, British National Archives. The vessel was a captured American privateer, an armed sloop with four cannon and eight swivel guns, which HMS *Unicorn* had brought into Newport on July 5. See Log of HMS *Renown,* July 5, 1777, ADM 51/776, British National Archives ("sailed into Newport his Majesty's ship *Unicorn* with 2 prizes"); Diary Entry, July 5, 1777, in Mackenzie, *Diary* 1:146 ("The *Unicorn* arrived this afternoon with a privateer sloop of 4 guns, 8 swivels and 40 men"). The author did not find the letter to Admiral Howe and does not know if it still exists.

32. Diary Entry, July 14, 1777, in Muenchhausen, *At General Howe's Side,* 21; see also Diary Entry, July 14, 1777, in Kemble, "Journal," *N.Y. Hist. Soc. Coll.* 124-25 (1884).
33. Diary Entry, July 14, 1777, in Kemble, "Journal," *N.Y. Hist. Soc. Coll.* 125 (1884).
34. Diary Entry, July 14, 1777, in Muenchhausen, *At General Howe's Side,* 21.
35. Captain John [illegible last name] to H. Percy, July 15, 1777, Hugh Percy Papers, British Manuscript Project, microfilm reel Aln 27, Library of Congress. From the rest of the letter, it is clear that the letter's author served in the army.
36. J. Bowater to B. Fielding, July 27, 1777, in Balderston and Syrett (eds.), *Lost Letters,* 140-41.
37. Diary Entry, July 14, 1777, in Tatum (ed.), *Serle Journal,* 238.
38. W. Howe to G. Germain, July 15, 1777, CO 5/94, British National Archives; *Newport Gazette,* July 24, 1777; H. Barry to H. Percy, July 22, 1777, Hugh Percy Papers, British Manuscript Project, microfilm reel Aln 27, Library of Congress.
39. Diary Entry, July 17, 1777, in MacVeagh (ed.), *Journal of Nicholas Cresswell,* 258.
40. Diary Entry, July 17, 1777, in Dexter (ed.), *Stiles Diary* 2:192.
41. J. Bowater to B. Fielding, July 27, 1777, in Balderston and Syrett (eds.), *Lost Letters,* 140-41.
42. John Howland Recollections, in Stone, *Life of Howland,* 87. In the 1800s, Howland became a historian and president of the Rhode Island Historical Society.
43. Williams, *Life of Barton,* Appendix, 131. The story ends, "Sam thought the General must have found out, on that occasion, 'where the shoe pinched.'"
44. J. Spencer to J. Trumbull, July 14, 1777, in "Trumbull Papers," *Mass. Hist. Soc. Coll.,* 7th Series, 3:80 (1904).
45. F. Smith to W. Howe, July 12, 1777, in Bartlett (ed.), *Records of R.I.* 8:281-82 and Hagist (ed.), *General Orders, R.I.,* Appendix II, 130. For the identity of Prescott's servant, see 1777 and 1778 muster rolls, 7th Regiment of Foot, WO 12/2474, British National Archives, where Carder is described in early 1777 as "on duty at Rhode Island," in early 1778 as on "General Prescott's leave," and in late 1778 (by which time Prescott had returned to Newport) as "on duty at Rhode Island." The author thanks Don N. Hagist for providing this information.
46. H. Barry to H. Percy, July 22, 1777, Hugh Percy Papers, British Manuscript Project, microfilm reel Aln 27, Library of Congress; see also Diary Entries, July 12 and 13, 1777, in Mackenzie, *Diary* 1:151 and 153.
47. S. Hopkins to H. Barry, July 13, 1777, in Bartlett (ed.), *Records of R.I.* 8:283.
48. Diary Entry, July 13, 1777, in Mackenzie, *Diary* 1:153; *Providence Gazette,* July 19, 1777.
49. J. Spencer to G. Washington, July 11, 1778, in Twohig et al. (eds.), *Washington Papers* 10:250.
50. R. Prescott Parole, July 14, 1777, copied in Peter Force Transcripts, Jonathan Trumbull Papers, Series 7E, microfilm reel 47, Library of Congress; Arnold, *History of the State of RI* 2:403-04, n.1.
51. J. Spencer to J. Trumbull, July 14, 1777, in "Trumbull Papers," *Mass. Hist. Soc. Coll.,* 7th Series, 3:80-81 (1904); *Providence Gazette,* July 19, 1777.

52. J. Campbell to H. Percy, March 7, 1778, in Hugh Percy Papers, British Manuscript Project, microfilm reel Aln 27, Library of Congress.

53. G. Washington to J. Trumbull, July 17, 1778, in Twohig et al. (eds.), *Washington Papers* 10:315. Stories of Prescott's continued abuse followed him even in Connecticut. During his stay at Lebanon, he reportedly dined at an inn kept by one Captain Alden. He was politely received, and in the course of the meal Mrs. Alden set upon the table a dish of succotash, whereupon Prescott, unfamiliar with the dish, roared, "What do you mean by offering me this hog's food?" and threw it to the floor. The woman retreated in tears to the kitchen. As the story goes, her husband then acquired a stout horsewhip and dealt with the boor as he deserved. *The Times and Hartford Advertiser,* March 2, 1824 (citing the *Concord Literary Journal*); Lossing, *Pictorial Field-Book of the Rev.* 1:603 and n. 1 (in addition to repeating the story, has engraving of the Alden Tavern and discusses its location in Lebanon); Fiske, *American Revolution,* 2:75. Alden's tavern did exist at this time, but the veracity of this story cannot be confirmed. The following humorous story was tied to the Connecticut tavern story: "The sequel of this story has recently been communicated by a gentleman at Nantucket, who retains a perfect recollection of all the circumstances. After Gen. Prescott was exchanged and restored to his command on [Aquidneck] Island, the inhabitants of Nantucket deputed Wm. Rotch, Dr. Tupper, and Timothy Folger to negotiate some concerns with him in behalf of the town. They were for some time refused admittance to his presence, but then the Dr. and Folger overcame the opposition and ushered themselves into the room. Prescott raged and stormed with great vehemence, until Folger was compelled to withdraw. After the Dr. announced his business, and the General had become a little calm, he said, 'Was not my treatment to Folger very uncivil?' The Dr. said yes. Then said Prescott, 'I will tell you the reason: he looked so much like the d___d Connecticut man that horse whipped me, that I could not endure his presence." *The Times and Hartford Advertiser,* March 2, 1824 (citing the *Concord Literary Journal*); Fessenden, *The New England Farmer,* 227; Lossing, *Pictorial Field-Book of the Rev.* 1:603, n. 1. The above story is likely not true, as William Rotch included a summary of this Newport meeting in his memoirs and described Prescott as well behaved throughout the meeting. William Rotch Recollections, in Rotch, *Memorandum Written in the Eightieth Year of His Life,* 9-14. Both of the above stories appeared in a September 1779 entry in Dr. James Thacher's wartime journal, but in the first story he does not mention the Aldens or Lebanon specifically, and in the second he garbles the proper names of the Nantucketers. See Diary Entry, Sept. 1779, in Thacher, *Military Journal,* 179. It was probably the case that Thacher heard both of these stories after the war and added them to this journal prior to its publication in 1823.

54. J. Trumbull to E. Williams, July 22, 1777, in Parsons (ed.), *Ezekiel Williams Letters,* 19-20; see also J. Trumbull to G. Washington, July 25, 1777, in Twohig et al. (eds.), *Washington Papers* 10:422.

55. Stiles, *History of Windsor* 1:659 and 769.

56. Quoting Dr. Horace C. Gillette, in ibid., 659. For Dr. Gillette's local history efforts, see id., 9.

57. W. Peck to E. Williams, Aug. 23, 1777, and E. Williams to J. Huntington, Aug. 28, 1777, in "Huntington Papers," *Conn. Hist. Soc. Coll.* 20:68-69 (1923). Ezekiel Williams was the Commissary of Prisoners of Connecticut; the other two writers were Colonel William Peck of Rhode Island and Jedidiah Huntington from Connecticut. These "necessaries" were sent by the British in Newport to Providence on July 31, 1777. Diary Entry, July 31, 1777, in Mackenzie, *Diary* 1:158. Prescott was sent additional "necessaries" in a flag-of-truce sent to Providence on November 15, 1777. P. Parker to N. Cooke, Nov. 15, 1777, in Morgan, Crawford et al. (eds.), *Naval Docs.* 10:499 (necessaries also sent for "Lt. Col. Campbell of the 71st Reg. and Lieut. Otway of the *Lark*").

58. J. Varnum to N. Cooke, July 20, 1777, in Jones (ed.), "Rev. Corr.," *Proceedings of the American Antiquarian Society* 36:2, 195 (Oct. 1926).
59. G. Washington to W. Howe, July 16, 1777, in Twohig et al. (eds.), *Washington Papers* 10:296.
60. Ibid.
61. G. Washington to C. Thomson, July 28, 1777, in ibid., 451.
62. W. Howe to G. Germain, Aug. 30, 1777, CO 5/94, British National Archives.
63. G. Washington to W. Howe, Sept. 5, 1777, and W. Howe to G. Washington, Sept. 6, 1777, in Twohig et al. (eds.), *Washington Papers* 11:152-53 and 161-62.
64. W. Howe to G. Germain, July 15, 1777, CO 5/94, British National Archives.
65. G. Germain to W. Howe, Sept. 6, 1777, in CO 5/94, British National Archives and Historical Manuscripts Commission (ed.), *Report on American Manuscripts* 1:129.
66. For another early version, see *London Chronicle*, Aug. 16-19, 1777 ("The intelligence brought by the *Lady Gage*, Capt. Loring, is that Gen. Prescott, who commanded at Rhode Island is, with his aide-de-camp, made prisoners"); see also *Adam's Weekly Courant*, Aug. 26, 1777 (Chester, England) ("A private letter from Portsmouth says sick and wounded soldiers, belonging to the Regiments of Foot Guards, brought from the *Lady Gage* transport, which is arrived").
67. *London Evening Post*, Aug. 21-23, 1777.
68. *Public Advertiser*, Aug. 22, 1777 (London); *London Evening Post*, Aug. 21-23, 1777.
69. See Gaston, "Richard Prescott and Mud Island: Epitomes of the American Revolution as Seen by London Poets," *Early American Literature* 11:2, 148 (Fall 1976). Gaston identified the anagrams as "the work of competent, though minor writers," like Soame Jenyns, an experienced member of the Board of Trade and Plantations who had been publishing poetry for the enjoyment of his friends since 1730; William Kenrick, a polemical writer known for his willingness to champion any profitable cause; and Edward Thompson, a navy commander and popular writer of satire known as "poet Thompson" among his fellow officers. Id., 147.
70. *London Evening Post*, Sept. 20, 1777; *Public Advertiser*, Sept. 24, 1777; *London Chronicle*, Sept. 23-25, 1777.
71. *London Chronicle*, Sept. 27-30, 1777.
72. A persistent (and unfounded) Newport legend holds that Prescott had an affair with Mary Overing, the wife of John Henry Overing. See Cummings, "Portrait of a Loyalist," Newport Restoration Foundation Report, 9.
73. J. Campbell to H. Percy, July 13, 1777, Hugh Percy Papers, British Manuscript Project, microfilm reel Aln 27, Library of Congress.
74. Diary Entry, July 11, 1777, in Mackenzie, *Diary* 1:150.
75. See text accompanying notes 49-58 and 74-76 in Chapter 5.
76. *London Evening Post*, Aug. 19-22, 1777.
77. *Gazetteer and New Daily Advertiser*, Aug. 29, 1777.
78. W. Howe to G. Germain, Jan. 17, 1778, CO 5/95, British National Archives.
79. W. Barrington to W. Howe, Sept. 2, 1777, in Headquarters Papers of the British Army, PRO 30/55, British National Archives and summarized in Historical Manuscripts Commission (ed.), *Report on American Transcripts*, 1:132.
80. *Morning Chronicle and London Advertiser*, Sept. 9, 1777.
81. Quoted in Williams, *Life of Barton*, Appendix, 129.
82. J. Spencer to G. Washington, Aug. 15, 1777, in Twohig et al. (eds.), *Washington Papers* 10:629 and 630, n.4; *Providence Gazette*, Aug. 2, 1777; Log of HMS *Diamond*, July 25-26, 1777, in Morgan, Crawford et al. (eds.), *Naval Docs. of the A.R* 9:691. The following August log entry likely refers to the two seamen who were taken on Prudence Island: "AM came down Lt. Harrington, with the flag of truce from Providence, by which we learned that Barney Handright and Thomas Hutchinson, seamen, were taken

off Prudence Island by the rebels and prisoners with them at Providence." Log of HMS *Diamond,* Aug. 8, 1777, in Abbass, *R.I. in the Rev.* 4:120.

83. J. Spencer to G. Washington, Aug. 15, 1777, in Twohig et al. (eds.), *Washington Papers* 10:629; see also *Providence Gazette,* Aug. 2, 1777; *Boston Gazette,* Aug. 14, 1777 (a "gentleman from Providence" supplied the information); J. Spencer to J. Trumbull, Dec. 2, 1777, copied in Peter Force Transcripts, Jonathan Trumbull Papers, Series 7E, microfilm reel 47, Library of Congress.

84. Bartlett (ed.), *Records of R.I.* 8:285-86; see also *Connecticut Courant,* July 18, 1777. The captain of the *Lark* tried desperately to obtain Otway and Brooks back in a prisoner exchange, but it took considerable time. J. Spencer to G. Washington, August 15, 1777, in Twohig et al. (eds.), *Washington Papers* 10:629. Otway was finally paroled and allowed to return to Newport in early March 1778. *Newport Gazette,* March 5, 1778.

85. *Providence Gazette,* Sept. 6, 1777; N. Cooke to H. Cooke, Sept. 6, 1777, in Jones (ed.), "Rev. Corr.," *Proceedings of the American Antiquarian Society* 36:347 (Oct. 1926); Diary Entry, Sept. 6, 1777, in Mackenzie, *Diary* 1:174.

86. The most useful descriptions of this raid are in Diary Entry, Sept. 5, 1777, Journals of Christopher French, in Morgan, Crawford et al. (eds.), *Naval Docs. of the A.R.* 9:881; Nathaniel Arnold Rev. War Pension Application and John Ash Rev. War Pension Application, National Archives Building; Diary Entry, Sept. 4, 1777, in Mackenzie, *Diary* 1:173. See also *Providence Gazette,* Sept. 6, 1777; *Newport Gazette,* Sept. 11, 1777; N. Cooke to H. Cooke, Sept. 6, 1777, in Jones (ed.), "Rev. Corr.," *Proceedings of the American Antiquarian Society* 36:347 (Oct. 1926); Log of HMS *Juno,* Sept. 4, 1777, in Morgan, Crawford et al. (eds.), *Naval Docs. of the A.R.* 9:874-75; Diary Entry, Aug. 20, 1777, in Laughton (ed.), "Journal of Bartholomew James," *Publications of the Navy Records Society* 6:45-46 (1896); J. Spencer to J. Trumbull, Sept. 9, 1777, copied in Peter Force Transcripts, Jonathan Trumbull Papers, Series 7E, microfilm reel 47, Library of Congress. For the wounded prisoner, see also List of Patients, Diseases and Treatments, Aug. 8, 1777-Nov. 15, 1777, Providence General Hospital Records, box 3, folder 175, R.I. Hist. Soc. ("James Quelch, prisoner taken on Prudence, wounded in his arm with a musket ball, belonging to the *Juno* frigate of 32 guns, marine"). For the taking of the equipment from the British soldier, see William Bissell Shearman Rev. War Pension Application, National Archives Building. Shearman hailed from Scituate, Rhode Island.

87. See Diary Entry, Aug. 20, 1777, in Laughton (ed.), "Journal of Bartholomew James," *Publications of the Navy Records Society* 6:45-46 (1896); Log of HMS *Juno,* Sept. 4, 1777, in Morgan, Crawford et al. (eds.), *Naval Docs. of the A.R.* 9:874-75; Diary Entries, Sept. 5, 1777, in Journals of Christopher French, in Morgan, Crawford et al. (eds.), *Naval Docs. of the A.R.* 9:881; Mackenzie, *Diary* 1:173.

88. Log of HMS *Juno,* Sept. 4, 1777, in Morgan, Crawford et al. (eds.), *Naval Docs. of the A.R.* 9:874-75.

89. Diary Entry, Sept. 5, 1777, Journals of Christopher French, in ibid., 881.

90. Diary Entry, Sept. 5, 1777, in Mackenzie, *Diary* 1:173.

91. *Newport Gazette,* Sept. 11, 1777. For the most complete description of military incidents in the Rhode Island theater of war, see Abbass, *A Chronology of the War in Rhode Island,* vol. I, in *Rhode Island in the Revolution: Big Happenings in the Smallest Colony.*

92. G. Washington to J. Spencer, Sept. 2, 1777, in Twohig et al. (eds.), *Washington Papers* 11:130.

CHAPTER EIGHT: THE GENERALS ARE EXCHANGED

1. G. Germain to W. Howe, Aug. 6, 1777, Headquarters Papers of the British Army, PRO 30/55, British National Archives and summarized in Historical Manuscripts Commission (ed.), *Report on American Manuscripts* 1:129.

2. Resolution, Aug. 7, 1777, in Ford (ed.), *Journals of the Continental Congress* 8:621. Another resolution of the same date authorized Washington to negotiate the exchange of prisoners of war "as he shall judge expedient, notwithstanding the resolution of Congress respecting Lieutenant Colonel Campbell, and the five Hessian field officers." Id., 621.

3. H Laurens to J. L. Gervais, Aug. 5, 1777, in Chesnutt et al. (eds.), *Laurens Papers* 11:420.

4. See Ryan, "Hidden Concord: Concord Gaol," at www.concordma/magazine/dec98/campbell. Campbell signed a parole on November 14, which is evidence that he was not released until that time. See Archibald Campbell Parole, Nov. 14, 1777, in Walcott, *Campbell*, 51, n. But the author believes that Campbell was paroled in August and that either the date of this parole was misread by Walcott or that a second parole was signed by him in November. Concord historian Michael D. Ryan wrote that Campbell "visited shops and homes and was well cared for by the people, jailer and especially Dr. Minot's daughter Mrs. Merrick (whose patriot prisoner son Tilly would one day be helped by Campbell)." Ryan, "Hidden Concord: Concord Gaol," at www.concordma/magazine/dec98/campbell.

5. Lt. Jakob Piel Diary Entry, Aug. 25, 1777, in Burgoyne (ed.), *Diaries of Hessian Officers*, 25.

6. G. Washington to W. Howe, Sept. 5, 1777, in Twohig et al. (eds.), *Washington Papers* 11:152-53.

7. W. Howe to G. Washington, Sept. 6, 1777, in ibid., 161.

8. W. Howe to G. Germain, Oct. 25, 1777, CO 5/94, British National Archives.

9. Alden, *General Charles Lee*, 184.

10. See, e.g., Langworthy, "Memoir of Major General Lee," in *Lee Papers* 4:136; Warren, *History ... of the Am. Rev.* 1:184, n.

11. W. Howe to G. Washington, Nov. 26, 1777 and G. Washington to W. Howe, Nov. 28, 1777, in Twohig et al. (eds.), *Washington Papers* 13:412-13 and 438.

12. W. Howe to H. Clinton, Nov. 27, 1777, Henry Clinton Collection 27:40, William L. Clements Library.

13. G. Germain to W. Howe, Sept. 3, 1777, CO 5/94, British National Archives; see also W. Howe to G. Germain, Jan. 17, 1778, in Davies (ed.), *Documents of the A.R.* 15:30 ("General Lee in the same manner will be admitted to his liberty upon parole in the place of General Prescott since the King has been pleased to consent he may be deemed and exchanged as a prisoner of war").

14. C. Lee Parole Agreement, Dec. 27, 1777, in *Lee Papers* 1:375-76.

15. C. Lee to G. Washington, Dec. 30, 1777, in Twohig et al. (eds.), *Washington Papers* 13:71. William Smith reported in his diary for January 24, 1778, "Mrs. Watkins, who lately came from New York, saw Lee walking the streets." Diary Entry, Jan. 24, 1778, in Sabine (ed.), *Historical Memoirs of William Smith* 1:290.

16. E. Boudinot to J. Loring, Dec. 29, 1777, and E. Boudinot to L. Pintard, Dec. 29, 1777, in Boyle (ed.), *Boudinot Letterbook*, 63-64.

17. E. Boudinot to H. Gates, March 21, 1777, in ibid., 117-18; H. Laurens to A. Campbell, Jan. 14, 1778, in Smith (ed.), *Letters of Delegates* 8:587 (Prescott has departed for New York City "as a tender in exchange for Major General Lee"); J. Webb to G. Washington, Jan. 30, 1778, in Twohig et al. (eds.), *Washington Papers* 13:417; R. Pigot to E. Percy, Jan. 23, 1778, Hugh Percy Papers, British Manuscript Project, microfilm reel Aln 27, Library of Congress ("I hear General Prescott is at New York"); C. Lumm to E. Percy, Feb. 5, 1778, id., ("General Prescott is now at New York").

18. *Norwich Packet*, Feb. 2, 1778, quoting from unidentified Connecticut newspaper.

19. G. Washington to C. Lee, Jan. 27, 1778, in Twohig et al. (eds.), *Washington Papers* 13:367.

20. See W. Howe to G. Washington, Jan. 19, 1778, in ibid., 280-81; W. Howe to G. Germain, Jan. 17, 1778, CO 5/95, British National Archives.
21. W. Howe to G. Washington, Jan. 19, 1778, in Twohig et al. (eds.), *Washington Papers* 13:536; W. Howe to G. Germain, March 5, 1778, in Davies (ed.), *Documents of the A.R.* 15:54.
22. G. Washington to W. Howe, Jan. 30, 1778, in Twohig et al. (eds.), *Washington Papers* 13:412; Resolutions, Dec. 19, 1777, and Jan. 21, 1778, in Ford (ed.), *Journals of the Continental Congress* 9:1037 and 10:78.
23. Diary Entry, Jan. 24, 1778, in Sabine (ed.), *Historical Memoirs of William Smith* 1:290.
24. C. Lumm to E. Percy, Feb. 5, 1778, Hugh Percy Papers, British Manuscript Project, microfilm reel Aln 27, Library of Congress.
25. Diary Entry, Sept. 26, 1777, in Burgoyne (ed.), *Waldeck Diary*, 43.
26. Elias Boudinot Recollections, in Boyle (ed.), *Boudinot Journal*, 74-76.
27. C. Lee to J. Robertson, undated [probably early 1778], Henry Clinton Collection 34:26, William L. Clements Library.
28. E. Boudinot to A. Campbell, March 24, 1777, in Boyle (ed.), *Boudinot Letterbook*, 120. In early March, despite Prescott being released on parole and joining the British garrison in New York City, General James Robertson, the British commander of the city, informed Boudinot that he had no instructions from Howe to release Lee on parole. E. Boudinot to G. Washington, March 2, 1778, in Twohig et al. (eds.), *Washington Papers* 14:18. During the delay, Lee won a $500 prize playing a lottery held by the New York City poor house. *New York Royal Gazette*, Feb. 7, 1778.
29. E. Boudinot to H. Gates, March 21, 1777, in Boyle (ed.), *Boudinot Letterbook*, 117-18.
30. G. Washington to W. Howe, March 9 and March 12, 1778, in Twohig et al. (eds.), *Washington Papers* 14:114 and 159-60.
31. C. Lee to H. Clinton, March 16, 1778, Henry Clinton Collection 32:14, William L. Clements Library. Interestingly, Alden did not quote from this letter.
32. Ibid; see also E. Boudinot to H. H. Fergusson, March 2, 1778, and E. Boudinot to J. Loring, March 8, 1778, in Boyle (ed.), *Boudinot Letterbook*, 96 and 99-100.
33. E. Boudinot to C. Lee, March 8, 1777, in Boyle (ed.), *Boudinot Letterbook*, 100-1; W. Howe to G. Washington, March 10, 1777, in Twohig et al. (eds.), *Washington Papers* 14:130. Howe later changed his mind. He wrote to General Clinton on March 17: "I have sent a letter through the rebel Commissary, Mr. Boudinot, granting permission for General Lee to come to this place by land; but having cause since that time to believe Mr. Washington will take the advantage of his passing through Jersey, I desire I am not too late in this application, that you will put a stop to his journey, as well as Major Williams's and Mr. Loring's, and that they may all come by sea." W. Howe to H. Clinton, March 17, 1778, Henry Clinton Collection, William L. Clements Library. However, either this letter did not arrive on time or Howe again changed his mind.
34. W. Howe to G. Germain, March 26, 1778, CO 5/95, British National Archives; Diary Entries, March 25, 1778, in Montresor, "Journals," *N.Y. Hist. Soc. Coll.* 482 (1881); Gruber (ed.), *Peebles Diary*, 171 and Whinyates (ed.), *Services of Downman*, 57; Diary Entry, March 26, 1778, in Muenchhausen, *At General Howe's Side*, 49; *Royal Pennsylvania Gazette* (Philadelphia), March 27, 1778; J. Morris to G. Washington, March 26, 1778, in Twohig et al. (eds.), *Washington Papers* 14:324. The route of Lee, Loring, and Williams, as provided in Loring's pass through American lines, was "from Brunswick to Cranberry and through Bordentown and Burlington from whence they may either go by water down the river or cross over to Bristol and then go down the usual road to Philadelphia." Pass for Joshua Loring, March 8, 1778, in Boyle (ed.), *Boudinot Letterbook*, 100; see also Continental Navy Board of the Middle Department to G. Washington, March 24, 1778, in Morgan, Crawford et al. (eds.), *Naval Docs. of*

the A.R. 11:774 ("General Lee passed through Crosswicks [in New Jersey] this day on his way to Philadelphia. It is said he is going to be exchanged"); *Connecticut Courant* (Hartford), April 7, 1778, with dateline Trenton, March 25, 1778 ("Yesterday Major General Lee passed through Bordentown from New York on his way to Philadelphia, where it is said he is likely to be exchanged").

35. J. Morris to G. Washington, March 26, 1778, in Twohig et al. (eds.), *Washington Papers* 14:324; W. Howe to G. Germain, March 26, 1778, CO 5/95, British National Archives. In anticipation of an exchange, Joshua Loring informed his British counterpart that the five Hessian field officers would be arriving soon from Virginia. E. Boudinot to H. H. Fergusson, March 2, 1778, in Boyle (ed.), *Boudinot Letterbook,* 96.

36. W. Smallwood to G. Washington, March 28, 1778, in Morgan, Crawford et al. (eds.), *Naval Docs. of the A.R.* 11:820 ("A gentleman of Philadelphia on Friday last informed me he saw General Lee in the Coffee House there").

37. Resolution, March 30, 1778, in Ford (ed.), *Journals of the Continental Congress* 10:295.

38. Ryan, "Hidden Concord: Concord Gaol," at www.concordma/magazine/dec98/campbell.

39. Elias Boudinot Recollections, in Boudinot, *Journal,* 77.

40. Ibid.

41. W. Howe to G. Washington, April 3, 1778, in Twohig et al. (eds.), *Washington Papers* 14:389.

42. A. Hamilton to N. Greene, April 3, 1778, in Syrett (ed.), *Hamilton Papers* 1:452-52; G. Washington to H. Laurens, April 4, 1778, in Twohig et al. (eds.), *Washington Papers* 14:403.

43. Diary Entry, March 26, 1778, in Muenchhausen, *At General Howe's Side,* 49; see also Diary Entry, March 25, 1778, in Montresor, "Journals," *N.Y. Hist. Soc. Coll.* 482 (1881). By using the term "another," the Hessian aide was likely referring to the first time Howe met with Lee in early 1777, when they discussed Lee sending Congress a letter requesting to send to him two or three American committee members.

44. C. Lee to B. Rush, June 4, 1778, in *Lee Papers* 2:398.

45. Ibid.

46. Diary Entry, April 5, 1778, in Montresor, "Journals," *N.Y. Hist. Soc. Coll.* 484 (1881).

47. Elias Boudinot Recollections, in Boudinot, *Journal,* 78.

48. Diary Entry, April 6, 1778, in Crane (ed.), *Drinker Diary* 297; see also J. Laurens to H. Laurens, April 5, 1778, in Simms (ed.), *Army Correspondence of John Laurens,* 154; Diary Entry, April 5, 1778, in Wild, "Journal of Ebenezer Wild," *Mass. Hist. Soc. Proceedings,* 2nd Series, 11:107 (1890-91).

49. Elias Boudinot Recollections, in Boudinot, *Journal,* 77-78.

50. W. Howe to G. Washington, April 3, 1778, in Twohig et al. (eds.), *Washington Papers* 14:389. For Lee's parole, see Parole, April 5, 1778, in *Lee Papers* 2:382.

51. H. Laurens to J. Duane, April 7, 1778, and T. Burke to R. Caswell, April 9, 1778, in Smith (ed.), *Letters of Delegates* 9:380 and 393.

52. T. McKean to S. McKean, April 9, 1778, and J. Banister to P. Henry, April 10, 1778, in ibid., 400-401.

53. Draft Letter from Congress to G. Washington, April 10, 1778, in Ford (ed.), *Journal of the Continental Congress* 10:332; see also H. Laurens to J. Laurens, April 9, 1778, in Chestnutt et al. (eds.), *Laurens Papers* 13:94.

54. Fleming, *Washington's Secret War,* 287-88.

55. H. Laurens to G. Washington, April 14, 1778, in Twohig et al. (eds.), *Washington Papers* 14:511 and 512, n. 10.

56. C. Lee to H. Laurens, April 17, 1778, in Chestnutt et al. (eds.), *Laurens Papers* 13:133.

57. Elias Boudinot Recollections, in Boudinot, *Journal*, 79.
58. Plan for the Formation of the American Army, undated (attached to letter dated April 13, 1778), in *Lee Papers* 2:383-89; Fleming, *The Secret War*, 288 ("mockery").
59. C. Lee to G. Washington, April 13, 1778, in *Lee Papers* 2:382-83.
60. C. Lee to H. Laurens, April 17, 1778, in Chestnutt et al. (eds.), *Laurens Papers* 13:133.
61. Randall, *Ethan Allen*, 428-29.
62. Ibid., 429.
63. Lt. Jakob Piel Diary Entries, Feb. 10 to April 20, 1778, in Burgoyne (ed.), *Diaries of Hessian Officers*, 28-29; Diary Entry, April 20, 1778, in Uhlendorf (ed.), *Baurmeister Journals*, 167.
64. G. Washington to C. Lee, April 22, 1778, in Twohig et al. (eds.), *Washington Papers* 14:585.
65. Ibid.
66. Moore, "The Treason of Charles Lee," in *Lee Papers* 2:401-2; C. Carroll to C. Carroll, Sr., April 20, 1778, in Smith (ed.), *Letters of Delegates* 9:448 (Lee had left York a few days previous "on his way to his farm in Virginia"); H. Laurens to J. C. Zahn, April 28, 1778, in id., 517 ("General Lee ... is now exchanged for General Prescott"); R. H. Lee to T. Jefferson, May 2, 1778, in id., 566 ("General Lee is fully exchanged and is sent for from Berkeley to attend the Army"). On his return trip, Lee stopped at York to press Congress to promote him to the post of lieutenant general, on the ground that other officers had attained the same rank as his—an annoyed Congress ignored the request, which in turn irritated Lee. C. Lee to President of Congress, May 13, 1778, in *Lee Papers* 2:392-93 (written from York, Pennsylvania); C. Carroll to C. Carroll, Sr., May 17, 1778, in Smith (ed.), *Letters of Delegates* 9:691; Journal Entry, May 13, 1778, in Ford (ed.), *Journals of the Continental Congress* 10:492 ("A letter, of this day, from General Lee, was read").
67. Randall, *Ethan Allen*, 429-30. The Americans had delayed allowing Campbell to enter New York City due to Howe's refusal to release Lee in March. E. Boudinot to J. Loring, March 8, 1778, in Boyle (ed.), *Boudinot Letterbook*, 100. On April 20, 1778, Campbell arrived at Morristown, New Jersey, ready to be taken to Elizabethtown, New Jersey, in exchange for Ethan Allen. G. Washington to A. Campbell, April 23, 1778, in Twohig et al. (eds.), *Washington Papers* 14:592.
68. Ethan Allen Recollections, in Allen, *Narrative*, 121-22.
69. See Ryan, "Hidden Concord: Concord Gaol," at www.concordma/magazine/dec98/campbell.
70. E. Allen to H. Laurens, May 9, 1778, in Chestnutt et al. (eds.), *Laurens Papers* 13:277-78.
71. Campbell, "Introduction," *Journal of an Expedition against the Rebels of Georgia*, x. For his services in Jamaica, Campbell was made a Knight of Bath on September 30, 1785. Upon his return to Scotland from Madras, India, he was immediately reelected to Parliament, but died of a severe cold in 1790. He was buried in Westminster Abbey, where his monument is next to that of the composer Handel. Id.; see also Campbell, J. L., "Campbell, Sir Archibald," *Oxford Dictionary of National Biography*, online edition, Jan. 2008.
72. W. Howe to G. Germain, Jan. 17, 1778, in CO 5/95, British National Archive and Historical Manuscripts Commission (ed.), *Report on American Transcripts*, 1:279.
73. *London Gazette*, March 21-24, 1778; *General Advertiser and Morning Intelligencer*, March 23, 1778 (London).
74. Prescott Court Martial Record, April 24, 1778, in Hagist (ed.), *General Orders, Rhode Island*, Appendix II, 133.
75. Ibid., 134.

76. W. Barrington to H. Clinton, Aug. 5, 1778, in Historical Manuscripts Commission (ed.), *Report on American Transcripts*, 1:278.
77. Boudinot, *Journal*, 80. Lafayette wrote of his relationship with Lee, "as one of them was a violent Anglomaniac and the other a French enthusiast, their relationship was never peaceful." "Memoirs of the Marquis de Lafayette," in Idzerda (ed.), *Lafayette Letters* 2:10.
78. A. Hamilton to E. Boudinot, July 26, 1778, in Syrett (ed.), *Hamilton Papers* 1:528; see also Lockhart, *The Drillmaster of Valley Forge*, 133.
79. Lockhart, *The Drillmaster of Valley Forge*, 188.
80. Willcox, *Portrait of a General*, 223-24 and 232-33.
81. Council of War Record, June 18, 1778, in Twohig et al. (eds.), *Washington Papers* 15:414-17; M. Lafayette to G. Washington, June 17, 1778, in id., 421-23; B. Arnold to G. Washington, June 18, 1778, in id., 431-32; J. Cadwalader to G. Washington, June 18, 1778, in id., 435-36; N. Greene to G. Washington, June 18, 1778, in id., 441-44; H. Knox to G. Washington, June 18, 1778, in id., 446-48; C. Lee to G. Washington, June 18, 1778, in id., 457-58; Lengel, *General George Washington*, 291.
82. C. Lee to G. Washington, June 18, 1778, in Twohig et al. (eds.), *Washington Papers* 15:457-58.
83. Council of War Minutes, June 24, 1778, in ibid., 521; Lengel, *General George Washington*, 295.
84. C. Lee to G. Washington, June 25, 1778, in Twohig et al. (eds.), *Washington Papers* 15:541-42; Lengel, *General George Washington*, 294.
85. Lee then made noises about changing his mind and leading the detachment, to Washington's irritation, but he again backed off. See "Memoirs of the Marquis de Lafayette," in Idzerda (ed.), *Lafayette Letters* 2:10; A. Hamilton to E. Boudinot, July 5, 1778, in Syrett (ed.), *Hamilton Papers* 1:511.
86. A. Hamilton to E. Boudinot, July 5, 1778, in Syrett (ed.), *Hamilton Papers* 1:510.
87. N. Greene to G. Washington, June 24, 1778, in Showman (ed.), *Greene Papers* 2:447-48.
88. M. Lafayette to G. Washington, June 24, 1778, in Twohig et al. (eds.), *Washington Papers* 15:529; Chernow, *Washington, A Life*, 293. Wayne refused to sign the council of war recommendation and advocated the same measures as Greene and Lafayette. A. Wayne to G. Washington, June 24, 1778, in Twohig et al. (eds.), *Washington Papers* 15:535.
89. G. Washington to M. Lafayette, June 25, 1778, in Twohig et al. (eds.), *Washington Papers* 15:539 and n. 1.
90. C. Lee to G. Washington, June 25, 1778, in ibid., 541.
91. M. Lafayette to G. Washington and G. Washington to C. Lee, June 26, 1778, in ibid., 552 and 556; Diary Entry, June 27, 1778, in McHenry, *Journal*, 5; Showman (ed.), *Greene Papers* 2:453; Lengel, *General George Washington*, 294-95.
92. Thayer, *The Making of a Scapegoat*, 46-47; see also J. McHenry Testimony, July 14, 1778, in *Lee Papers* 3:78 (during the battle, Lee accused Scott of retreating without orders; Maxwell retreated too without orders); Tench Tilghman Testimony, July 14, 1778, in *Lee Papers* 3:81 (Lee told him Scott "had quitted very advantageous position without orders").
93. H. Clinton to G. Germain, July 5, 1778, in *Lee Papers* 2:461-66; Henry Clinton Recollections, in Willcox (ed.), *Clinton Narrative*, 93; Willcox, *Portrait of a General*, 234.
94. John S. Brooks Testimony, July 23-24, 1778, Lee Court Martial, in *Lee Papers* 3:146, 149, and 150-51.
95. Marquis de Lafayette Testimony, July 5, 1778, in ibid., 16-17; Charles Lee Closing Statement, Aug. 9, 1778, in id., 191.

96. Charles Lee Closing Statement, Aug. 9, 1778, Lee Court Martial, in *Lee Papers* 3:191.
97. Ibid.
98. Tench Tilghman Testimony, July 14, 1778, Lee Court Martial, in ibid., 81.
99. Evan Edwards Testimony, July 25, 1778, Lee Court Martial, in *Lee Papers* 3:166-67 and 173; John F. Mercer Testimony, July 19, 1778, in id., 112-13; Thayer, *The Making of a Scapegoat*, 54.
100. John F. Mercer Testimony, July 19, 1778, Lee Court Martial, in *Lee Papers* 3:113; see also Charles Lee Closing Statement, Aug. 9, 1778, in id., 200 ("I had answered . . . I myself should be one of the last to leave the field").
101. Jenkins and Jenkins, *Monmouth Court House*, 208-9; Lengel, *General George Washington*, 301-2.
102. Thayer, *The Making of a Scapegoat*, 55-56; Morrissey, *Monmouth Courthouse*, 70-71; Lockhart, *The Drillmaster of Valley Forge*, 161-62.
103. James McHenry Testimony, July 14, 1778, Lee Court Martial, in *Lee Papers* 3:79. Lee, in a follow-up question as part of his defense, admitted making this damaging statement. Charles Lee Question, in id.
104. J. Laurens to H. Laurens, June 30, 1778, in Chesnutt et al. (eds.), *Laurens Papers* 13:535. See also Diary Entry, June 28, 1778, in Martin, *A Narrative of a Revolutionary Soldier*, 112-14; J. McHenry to J. Cox, July 1, 1778, in Montgomery, "Battle of Monmouth," in *Magazine of American History* 3:358 (June 1879) (Greene's artillery supporting Wayne); Diary Entry, June 28, 1778, in Brown and Peckham (eds.), *Journals of Henry Dearborn*, 128 ("We pursued until we got possession of the field of battle. . . . The enemy retreated across a morass and formed"); Thayer, *The Making of a Scapegoat*, 61-62.
105. Jenkins and Jenkins, *Monmouth Court House*, 231.
106. J. McHenry to J. Cox, July 1, 1778, in Montgomery, "Battle of Monmouth," *Magazine of American History* 3:358 (June 1879). Writing a day earlier from the American army's camp, McHenry wrote that Lee "either from false information of the enemies' force and disposition, or from some causes not yet fully understood, gave orders to retreat." J. McHenry to G. Lux, June 30, 1778, in id. 355-56.
107. C. Lee to G. Washington, July 1 [should be June 30], 1778, in Twohig et al. (eds.), *Washington Papers* 15:594-95.
108. G. Washington to C. Lee, June 30, 1778, in ibid., 595-96.
109. Charles Lee Closing Statement, Aug. 9, 1778, Lee Court Martial, in *Lee Papers* 3:206.
110. C. Lee to G. Washington, June 28 [should be 30], 1778, in Twohig et al. (eds.), *Washington Papers* 15:596.
111. G. Washington to C. Lee, June 30, 1778, in ibid., 595-96.
112. C. Lee to G. Washington, June 30, 1778, in ibid., 596-97.
113. A. Wayne and C. Scott Memorandum, June 30, 1778, quoted in ibid., 597-98.
114. G. Washington to C. Lee, June 30, 1778, in ibid., 597 and n. 2; J. McHenry to G. Lux, June 30, 1778, in Montgomery, "Battle of Monmouth," *Magazine of American History* 3:356 (June 1879) ("This evening General Lee was arrested").
115. J. Penn to R. Caswell, July 15, 1778, in Smith (ed.), *Letters of Delegates* 10:288.
116. E. Boudinot to A. Hamilton, July 8, 1778, in ibid., 10:238.
117. C. Lee to R. Morris, July 3, 1778, in *Lee Papers* 2:457.
118. For the entire record of the court martial, see *Lee Papers* 3:1-208. For Lee's sentence, see id., 208. For a detailed discussion of the court's sentence by historians sympathetic to Lee, see Thayer, *The Making of a Scapegoat, passim* and Alden, *General Charles Lee*, chapter 15.
119. See Lengel, *General George Washington*, 305.

120. Jenkins and Jenkins, *Monmouth Court House*, 230. The authors continued, "Perhaps not, but Lee is, unfortunately, more remembered for his abrasive personality, massive ego, total lack of diplomatic ability, and lack of faith in the military ability of the soldiers under his command, and the fault for that lies strictly with him. Thomas Fleming's conclusion was that Lee was not 'a great general. His total failure at Monmouth to reconnoiter the terrain; his indecision and hesitation, which allowed Clinton to outmaneuver him; his failure to inspire either confidence or cooperation in his subordinates—all these mark him as a third rate leader of men,' is perhaps too harsh, but considering Lee's personal behavior throughout his career, perfectly understandable." Id. In the note supporting Fleming's quote (in which the authors cited Fleming, "The 'Military Crimes' of Charles Lee," *American History Magazine* 19:3 [April 1968]), the authors added the following: "Fleming advised that although he would not be quite so damning in his opinion of Lee today, he nonetheless thought it best for the country that the general was removed from active duty. Thomas Fleming e-mail message to the authors (Jenkins and Jenkins), January 24, 2010." Jenkins and Jenkins, *Monmouth Court House*, 278, n. 51.

121. Quoted in Willcox (ed.), *Portrait of a General*, 235; see also Henry Clinton Recollections, in Willcox (ed.), *Clinton Narratives*, 96; H. Clinton to G. Germain, July 5, 1778, in *Lee Papers* 2:461-67. After the war, Benedict Arnold, in England after turning traitor in 1780, told Clinton that most American generals privately agreed with Lee's version of the Battle of Monmouth. Henry Clinton Recollections, in Willcox (ed.), *Clinton Narratives*, 96, n. 19.

122. Alden, *General Charles Lee*, 238; Shy, "Charles Lee: The Soldier as Radical," in Billias (ed.), *George Washington's Generals and Opponents*, 45. In addition, military historian Paul David Nelson recently wrote that "only the charge of disrespect to Washington had any merit at all." Nelson, "Charles Lee," in Fremont-Barnes and Ryerson (eds.), *Encyclopedia of the American Rev. War* 2:700.

123. Shy, "Charles Lee: The Soldier as Radical," in Billias (ed.), *George Washington's Generals and Opponents*, 45.

124. Thayer, *The Making of a Scapegoat*, 79. John Shy labeled the sentence "absurd." Shy, "Charles Lee: The Soldier as Radical," in Billias (ed.), *George Washington's Generals and Opponents*, 45. Alden wrote that if Lee "was actually guilty as found on the first and second charges, the death penalty could have been imposed." Alden, *General Charles Lee*, 238.

125. G. Morris to G. Washington, Oct. 26, 1778, in Twohig et al. (eds.), *Washington Papers* 17:588.

126. B. Rush to W. Gordon, Dec. 10, 1778, in Butterfield (ed.), *Letters of Rush* 1:220. See also Shy, "Charles Lee: The Soldier as Radical," in Billias (ed.), *George Washington's Generals and Opponents*, 45-46; Alden, *General Charles Lee*, 253-54.

127. See Resolution, Dec. 5, 1778, in Ford (ed.), *Journals of the Continental Congress* 12:1194-95; H. Laurens to G. Washington, Dec. 7, 1778, in Twohig et al. (eds.), *Washington Papers* 18:373. Massachusetts and Georgia voted to reject the verdicts; Rhode Island, Connecticut, New York, Pennsylvania, North Carolina and South Carolina voted to affirm; New Hampshire and Maryland were divided; and New Jersey and Delaware lacked a quorum to cast ballots. On an individual basis, voting to reject included Samuel Adams and James Lovell of Massachusetts, and William Whipple of New Hampshire (who was also a state brigadier general); voting to affirm included Gouverneur Morris and James Duane of New York, Roger Sherman and Oliver Ellsworth of Connecticut, and Henry Laurens and William Drayton of South Carolina. Washington issued the charges, conviction, and sentence in his general orders of December 22, 1778. General Orders, Dec. 22, 1778, in Twohig et al. (eds.), *Washington Papers* 18:486-87.

128. General Lee's Vindication to the Public, in *Pennsylvania Packet*, Dec. 3, 1778, and *Lee Papers* 3:255-65.
129. G. Washington to J. Reed, Dec. 12, 1778, in Twohig et al. (eds.), *Washington Papers* 18:397-98.
130. For more on the *code duello*, see Schaefer, "The Whole Duty of Man: Charles Lee and the Politics of Reputation, Masculinity, and Identity during the Revolutionary Era, 1755-1783," doctoral dissertation, University of Toledo (May 2006), 204-35.
131. Quoted in Massey, *John Laurens*, 125.
132. Account of a Duel between Major General Charles Lee and Lieutenant Colonel John Laurens, Dec. 24, 1778, in Syrett (ed.), *Hamilton Papers* 1:603. For a view of the duel from the perspective of Evan Edwards, Lee's second at the duel, see Graydon, *Memoirs*, 323-24. Special rules applied to a duel by proxy. Laurens's biographer, Gregory D. Massey, noted that because Laurens was the aggressor, first challenging Lee to a duel, under the *code duello*, he should not have been permitted to act as a proxy for Washington. Massey, *John Laurens*, 125.
133. Quoted in Moultrie, *Memoirs of the American Revolution* 1:141; Dabney and Dragan, *William Henry Drayton*, 134 (citing letter from Richard Huston to Isaac Hayne, June 24, 1776, *Charleston Year Book*, 320 [1895]).
134. Quoted in Schaefer, "The Whole Duty of Man: Charles Lee and the Politics of Reputation, Masculinity, and Identity during the Revolutionary Era, 1755-1783," doctoral dissertation, University of Toledo (May 2006), 229-30, citing Hezekiah Niles, *Principles and Acts of the Revolution in America*, reprinted by New York, NY: Burt Franklin, 1971, 93 (originally published in 1822).
135. Dabney and Dargan, *William Henry Drayton*, 154-55.
136. C. Lee to W. H. Drayton, March 15, 1779, in *Lee Papers* 3:317.
137. Ibid., 318. For a detailed account of this affair, see Schaefer, "The Whole Duty of Man: Charles Lee and the Politics of Reputation, Masculinity, and Identity during the Revolutionary Era, 1755-1783," doctoral dissertation, University of Toledo (May 2006), 229-35 and Dabney and Dragan, *William Henry Drayton*, 154-56.
138. C. Lee to President of Congress, undated (probably Jan. 1779), in *Lee Papers* 4:405.
139. "Charles Lee", in Selesky (ed.), *Encyclopedia of the American Rev.* 1:613; Nelson, "Charles Lee," in Fremont-Barnes and Ryerson (eds.), *Encyclopedia of the American Rev. War* 2:700.
140. C. Lee to President of Congress, Jan. 30, 1780, in *Lee Papers* 4:407-9.
141. Langworthy, *Memoirs of Lee*, 40.
142. Quoted in Sparks, *Life of Charles Lee*, 187.
143. A Berkeley County historian wrote in an 1890 publication: "The house of Gen. Lee was a one-storied affair, but evidently comfortable for the period and not at all in accordance with the descriptions given by historians from Bancroft on down, who try to make it appear that Lee lived in a hovel with his dogs, etc. His will gives contradiction to those assertions, for a man who has a housekeeper and a valet, or personal servant, and slaves, in addition to a number of horses, fillies and milk cows, can hardly be considered as living in a 'hovel,' in destitution with canines." Norris (ed.), *History of the Lower Shenandoah Valley*, 241. While the author makes some excellent points, it is clear that Lee suffered from financial problems. Lee may have had difficulty paying for improvements to his house's interior, when Langworthy visited him. See also Alexander R. Boteler Recollections, 1860, in id. ("Soon afterward, we found ourselves in front of the former residence of Gen. Charles Lee, of Revolutionary notoriety. The house is a long, low, quaint looking building with a high pitched roof and irregularly placed chimneys."); an unidentified correspondent of the *Petersburg Express*, "Revolutionary Men and Reminiscences," in the *Charleston Mercury* (Charleston, South Carolina), Nov. 8, 1856, and *The Daily Globe* (Washington, D.C.), Jan. 3, 1857 ("Lee's house is a hundred

paces from the little assemblage of houses called by his name, and is an oblong building of stone, with chimneys at each end and midway—low, with a rude porch . . . above the rough door, and with a few outhouses"). The area where Lee's house stood was named after him—Leetown, West Virginia, in Jefferson County. Other towns named after Charles Lee were Lee, Massachusetts, and Lee, New Hampshire.

144. For his military colony, see "A Sketch of a Plan for the Formation of a Military Colony," undated (probably 1779), in *Lee Papers* 3:323-30. Lee refused to allow merchants and lawyers in his colony.

145. C. Lee to R. Morris, Aug. 19, 1782, in Cantanzariti et al. (eds.), *Morris Papers* 6:225.

146. Ibid.; R. Morris to C. Lee, July 26, 1782, in id., 29 and R. Morris and J. Morris to E. Randolph, Oct. 7, 1782, in id., 524; J. Vaughn to W. T. Franklin, Oct. 1782, Sol Feinstone Collection, American Philosophical Society (price for farm).

147. Langworthy, *Memoirs of Lee*, 59. The Sign of the Conestoga Wagon was a long-established tavern on Market Street. Advertisements for it ran in the July 11, 1734, and February 26, 1750, editions of the *Pennsylvania Gazette*; some delegates would stay there during the Constitutional Convention of 1787; and it was still in business in the early 1800s. See Graham, "The Taverns of Colonial Philadelphia," *Transactions of the American Philosophical Society*, New Series, 43:1, 319 (1953). William Moore advertised in the August 16, 1777, edition of the *Pennsylvania Evening Post* that he had become the new proprietor of "that noted inn, known by the Sign of the Conestoga Wagon, in Market-Street, where gentlemen travelers and others may depend upon the best accommodation and attendance." Benjamin Thompson may have been the tavern's proprietor when Lee died there, as Thompson announced his move from the Sign of the Conestoga to a new nearby inn in 1784. Advertisement in *Independent Gazetteer*, July 31, 1784. In 1789, former major general Samuel Parsons of the Continental army from Connecticut stayed there on his way to serve as Chief Judge of the Northwestern Territory; he mentioned that its proprietor was Samuel Nichols, who was a former leader of the marines during the Revolutionary War. S. Parsons to his wife, March 16, 1789, in Hall, *Life of Parsons*, 554; see also Watson, *Annals of Philadelphia* 3:294 (referring to a 1789 notice of a meeting held at the tavern, run by Samuel Nichols). In 1806, Henry Knerr advertised that he had become the new proprietor of the tavern, promising that "he intends to keep everything, appertaining to that line of business, of the best quality." Advertisement in *Aurora General Advertiser* (Philadelphia), June 7, 1806 (giving as its then address 140 Market Street). One source stated that its location was on the south side of Market Street between Fourth and Fifth streets. Graham, "The Taverns of Colonial Philadelphia," *Transactions of the American Philosophical Society*, New Series, 43:1, 319 (1953). Another source stated that it was located on the north side of Market Street. Watson, *Annals of Philadelphia* 3:294. A historian in 1921 gave as its address 410 Market Street, based on a history of Market Street the author had read. Robins, "Charles Lee," *Penn. Mag. of Biography and History* 45:91 (1921). In describing Lee's death, the inn is sometimes portrayed as run-down or shabby. See, e.g., Jones, *History of New York* 2:352; Montross, *Rag, Tag and Bobtail*, 288. But this seems unlikely, given its location and that Parsons and delegates to the Constitutional Convention stayed there.

148. John Bernard Recollections, in Bernard, *Retrospections of America*, 103. Lee's first biographer, Edward Langworthy, wrote, "A friend of the Editor's was at the inn when he took his departure from this world. The servants informed him that General Lee was dying; upon which he went into the room; he was then struggling with the king of terrors, and seemed to have lost his senses; the last words he heard him speak were, 'Stand by me, my brave grenadiers!'" Langworthy, *Memoirs of Lee*, 59. The friend of Bernard's and Langworthy's may have been the author of a column in Philadelphia titled "The

Anti-Lounger." The author of this column wrote in 1805: "I always leave the Conestoga Wagon with a melancholy impression. In a room on the first floor (called now number 7) died Major General Lee, once the second in command of the Army of the United States. I was present when Life's feverish Dream was with the General. I witnessed his last struggles, for there seemed to be a conflict between him and the King of Terrors. He seemed to have lost his senses. The last words I heard him utter were 'stand by me, my brave Grenadiers.'" Unknown Author, "The Anti-Lounger," *Poulson's American Daily Advertiser*, Jan. 29, 1805. It is also possible that this author was plagiarizing from Langworthy's book on Lee.

149. Ebenezer Hazard to J. Belknap, Jan. 29, 1783, in "Belknap Papers," Massachusetts Hist. Soc. Coll., 184 (1877). The entire description is as follows: "General Lee died in the second story of a tavern, after a few days' illness, in some degree his own physician and but badly attended, except by two faithful dogs, who frequently attempted in vain to awaken their dead master. They laid themselves down by his corpse for a considerable time, so long that it became necessary for new masters to remove them." The editors of the Belknap Papers wrote in a note for this letter that "This account of the death of General Charles Lee was probably communicated to [Ebenezer] Hazard by Dr. Clarkson of Philadelphia." Id.

150. *Independent Gazetteer* (Philadelphia), Oct. 5, 1782, and quoted in *Lee Papers*, 4:161; Registry of Burials, Oct. 4, 1782, Christ Church Archives.

151. Ibid; Diary Entry, Robert Morris, Oct. 4, 1782, in Cantanzariti et al. (eds.), *Morris Papers* 6:490; J. Vaughn to W. T. Franklin, Oct. 1782, Sol Feinstone Collection, American Philosophical Society; see also Diary Entry, Oct. 4, 1782, in "Extracts from the Diary of Jacob Hiltzheimer," *Penn. Mag. of History and Biography* 16:162 (1892) ("Gen. Lee late of our army and just from his farm in Virginia, was today buried in Christ Church yard.").

152. Diary Entry, Robert Morris, Oct. 4, 1782, in Cantanzariti et al. (eds.), *Morris Papers* 6:490.

153. Norris (ed.), *History of the Lower Shenandoah Valley*, 241.

154. Charles Lee Will, undated [about 1782], in *Lee Papers* 4:31. The will was published in the January 31, 1784, edition of Eleazer Oswald's *Independent Gazetteer*. Oswald changed the full names of individuals named in the published text to their respective initials. The will in this published version was dated 1782. The will, taken from the original filed in the clerk's office in Berkeley County, was published in its entirety in Norris (ed.), *History of the Lower Shenandoah Valley*, 238-40.

155. Ebenezer Hazard to J. Belknap, Jan. 29, 1783, in "Belknap Papers," *Massachusetts Hist. Soc. Coll.*, 5th Series, 2:184 (1877).

156. "Disinterment of the Remains of Major-General Charles Lee, at Christ Church, Philadelphia," *Historical Magazine* 5:370-71 (1861); Clark, *Record of the Inscriptions on the Tablets and Gravestones of Christ Church*, 13. Edward Clark explained that Christ Church was forced to move Lee's remains and those of others after the city took eight feet of its burial ground as part of a street widening project. Clark wrote that Lee's remains were placed in a new coffin, which was buried "between the first and second windows east of the S. W. door of the Church." Clark, *Record of the Inscriptions on the Tablets and Gravestones of Christ Church*, 13. The *Historical Magazine* wrote of Lee's remains that only "his wig remained in good preservation."

157. See www.findagrave.com (search for Charles Lee and view images). The plaque was a gift of Samuel White Patterson (id.), author of a biography of Lee called *Knight Errant of Liberty, The Triumph and Tragedy of General Charles Lee*.

158. See McBurney, *Rhode Island Campaign*, passim; "Circumstances Relative to the Misunderstanding Between Gen. Pigot and Gen. Prescott, the 29th Aug. 1778," in Mackenzie, *Diary* 2:402-3.

159. See McBurney, "British Treatment of Prisoners During the Occupation of Newport, 1776-1779: Disease, Starvation and Death Stalk the Prison Ships," *Newport History* 79:263, 16-20 (Fall 2010).

160. J. Hill to C. Waller, May 30, 1779, Jonathan Trumbull Papers, Peter Force Transcripts, series 7E, microfilm reel 48, Manuscript Division, Library of Congress.

161. Don N. Hagist, in an email to the author, dated May 26, 2013, stated that Barrington's promotion to captain did not occur on December 10, 1778, as stated in Baule and Gilbert (eds.), *British Army Officers*, 10 and Ford (ed.), *British Officers Serving in the A.R.*, 24. Hagist consulted John Houlding, an expert in the field whom Hagist explained has taken information directly from the Succession Rolls at the British National Archives, and Hagist said that that source indicated Barrington was officially promoted to captain on June 6, 1777. Hagist, in the same email, also said that muster records of the 7th Regiment indicated that Barrington had been promoted on October 25, 1777, which was when he was still a captive. Hagist is the author of the recently published *British Soldiers, American War, Voices of the American Revolution* (Yardley, PA: Westholme, 2012).

162. Diary Entry, Dec. 21, 1778, in Mackenzie, *Diary* 2:434; J. Sullivan to H. Laurens, Dec. 20, 1778, in Hammond (ed.), *Sullivan Letters* 2:463-64 (a British captain is one of the prisoners); *Independent Chronicle*, Jan. 8, 1779 (Barrington one of the prisoners). Barrington, who was married in New York City about June of 1778, retired from the army on September 2, 1779. See email from Don N. Hagist in note immediately above. After that, he disappears from the pages of history—he is not mentioned in British newspapers or in biographies of British officers.

163. Johann Conrad Dohla Diary Entry, Oct. 25, 1779, in Burgoyne (ed.), *Hessian Diary*, 113; H. Gates to H. Laurens, Oct. 27, 1779, Horatio Gates Papers, N.Y. Hist. Soc.; Willcox, *Portrait of a General*, 291-92.

164. *Morning Chronicle and London Advertiser*, Feb. 2, 1780; Rivington's *Royal Gazette*, Dec. 9, 1780; *London Chronicle*, March 12, 1782.

165. Boatner, *Encyclopedia of the A. R.*, 887; Wheater, *Historical Record of the Seventh Royal Regiment of Fusiliers*, 230; *London Gazette*, Nov. 26, 1782 (announcing appointment of Prescott as lieutenant general); *London Gazette*, Oct. 25, 1788 (announcing the replacement as colonel of the 7th Regiment "lieutenant general Richard Prescott dec."); *Daily Advertiser* (London), Nov. 1, 1788 (advertisement requesting creditors of the recently deceased "lieutenant general Richard Prescott late of Queen-Anne-Street West, in the County of Middlesex" to contact the named attorney).

166. See also W. Barrington to W. Howe, Sept. 2, 1777, CO 5/94, British National Archives (attaching list of promotions, including Harcourt's appointment, as of August 29, 1777).

167. Extract of a Letter from Chatham, Sept. 17, 1777, in *Daily Advertiser*, Sept. 19, 1777 and quoted in Scull, *The Evelyns in America*, 228, n. A more detailed description of the tragedy is set forth in Extract of a Letter from Oxford, Sept. 17, 1777, in *General Evening Post* (London), Sept. 18-19, 1777, *Gazetteer and New Daily Advertiser* (London), Sept. 19, 1777, and *Morning Chronicle* (London), Sept. 19, 1777.

168. *London Evening Post*, Sept. 18-21, 1777.

169. W. Harcourt to Lord Nuneham, Dec. 17, 1776, in Scull, *The Evelyns in America*, 226 and Harcourt (ed.), *Harcourt Papers* 11:181.

170. W. Harcourt to Earl Harcourt, Mar. 17, 1777, in Harcourt (ed.), *Harcourt Papers* 11:208-9.

171. W. Harcourt to Earl Harcourt, May 31, 1777, in ibid., 213.

172. W. Harcourt to Lord Nuneham, Nov. 29, 1777, in ibid., 224.

173. W. Harcourt to Earl Harcourt, March 17, 1777, in Harcourt (ed.), *Harcourt Papers* 11:207.

174. W. Harcourt to Earl Harcourt, Nov. 29, 1777, in ibid., 225.

175. Fleming, *Washington's Secret War,* 50.
176. W. Howe to G. Germain, Jan. 19, 1778, in Davies (ed.), *Documents of the A.R.* 13:227 (Harcourt returning to England with dispatches dated late December of 1777).
177. See Hargrove, *General John Burgoyne,* 232; C. Jenkinson to King George III, Oct. 18, 1779, in Fortescue (ed.), *Correspondence of King George the Third* 4:466; *London Public Advertiser,* Oct. 22, 1779; *London Gazette,* Oct. 30, 1779. The 16th Regiment of Light Dragoons had returned from America to England in December of 1778.
178. *London Gazette,* Oct. 21, 1780.
179. *Dictionary of National Biography* 8:1211; *Royal Military Calendar* 1:281-82; see also Scull, *The Evelyns in America,* 209-10 (which is not always accurate on the years of events, such as Harcourt's service in Holland and the date of his death); *London Gazette,* Nov. 26, 1782 (appointed major general); Mary Harcourt to Countess Harcourt, Sept. 1790, in Harcourt (ed.), *Harcourt Papers* 11:255 (the "Queen, the Princess Royal, Lady Chesterfield, and General Harcourt" play together at "casino," while Mary Harcourt sometimes makes a "fourth . . . at cribbage" with another set of notables); *The Times* (London), May 4, 1793 (appointed to command a brigade of cavalry); *London Gazette,* Oct. 19, 1793 (appointed lieutenant general); W. Harcourt to Earl Harcourt (William's brother), May 11, 1794, in Harcourt (ed.), *Harcourt Papers* 11:242 (describing Harcourt's role as commander of the British cavalry in a successful action in Holland against the enemy, seizing "10 or 11 pieces of artillery, and about 1,500 killed and prisoners"); *London Gazette,* Jan. 9, 1798 (appointed general).
180. *Dictionary of National Biography* 8:1211; "In Honour of a Hero," at www.stgeorges-windsor.org (search for William Harcourt). Sculpted by Robert William Sievier in 1832, the statue stands 76 inches high on a stone base and shows Harcourt in his coronation robes. A plaster model, identical to the white marble figure at St. George's, now stands in the south transept of Stanton Harcourt. See "In Honour of a Hero," at www.stgeorges-windsor.org (search for William Harcourt).

CHAPTER NINE: THE ORDEAL OF WILLIAM BARTON
1. General Assembly Resolution, Feb. 1778 session, in Bartlett (ed.), *Records of R.I.* 8:355-56; N. Cook to W. Barton, Feb. 14, 1778, in id., 358. Barton had been selected to lead the Second Rhode Island State Regiment as its colonel in December of 1777. General Assembly Resolution, Dec. 1777 session, in id., 328.
2. Rhode Island Council of War to R. Pigot, Providence, April 25, 1778, Letters from the Governor, vol. 3, R.I. State Archives; Rhode Island Council of War Records, April 24 and 27, 1778, in id.
3. Diary Entry, April 28, 1778, in Mackenzie, *Diary* 1:271-72; see also R. Pigot to N. Cooke, April 28, 1778, Letters to the Governor, vol. 12, R.I. State Archives; A List of American Prisoners at Rhode Island, 29 Apr. 1778, folio 85, Council of War Papers, Prisoner Exchanges and Miscellaneous Papers, 1775-1781, in id.
4. McBurney, *The Rhode Island Campaign,* 49-60.
5. Ibid., 61-62.
6. H. Laurens to W. Barton, June 20, 1778, in Williams, *Life of Barton,* 110.
7. See McBurney, *Rhode Island Campaign,* chapters 4-9.
8. H. Gates to W. Greene, June 15, 1779, in Horatio Gates Papers, microfilm reel 19, N.Y. Hist. Soc. Barton advertised for troops to fill his "light corps" in the July 1, 1779, edition of Providence's *The American Journal and General Advertiser.*
9. H. Gates Orders to E. Bowen, June 30, 1779, in Horatio Gates Papers, microfilm reel 19, N.Y. Hist. Soc.
10. H. Gates Orders to W. Barton, July 24, 1779, in ibid.
11. H. Gates Orders to W. Barton, Aug. 16, 1779, in ibid. It appears that Barton raised only about 100 light troops for his corps. See Weekly Return of the Troops in Rhode Island Commanded by General Horatio Gates, Sept. 11, 18 and 25, 1779, in id.

12. W. Barton to H. Gates, Oct. 10 and 13, 1779, in ibid.; General Orders, Oct. 26, 1779, James Webb's Orderly Book. Col. Henry Sherburne's Regiment, Revolutionary War Records, Box 2, Folder 1, R.I. Hist. Soc.
13. General Assembly Resolution, Feb. 1780 session, in Bartlett (ed.), *Records of R.I.* 9:29-30.
14. See *Providence Patriot,* June 18, 1814 (advertisement by Benjamin Howland, tailor, now occupying General Barton's old store); *Rhode Island American,* Oct. 8, 1816 (advertisement by Daniel Russell, boot and shoe manufacturer and seller, occupying "the shop of General William Barton").
15. General Assembly Committee Reports and Resolutions, June 1782 and Aug. 1782 sessions, in Bartlett (ed.), *Records of R.I.* 9:570 and 592-93. Barton put the South Kingstown lot up for sale in 1783. Advertisement, *Providence Gazette,* Aug. 16, 1783.
16. Memorial of William Barton to the Continental Congress, April 28, 1785, Papers of the Continental Congress, Memorials Addressed to Congress 1775-1789, M247, microfilm reel 48, item 41, I, folio 423; see also Committee Appointment, May 2, 1778, in Ford (ed.), *Journal of the Continental Congress* 28:325, n. 1. The congressional committee appointed to consider Barton's memorial consisted of William Grayson, James McHenry, and Rhode Islander David Howell. Id.
17. Committee Report, May 11, 1785, in Ford (ed.), *Journal of the Continental Congress* 28:347.
18. Resolution, Sept. 7, 1785, in ibid., 29:684.
19. W. Barton to Z. Andrews, Sept. 6, 1785 (from New York City), box 44, folder 8, Newport Hist. Soc. Barton must have written this letter on September 7, the date Congress enacted the resolution relating to him, and not on September 6.
20. Ibid.
21. See partial lists of deputies to the General Assembly, in Bartlett (ed.), *Records of R.I.* 9:539 (May 1782) and 10:281 (May 1788); *United States Chronicle* (Providence), Aug. 28, 1788 (Barton elected Aug. 1788), and March 14, 1789 (Barton serving in March 1789 session). Around this time, a William Barton was elected to serve in the General Assembly from Warren, where Colonel William Barton was born. *See* Bartlett (ed.), *Records of R.I.* 10:192 (May 1786) and 10:427 (May 1791). This man was another William Barton, who was also from Warren and who served as a private in the Bristol County militia as a young man and rose to become chief justice of the Court of Common Pleas; he also served as town clerk for Bristol for about thirty years. See William Barton, Index Cards Showing Military Service in the Revolutionary War, R.I. State Archives (service as a private from Warren in a Bristol County alarm company in 1778 and 1779 and in the Bristol County militia in 1780 and 1781); death notice for "William Barton, aged 64" of Warren in *Bristol County Register,* Aug. 19, 1809, *Rhode Island Republican,* Aug. 23, 1809, and *New York Gazette,* Aug. 24, 1809. A William Barton was also selected as tax collector for Bristol County in 1785 and 1786. General Assembly Resolutions, in Bartlett (ed.), *Records of R.I.* 10:96 (May 1785) and 10:194 (May 1786). The author suspects that William Barton, the hero of Prescott's capture, served only in Providence posts.
22. General Assembly Resolutions, in Bartlett (ed.), *Records of R.I.* 10:284 (May 1788; adjutant general); Arthur Skinner Certification, May 10, 1790, William Barton Papers, MSS 921, R.I. Hist. Soc. (Skinner certified that he has been "satisfied with the conduct of Brigadier General William Barton since his appointment to that office"); Note of the Minutes of the Brigade of Providence County, May 19, 1791, in id. (voting for "Brigadier General William Barton" for Brigadier General of Providence County); Order from Brigadier General William Barton to Colonel William Aldrich, Sept. 18, 1794, in id.; Order from Major General Martin to Brigadier General William Barton, Dec. 19, 1797, in id.; *Newport Mercury,* May 20, 1794 ("Brigadier General Barton" and

the state governor tour the works of "Fort Washington on Goat Island" just outside of Newport Harbor); Smith, *Civil and Military List of R.I.* 1:516 (appointed inspector general of the state militia, May 1793); id., 529 (appointed Brigadier General of the Providence County Brigade, of the state militia, May 1794; id., 545 (same, May 1795); id., 559 (same, May 1796); id., 573 (same, May 1797); id., 587 (same, May 1798; id., 2:21 (same, May 1801); id., 37 (same, May 1802). Smith's list is not complete.

23. See Bartlett (ed.), *Index to Acts and Resolves of R.I.* (elected major general June 3, 1802); Smith, *Civil and Military List of R.I.* 2:35 (appointed major general June 1802); id., 50 (same, May 1803); id., 66 (same, May 1804); id., 80 (same, June 1805); id., 105 (same, May 1807); id., 118 (same, May 1808); see also *Providence Gazette,* May 7, 1808 ("William Barton, Esq. re-appointed Major General of the Militia of the State").

24. R. Morris to D. Humphreys, June 15, 1784, in Cantanzariti et al. (eds.), *Morris Papers* 9:392 and Humphreys, *Life of Humphreys,* 324. As reported in the *New York Journal* article of June 1, 1786, other recipients included Colonel Marinus Willett of New York, who successfully defended Fort Schuyler (also called Fort Stanwix) in a siege in 1777; Colonel Samuel Smith of the Maryland Continental line "for the defense of Mud Island" in the Delaware River; Colonel Tench Tilghman of Maryland, aide-de-camp to General Washington, "[i]n testimony of Congress's high opinion of his merit and ability"; Colonel Return Jonathan Meigs of the Connecticut Continental line, "[f]or his prudence, activity, enterprise and valor in an expedition to Long Island," in which twelve brigs and sloops were destroyed and ninety Loyalist militiamen taken prisoner at Sag Harbor; Colonel Christopher Greene of the Rhode Island Continental line, for his "[d]efense of Red Bank on the Delaware River"; Colonel Andrew Pickens of the South Carolina militia "for his spirited conduct in the action of the Cowpens"; Colonel David Humphreys, aide-de-camp to General Washington, "as a mark of esteem"; Commodore John Hazelwood, commander of the naval force of the state of Pennsylvania, "[f]or his gallant defense of his country against the British fleet, whereby two of their men-of-war were destroyed and four others compelled to retire"; Captain William Pierce of Virginia, aide-de-camp to General Nathaniel Greene, "who bore Gen. Greene's dispatches, giving an account of the victory" at Eutaw Springs. For the awards of the swords by the Continental Congress, see Ford (ed.), *Journal of the Continental Congress* 8:579-80 (Meigs and Barton); 9:771-72 (Willet) and 862 (Greene, Smith and Hazelwood); 19:247 (Pickens); 21:1082 (Tilghman), 1085 (Pierce), and 1108 (Humphreys).

25. It is somewhat of a mystery as to whether credit for making the swords should be given to Claude-Raymond Liger, his son, Pierre-Ambroise Liger, or both. The Metropolitan Museum of Art's description of Colonel Marinus Willet's sword states that the tradesman who made the sword was "C. Liger (French, Paris, recorded 1770-93)." Description of Smallsword of Col. Marinus Willet, Metropolitan Museum of Art, American Wing, Gallery 753 and at www.metmuseum.org/collections (search "marinus willett"). The Smithsonian Museum also credits "C. Liger, Paris" for making the sword awarded to Return Jonathan Meigs. See Continental Congress Sword Presented to Colonel Return J. Meigs, American Stories on-line exhibition, at www.si.edu (for how to access this sword online, see bibliography to this book, under Unpublished Records and "Continental Congress Sword"). Thus, both museums credit Claude-Raymond Liger. By a web-engine search of the name Pierre-Ambroise Liger conducted on June 3, 2013, the author found two useful French sources. The first one is a family tree of the Liger family, prepared by Antonio Liger on GeneaNet, which lists a Claude-Raymond Liger (1720-1802) and his son, Pierre-Ambroise Liger (1752-1806). A second result of this search, authored by Thierry Straub in 2000, lists a Pierre-Ambroise Liger residing in Paris in 1776, and describes him as a "maître fourbisseur" (master sword maker) who was born on April 4, 1752, the son of Claude-Raymond Liger. Emily Schulz, deputy

director and curator of The Society of the Cincinnati, showed the author a 2009 email from a Belgian researcher, who found a reference to Liger searching online French sources. The information indicated that the sword maker's full name was Pierre-Ambroise Liger; he was promoted to the post of master fourbisseur in 1757; in 1770 he was fourbisseur for the Duc de Chartres and the Comte de Clermont; and in 1793 he was responsible for a study to improve the fabrication of edged weapons. The email further notes that Liger's workshop stood at 192 Rue Coquillière in Paris and that his signature appeared on items until the early 1800s, although it is not known if his workshop was eventually taken over by his son. The source of this information, according to this email, is: Jean-Jacques Buigné and Pierre Jarlier, *Le "Qui est qui" de l'arme en France de 1350 à 1970,* Tome 1, France: La Tour du Pin, Édition du Portail, 2001. American sword expert Harold L. Peterson examined the sword awarded to Colonel Meigs and found that the "reverse side at the hilt bears the inscription "LIGER/ Fourbisseur/ De S: A:/ Msgr/ Le Duc/ De Chartre/ & Comte/ De Clermont/ Rue/ Coquillière/ à Paris." Peterson, *The American Sword, 1775-1945,* 192. This information is consistent with that found in the email described in the above paragraph. It appears that French authors Buigné and Jarlier may have confused Claude-Raymond Liger and Pierre-Ambroise Liger, based on their birthdates in the Liger family tree. Given that Pierre-Ambroise was born in 1752, it must have been Claude-Raymond who was promoted to the post of master fourbisseur in 1757 and was working in 1770 as fourbisseur for the Duc de Chartres and the Comte de Clermont. By 1793, either of them could have been responsible for a study to improve the fabrication of edged weapons. But given that Claude-Raymond would have been seventy-three years old at that time, it was probably Pierre-Ambroise who did that work. In 1786, when the last of the swords contracted for by Humphreys were delivered to him, Claude-Raymond was sixty-six years old and Pierre-Ambroise was thirty-four years old. The author suspects, but cannot be sure, that at that time, Claude Raymond Liger still controlled the shop, but that Pierre-Ambroise Liger was performing more work than his father.

26. The same announcement and material relating to the ceremonial swords brought back by Humphreys that appeared in the *New York Journal* was reported in the June 5, 1786, edition of Hartford's *Connecticut Courant* and the June 7, 1786, edition of the *Pennsylvania Herald.*

27. D. Humphreys to H. Knox, May 22, 1786, in Humphreys, *Life of Humphreys,* 355; see also H. Knox to D. Humphreys, May 25, 1786, in id., 356 (confirming receipt of the "ten elegantly mounted swords" with the names of the applicable officers "engraved thereon").

28. H. Knox to W. Barton, Aug. 1, 1786, in *Massachusetts Gazette,* March 23, 1787, and *Newport Mercury,* April 2, 1787, and Williams, *Life of Barton,* 111-12.

29. W. Barton to H. Knox, Aug. 10, 1786, in *Massachusetts Gazette,* March 23, 1787, and *Newport Mercury,* April 2, 1787. The grip of Barton's sword is inscribed with "Congress/to/Col. William Barton/July 25, 1777." In addition, the scabbard, covered in cloth with silver trim, has a silver chain and belt loop. See image and description of Barton's sword on the website for artifacts at the Rhode Island Historical Society, www.rihs.org. The call number for the ceremonial sword and scabbard at the Rhode Island Historical Society is 1933.3.1.

30. W. Barton to T. L. Halsey, Nov. 8, 1787, in Williams, *Life of Barton,* 113-14. The author has not found a copy of this narrative. The author reviewed copies of outgoing correspondence from the New York City French Consulate, as well as from the Boston French Consulate, from 1782 through 1792, but did not find Barton's missive. See French Copying Project, Archives du Ministère des Affaires Étrangères, B1, Correspondence Consulaire et Commerciale, New York (1783-1792), volumes 909-10, reels 4 and 5, and Boston (1779-92), volumes 209, reels 1 and 2, Library of Congress.

The workers on the French copying project admitted that they did not necessarily copy every item of correspondence.

31. Letter to the editor, from unidentified source sympathetic to Barton, in *North Star* (Danville, Vermont), June 7, 1821.

32. See Conley, *Democracy in Decline,* 80-142.

33. See list of constitutional convention delegates in Staples, *Rhode Island in the Continental Congress,* 641 (March 1790); Providence and 672 (May 1790); Providence; Barton voted in favor of ratification).

34. Summary of William Barton Statements, March 3, 1790, in Foster, *Minutes of the Convention,* 54.

35. Summary of William Barton Statements, March 6, 1790, in ibid., 78-79 and 88.

36. R. Flint to A. Hamilton, June 14, 1790, with unsigned memorandum attached, quoted in Hunt (ed.), *Calendar of Applications and Recommendations for Office,* x and 44. Flint gained his knowledge from speaking with an unidentified man, probably a Rhode Island Federalist, or possibly a Connecticut merchant with ties to Providence. Id., x. Flint was originally from Connecticut and had moved to New York City.

37. D. Owen to G. Washington, May 29, 1790, in Twohig et al. (eds.), *Washington Papers (Presidential Series)* 5:440; J. Bowen to G. Washington, June 19, 1790, id., 533 (Barton had returned to Rhode Island carrying Washington's federal appointments); Bartlett (ed.), *Index to Acts and Resolves of R.I.* (an act reimbursing Barton "for expenses to New York on business connected with the adoption of the Constitution of the United States;" enacted May 22, 1798).

38. W. Barton to G. Washington, Sept. 3, 1789, in Twohig et al. (eds.), *Washington Papers (Presidential Series)* 3:596.

39. John Swan of Baltimore, who served as a major in the dragoons during the Revolutionary War, introduced Barton to Michael Jenifer Stone of Maryland and recommended him for a federal post, explaining that "This gentleman's active conduct during the revolution speaks forcibly in his favor." J. Swan to M. J. Stone, June 8, 1790, quoted in Twohig et al. (eds.), *Washington Papers (Presidential Series)* 5:506, n. 1. Stone then forwarded the recommendation to President Washington. M. J. Stone to G. Washington, June 9, 1790, in id., 506. For Washington's appointment of Barton, see G. Washington to U.S. Senate, June 14, 1790, quoted in id., n. 1; see also G. Washington to U.S. Senate, March 6, 1792, in id., 10:41-42 (listing appointments made during recess of the U.S. Senate, including Barton's as Inspector of the Surveys and Ports for Providence, Rhode Island). William Barton of Rhode Island is sometimes mistaken by editors of historical records as William Barton of Pennsylvania. Both sought federal appointments at about the same time. The latter was a well-educated attorney whose uncle was the renowned scientist David Rittenhouse of Philadelphia.

40. W. Barton to B. Bourne, Feb. 3, 1796, Benjamin Bourne Papers, MSS 11, R.I. Hist. Soc.

41. Carter, *The Bartons' Quest for Liberty,* 22-23. Seth Barton had served as a first lieutenant in Colonel Robert Elliott's Rhode Island State Regiment of Artillery during the Revolutionary War, and after accumulating sufficient money as a merchant in Baltimore, purchased a farm in Virginia. Id. Thomas B. Barton, apparently one of Seth's sons, while residing in Virginia, was contacted in 1820 about providing financial assistance to William Barton, but he refused. See M. Hall to T. B. Barton, Jan. 26, 1820, MSS 9006, Manuscripts, vol. 8, p. 85, R.I. Hist. Soc.

42. *Daily Advertiser* (New York), Jan. 6, 1809; *Massachusetts Spy,* March 7, 1810 ("The petitions of Mrs. Hamilton and General Barton of Rhode Island were before the House and occupied a great part of the day"); *Farmer's Repository,* March 2, 1810 (Barton's and Hamilton's petitions defeated by a vote of 63-62). Mrs. Hamilton was the widow of Alexander Hamilton.

43. "American Gallantry," in *The Port Folio,* 2nd Ser., 8:3, 245-51 (Sept. 1812).

44. The Rhode Island Historical Society has in its collections the original handwritten version of Barton's narrative that was signed by Barton and relied on by the editors of *The Port Folio*. Barton, "Narrative of the Capture of Major General Prescott," undated (probably around 1812), MSS 9003, vol. III, folder 13, R.I. Hist. Soc.
45. *The Port Folio*, 2nd Ser., 8:4, 436 (Oct. 1812).
46. Letter to the editor, from unidentified source sympathetic to Barton, in *North Star* (Danville, Vermont), June 7, 1821.
47. This supposition is based on the statement by the editor of *The Port Folio* that "Only one copy has been taken previous to the publication, and that was done at the request of our former friend and ally the unfortunate Louis XVI, of France, by whom it was read and admired." This comment suggests that the version sent to the French and the one published in *The Port Folio* were the same.
48. General Assembly Resolution, Oct. 23, 1781, in Walton (ed.), *Records of the Governor and Council of Vermont* 2:122. For conferring with Ira Allen, see Wilbur, *Ira Allen*, 324.
49. General Assembly Resolution, Oct. 23, 1781, in Walton (ed.), *Records of the Governor and Council of Vermont* 2:122.
50. General Assembly Resolution, Oct. 16, 1784, in ibid., 3:55. The original grant was confirmed in 1788. Report of Land Commissioners, March 15, 1788, in id., 180.
51. General Assembly Resolution, Oct. 17, 1789, in ibid., 3:192.
52. Young, *A History of Barton, Vermont*, 2-3.
53. Ibid., 6.
54. For the summary of the legal proceedings by an author unsympathetic to Barton, see "Gen. Barton," *Vermont Watchman and State Gazette*, Aug. 23, 1831, quoted in Walton (ed.), *Records of the Governor and Council of Vermont* 8:307-9, which was a defense of Herman Allen against charges that Barton was harshly treated in Vermont. This article originally appeared in Danville's *North Star*, Dec. 7, 1824. For the summary of the legal proceedings by an author sympathetic to Barton, see "General Barton," *Spooner's Vermont Journal*, Oct. 4, 1824, which was reprinted in the *Rhode Island Republican*, Oct. 14, 1824. For more on the litigation, see copy of letter from W. Mattocks to H. Newcomb, Nov. 1, 1824, MSS 9006, Manuscripts, vol. 8, p. 92, R.I. Hist. Soc. and Blackington, "Case of the Rejected Hero," *Vermont Life* 13:1, 52-54 (Aug. 1958).
55. Quoted in "General Barton," *Spooner's Vermont Journal*, Oct. 4, 1824.
56. Ibid.
57. "Gen. Barton," *Vermont Watchman and State Gazette*, Aug. 23, 1831, quoted in Walton (ed.), *Records of the Governor and Council of Vermont* 8:307-9. More legal proceedings continued until 1816, all of which went against Barton. Id.
58. John Howland Recollections, in Williams, *Life of Barton*, 98-99.
59. Letter to the editor of the *National Intelligencer*, from "A Vermonter," Sept. 25, 1824, quoted in the *Essex Register*, Oct. 7, 1824.
60. *Providence Patriot*, Feb. 5, 1814.
61. An Act Concerning Invalid Pensioners, enacted by the Senate and House of Representatives of the United States of America, approved by President James Madison, March 3, 1815, quoted in *Daily National Intelligencer*, March 8, 1815; William Barton Rev. War Pension Application, National Archives Building; letter to the editor, from unidentified source sympathetic to Barton, in *North Star* (Danville, Vermont), June 7, 1821; R.I. Pension Roll 1835, p.4, R.I. State Archives (pension commenced January 1, 1815; relinquished for benefits of the Act of May 15, 1828).
62. "Gen. Barton," *Vermont Watchman and State Gazette*, Aug. 23, 1831, quoted in Walton (ed.), *Records of the Governor and Council of Vermont* 8:309.
63. S. B. Barrell to W. Barton, Dec. 4, 1818, William Barton Papers, MSS 921, folder 5, R.I. Hist. Soc. ("$600, the amount for which you are actually confined in prison; the

sum of $2,600 which includes the amount of the judgment obtained against you"). There is some support for the $2,600 amount. See Summons for William Barton to Appear at the Supreme Court of Vermont in Danville on the Third Tuesday of August 1812, signed by Chief Judge Royal Flynn, id., Folder 4 (judgments obtained by Herman Allen and Samuel Fitch for Barton's failure to convey to them six lots of land, with monetary damages for the lots of $500, $460, $460, $460, $260, and $190, respectively, for a total of $2,330); judgments in next note totalling $320.01.

64. Transcripts from the Docket of Orleans County Court, Entries Related to William Barton from March 1810 to June 27, 1814, Certified by the Court Clerk, June 27, 1814, ibid. (Solomon Wadhams versus William Barton, Sept. 1, 1812, damages of $195.54 and costs of $23.24; Jonathan Allyn versus William Barton, March 8, 1813, damages of $50.13 and costs of $51.10.)

65. S. B. Barrell to W. Barton, March 3, 1819, MSS 9006, Manuscripts, vol. 8, p. 84, R.I. Hist. Soc.

66. W. Barton to D. Chase, Oct. 10, 1818, in author's private collection.

67. S. Crafts to W. Barton, Feb. 11, 1820, MSS 9006, Manuscripts, vol. 8, p. 86, R.I. Hist. Soc.; see also Petition of William Barton to United States Congress, Dec. 1818, Danville, Vermont, in id., p. 84.

68. W. Barton to J. Monroe, Dec. 15, 1820, MSS L2012F135 M, Library of The Society of the Cincinnati.

69. Report of the Committee on Insolvency, 1821, quoted in *Vermont Journal*, Nov. 19, 1821 (Nov. 5, 1821, journal of legislative proceedings), and Walton (ed.), *Records of the Governor and Council of Vermont* 8:308-9, n. 3.

70. For the first advertisements for the pamphlet, see *Spooner's Vermont Journal*, Oct. 21 and 22, and Nov. 12 and 19, 1821. The text of the narrative was ultimately published in the October 11, 1824, edition of *Spooner's Vermont Journal* and in other newspapers, such as the *Connecticut Herald* (New Haven), Nov. 9, 1824, and *Hallowell Gazette* (Hallowell, Maine), Nov. 10, 1824.

71. J. B. Barton to W. Barton, Feb. 15, 1821, William Barton Papers, MSS 921, Folder 2, R.I. Hist. Soc.

72. According to a Barton family genealogy, William Barton, Jr., was born on December 16, 1771, and died in 1818 in Enfield, Connecticut; Henry Barton was born on November 18, 1780, and died on November 14, 1814, in Savannah, Georgia; and Robert Carver Barton was born on December 19, 1782, and died in September of 1824 in Marietta, Illinois, while serving as a lieutenant in the United States Army. Barton Family Genealogy, R.I. Hist. Soc., 17.

73. "Gen. Barton," *Vermont Watchman and State Gazette*, Aug. 23, 1831, quoted in Walton (ed.), *Records of the Governor and Council of Vermont* 8:309.

74. Copy of letter from W. Mattocks to H. Newcomb, Nov. 1, 1824, MSS 9006, Manuscripts, vol. 8, p. 92, R.I. Hist. Soc.

75. M. Hall to T. B. Barton, Jan. 26, 1820, MSS 9006, Manuscripts, vol. 8, p. 85, R.I. Hist. Soc.

76. W. Barton to D. Chase, Oct. 10, 1818, in author's private collection.

77. Letter from "Montague" (a pen name) to Mrs. E. Waring of Newport, R.I., April 6, 1822, in *Saratoga Sentinel*, April 24, 1822, and reprinted in *Rhode Island Republican*, May 10, 1822.

78. *Essex Register*, Sept. 30, 1824 (italics in original); see also *The Times and Hartford Advertiser*, Sept. 7, 1824; *American Repertory* (Burlington, Vermont), Dec. 25, 1821.

79. Lossing, *Pictorial Field-Book* 1:643, n. 1 (quoting part of the poem). For the entire poem, titled "The Prisoner for Debt," see Griswold (ed.), *Readings in American Poetry*, 211-13; Birdsall and Jones (eds.), *A Century of American Literature*, 88-89.

80. Nolan (ed.), *Lafayette in America Day by Day*, 73-83 (reached Providence August 1,

1778, and left Providence September 28, 1778) and 230-31 (in Providence from October 23 to 26, 1784, not including an overnight trip to Newport). During the war, Lafayette's only other visit to Rhode Island was a short visit to Newport from July 24 to August 5, 1780, to meet with commanders of French troops then occupying Newport. Id., 118-20. Barton could have met with Lafayette during that trip too if he had travelled to Newport.

81. "Gen. Lafayette's Last Act in America," *North Star* (Danville), Dec. 6, 1825, quoted in Walton (ed.), *Records of the Governor and Council of Vermont* 7:502. The *North Star* report stated that Lafayette sent the payment while he was in New York City aboard the *Brandywine*. But Lafayette departed New York City for the last time on July 14, 1825. Nolan (ed.), *Lafayette in America Day by Day*, 295. He sailed for France from Washington, D.C., on September 9, 1825. Id., 305. Thus, Lafayette may have written the payment for Barton just before his departure from Washington, D.C., in September, but his correspondence took some time to reach Fletcher in Vermont. Lafayette arrived in Windsor, Vermont, on June 28, 1825, and the same day visited Woodstock and Royalton, arriving in Montpelier in the evening. The next day he visited Burlington, before taking a steamer down the Hudson River for Whitehall, New York. Id., 294.

82. See *Literary Cadet and Rhode Island Statesmen*, May 13, 1826, quoting *St. Thomas Tidende* (Virgin Islands) ("We think that Gen. Barton's gratitude to the humane and generous Frenchman can be equaled only by the *contempt* which he must feel for his *ungrateful* countrymen. The people of the United States have bestowed many and great favors on Lafayette, and very meritoriously—but should they neglect their old and gallant countrymen who fought in the same cause and devoted the best part of their lives to the same service?").

83. Lavesseur, *Lafayette in America in 1824 and 1825*, 272-74; Parker, *Recollections of General Lafayette on his Visit to the United States in 1824 and 1825*, 35.

84. See also *Boston Commercial Gazette*, Dec. 15, 1825 ("The unfortunate and brave revolutionary worthy, Gen. Barton of Rhode Island, who has been imprisoned for debt for 13 years in Vermont, has recently been liberated by the bounty of Gen. Lafayette").

85. Excerpt of letter from unidentified gentleman in New York to the *Boston Commercial Gazette*, quoted in *Boston Commercial Gazette*, Dec. 29, 1825; quoted in *Essex Register* (Salem, Massachusetts), Jan. 2, 1826, and *North Star* (Danville), Jan. 3, 1826, and Walton (ed.), *Records of the Governor and Council of Vermont* 7:502. See also *Providence Patriot*, Dec. 17, 1825 (Barton arrived at his home in Providence the previous day).

86. *Rhode Island American*, July 18, 1826.

87. *Providence Patriot*, June 27, 1827.

88. *Rhode Island Republican*, July 10, 1828; see also *Newport Mercury*, July 12, 1828 ("The scene, and the incidents connected with it, were recalled to his memory on entering the house ... although upwards of half a century had elapsed since it occurred; and many of the circumstances connected with the surprise and removal of the general from the house were related by him with much minuteness and feeling"); *Literary Cadet and Rhode Island Statesman*, July 2, 1828.

89. Bank Draft of the Bank of the United States, March 10, 1830, William Barton Papers, MSS 921, R.I. Hist. Soc.

90. According to the *National Gazette* (Philadelphia), January 13, 1829, there were only twenty-six surviving officers from the Revolutionary War: five colonels (including Barton), four lieutenant colonels, and seventeen majors.

91. *Rhode Island American*, Oct. 25, 1831.

92. Ibid. The newspaper also stated that "the remains of General Barton were interred today under military honors.... As a further mark of respect, the flags of the shipping

and alarm posts were suspended at half-mast." The October 31, 1831, edition of the *Rhode Island Republican* noted, "The capture of Gen. Prescott . . . was one of the most hazardous achievements of those times of daring." Barton's widow, Rhoda, received a pension as the widow of a Revolutionary War veteran under the Act of July 4, 1836. She died on December 15, 1841. William Barton Rev. War Pension Application, National Archives Building.

93. For an image of Barton's gravesite marker, see www.findagrave.com (search for William Barton).

94. See, e.g., Farmer and Moore (eds.), *Collections, Historical and Miscellaneous; and Monthly Literary Journal* 3:371-78 (Concord, NH: J. B. Moore, 1824); *American Anecdotes, Original and Select,* 121-33 (Boston, MA: Putnam and Hunt, 1830); Watson (ed.), *The Old Bell of Independence; or, Philadelphia in 1776,* 156-69 (Philadelphia, PA: Lindsay and Blakiston, 1852). In 1899, a historical novel for juveniles based on Barton's capture of Prescott was published. See William B. Chapman, *The Young Minuteman: A Story of the Capture of General Prescott* (New York: A. L. Burt, 1899).

95. This poem was originally published in 1835 in the *Old Colony Memorial* magazine. It was also printed in several newspapers later that year: *Richmond Inquirer* (Richmond, Virginia), June 23, 1835; *Saratoga Sentinel* (Saratoga Springs, New York), July 14, 1835; and *Manufacturers' and Farmers' Journal* (Providence, R.I.), June 25, 1835. These newspapers reported that the poem was "from the *Plymouth Memorial,*" whose formal name was the *Old Colony Memorial* and was published in Plymouth, Massachusetts. The author has been unable to find the edition of the *Old Colony Memorial* that contains the original published version of this poem. The poem thereafter survived in popular books and collections of songs marketed between 1842 and 1893. McCarty, *Songs, Odes, and Other Poems,* 366-69 (1842); *The Union Song Book,* 127-29 (1857); Duyckinck et al., *Cyclopedia of American Literature* 1:469 (1875); Barney, *Songs of the Rev.,* 42-43 (1893). A second, earlier poem about Barton's capture of Prescott first appeared in Catherine R. Williams's 1839 biography of William Barton. Williams, *Life of Barton,* Appendix, 128-30. It was reprinted in 1875. Duyckinck et al., *Cyclopedia of American Literature* 1:469. This poem is also discussed in the text of the Appendix to this book accompanying note 25.

96. Located at Highland Avenue in Tiverton, it is not clear when Fort Barton was named. Historian and archeologist D. K. ("Kathy") Abbass wrote of Fort Barton: "Fort Barton is a Revolutionary War fortification sited on an outcropping of granite 110 feet above the Sakonnet River to the west. No structures remain from the 18th century, but the earthworks are still discernible. Now a landscaped park, the park contains an observation tower erected in 1970. The site here was an advantageous location for a battery of guns. On June 11, 1777, Mackenzie says, 'Yesterday and today the rebels have been busily employed in making a work on a hill above Howland's Ferry where their guns have been placed all winter. It appears to be very extensive, and must cost them a great deal of labor, as there is little or no soil on the hill.' [Citing Diary Entry, June 28, 1777, in Mackenzie, *Diary* 1:413.] On June 28th, the Americans erected a flagstaff and raised their colors at the fort. On the 29th, he describes the fort as 'irregular in its figure, but very extensive. From the situation, it must be strong.' Id., 144. A week later, Barton led his raid. Presumably, this led to the fort being named Fort Barton." Abbass, *R.I. in the Rev.* 4:121. Abbass also wrote, "By June 28 the American fort at Tiverton was complete and flew the rebel colors 'on which occasion they fired an 18 lb shot at our Guard near the [Howland's] Bridge, which fell short.'" Abbass, *R.I. in the Rev.* 1:305 (citing Diary Entry, June 28, 1777, in Mackenzie, *Diary* 1:144). But Abbass did not state when the Revolutionary War fort was named Fort Barton. While the author is confident that Fort Barton was named after William Barton, he has not found documents indicating when the fort was named. The official information for the park states that it was named after William Barton by the Continental Congress shortly after his capture of General

Prescott, but the author has not found any support for that statement. As a state fort, it would have been unusual for Congress to have named it. The earliest date the author has found a reference to Fort Barton is 1847, when a Revolutionary War commemoration was held there. John Howland Recollections, in Stone (ed.), *Life of Howland*, 280. The author has made a close examination of the first major effort by New England to oust the British from Newport, called Spencer's Expedition, which occurred in September and October of 1777. See McBurney, *Rhode Island Campaign*, chapter 2. Much activity occurred in and around the Tiverton fort overlooking Howland's Ferry, but the author saw no reference to it as Fort Barton. American commander general Joseph Spencer ordered the fort to be manned with artillery pieces from Colonel Thomas Crafts's Massachusetts State Artillery Regiment in order to prevent British warships sailing up the Sakonnet River and interfering with planned New England landings on Aquidneck Island. Spencer's General Orders, Oct. 16, 1777, in Enquiry into the Causes of the Failure of the Expedition Against R.I., Robert Treat Paine Papers, Mass. Hist. Soc. ("Col. Elliot will appoint a sufficient number of officers and men to defend the fort at Fogland Ferry and to intercept, stop or sink any of the King's ships that may attempt to pass the same or annoy us in our landing. Col. Crafts will also appoint a sufficient number at Howland's Ferry for the same purpose.") Crafts's Artillery Regiment had four brass 4-pounders and a 10-inch howitzer, all fully equipped. Examination of Col. Thomas Crafts, Feb. 1778, in id. Colonel John Waterman, commander of the 1st Kent County Regiment of Rhode Island militia, ordered his men on October 25, 1777, to parade in the "Holler Back" (hollow back) of the fort at Tiverton at 3:00 p.m., without naming the fort. Col. John Waterman Regimental Order, Oct. 25, 1777, Rev. War Papers, box 3, folder 21, R.I. Hist. Soc. As reported by the *Newport Mercury*, in 1794 William Barton, in his capacity as brigadier general of the Rhode Island state militia, toured the defenses of Newport, including "the battery at Howland's Ferry, a block house erected to secure a safe passage for our country friends to assist us, or in case of misfortune to retreat." *Newport Mercury*, May 20, 1794. The article did not call the Howland's Ferry works Fort Barton, despite William Barton touring it. Upon Barton's death in 1831, none of the obituaries mentioned Fort Barton being named after him. The author suspects that Fort Barton was named for William Barton sometime after his death in 1831 and before 1847, when John Howland mentioned its name. There is currently a Fort Barton Elementary School in Tiverton, Rhode Island.

Appendix: Some Minor Participants

1. Extract of a Letter from New York, Dec. 17, 1776, in *London Chronicle*, March 1-4, 1777, and *Scots Magazine* 39:80 (1777) (identifying the author as James Baird). For a complete history of the death of Geary and the subsequent treatment of his gravesite, see Riddle, *Brigade Dispatch* 23:4, 18-26 (Autumn 1992); some other material, is at Riddle, "The Ambush of Geary's Dragoons," www.doublegv.com/ggv/battles/geary.

2. *Proceedings of the N. J. Hist. Soc.*, 2nd Series, 11:166 (1892) (based on recollections of family that kept Geary's artifacts); Riddle, "The Ambush of Geary's Dragoons," *Brigade Dispatch* 23:4, 22-23 (Autumn 1992).

3. W. Harcourt to F. Geary, Dec. 18, 1776, in Force (ed.), *American Archives*, 5th Ser., 3:1277. See also Diary Entry, Dec. 13, 1776, in Lydenberg (ed.), *Robertson Diary*, 116 ("Another patrol of an officer and eight [dragoons] this day went towards Flemington, the officer was killed"); Baule and Gilbert, *British Officers*, 72 (Geary killed in action at Flemington on December 14, 1776); Extract of a letter from New York, Jan. 8, 1777, in *St. James's Chronicle* (London), March 4, 1777.

4. Quoted in Riddle, "The Ambush of Geary's Dragoons," *Brigade Dispatch* 23:4, 24-25 (Autumn 1992) (quoting from the Hunterdon County Historical Society, *Centennial*

Newsletter Series 21:1, 438 (Winter 1985); see also Vosseller, *History of the Hunterdon County Historical Society,* 10; *Proceedings of the N.J. Hist. Soc.,* 2nd Series, 11:166 (1892) (New Jersey historian William Stryker confirmed at a May 21, 1891 meeting of the New Jersey Historical Society that the buttons shown at the meeting by Elias Vosseller of the Hunterdon County Historical Society were from the 16th Regiment of Light Dragoons). Unfortunately, the buttons since that time have been lost; the Hunterdon County Historical Society was in June of 2013 unable to locate them, even after a thorough search. Email from Terry A. McNealy, Librarian, Hunterdon County Historical Society, to the author, June 20, 2013.

5. Riddle, "The Ambush of Geary's Dragoons," *Brigade Dispatch* 23:4, 26 (Autumn 1992, quoting from the Hunterdon County Historical Society, *Centennial Newsletter Series* 21:1, 438 [Winter 1985]).

6. Hagist, "Deserter: Walter Graham, 22nd Regiment of Foot," July 19, 2009, in redcoat76.blogspot.com.

7. Rhode Island Council of War Records, vol. 2, July 24, 1777, R.I. State Archives.

8. Rhode Island Council of War Records, vol. 2, Aug. 7, 1777, in ibid; N. Cooke to R. Pigot, May 2, 1778, in Letters from the Governor, vol. 2, R.I. State Archives; see also R. Pigot to N. Cooke, April 28, 1778, Letters to the Governor, vol. 12, R.I. State Archives. The Rhode Island Council of War minutes for August 7, 1777, stated that Buffum "went on the expedition to Rhode Island and was made a prisoner." The only expedition to Rhode Island prior to this time was an aborted one in March of 1777. However, Rhode Island Council of War minutes for March 21, 1777, stated the following: "Samuel Buffum, late of Newport, made his escape from the mainland to the enemy upon Rhode Island [Aquidneck Island]." The Council of War ordered the sheriff of Kent County to watch over his estate. Rhode Island Council of War Records, vol.1, March 21, 1777, R.I. State Archives. It may have been the case that the Council of War only after this March 1777 meeting learned that Buffum had been captured during a raid on Aquidneck Island by patriot forces and therefore was not a disloyal soldier who tried to escape to Newport. On the other hand, Governor Cooke's letter to General Pigot indicated that Buffum may have suffered from a mental disability. N. Cooke to R. Pigot, May 2, 1778, in Letters from the Governor, vol. 2, id.

9. N. Cooke to R. Pigot, May 2, 1778, in Letters from the Governor, vol. 2, R.I. State Archives.

10. Ibid.

11. Hagist, "Deserter: Walter Graham, 22nd Regiment of Foot," July 19, 2009, in redcoat76.blogspot.com.

12. From a Hessian in Rhode Island to his Brother, June 24, 1777, in Pettengill (ed.), *Letters from America,* 165-66.

13. See Walter Graham, Index of Military Service in the Revolutionary War, R.I. State Archives (citing military returns, S.A. II 17).

14. Holbrook, *Rhode Island 1782 Census.* There was also no Graham listed in a March 1777 census in Rhode Island and in a 1774 census there was only one Graham family in Rhode Island (headed by Malcolm Graham and residing in Newport). See Chamberlain (ed.), *Rhode Island 1777 Military Census* and Bartlett (ed.), *Census of Rhode Island 1774,* 15.

15. *Heads of Families at the First Census, 1790, Massachusetts,* 22. Graham's listing also records a second adult white female residing in the household. She could have been an adult child, or she could have been a relative of Graham's wife, perhaps her mother.

16. Abel Potter Rev. War Pension Application, 1832, in Dann (ed.), *Revolution Remembered,* 24 and National Archives Building.

17. After the war, Abel Potter moved from Rhode Island to Vermont and later to upstate New York. Abel Potter Rev. War Pension Application, National Archives

Building. For Abel Potter residing as a head of household in Pownal, Vermont, in the 1800 census, see *Heads of Families at the Second Census, 1800, Vermont*, 35. This listing records Potter as having in his household an adult female (his wife, presumably) and a son aged from 10 to 15 (perhaps the same son who went to Graham's classroom). Abel Potter also appeared as residing in Pownal in the 1810 census. Jackson et al. (eds.), *Vermont 1810 Census Index*, 39. There are several male adult Grahams listed in the censuses of 1800 and 1810 as residing in Bennington County, where Pownal was located—these could have been Walter Graham's sons. See *Heads of Families at the Second Census, 1800, Vermont*, 26-28; Jackson et al. (eds.), *Vermont 1810 Census Index*, 32. It should also be noted that Walter Graham could have resided in 1790 in the part of Adams, Massachusetts, that later broke off to become North Adams—this area is only eight miles from Pownal.

18. Hall and Hall, *The Local History of Bennington, 1860-1883*, 11.

19. Bartlett (ed.), *Census of Rhode Island of 1774*, 239. Native Americans constituted 2.5 percent of Rhode Island's population in 1774. Id.

20. Historian John Wood Sweet compared the names of African-American soldiers who had served in the 1st Rhode Island Regiment since 1777 and those who were on the list as enrolling in the regiment during the winter and spring of 1778. He found that at least twenty-three had served since 1777. Sweet, *Bodies Politic*, 439, n. 44. Sweet's book contains the best and most complete analysis of men of color from New England serving in the Revolutionary War. Id., 183-224.

21. Diary Entry, Aug. 3, 1777, in Thacher, *Journal*, 86.

22. The obituary published in the November 3, 1821, edition of the *Providence Gazette* did not provide Prince's last name. It did state that Prince was from Plymouth, Massachusetts. The 1800 federal census lists a Prince, with no last name, residing in Plymouth in a household of seven free persons of color. Jackson (ed.), *Massachusetts 1800 Census*, 835. In the 1790 federal census, the only Prince residing in Plymouth was named Prince Goodwin, and he was listed as head of a household of eight free persons of color. *Heads of Families at the First Census, 1790, Massachusetts*, 178. Prince Goodwin was also listed as heading a household in Plymouth County in the 1810 federal census. Jackson et al. (eds.), *Massachusetts 1810 Census Index*, 721. The author believes that all of these references refer to the same man, Prince Goodwin. A Bristol County, Massachusetts, historian wrote that Prince's identity was Prince Pierce of Dighton, Massachusetts. See Hurd (ed.), *History of Bristol County* 1:227, n. 2; Dighton Town Resolution, March 1, 1781, quoted in id., 227. Prince was the slave of Captain John Pierce of Dighton. Id. However, there is no other evidence that Prince Pierce was the same Prince referred to in the obituary, which stated that Prince resided in Plymouth, not Dighton.

23. The entry for William Barton in a book of short American biographies, published in 1857, identifies Prince as knocking his head against Prescott's door, but it solely relied on Prince's obituary in the *Providence Gazette*. Allen, *American Biographical Dictionary*, 69. A blatantly racist version of Prince's role, which has factual inaccuracies as well, is set forth in Hurd, *History of Bristol County* 1:227, n. 2.

24. S. B. Barrell to W. Barton, Sept. 24, 1818, MSS 9006, Shepley Papers, vol. 8, p. 82, R.I. Hist. Soc.

25. This ballad and its racial implications are discussed in Sweet, *Bodies Politic*, 219-20.

26. See MacGunnigle (ed.), *Regimental Book, Rhode Island Regiment for 1781*, 36, 53, 79, 112, and 125 (Watson's service in the 1st Regiment of Rhode Island Continentals); Guy Watson Rev. War Pension Application, 1818, National Archives Building; Hazard, *Jonny-Cake Papers*, 341 (mixed heritage).

27. See McBurney, *Rhode Island Campaign*, 47-48.

28. Same sources as in the note two notes above.

29. Thomas R. Hazard Recollections, in Hazard, *Jonny-Cake Papers*, 341.
30. *Rhode Island Republican*, July 8, 1828. No other mention was made of Watson's role in the operation.
31. *Literary Subaltern*, quoted in *Easton Gazette* (Easton, Maryland), Jan. 14, 1832, and *American Advocate* (Hallowell, Maine), Feb. 31, 1832. The *Literary Subaltern* was published in Providence from 1829 to 1833.
32. See, e.g., *Public Ledger* (Philadelphia), March 23, 1837; *The Pittsfield Sun* (Massachusetts), March 30, 1837; *Ithaca Herald* (Ithaca, New York), April 12, 1837. For the date of Watson's death, see Gunning, *Selected Final Pension Payment Vouchers*, 258 (Watson had no surviving widow but did leave a married child, Sarah Hazard).
33. Williams, *Life of Barton*, 52-53. Williams could have gained information about the raid by talking with Samuel Corey, one of the then surviving members of the raid. See id., 56 (Corey living in 1839 in Rhode Island).
34. Lossing, *Pictorial Field-Book of the Rev.* 1:645. Historian John Wood Sweet believes that Sisson was the man who crashed his head into Prescott's door. Sweet, *Bodies Politic*, 219.
35. The author has discovered that the first attempt to publish the names of the participants in Barton's raid was made in 1824, when Barton's narrative of the raid was first published. See *Spooner's Vermont Journal* (Windsor, Vermont), Oct. 11, 1824. This list contains thirty-seven names and was probably made with the assistance of William Barton.
36. See Williams, *Life of Barton*, Appendix, 127-28. The publisher of the 1824 list cited in the above note misspelled several names—he may have had difficulty reading Barton's atrocious handwriting. Catherine R. Williams apparently started with this list, as parts of her list are in the same order as the 1824 one. See notes 2 and 3 in chapter 6. However, she corrected the spelling of a number of the names and added to the list the following persons: John Hunt, Thomas Austin, Jack Sisson ("the Black, and boat steerer"), and Howe or Whiting ("boat steerer"). She was able to speak with several surviving participants, including Samuel Cory, who could have provided the additional names.
37. MacGunnigle (ed.), *Regimental Book, Rhode Island Regiment for 1781*, 75.
38. John Howland Recollections, in Stone, *Life of Howland*, 87. The historian Edward Peterson, probably based on Howland's recollections, stated that the man who crashed through Prescott's door was Quako Honeyman, Prescott's former servant who had given intelligence to Barton. Peterson, *History of R.I.*, 215. But another historian, Sidney Rider, rejected this idea, on the logical ground that he would not have been permitted to go on the mission since if he were caught, he would have been hanged. Rider, *Historical Inquiry*, 67.
39. General Assembly Resolution, Jan. 1782 session, in Bartlett (ed.), *Records of R.I.* 11:509-10. For more on this topic, see notes 2 and 3 in chapter 6.
40. MacGunnigle (ed.), *Regimental Book, Rhode Island Regiment for 1781*, 44, 98, 111 and 125; Richard Rhodes Rev. War Pension Application, 1818, National Archives Building.
41. Richard Rhodes Rev. War Pension Application, 1818, National Archives Building.
42. Elisha Baker Rev. War Pension Application, 1832, National Archives Building. While Baker is not mentioned in any of the lists of the names of soldiers who participated in Barton's raid, several names were omitted from the lists, so it is possible that Baker actually was a participant. See note 25 in chapter 6. Even so, his claim that he and Barton entered Prescott's bedroom by going through a window leads the author to question the entire credibility of his claim. The author has found three other pension applications of soldiers who claimed that they were members of Barton's party, but are not on any list of participants—Peleg Sherman, John Austin, and Robert Babcock.

Peleg Sherman Rev. War Pension Application, John Austin Rev. War Pension Application, and Robert Babcock Rev. War Pension Application, id. Thomas Austin was included in Williams's list—it could have been John Austin who was the actual participant. Similarly, Jack Sherman was included in Williams's list—it could have been Peleg Sherman who actually participated in the raid.

43. Abel Potter Rev. War Pension Application, 1832, in Dann (ed.), *Revolution Remembered*, 22-26 and National Archives Building; John Hunt Rev. War Pension Application, 1837, National Archives Building and quoted in part in Cowell, *Spirit of '76*, 148. A purported participant in the raid from Exeter, Rhode Island, recalled many years later in his pension application that Barton had a man "with them and [Barton] made him burst the door in with his head. Barton stood over him with drawn sword and told him the door must come open or his head would come off." Quoted in Simister, *A Short History of Exeter, Rhode Island*, 24. The author has not found this pension application. While the author believes credence generally should be shown to recollections in pension applications, in this case the incident was so well known that the recollection may have been repeating inaccurate lore that was passed around or published in newspapers.

44. Fowler, *History of Fall River*, 26. Catherine R. Williams wrote of Page, similarly to Fowler: "After leaving the Overing house with their prisoner, this man recollected that General Prescott's sword was left behind, and imagining that he could find it and regain the company, he returned back to the house, and groped his way to the room, found the sword and overtook the company before they regained the shore, and presented the sword to Colonel Barton." Williams, *Life of Barton*, Appendix, 127-28.

45. Recollections of Dr. Harris, 1842, before the Congregational and Presbyterian Anti-Slavery Society, at Francestown, New Hampshire, quoted in Nell, *Colored Patriots*, 129-30; see also McBurney, *Rhode Island Campaign*, 187-93.

BIBLIOGRAPHY

PUBLISHED PRIMARY SOURCES: DIARIES, LETTERS, AND OTHER

Abbass, D. K., ed. "Transcripts of Archival Materials from the Public Records Office/National Archives in London." (Royal Navy Ship Logs.) In *Bibliography and Appendices.* Vol. 4. *Rhode Island in the Revolution: Big Happenings in the Smallest Colony.* USDI National Park Service, American Battlefield Protection Program. 2nd ed., 2006. (Copies at R.I. State Archives, U.S. Naval War College at Newport, and other Rhode Island libraries.)

Acomb, Evelyn M., ed. *The Revolutionary Journal of Baron Ludwig von Closen, 1780-1783.* Chapel Hill, NC: University of North Carolina Press, 1958.

Adams, Charles Francis, ed. *Familiar Letters of John Adams and his Wife Abigail Adams, During the Revolution.* Boston, MA: Houghton Mifflin Company, 1875.

Allen, Ethan. *A Narrative of Colonel Ethan Allen's Captivity, from the Time of his being Taken by the British, Near Montreal, on the 2th Day of September, in the Year 1775, to the Time of his Exchange, on the 6th day of May, 1778.* New York, NY: The Georgian Press, 1930. Originally published in Philadelphia by Bell, 1779.

Allen, James. "Diary of James Allen, Esq., of Philadelphia, Counselor-at-Law, 1776-1778." *Pennsylvania Magazine of History and Biography* 9:3, 278-96 (Oct. 1885).

Atkinson, C. T. "British Forces in North America, 1774-1781: Their Distribution and Strength." *Journal of the Society for Army Historical Research* 16:2-23 (1937).

Balderston, Marion and David Syrett, eds. *The Lost War: Letters from British Officers during the American Revolution.* New York, NY: Horizon Press, 1975.

Ballagh, James Curtis, ed. *The Letters of Richard Henry Lee.* 2 vols. New York, NY: Macmillan Co., 1911-14. Reprinted by Da Capo Press, 1970.

"Bamford's Diary: The Revolutionary Diary of a British Officer." (William Bamford). *Maryland Historical Magazine* 28:240-59 and 296-314 (Dec. 1932) and 9-26 (March 1933).

Barnes, G. R. and J. H. Owen, eds. *The Private Papers of John, Earl of Sandwich, First Lord of the Admiralty, 1771-1782.* Vol. 1. England: Naval Records Society, 1932.

Barney, Samuel E., ed. *Songs of the Revolution.* New Haven, CT: Tuttle, Morehouse and Taylor, 1893. Reprinted by Kessenger Publishing, 2004.

Bartlett, John R., ed. *Census of the Colony of Rhode Island and Providence Plantations, 1774.* Lambertville, NJ: Hunterdon, 1984. Originally published in 1854.

_____. *Index to the Printed Acts and Resolves of, and of the Petitions and Reports to, the General Assembly of the State of Rhode Island and Providence Plantations, from the Year 1758 to 1850.* Providence, RI: Knowles, Anthony and Co., 1856.

———. *Records of the Colony of Rhode Island and Providence Plantations in New England.* 10 vols. Providence, RI: A.C. Greene and Bros, 1856-65. Reprinted by AMS Press, 1968.

Bates, Albert C., ed. "The Wyllys Papers: Correspondence and Documents Chiefly of Descendants of Gov. George Wyllys of Connecticut 1590-1796." *Collections of the Connecticut Historical Society.* Vol. 21 (1924).

Baule, Steven M. and Stephen Gilbert, eds. *British Army Officers Who Served in the American Revolution, 1775-1783.* Westminster, MD: Heritage Books, 2004.

"The Belknap Papers." *Massachusetts Historical Society Proceedings.* 5th Series, Vol. 2 (1877) and 6th Series, Vol. 4 (1891).

Benians, E. A., ed. *A Journal by Thos. Hughes for his Amusement, & Designed for his Perusal by the Time He Attains Age 50 if He Lives So Long (1778-1779).* (Thomas Hughes). Cambridge, England: Cambridge University Press, 1947.

Bernard, John. *Retrospections of America, 1797-1811.* New York, NY: Benjamin Blom, 1969. First published in 1887.

Birdsall, William Wilfred and Rufus M. Jones, eds. *A Century of American Literature and the Lives and Portraits of Our Favorite Authors.* Philadelphia, PA: John C. Winston Co., 1901.

Boudinot, Elias. *Journal; or, Historical Recollections of American Events During the Revolutionary War.* Philadelphia, PA: Frederick Bourquin, 1894. Reprinted by New York Times and Arno Press, 1968.

"Bowdoin and Temple Papers." *Massachusetts Historical Society Proceedings.* 6th Series, Vol. 9 (1897).

Boyd, Julian, ed. *Papers of Thomas Jefferson.* Vols. 1-5 and 16. Princeton, NJ: Princeton University Press, 1950-52 and 1961.

Boyle, Joseph Lee, ed. *From Redcoat to Rebel: The Thomas Sullivan Journal.* Bowie, MD: Heritage Books, 1997.

———. *"Their Distress is almost intolerable." The Elias Boudinot Letterbook, 1777-1778.* Bowie, MD: Heritage Books, 2002.

Bradford, S. Sydney, ed. "A British Officer's Revolutionary War Journal, 1776-1778." *Maryland Historical Magazine* 56:2, 150-75 (June 1961).

Bray, Robert C. and Paul E. Bushnell, eds. *Diary of a Common Soldier in the American Revolution, 1775-1783.* (Jeremiah Greenman). DeKalb, IL: Northern Illinois University Press, 1978.

"British Army Orders: Gen. Sir William Howe, 1775-1778, Gen. Sir Henry Clinton, 1778; and Gen. Daniel Jones, 1778." *New York Historical Society Collections* 251-585 (1884).

Brown, Lloyd A. and Howard H. Peckham, eds. *Revolutionary War Journals of Henry Dearborn, 1775-1783.* New York, NY: Da Capo Press, 1971. Originally published by J. Wilson and Son, 1887.

Bunbury, Henry. *The Correspondence of Sir Thomas Hanmer, Bart., Speaker of the House of Commons. With a Memoir of his Life. To which are Added, Other Relicks of a Gentleman's Family.* London: E. Moxon, 1838.

Burgoyne, Bruce E., ed. *Defeat, Disaster and Dedication: the Diaries of the Hessian Officers Jakob Piel and Andreas Wiederhold.* Bowie, MD: Heritage Books, 1997.

____. *Diaries of a Hessian Chaplain and the Chaplain's Assistant.* (Henrich Kuemmel and Valerie Asteroth). Pennsauken, NJ: Johannes Schwalm Historical Association, 1990.

____. *The Diary of Lieutenant von Bardeleben and Other von Donop Regiment Documents.* Bowie, MD: Heritage Books, 1998.

____. *A Hessian Diary of the American Revolution.* (Johann Conrad Dohla). Norman, OK: University of Oklahoma Press, 1990.

____. *A Hessian Report on the People, the Land, the War: Eighteenth Century America, as Noted in the Diary of Chaplain Philipp Waldeck, 1776-1780.* Bowie, MD: Heritage Books, 1995.

Bushnell, Charles I., ed. *Journal of Solomon Nash, a Soldier of the Revolution, 1776-1777.* New York, NY: Privately printed, 1861.

Butterfield, Lyman H., ed. *Adams Family Correspondence.* Vol. 2. Cambridge, MA: Belknap Press of Harvard University, 1963.

____. *Benjamin Rush Letters.* 2 vols. Princeton, NJ: Princeton University Press, 1951.

Butterfield, Lyman H., Wendell D. Garrett, and Marjorie E. Sprague, eds. *The Adams Papers: Diary and Autobiography of John Adams.* 4 vols. Cambridge, MA: Belnap Press of Harvard University, 1962-63.

Catanzarti, John and James E. Ferguson, eds. *The Papers of Robert Morris, 1781-1784.* Vols. 6 and 9. Pittsburgh, PA: University of Pittsburgh Press, 1984 and 1999.

Chamberlain, Mildred M., ed. *The Rhode Island 1777 Military Census.* Baltimore, MD: Genealogical Publishing Co., 1983.

Chestnutt, David R., James C. Taylor, and Peggy J. Clark, eds. *The Papers of Henry Laurens.* Vols. 12-14. Columbia, SC: University of South Carolina Press, 1990-94.

Clark, Edward L. *Record of the Inscriptions on the Tablets and Grave-Stones in the Burial-Grounds of Christ Church, Philadelphia.* Philadelphia, PA: Collins, 1864.

Coldham, Peter W. *American Migrations, 1765-1799, The Lives, Times and Families of Colonial Americans Who Remained Loyal to the British Crown before, during and after the Revolutionary War, as Related in their own Words and Through Their Correspondence.* Baltimore, MD: Genealogical Publishing Co., 2000.

Commager, Henry Steele and Richard B. Morris, eds. *The Spirit of Seventy-Six: The Story of the American Revolution as Told by Participants.* New York, NY: Da Capo Press, 1995.

Crane, Elaine Forman, ed. *The Diary of Elizabeth Drinker: The Life Cycle of an Eighteenth-Century Woman.* Philadelphia, PA: University of Pennsylvania Press, 2013.

Cushing, Harry A., ed. *The Writings of Samuel Adams.* Vols. 3-4. New York, NY: G. P. Putnam's Sons, 1907-08.

Dann, John C., ed. *The Revolution Remembered, Eyewitness Accounts of the War for Independence.* Chicago, IL: University of Chicago Press, 1980.

Davies, K.G., ed. *Documents of the American Revolution, 1770-1783.* Colonial Office Series 12. 21 vols. Dublin, Ireland: Irish University Press, 1972-81.

Dawson, Henry B., ed. *Diary of David How, a Private in Colonel Paul Dudley Sargent's Regiment of the Massachusetts Line, in the Army of the American Revolution*. Morrisania, NY: Privately Printed, 1865.

The Deane Papers. Vol. 1. (Silas Deane). *Collections of the New-York Historical Society*. 1887.

Dexter, Franklin B., ed. *Literary Diary of Ezra Stiles*. 2 vols. New York: Charles Slocum Co., 1901.

"Disinterment of the Remains of Major-General Charles Lee, at Christ Church, Philadelphia." *The Historical Magazine* 5:370-71 (1861).

Dornfest, Walter T. *Military Loyalists of the American Revolution. Officers and Regiments, 1775-1783*. Jefferson, NC: McFarland and Co., 2011.

Duffy, John J., ed. *Ethan Allen and His Kin. Correspondence, 1772-1819*. Vol. 1. Hanover, NH: University Press of New England, 1998.

Duyckinck, Evert A. and George L. Duyckinck, eds. *Cyclopedia of American Literature. Embracing Personal and Critical Notices of Authors and Selections from Their Writings, from the Earliest Period to the Present Day, with Portraits, Autographs, and other Illustrations*. Vol. 1. Philadelphia, PA: Wm. Rutter and Co., 1875.

Egerton, Edward H., ed. *The Royal Commission on the Losses and Services of American Loyalists, 1783 to 1785*. Oxford, England: The Roxburghe Club, 1915.

"Extracts from the Diary of Jacob Hiltzheimer of Philadelphia, 1768-1799." *Pennsylvania Magazine of History and Biography* 16:93-102, 160-77 and 412-22 (1892).

Farmer, J. and J. B. Moore, eds. *Collections, Historical and Miscellaneous; and Monthly Literary Journal*. Vol. 3. Concord, NH: J. B. Moore, 1824.

Fitzpatrick, John C., ed. *The Writings of George Washington from the Original Manuscript Sources, 1745-1799*. Vols. 11-24. Washington, D.C.: Library of Congress, 1934-38.

Force, Peter, ed. *American Archives*. 5th Series, Vol. 3. Washington, D.C.: M. St. Clair Clarke and Peter Force, 1853.

Ford, Paul L., ed. *The Journals of Hugh Gaine, Printer*. 2 vols. New York, NY: Dodd, Mead and Company, 1902.

Ford, Worthington C., ed. *British Officers Serving in the American Revolution, 1775-1783*. Brooklyn, NY: Historical Printing Club, 1897.

____. *Correspondence and Journals of Samuel B. Webb*. Vol. 2. New York: Wickersham Press, 1893.

____. *The Journals of the Continental Congress*. 34 vols. Washington, D.C.: Library of Congress, 1905-37.

____. "Some Papers of Aaron Burr." *Proceedings of the American Antiquarian Society* 29:1, 43-128 (1920).

Fortescue, Sir John, ed. *The Correspondence of King George the Third from 1760 to December 1783*. Vols. 3-4. London: Frank Cass and Co., 1967.

Foster, Theodore. *Minutes of the Convention Held at South Kingstown, Rhode Island, in March, 1790, Which Failed to Adopt the Constitution of the United States*. Annotations by Robert C. Cotner. Freeport, NY: Books for Libraries Press, 1970.

Goodwin, John. "Military Journal Kept in 1777, During the Rhode Island Expedition, by John Goodwin of Marblehead, Mass., First Lieutenant in Capt. Nathaniel Lindsey's Company in Col. Timothy Pickering's Regiment." *Essex Institute Historical Collections* 45:205-21 (July 1909).

Greene, Fleet S. "Newport in the Hands of the British: A Diary of the Revolution." *The Historical Magazine* 4:1, 1-4, 34-38, 69-72, 105-7, 134-37, 172-73 (Jan. 1860).

Griswold, Rufus W., ed. *Readings in American Poetry.* New York, NY: John C. Riker, 1843.

Gruber, Ira D., ed. *John Peebles' American War: The Diary of a Scottish Grenadier, 1776-1782.* Mechanicsburg, PA: Stackpole Books, 1998.

Gunning, Kathryn McPherson. *Selected Final Pension Payment Vouchers, 1818-1864.* Westminster, MD: Willow Bend Books, 1999.

Hagist, Don N., ed. *General Orders, Rhode Island: December 1776-January 1778.* Bowie, MD: Heritage Books, 2001.

Hall, Charles S. *Life and Letters of Samuel Holden Parsons.* New York, NY: Osteningo Publishing Co., 1905.

Hammond, Otis G., ed. *Letters and Papers of Major-General John Sullivan, Continental Army.* Vol. I. Concord, NH: New Hampshire Historical Society, 1930.

Hanger, George. *An Address to the Army; in Reply to Strictures, by Roderick M'Kenzie, (Late Lieutenant in the 71st Regiment) on Tarleton's History of The Campaigns of 1780 and 1781.* London: James Ridgeway, 1789.

Harcourt, Edward William, ed. *The Harcourt Papers.* Vol. 11. Oxford, England: James Parker and Co., 1885.

Heads of Families at the First Census of the United States Taken in the Year 1790, Massachusetts. Washington, D.C.: Government Printing Office, 1907.

Heads of Families at the First Census of the United States Taken in the Year 1790, Rhode Island. Washington, D.C.: Government Printing Office, 1907.

Heads of Families at the First Census of the United States Taken in the Year 1790, Vermont. Washington, D.C.: Government Printing Office, 1907.

Heads of Families at the Second Census of the United States Taken in the Year 1800, Vermont. Montpelier, VT: Vermont Historical Society, 1938.

"Heath Papers." *Collections of the Massachusetts Historical Society.* 7th Series, 4:1-285 (1904).

Heath, William. *Heath's Memoirs of the American War.* Boston, MA: Thomas and E. T. Andrews Co., 1798. Reprinted by Books for Libraries Press, 1970.

Heitman, Francis B. *Historical Register of Officers of the Continental Army During the War of the Revolution.* Baltimore, MD: Genealogical Publishing Society, 1969. Originally published in 1914.

Historical Manuscripts Commission. *Report on American Manuscripts in the Royal Institution of Great Britain.* V. 1. London: Mackie and Co., Ld., 1904.

Holbrook, Jay M., ed. *Rhode Island 1782 Census.* Oxford, MA: Holbrook Research Institute, 1979.

Hunt, Gaillard. *Calendar of Applications and Recommendations for Office During the Presidency of George Washington.* Washington, D.C.: Government Printing Office, 1901.

"Huntington Papers: Correspondence of the Brothers Joshua and Jedediah Huntington During the Period of the American Revolution, 1771-1783." *Collections of the Connecticut Historical Society*. Vol. 20 (1923).

Idzerda, Stanley J., ed. *Lafayette in the Age of the American Revolution: Selected Letters and Papers, 1776-1790*. Vol. 2. Ithaca, NY: Cornell University Press, 1979.

Jackson, Ronald Vern, ed. *Massachusetts 1800 Census Index*. Provo, UT: Accelerated Indexing Systems, 1973.

Jackson, Ronald Vern, Gary Ronald Teeples, and David Schaefermeyer, eds. *Vermont 1810 Census Index*. Bountiful, UT: Accelerated Indexing Systems, 1976.

Johnston, Henry P. *Record of Connecticut Men in the Military and Naval Service During the War of the Revolution, 1775-1783*. Hartford, CT: Adjutant General's Office, 1889.

Jones, Matt B. "Revolutionary Correspondence of Governor Nicholas Cooke, 1775-1781." *Proceedings of the American Antiquarian Society* 36:2, 231-353 (Oct. 1926).

"Journal of Sergeant William Young, Written During the Jersey Campaign in the Winter of 1776-1777." *Pennsylvania Magazine of History and Biography* 8:3, 255-78 (1884).

Kemble, Stephen. "Journals of Lieut.-Col. Stephen Kemble, 1773-1789." *Kemble Papers*. Vol. 1. *New York Historical Society Collections* 16:1-287 (1883).

Ketchum, Richard, ed. "New War Letters of Banastre Tarleton." *New York Historical Society Quarterly* 51:1, 61-81 (Jan. 1967).

Lamb, Roger. *An Original and Authentic Journal of Occurrences During the Late American War, from the Commencement to the Year 1783*. Dublin: Wilkinson and Courtney, 1809. Reprinted by New York Times and Arno Press, 1968.

Laughton, John K., ed. *Journal of Rear-Admiral Bartholomew James, 1752-1828*. London: Navy Records Society, 1896.

———. "Journals of Henry Duncan, Captain, Royal Navy, 1776-1782." *The Naval Miscellany*. London: Navy Records Society, 1902, 107-219.

Laurens, John. *The Army Correspondence of Colonel John Laurens in the Years 1777-78*. New York: Bradford Club, 1867. Reprinted by New York Times, 1969.

Lavasseur, Auguste. *Lafayette in America in 1824 and 1825. Journal of a Voyage to the United States*. Manchester, NH: Lafayette Press Inc., 2006. Translated by Alan R. Hoffman. Originally published in French in 1829.

Lee, Henry. *Memoirs of the War in the Southern Department of the United States*. 2 vols. New York, NY: University Publishing Company, 1869. Originally published in Philadelphia, PA, by Bradford and Inskeep, 1812.

Lee Papers, 1754-1811. 4 vols. (Charles Lee). *Collections of the New-York Historical Society*. 1872-75.

Lesser, Charles H., ed. *The Sinews of Independence: Monthly Strength Reports of the Continental Army*. Chicago, IL: University Press of Chicago, 1976.

Lydenberg, Harry M., ed. *Archibald Robertson, Lieutenant Colonel, Royal Engineers: His Diaries and Sketches in America, 1762-1780*. New York, NY: New York Public Library, 1930.

MacGunnigle, Bruce C. *Regimental Book. Rhode Island Regiment for 1781 &c.* East Greenwich, RI: Rhode Island Society of the Sons of the American Revolution, 2011.

Mackenzie, Frederick. *Diary of Frederick Mackenzie, Giving a Daily Narrative of His Military Service as an Officer of the Regiment of Royal Welch Fusiliers During the Years 1775-1781 in Massachusetts, Rhode Island and New York.* Cambridge, MA: Harvard University Press, 1930. Reprinted by New York Times, 1969.

MacVeagh, Lincoln, ed. *The Journal of Nicholas Cresswell, 1774-1777.* New York: The Dial Press, 1924.

"Martin Hunter's Journal: America 1774-1778." *The Valley Forge Journal: A Record of Patriotism and American Culture* 4:1, 1-34 (June 1988).

McCarty, William, ed. *Songs, Odes, and Other Poems, on National Subjects, Compiled from Various Sources. Part Second—Naval.* Philadelphia, PA: Privately Published, 1842.

Mervers, Frank C., ed. *The Papers of Josiah Bartlett.* Hanover, NH: University Press of New England, 1979.

Montgomery, Thomas H. "The Battle of Monmouth Described by Dr. James McHenry, Secretary to General Washington." *Magazine of American History* 3:355-63 (June 1879).

Montresor, John. "Journals of Captain John Montresor." *New York Historical Society Collections* (1881).

Moore, Frank. *Diary of the American Revolution, from Newspapers and Original Documents.* 2 vols. Hartford, CT: The J. B. Burr Publishing Co., 1875. Reprinted by New York Times, 1969.

Morgan, William J., Michael J. Crawford, and William B. Clark, eds. *Naval Documents of the American Revolution.* Vols. 2-11. Washington, D.C.: U.S. Naval Department, 1966-2005.

Muenchhausen, Friedrich von. *At General Howe's Side 1776-1783: The Diary of General Howe's Aide de Camp, Captain Friedrich von Muenchhausen.* Translated by Ernst Kipping and annotated by Samuel Steele Smith. Monmouth Beach, NJ: Philip Freneau Press, 1974.

Nolan, J. Bennett, ed. *Lafayette in America Day by Day.* Baltimore, MD: Johns Hopkins University Press, 1934.

Parker, A. A. *Recollections of General Lafayette on his Visit to the United States in 1824 and 1825.* Keene, NH: Sentinel Printing Company, 1879.

Parsons, John C., ed. *Letters and Documents of Ezekiel Williams of Wethersfield, Connecticut: Deputy Commissary General of Prisoners of War within the State of Connecticut (1777-c. 1783).* Connecticut: The Acorn Club, 1976.

Pettengill, Ray W., ed. *Letters from America, 1776-1779: Being Letters of Brunswick, Hessian, and Waldeck Officers with the British Armies During the Revolution.* Boston, MA: Houghton Mifflin, 1924. Reprinted by the Kennikat Press, 1964.

Powell, William S., ed. "A Connecticut Soldier Under Washington: Elisha Bostwick's Memoirs of the First Years of the Revolution." *William and Mary Quarterly Historical Magazine,* 3rd Series, 6:94-107 (1949).

Proceedings of *the New Jersey Historical Society.* 2nd Series. Vol. 11. (1892).

Quincy, Eliza S. M. *Memoir of the Life of Eliza S. M. Quincy*. Boston, MA: John Wilson and Son, 1861.

Quincy, Josiah, ed. *The Journals of Major Samuel Shaw. The American Consul at Canton*. Boston, MA: Wm. Crosby and H. P. Nichols, 1847.

Rau, Louise, ed. "Sergeant John Smith's Diary of 1776." *Mississippi Valley Historical Review* 20:247-70 (June 1933).

Reed, Joseph. "General Joseph Reed's Narrative of the Movements of the American Army in the Neighborhood of Trenton in the Winter of 1776." *Pennsylvania Magazine of History and Biography* 16:391-401 (1892).

"Revolutionary Correspondence from 1775 to 1782." *Rhode Island Historical Society Collections* 6:107-304 and 371-77 (1867).

Rodney, Thomas. *The Diary of Captain Thomas Rodney, 1776-1777*. Wilmington, DE: Papers of the Historical Society of Delaware, 1888.

Rotch, William. *Memorandum Written in the Eightieth Year of His Age*. Boston, MA: Houghton Mifflin Company, 1916.

The Royal Military Calendar, or Army Service and Commission Book. Vols. 1-5, 3rd edition. London: A. J. Valpy, 1820.

Rush, Benjamin. *Autobiography*. Princeton, NJ: Princeton University Press, 1948.

Ryan, Dennis P., ed. *A Salute to Courage: The American Revolution as Seen Through the Writings of Wartime Officers in the Continental Army and Navy*. New York, NY: Columbia University Press, 1979.

Ryden, George H., ed. *Letters to and from Caesar Rodney, 1756-1784*. Philadelphia, PA: University of Pennsylvania Press, 1933.

Sabine, William H. W., ed. *Historical Memoirs of William Smith*. New York, NY: W. H. W. Sabine, 1956. Reprinted by New York Times and Arno Press, 1969.

Sargent, Winthrop, ed. *The Loyalist Poetry of the Revolution*. Philadelphia, PA: Collins, 1857. Also published by Milford House in 1972.

Scheer, George F. and Hugh F. Rankin. *Rebels and Redcoats: The American Revolution Through the Eyes of Those Who Fought and Lived It*. New York, NY: New American Library, 1957.

Showman, Richard K., ed. *The Papers of General Nathaniel Greene*. Vols. 1-3. Chapel Hill, NC: University of North Carolina Press, 1976-83.

Smith, Joseph J., ed. *Civil and Military List of Rhode Island*. 2 vols. Providence, RI: Preston and Rounds, 1900-1901.

Smith, Paul H., ed. *Letters of Delegates to Congress, 1774-1789*. Vols. 2-14. Washington, D.C.: 1977-1987.

Staples, William R. *Rhode Island in the Continental Congress*. Providence, RI: Providence Press Co., 1870.

Stevens, Benjamin F., ed. *Facsimiles of Manuscripts in European Archives Relating to America, 1773-1783*. Vol. 23. London: Whittingham and Co., 1895.

Stirke, Henry. "A British Officer's Revolutionary War Journal." Edited by S. Sidney Bradford. *Maryland Historical Magazine* 56:150-70 (June 1961).

Stone, Edwin M. *The Life and Recollections of John Howland*. Providence, RI: George H. Whitney, 1857.

Stone, William L., ed. *Letters of Brunswick and Hessian Officers During the American Revolution*. Albany, NY: Joel Munsell's Sons, 1891. Reprinted by Da Capo Press, 1970.

Syrett, David and R. L. DiNardo, eds. *The Commissioned Sea Officers of the Royal Navy, 1660-1815.* London: Scolar Press, 1994.

Syrett, Harold C., ed. *The Papers of Alexander Hamilton.* Vol. 1. New York, NY: Columbia University Press, 1961.

Tatum, Edward H., ed. *The American Journal of Ambrose Serle, Secretary to Lord Howe, 1776-1778.* San Marino, CA: The Huntington Library, 1940. Reprinted by New York Times, 1969.

Taylor, Robert J., ed. *Papers of John Adams.* Vols. 5-6. Cambridge, MA: Belknap Press of Harvard University, 1983.

Thacher, James. *A Military Journal During the American Revolutionary War from 1775 to 1783.* Boston, MA: Richardson and Lord, 1823. Reprinted by Corner House Historical Publications, 1998.

The Union Song Book. A Choice and Well-Selected Collection of the Most Popular, Sentimental, Patriotic, Naval, and Comic Songs. New York, NY: Leavitt and Allen, 1857.

"Trumbull Papers." *Collections of the Massachusetts Historical Society,* 7th Series, Vol. 3 (1902).

Tustin, Joseph P., ed. *Diary of the American War: A Hessian Journal.* (Diary of Johann von Ewald). New Haven, CT: Yale University Press, 1979.

Twohig, Dorothy; Philander D. Chase, Theodore J. Crackel, and W. W. Abbot, eds. *The Papers of George Washington. Revolutionary War Series.* Vols. 1-18. Charlottesville, VA: University Press of Virginia, 1985-2010.

Twohig, Dorothy and W. W. Abbot, eds. *The Papers of George Washington. Presidential Series.* Vol. 5. Charlottesville, VA: University Press of Virginia, 1996.

Tyler, Moses Coit, ed. *The Literary History of the American Revolution, 1763-1783.* New York, NY: Burt Franklin, 1970.

Uhlendorf, Bernhard A., ed. *Revolution in America: Confidential Letters and Journals, 1776-1784, of Adjutant General Major Baurmeister of the Hessian Forces.* New Brunswick, NJ: Rutgers University Press, 1957.

Walton, Eliakim. P., ed. *Records of the Governor and Council of the State of Vermont.* Vols. 2-8. Montpelier, VT: Steam Press of J. and J. M. Poland, 1874-80.

Warren-Adams Letters. Collections of the Massachusetts Historical Society. 2 vols. (1917-25).

Whinyates, F. A. *The Services of Lieut.-Colonel Francis Downman, R.A., in France, North America, and the West Indies, between the Years 1758 and 1784.* Woolwich, England: Royal Artillery Institution, 1898.

Wilkinson, James. *Memoirs of My Own Times.* Vol. 1. Philadelphia, PA: Abraham Small, 1816.

Willcox, William B., ed. *The American Rebellion, Sir Henry Clinton's Narrative of His Campaigns, 1775-1782.* New Haven, CT: Yale University Press, 1954.

Willcox, William B. and Claude A. Lopez, eds. *The Papers of Benjamin Franklin.* Vols. 22-27. New Haven, CT: Yale University Press, 1982-88.

PUBLISHED SECONDARY SOURCES: BOOKS

Abbass, D.K. *Rhode Island in the Revolution: Big Happenings in the Smallest Colony.* Part I: *A Chronology of the War in Rhode Island.* Part II: *The Ships Lost* in Rhode Island. Part III: *The Land Sites.* Part IV: *Bibliography and Appendices.* 4 vols. USDI National Park Service, American Battlefield Protection Program. 2nd ed., 2006. (Copies at R.I. State Archives, U.S. Naval War College at Newport, and other Rhode Island libraries.)

Alden, John R. *The American Revolution, 1775-1783.* New York, NY: Harper and Row, 1954.

____. *General Charles Lee: Traitor or Patriot?* Baton Rouge, LA: Louisiana State University Press, 1951.

____. *A History of the American Revolution.* New York, NY: Knopf, 1969.

Allen, William. *The American Biographical Dictionary: Containing an Account of the Lives, Characters, and Writings of the Most Eminent Persons Deceased in North America from Its First Settlement.* 3rd edition. Boston, MA: John P. Jewett and Company, 1857.

Arnold, Samuel Greene. *History of the State of Rhode Island and Providence Plantations.* 2 vols. New York, NY: D. Appleton and Co., 1859-60.

Barber, John W. and Henry Howe. *Historical Collections of the State of New Jersey; Containing a General Collection of the Most Interesting Facts, Traditions, Biographical Sketches, Anecdotes, Etc. Relating to its History and Antiquities, with the Geographical Descriptions of Every Township in the State.* New York, NY: S. Tuttle, 1845.

Bass, Robert D. *The Green Dragoon: The Lives of Banastre Tarleton and Mary Robinson.* New York, NY: Henry Holt and Company, 1957.

Bayles, Richard M. *History of Newport County, Rhode Island. From the Year 1638 to the Year 1887, Including the Settlement of the Towns, and Their Subsequent Progress.* New York, NY: I. E. Preston and Co., 1888.

Bilby, Joseph G. and Katherine Bilby Jenkins. *Monmouth Court House. The Battle that Made the American Army.* Yardley, PA: Westholme, 2010.

Billias, George Athan, ed. *George Washington's Generals and Opponents: Their Exploits and Leadership.* New York, NY: Da Capo Press, 1994.

The Biographical Cyclopedia of Representative Men of Rhode Island. Providence, RI: National Biographical Publishing Co., 1881.

Blanco, Richard L. *The American Revolution. An Encyclopedia.* 2 vols. New York and London: Garland Publishing, 1993.

Boatner, Mark M. *Encyclopedia of the American Revolution.* New York, NY: David McKay Co., 1974.

Bowman, Larry G. *Captive Americans: Prisoners During the American Revolution.* Athens, OH: Ohio University Press, 1976.

Buigné, Jean-Jacques and Pierre Jarlier. *Le "Qui est qui" de l'Arme en France de 1350 à 1970.* Volume 1. France: La Tour du Pin, Édition du Portail, 2001.

Burrows, Edwin G. *Forgotten Patriots. The Untold Story of American Prisoners During the Revolutionary War.* New York, NY: Basic Books, 2008.

Carter, Peyton F. III. *The Barton's Quest for Liberty. One Family's Sojourn Through Rhode Island and Virginia During the Nation's Formative Years.* Higginson Book Company, 2003. In the Rhode Island Historical Society Library.

Cecere, Michael. *Wedded to My Sword. The Revolutionary War Service of Light Horse Harry Lee.* Westminster, MD: Heritage Books, 2012

Chernow, Ron. *Washington: A Life.* New York, NY: Penguin Press, 2010.

Coffin, Charles. *The Lives and Services of Major General John Thomas, Colonel Thomas Knowlton, Colonel Alexander Scammell, Major General Henry Dearborn.* New York, NY: Egbert, Movey and King, 1845.

Conley, Patrick T. *Democracy in Decline. Rhode Island's Constitutional Development, 1776-1841.* Providence, RI: Rhode Island Historical Society, 1977.

Cowell, Benjamin. *Spirit of "76" in Rhode Island. Or, Sketches of the Efforts of the Government and People in the War of the Revolution.* Boston, MA: A. J. Wright, 1850.

Cox, Caroline. *A Proper Sense of Honor: Service and Sacrifice in Washington's Army.* Chapel Hill, NC: University of North Carolina Press, 2004.

Crane, Elaine Forman. *A Dependent People: Newport, Rhode Island, in the Revolutionary War.* New York, NY: Fordham University Press, 1985.

Crocker, Thomas E. *Braddock's March. How the Man Sent to Seize a Continent Changes American History.* Yardley, PA: Westholme, 2011.

De Fonblanque, Edward B. *Political and Military Episodes in the Latter Half of the Eighteenth Century Derived from the Life and Correspondence of the Right Hon. John Burgoyne, General, Statesman, Dramatist.* London: Macmillan and Company, 1876. Reprinted by the Gregg Press in 1972.

Dictionary of National Biography. Vol. 8. Edited by Leslie Stephen and Sidney Lee. New York, NY: Macmillan, 1886. Reprinted by Oxford University Press in 1968.

Dictionnaire de Biographie Française. Vol. 15. Sous la direction de J. Balteau, M. Barroux, and M. Prévost. Paris: Letouzey et Ané, 1933.

Di Ionno, Mark. *A Guide to New Jersey's Revolutionary War Trail for Families and History Buffs.* New Brunswick, NJ: Rutgers University Press, 2000.

Diman, J. Lewis. *The Capture of General Richard Prescott by Lt.-Col. William Barton. An Address Delivered at the Centennial Celebration of the Exploit at Portsmouth, R.I., July 10, 1877.* Providence, RI: Sidney S. Rider, 1877.

Dwyer, William M. *The Day is Ours! November 1776-January 1777: An Inside View of the Battles of Trenton and Princeton.* New York, NY: Viking Press, 1983.

Edgar, Gregory T. *Campaign of 1776: The Road to Trenton.* Bowie, MD: Heritage Books, 1995.

Fessenden, Thomas G. *The New England Farmer. Containing Essays, Original and Selected, Relating to Agriculture and Domestic Economy.* Vol. II. Boston, MA: William Nichols, 1824.

Field, Edward, ed. *History of the State of Rhode Island and Providence Plantations.* 3 vols. Boston, MA: Mason Publishing Co., 1902.

____. *Revolutionary Defences in Rhode Island. An Historical Account of the Fortifications and Beacons Erected During the American Revolution, with Muster Rolls of the Companies Stationed Along the Shores of Narragansett Bay.* Providence, RI: Preston and Rounds, 1896.

Fischer, David Hackett. *Washington's Crossing.* New York, NY: Oxford University Press, 2004.

Fleming, Thomas. *1776. Year of Illusions.* New York, NY: W. W. Norton and Co., 1975.

____. *Washington's Secret War. The Hidden History of Valley Forge.* New York, NY: Smithsonian Books, 2005.

Fowler, Orin. *History of Fall River with Notices of Freetown and Fall River.* Fall River, MA: Almy and Milne, 1862. Original version published in 1841.

Freeman, Douglas S. *George Washington.* 7 vols. New York, NY: Charles Scribner's Sons, 1948-54.

Geake, Robert A. *Historic Taverns of Rhode Island.* Charleston, SC: History Press, 2012.

Gordon, William. *The History of the Rise, Progress and Establishment of the Independence of the United States of America, Including an Account of the Late War.* Vol. 2. Freeport, NY: Books for Libraries Press, 1969. First published in New York, NY, in 1789.

Griffin, Martin I. *Stephen Moylan, Muster-Master General, Secretary and Aide-de-Camp to Washington, Quartermaster-General, Colonel of Fourth Pennsylvania Light Dragoons and Brigadier-General of the War for American Independence. The First and Last President of the Friendly Sons of St. Patrick of Philadelphia.* Philadelphia, PA: Privately Printed, 1909.

Griffith, Samuel B. *The War for American Independence: from 1760 to the Surrender at Yorktown in 1781.* Urbana, IL: University of Illinois Press, 2002.

Gruber, Ira D. *The Howe Brothers and the American Revolution.* Chapel Hill, NC: University of North Carolina Press, 1972.

Hargrove, Richard J. *General John Burgoyne.* Newark, DE: University of Delaware Press, 1983.

Hartmann, John W. *The American Partisan. Henry Lee and the Struggle for Independence, 1776-1780.* Shipppensburg, PA: Burd Street Press, 2000.

Harvey, Robert. *"A Few Bloody Noses." The American War of Independence.* Woodstok, VT: Overlook Press, 2002.

Hazard, Thomas R. *The Jonny-Cake Papers.* Boston, MA: Merrymount Press, 1915.

Humphreys, Frank Landon. *Life and Times of David Humphreys. Soldier—Statesman—Poet.* Vol. 1. New York, NY: G. P. Putnam's Sons, 1917.

Hurd, D. Hamilton, ed. *History of Bristol County, Massachusetts.* New York, NY: Lewis Historical Publishing Co., 1924.

Irving, Washington. *The Life of George Washington.* Vols. 3 and 4. New York, NY: G.P. Putnam, 1858-59.

Jones, E. Alfred. *The Loyalists of New Jersey: Their Memorials, Petitions, Claims, Etc. from English Records.* Newark, NJ: New Jersey Historical Society, 1927.

Jones, Thomas. *History of New York During the Revolutionary War.* 2 vols. New York, NY: New York Historical Society, 1879. Reprinted by New York Times, 1968.

Kelly, C. Brian. *Best Little Stories from the American Revolution: More Than 100 True Stories.* Naperville, IL: Sourcebook, Inc., 1999.

Ketchum, Richard. *The Winter Soldiers.* Garden City, NY: Doubleday & Co., 1973.

Langworthy, Edward. *The Life and Memoirs of the Late Major General Lee, Second in Command to General Washington, During the American Revolution, to which are Added, His Political and Military Essays. Also Letters to and from Many Distinguished Characters both in Europe and America.* Philadelphia, PA: Richard Scott, 1813.

Lefferts, Charles M. *Uniforms of the American, British, French and German Armies in the War of the American Revolution, 1775-1783.* New York, NY: New York Historical Society, 1926. Reprinted by We, Inc., 1971.

Lefkowitz, Arthur S. *The Long Retreat: The Calamitous Defense of New Jersey, 1776.* New Brunswick, NJ: Rutgers University Press, 1999.

Lengel, Edward G. *General George Washington: A Military Life.* New York, NY: Random House, 2005.

Littell, John. *Family Records, or Genealogies of the First Settlers of Passaic Valley (and Vicinity) Above Chatham—with Their Ancestors and Descendants, as Far as can now be Ascertained.* Feltville, NJ: Stationers' Hall Press, 1851.

Lockhart, Paul. *The Drillmaster of Valley Forge: The Baron de Steuben and the Making of the American Army.* New York, NY: Smithsonian Books, 2008.

Lossing, Benson. J. *The Pictorial Field-Book of the Revolution.* 2 vols. New Rochelle, NY: Caratzas Bros., 1976. Originally published in New York, NY by Harper and Brothers in 1850.

Lowell, Edward J. *The Hessians and the Other German Auxiliaries of Great Britain in the Revolutionary War.* Williamstown, MA: Cornet House, 1970. Reprint of 1884 edition.

Massey, Gregory D. *John Laurens and the American Revolution.* Columbia, SC: University of South Carolina Press, 2000.

Mayo, Lawrence Shaw. *Jeffrey Amherst: A Biography.* New York, NY: Longman's, Green and Co., 1916.

McBurney, Christian M. *The Rhode Island Campaign: The First French and American Operation in the Revolutionary War.* Yardley, PA: Westholme, 2011.

McCullough, David. *1776.* New York, NY: Simon and Schuster, 2005.

Mellick, Andrew D., Jr. *The Story of an Old Farm. Life in New Jersey in the Eighteenth Century.* Somerville, NJ: Unionist Gazette, 1889.

Messler, Abraham. *Centennial History of Somerset County.* Somerville, NJ: C. M. Jameson, 1878.

Moore, George H. *The Treason of Charles Lee. Major General, Second in Command in the American Army of the Revolution.* New York, NY: Charles Scribner, 1860. Also in *Lee Papers, 1754-1811,* vol. 4, *Collections of the New-York Historical Society* (1875), pages 335-427.

Nell, William C. *The Colored Patriots of the American Revolution.* New York, NY: New York Times and Arno Press, 1968. Originally published in Boston, MA, in 1851.

Nelson, Paul David. *General James Grant. Scottish Soldier and Royal Governor of East Florida.* Gainesville, FL: University Press of Florida, 1993.

———. *Sir Charles Grey, First Earl Grey: Royal Soldier, Family Patriarch.* Madison, NJ: Fairleigh Dickinson University Press, 1996.

Norris, J. E. *History of the Lower Shenandoah Valley, Counties of Frederick, Berkeley, Jefferson and Clarke.* . . . Chicago, IL: A. Warner and Co., 1890.

Patterson, Samuel White. *Knight Errant of Liberty. The Triumph and Tragedy of General Charles Lee.* New York, NY: Lantern Press, 1958.

Paul, Edward J. *The Part Borne by Sergeant John White Paul, of Col. John Topham's Regiment of the Rhode Island Brigade, in the Capture of Brigadier General Richard Prescott, Commander of the British Forces, Near Newport, R.I., in 1777.* Milwaukee, WI: Swain and Tate, 1887.

Peterson, Edward. *History of Rhode Island.* New York, NY: John S. Taylor, 1853.

Peterson, Harold L. *The American Sword, 1775-1945. A Survey of the Swords Worn by the Uniformed Forces of the United States from the Revolution to the Close of World War II.* New Hope, PA: Robert Halter, The River House, 1954.

Phillips, Kevin. *1775. A Good Year for Revolution.* New York, NY: Penguin Press, 2012.

Ramsay, David. *The History of the American Revolution.* Indianapolis, IN: Liberty Classics, 1990. Originally published in Philadelphia, PA, in 1793.

Randall, Willard Sterne. *Benedict Arnold: Patriot and Traitor.* New York, NY: William Morrow, 1990.

____. *Ethan Allen: His Life and Times.* New York, NY: W. W. Norton and Co., 2011.

Ross, Arthur A. *Discourse, Embracing the Civil and Religious History of Rhode-Island.* Providence, RI: H. H. Brown, 1838.

Royster, Charles. *Light-Horse Harry Lee and the Legacy of the American Revolution.* New York, NY: Alfred A. Knopf, 1981.

Sabine, Lorenzo. *Biographical Sketches of Loyalists of the American Revolution.* 2 vols. Boston, MA: Little, Brown, and Co., 1864.

Schecter, Barnet. *The Battle for New York. The City at the Heart of the American Revolution.* New York, NY: Penguin Press, 2002.

Schroder, Walter K. *The Hessian Occupation of Newport and Rhode Island, 1776-1779.* Westminster, MD: Heritage Books, 2005.

Scull, G. D. *The Evelyns in America, Compiled from Family Papers and Other Sources, 1608-1805.* Oxford, England: James Parker and Co., 1881

Selesky, Harold E. *Encyclopedia of the American Revolution.* 2nd Edition. Vols. 1-2. Detroit, MI: Charles Scribner's Sons, 2006.

Seymour, Joseph. *The Pennsylvania Associators, 1747-1777.* Yardley, PA: Westholme, 2012.

Simister, Florence. *A Short History of Exeter, Rhode Island.* Exeter, RI: Exeter Bicentennial Commission, 1978.

Snape, Sue Ellen. *Mighty Liberty Men.* Rehoboth, MA: Rehoboth Revolutionary War Bicentennial Commission, 1976.

Sparks, Jared. "Lives of Charles Lee and Joseph Reed." In *The Library of American Biography.* Edited by Jared Sparks. Vol. 13. Boston, MA: C. C. Little and J. Brown, 1846.

Stedman, Charles. *The History of the Origin, Progress, and Termination of the American War.* 2 vols. London: J. Murray, 1794. Reprinted by New York Times, 1969.

Stiles, Henry R. *The History and Genealogies of Ancient Windsor, Connecticut, Including East Windsor, South Windsor, Bloomfield, Windsor Locks, and Ellington. 1635-1891.* Hartford, CT: Case, Lockwood and Brainard Company, 1891.

Stokes, I. N. Phelps. *The Iconography of Manhattan Island, 1498-1909.* Vol. 5. New York, NY: Robert H. Dodd, 1926.

Stryker, William S. *The Battles of Trenton and Princeton.* Cambridge, MA: Riverside Press, 1898.

Swan, Frank. *General William Barton. A Biographical Sketch.* Providence, RI: Roger Williams Press, 1947.

Sweet, John Wood. *Bodies Politic: Negotiating Race in the American North, 1730-1830*. Baltimore, MD: The Johns Hopkins University Press, 2003.
Thane, Elwyth. *The Family Quarrel, A Journey Through the Years of the Revolution*. New York, NY: Duell, Sloan and Pearce, 1959.
Thayer, Theodore. *Colonial and Revolutionary Morris County*. Morris County, NJ: Morris County Heritage Commission, 1975.
____. *The Making of a Scapegoat: Washington and Lee at Monmouth*. Port Washington, NY: Kennikat Press, 1976.
Trevelyan, George O. (Sir). *The American Revolution*. Vols. III-IV. New York, NY: Longmans, Green, 1928-29.
Tucker, William Howard. *History of Hartford, Vermont 1761-1889*. Burlington, VT: The Free Press Association, 1889.
Updike, Wilkins. *History of the Episcopal Church in Narragansett, Rhode Island*. Boston, MA: Merrymount Press, 1907. Originally published by Henry M. Oderank, 1847.
Vanderpool, Ambrose E. *History of Chatham, New Jersey*. New York, NY: Charles Francis Press, 1921.
Vosseller, Elias. *History of the Hunterdon County Historical Society*. Flemington, NJ: Hunterdon County Historical Society, 1894.
Wade, Hebert T. and Robert A. Lively, *This Glorious Cause. The Adventures of Two Company Officers in Washington's Army*. Princeton, NJ: Princeton University Press, 1958.
Walcott, Charles H. *Sir Archibald Campbell of Inverneill, Sometime Prisoner of War in the Jail at Concord, Massachusetts*. Boston, MA: Beacon Press, 1898.
Ward, Christopher. *The War of Revolution*. 2 vols. New York: Macmillan, 1952.
Warren, Mercy Otis. *History of the Rise, Progress and Termination of the American Revolution*. 3 vols. Boston, MA: Manning and Loring, for E. Larkin, 1805.
Watson, John F. *Annals of Philadelphia, and Pennsylvania, in the Olden Time....* Vol. 3. Philadelphia, PA: Edwin S. Stuart, 1887.
Wheater, W. *Historical Record of the Seventh Royal Regiment of Fusiliers*. Leeds, England: Privately printed, 1875.
White, Donald Wallace. *A Village at War. Chatham, New Jersey, and the American Revolution*. Rutherford, NJ: Fairleigh Dickinson University Press, 1979.
Wilbur, James Benjamin. *Ira Allen: Founder of Vermont, 1751-1814*. Vol. 1. Boston, MA: Houghton Mifflin Company, 1928.
Willcox, William B. *Portrait of a General: Sir Henry Clinton in the War of Independence*. New York, NY: Alfred A. Knopf, 1964.
Williams, Catherine R. *Biography of Revolutionary Heroes: Containing the Life of Brigadier General William Barton, and also of Captain Stephen Olney*. Providence, RI. Privately printed, 1839.
Young, Darlene. *History of Barton, Vermont*. Barton, VT: Crystal Lake Falls Historical Association, 1998.

PUBLISHED SECONDARY SOURCES: ARTICLES

Abbass, D.K. "Ethan Allen and Rhode Island in the Revolution." In *Rhode Island in the Revolution: Big Happenings in the Smallest Colony*. Part IV:

Bibliography and Appendices. Vol. 4, 456-62. USDI National Park Service, American Battlefield Protection Program. 2nd ed., 2006. (Copies at R.I. State Archives, U.S. Naval War College at Newport, and other Rhode Island libraries.)

Blackington, Alton Hall. "The Case of the Rejected Hero." *Vermont Life* 13:1, 52-57 (Aug. 1958).

Campbell, Colin. "Introduction." In Campbell, Archibald, *Journal of an Expedition Against the Rebels of Georgia in North America under the Orders of Archibald Campbell Esquire, Lieut. Col. of His Majesty's 71st Regimt., 1778.* Darien, GA: The Ashantilly Press, 1981. Pages ix-xv.

Conway, Stephen. "British Army Officers and the American War for Independence." *The William and Mary Quarterly,* 3rd Series, 41:2, 265-76 (April 1984).

Curfman, Robert Joseph. "Captain George Whitehorne and Some of his Descendants." *The New England Historical and Genealogical Register* 146:16 (1992).

Fleming, Thomas. "The 'Military Crimes' of Charles Lee." *American Heritage Magazine* 19:3, 12-15 and 83-89 (April 1968).

Gaston, James C. "Richard Prescott and Mud Island: Epitomes of the American Revolution as Seen by London Poets." *Early American Literature.* Vol. XI, No. 2, 147-55 (Fall 1976).

Graham, Robert Earle. "The Taverns of Colonial Philadelphia." *Transactions of the American Philosophical Society,* New Series, 43:1, 318-25 (1953).

Irwin, Richard. "The Capture of General Lee." *The North Jersey Highlander* 17:4, 13-20 (Winter 1981).

McBurney, Christian. "British Treatment of Prisoners During the Occupation of Newport, 1776-1778: Disease, Starvation and Death Stalk the Prison Ships." *Newport History* 79:263, 1-41 (Fall 2010).

Morgan, Jr., Curtis F. "A Merchandise of Small Wares: Nathanael Greene's Northern Apprenticeship, 1775-1780." In Gregory Massey and James Piecuch, eds., *General Nathanael Greene and the American Revolution in the South.* Columbia, SC: University of South Carolina Press, 2012. Pages 29-55.

Riddle, Gilbert. "From Fact to Fantasy. The British 16th Light Dragoons and the Raid on Flemington, New Jersey, December 14, 1776." *The Brigade Dispatch* 23:4, 18-26 (Autumn 1992).

Rider, Sidney S. *An Historical Inquiry Concerning the Attempt to Raise a Regiment of Slaves by Rhode Island, During the War of the Revolution.* Providence, RI: Privately printed, 1880.

Robins, Edward. "Charles Lee—Stormy Petrel of the Revolution." *Pennsylvania Magazine of Biography and History* 45:66-97 (Jan. 1921).

Scheer, George F. "The Sergeant Major's Strange Mission." *American Heritage.* 8:6, 26-29 and 98 (Oct. 1957).

Shy, John. "Charles Lee: The Soldier as Radical." In Billias, George A. ed., *George Washington's Generals and Opponents.* New York, NY: Da Capo Press. Pages 22-53.

Simpson, Alan and Mary M. Simpson, "A New Look at How Rochambeau Quartered his Army in Newport (1780-1781)." *Newport History* 72-73:249-50, 91-121 (Fall 2003-Spring 2004).

"Traditions of the American War of Independence." *The United Service Journal and Naval and Military Magazine* 438-52 (Dec. 1834).

Voorhees, Oscar M. "The Whitaker Family of Somerset County." *Somerset County Historical Quarterly.* Vol. 2, 98-109. Somerville, NJ: Somerset County Historical Society, 1913.

UNPUBLISHED RECORDS

"A Plan of the Town of Newport in Rhode Island," by Charles Blaskowitz, 1777, Geography and Map Division, Library of Congress.

"A Walking Tour of Historic Basking Ridge Village." Basking Ridge, NJ: The Historic Society of the Somerset Hills, Undated. At www.historicalsociety-ofsomersethills.org (click on Enter Site; click on Tours; click on Walking Tour of Historic Basking Ridge Village). Accessed April 2013.

Barton Family Genealogy. Privately printed, 1942. Library call number CS.71, .B336 (1942). In the Rhode Island Historical Society Library.

Baskin, Marg. "Banecdotes: the Tarleton Nursery School . . . and Tavern?" At www.home.golden.net/marg/bansite/banecdotes.77nursery school. Accessed June 8, 2013.

Brown, John Brewer. *Swords Voted to Officers of the Revolution by the Continental Congress, 1775-1784.* Pamphlet. Washington, D.C.: The Society of the Cincinnati, 1965.

Campbell, J. L. "Campbell, Sir Archibald." *Oxford Dictionary of National Biography.* Online edition, Jan. 2008. Accessed April 6, 2013.

Continental Congress Sword Presented to Colonel Return J. Meigs. National Museum of American History, Smithsonian Museum. American Stories online exhibition at www.si.edu. Accessed July 19, 2013.

Cummings, April. "Portrait of a Loyalist: Research Findings for the Nichols-Overing House." Newport Restoration Foundation. August 2005. With appendices, at the Newport Restoration Foundation headquarters building in Newport at 51 Touro Street. Without appendices, available on the Newport Restoration Foundation's website, www.newportrestoration.org. Accessed June 4, 2013.

Davis Family Genealogy. At www.davistree.info/ (search for James Compton). Accessed May 20, 2013.

Description of Smallsword of Col. Marinus Willet (1740-1830). Metropolitan Museum of Art, New York City, American Wing, Gallery 753. And at www.metmuseum.org/collections (search "Marinus Willett"). Accessed June 20, 2013.

Find a Grave. At www.findagrave.com.

Gaston, James Clinton. "An Anthology of Poems Dealing with the American Revolution Taken from Prominent London Magazines and Newspapers, 1763-1783." Doctoral Dissertation, University of Oklahoma, 1975.

Hagist, Don N. "Deserter: Walter Graham, 22nd Regiment of Foot." July 19, 2009. At redcoat76.blogspot.com. Accessed March 14, 2013.

History of the 16th Queen's Light Dragoons. At www.16thqueenslightdragoons.blogspot.com (website for modern American reenactors of the 16th Regiment of Light Dragoons). Accessed June 2013.

"In Honour of a Hero." At www.stgeorges-windsor.org (search for William Harcourt). Accessed October 8, 2013.

McGeachy, Robert A. "The American War of Lieutenant Colonel Archibald Campbell of Inverneill." At www.earlyamerica.com/review/2001_summer_fall/ amer_war.html. Accessed March 7, 2013.
Moran, Donald N. "Revolutionary War Presentation Swords." At www.revolutionarywararchives.org. Accessed October 24, 2012.
"Morristown" Pamphlet. Morristown National Historical Park. National Park Service, 2013.
The On-Line Institute for Advanced Loyalist Studies, at www.royalprovincial.com. Hosted by Todd Braisted. Accessed December 2012 and January 2013.
Riddle, Gilbert. "The Ambush of Geary's Dragoons." At www.doublegv.com/ggv/battles/geary. Accessed on May 14, 2013.
Ryan, D. Michael. "Hidden Concord: Concord Gaol." At www.concordma/magazine/dec98/campbell. Accessed August 30, 2012 and July 19, 2013. Originally published in *Concord Magazine* (Dec. 1988).
Schaefer, James J. "The Whole Duty of Man: Charles Lee and the Politics of Reputation, Masculinity, and Identity During the Revolutionary Era, 1755-1783." Doctorate dissertation, University of Toledo (May 2006).
"South Carolina in the Revolution, An Exhibition from the Library and Museum Collections of The Society of the Cincinnati." Society of the Cincinnati pamphlet, 2004.
Widow White's Tavern. At www.t3consortium/drafts/widowhites.php. Accessed September 10, 2013.

NEWSPAPERS AND MAGAZINES

Adam's Weekly. 1777. (Chester, England).
American Advocate. 1832. (Hallowell, ME).
The American Journal and General Advertiser. 1779. (Providence, RI).
The American Repertory. 1821. (Burlington, VT).
The Annual Register, Or, a View of the History, Politics, Literature for the Year. Submitted by Wm. T. Sherman. 1777. (London).
The Athenaeum. Journal of Literature, Science, and the Fine Arts. 1831. (London).
Boston Chronicle. 1776-78. (Boston, MA).
Boston Commercial Gazette. 1825. (Boston, MA).
Boston Gazette. 1776-78. (Boston, MA).
Bristol County Register. 1809. (Bristol, RI).
Charleston Mercury. 1856. (Charleston, SC).
Connecticut Courant. 1776-78 and 1786. (Hartford, CT).
Connecticut Gazette. 1776-78. (New London, CT).
Connecticut Herald. 1824. (New Haven, CT).
Connecticut Journal. 1778. (Hartford, CT).
Constitutional Gazette. 1776. (New York, NY).
Continental Journal. 1777. (Boston, MA).
Daily Advertiser. 1788. (London).
Daily Advertiser. 1809. (New York, NY).
The Daily Globe. 1857. (Washington, D.C.).
Daily National Intelligencer. 1815. (Washington, D.C.).
Easton Gazette. 1832. (Easton, MD).

Edinburgh Advertiser. 1777. (Edinburgh, Scotland).
Essex Journal. 1824. (Essex, NH).
Essex Register. 1826. (Essex, MA).
Farmer's Repository. 1810. (Charlestown, VA [WV]).
Freeman's Journal. 1776-77. (Portsmouth, NH).
Gazetteer and New Daily Advertiser. 1777. (London).
General Evening Post. 1777. (London).
The Gentleman's Magazine. 1777-78. (London).
Hallowell Gazette. 1824. (Hallowell, ME).
Independent Chronicle. 1776-79. (Boston, MA).
Ithaca Herald. 1837. (Ithaca, NY).
Literary Cadet and Rhode Island Statesmen. 1826 and 1828. (Providence, RI).
London Chronicle. 1776-82.
London Gazette. Many dates.
The London Magazine, or Gentleman's Monthly Intelligencer. 1777-78.
London Packet or New Lloyd's Evening Post. 1777.
London Public Gazette. 1779.
Manufacturers' and Farmers' Journal. 1835. (Providence, RI).
Massachusetts Gazette. 1787. (Boston, MA).
Massachusetts Spy. 1810. (Worcester, MA).
The Mirror of Literature, Amusement, and Instruction. 1831. (London).
Morning Chronicle and London Advertiser. 1777 and 1780. (London).
Morning Post. 1776. (London).
National Gazette. 1829. (Philadelphia, PA).
National Intelligencer. 1824. (Washington, D.C.).
New England Chronicle. 1777. (Boston, MA).
New Jersey Gazette. 1778-80. (Brunswick, NJ).
New Jersey Journal. 1780. (Elizabethtown, NJ).
New York Gazette and Weekly Mercury. 1777-81 and 1809. (New York, NY).
New York Journal. 1786. (New York, NY).
Newport Gazette. 1777-78. (Newport, RI. Originals in R.I. Historical Society and Library of Congress).
Newport Mercury. Many years. (Newport, RI).
North Star. 1821-25. (Danville, VT).
Norwich Packet. 1776-78. (Norwich, CT).
Pennsylvania Evening Post. 1777-78. (Philadelphia, PA).
Pennsylvania Packet. 1777-81. (Philadelphia, PA).
Pennsylvania Herald. 1786. (Philadelphia, PA)
The Pittsfield Sun. 1837. (Pittsfield, MA).
The Port Folio. 1812 (Philadelphia, PA).
Poulson's American Daily Advertiser. 1805. (Philadelphia, PA).
Providence Gazette and Country Journal. 1776-78. (Providence, RI).
Providence Patriot, Columbian Phenix. 1814, 1825, and 1827. (Providence, RI).
Public Ledger. 1837. (Philadelphia, PA).
The Remembrancer; or, Impartial Repository of Public Events. 1777-78. (London).
Rhode Island American. 1826 and 1831. (Providence, RI).
Rhode Island Republican. Many years. (Providence, RI)

Richmond Inquirer. 1835. (Richmond, VA).
Rivington's Royal Gazette. 1776-81. (New York, NY).
Royal Pennsylvania Gazette. 1778. (Philadelphia, PA).
Saratoga Sentinel. 1822 and 1835. (Saratoga Springs, NY).
The Scots Magazine. 1776-78. (Edinburgh, Scotland).
Spooner's Vermont Journal. 1821-24. (Windsor, VT).
St. James's Chronicle or the British Evening Post. 1777. (London).
The Times. 1793. (London).
The Times and Hartford Advertiser. 1824. (Hartford, CT).
United States Chronicle. 1788. (Providence, RI).
Vermont Watchman and State Gazette. 1831. (Montpelier, VT).

UNPUBLISHED PRIMARY SOURCES

American Philosophical Society (Philadelphia, PA):
    Garvan Collection
    Sol Feinstone Collection of the American Revolution
Boston Public Library (Boston, Massachusetts):
    American Manuscripts, Rare Books and Manuscripts
British National Archives (Kew, England):
    Correspondence between Germain and Howe, CO 5/92-95
    War Office Papers, Regimental Roster, 16th Light Dragoons, WO 12/1246
    Various ships' logs
Brown University Library (Providence, RI):
    Revolutionary War Broadsides, microfiche
Christ Church Archives (Philadelphia, PA):
    Registry of Burials
Hatcher Graduate Library, University of Michigan (Ann Arbor, Michigan):
    Hugh Percy Papers, Duke of Northumberland Library at Alnwick Castle, British Manuscript Project, Letters and Papers relating to the American War, F286/49 to F289/52, microfilm reels 2005 and 2006
Library of Congress, Manuscript Reading Room (Washington, D.C.):
    Correspondence between Germain and Howe, CO 5/92-95, transcripts
    George Washington Papers, microfilm
    French Copying Project, Archives du Ministère des Affaires Étrangères, B1, Correspondence Consulaire et Commerciale
    Journal of Lieutenant-Colonel Christopher French, 1756-1778, MMC-1869, microfilm
    Peter Force Transcripts:
        Jonathan Trumbull Papers, Series 7.E, Entry 143, microfilm
        Massachusetts Council Records, Series 7.E, Entry 82, microfilm
Library of Congress, Microform Reading Room (Washington, D.C.):
    Hugh Percy Papers, Duke of Northumberland Library at Alnwick Castle, British Manuscript Project, Letters and Papers relating to the American War, F286/49 to F289/52, microfilm reels Aln 25, 26 and 27
Library of The Society of the Cincinnati (Washington, D.C.):
    Miscellaneous Correspondence

Massachusetts Historical Society (Boston, MA):
    Robert Treat Paine Papers, microfilm
    William Heath Papers, microfilm
Morristown National Historical Park (Morristown, NJ):
    Journal of the Regiment von Huyn, Translation from the Lidgerwood Collection
National Archives Building (Washington, D.C.):
    Papers of the Continental Congress, microfilm
    Revolutionary War Pension Application Records, microfilm
New York Historical Society Library (New York, NY):
    British Orderly Books, microfilm
    Early American Orderly Books Collection, microfilm
    Horatio Gates Papers, microfilm
Newport Historical Society (Newport, RI):
    William Barton Correspondence
    Princeton University Library (Princeton, NJ)
    Thomas Glyn, Journal of the American Campaign, 1776-77, Department of Rare Books and Special Collections, Manuscripts Collection, mss CO199 (no. 380)
    John Clark, Jr., "Map of the Raritan River & Adjacent Country, with a Plan of the Roads," February 11, 1777, Department of Rare Books and Special Collections, Manuscript Maps Collection, Box 3, Folder MS Map 4.
Rhode Island Historical Society (Providence, RI):
    Benjamin Bourne Papers, MSS 11
    Barton, William, A Narrative of the Particulars of the Capture of Major General Prescott & his Aide-de-Camp Major Barrington, MSS 9003
    Miscellaneous Correspondence and Records, Manuscripts, MSS 9003 and MSS 9006
    William Barton Papers, MSS 921
Rhode Island State Archives (Providence, RI):
    Admiralty Records, 1777-1780
    Council of War Records, vols. I-II, 1776-1781
    Index of Military Service Records, 1775-1783
    Letters from the Governor of Rhode Island, 1776-1779
    Letters to the Governor of Rhode Island, 1776-1779
    Military Papers, Revolutionary War, 1775-1782
    Petitions to the Rhode Island General Assembly, 1775-1787, microfilm
    Prisoner Exchanges and Miscellaneous, 1775-1781
The Royal Artillery Institution, Old Royal Military Academy (Woolwich, London, England):
    Particulars of the Attack of Rhode Island in August 1778, Anonymous. (Diary probably by a British artillery officer.)
William L. Clements Library, University of Michigan (Ann Arbor, MI):
    Frederick Mackenzie Papers
    Henry Clinton Papers
    Loftus Cliffe Papers
    Schoff Revolutionary War Collection

ACKNOWLEDGMENTS

I am most grateful to the outstanding librarians and archivists at the institutions set forth in the bibliography to this book for their helpful and unfailing assistance. That is one of the pleasures of working in this field.

In particular, I thank Eric Olsen, ranger and historian at Morristown National Historical Park, for providing me with original sources that I did not have relating to Lee's capture. He also gives a great tour of the park's Ford Mansion. Bert Lippincott of the Newport Historical Society provided me with a William Barton letter I had not seen. Dennis Conrad at the Early History Branch of the Naval History & Heritage Command provided access to useful naval sources. Emily Schulz of The Society of the Cincinnati generously shared information she had collected about the fifteen ceremonial swords that the Continental Congress awarded during the Revolutionary War. Kirsten Hammerstrom of the Rhode Island Historical Society took time to show me William Barton's ceremonial sword. Ken Carlson at the Rhode Island State Archives deserves special mention for his cheerful assistance over the course of many years.

I extend a special thanks to Nicholas Henderson, who did excellent research for me at the William L. Clements Library at the University of Michigan. Thomas McCord, a work colleague of mine, did some useful research at the Boston Public Library. I used in this book material that Kari Best obtained for me as a student researcher at Brown University. I am also very thankful to my neighbor, Bert Caudron, for his French translations and his splendid proofreading of some drafts and galleys.

I am grateful most of all to Dennis Conrad for reviewing and commenting on the draft chapters of this book. Don N. Hagist also reviewed and commented on several chapters of this book and provided me with muster rolls of the 16th Regiment of Light Dragoons. They are terrific historians who showed great generosity with their valuable time. I also thank Bruce H. Franklin, publisher of Westholme Publishing, for supporting this project. Any errors that remain in this book are my own.

When using original sources I have, when possible, cited to publications. For the convenience of the reader, I have corrected spelling, grammar and punctuation in quoted material. Please check the bibliography for the full citations to published and unpublished sources referred to in the footnotes.

Last but not least, I thank my (British) wife, Margaret, for her support of this project. We just celebrated the thirtieth year of our wonderful marriage.

INDEX

Abbass, D. K., 89–90, 249n26, 270n45, 297–298n95
Abercrombie, James, 3, 4
Adamant, 86
Adams, Abigail, 6–7, 97–98, 141
Adams, Ebenezer, 129, 139, 157, 267n25
Adams, John, 5, 7, 8, 97–98, 141, 207
Adams, Samuel, 5, 88, 250n37, 285n127
Alden, Captain, 275n53
Alden, John R., 179, 220n7, 233n59, 285n123
Alert, 81
Allen, Ethan, 84, 85–86, 87, 88–90, 112, 167, 169–170, 185, 198
Allen, Herman, 199–200, 201, 295n54
Allen, Ira, 198, 199
Allen, James, 146
Allen, Timothy, 150
Amazon, 269n36
Annual Register, 69, 90, 103
Anthony, Burrington, 113–114
Anthony, Elisha, 115
Antill, Edward, 87
Arnold, Benedict, 54, 107, 113, 152, 284n121
Arnold, David, 139
Auchmuty, Robert Nicholas, 272n63
Austin, John, 302n42
Austin, Thomas, 116, 267n25

Babcock, Joshua, 126
Babcock, Robert, 302n42
Baird, James, 40, 50, 237–238n98
Baker, Elisha, 218
Banister, John, 110, 117
Banister, Thomas, 192
Bardeleben, Johann Heinrich von, 235n70
Barrell, Samuel Brown, 201, 202, 214, 271n50
Barrington, William (Lieutenant), 122, 134, 136, 139, 147–148, 150, 162, 185, 194, 210, 262n2
Barrington, William (Secretary of War), 6, 155–156, 171, 230n36
Barry, Henry ("Harry"), 142, 148–149

Bartlett, Josiah, 57
Barton, John B., 200, 202, 207, 267n25
Barton, Rhoda, 202, 207, 297n92
Barton, Seth, 197
Barton, Thomas B., 203
Barton, William: E. Adams and, 157; background of, 108–110; Coffin and, 123; Constitution and, 195–196; in debtor's prison, 200–205; later career of, 189–193; on Lee, 111; map of raid by, 135, 145; pension for, 200; plan of, 116–117, 124–125, 126–127; in politics, 196–197; praise for, 140–141, 142, 143, 144, 146, 156; on raid, 127–130, 131–134, 136–137, 138–139, 148; recounting of raid by, 155, 213, 216; release of, 207; return to Rhode Island and, 207–208; sword for, 193–195, 207; sympathy for, 203–205; in Vermont, 197–205
Bernard, John, 5, 183–184
Bilby, Joseph, 175–176, 178
Bird, Otway, 29
Bloomfield, Joseph, 239n20
Boisbertrand, René-Etienne Henry Vic Gaiault de, 28–29, 32, 45–46, 48, 58, 99–100
Boston Commercial Gazette, 207
Boston Palladium, 207
Boudinot, Elias, 63, 162, 164–165, 166–168, 177–178
Bowater, John, 102, 116, 146–147, 163
Bowdoin, James, 10, 13, 96
Bowen, Ephraim, 191
Boyd, Thomas, 82
Boylston, Edward, 82
Braddock, Edward, 220n8
Bradford, William, Jr., 28, 29, 32, 45, 46, 48, 52, 58, 59, 65–66, 68, 237n95
Brandywine, 206
Brandywine, Battle of, 178
Bretthauer, Balthasar, 251n61
Brooklyn, Battle of, 1, 11, 81, 83, 257–258n32
Brooks, Francis, 157
Brown, Samuel, 29
Buffum, Samuel, 211
Buigné, Jean-Jacques, 292n25

328 *Index*

Bullion's Tavern, 241n55
Bunker Hill, Battle of, 107, 113
Burgoyne, John, 4, 36, 153, 161, 168, 187
Burr, Aaron, 183
Burrows, Edwin, 82
Butler, William, 162

Cadwalader, John, 21, 57, 74, 75
Cadwalader, Thomas, 88
Caldwell, James, 30
Campbell, Archibald: exchange of, 98, 102, 151, 155, 162, 163, 165, 167, 169, 278n2; later career of, 170, 187–188; parole of, 160–161; portrait of, 93; retaliation and, 92, 93–97, 100–101; treatment of, 95–96
Campbell, John, 124, 138, 144, 146, 150, 154, 185, 190–191
Carder, Isaac, 148, 150
Carleton, Guy, 84, 86, 87
Carver, Rhoda, 108
Cato, 125
Centurion, 101–102, 116, 147, 150, 160, 161, 163, 164
Chace, Samuel, 139
Charlotte, Queen, 35, 36
Chase, Dudley, 201, 203
Chatham, 122, 132, 133, 138–139, 146, 269n36
Clark, Edward, 288n155
Clarke, John M., 119, 126
Cliffe, Loftus, 75
Clinton, Henry: evacuation by, 172, 186; Howe and, 67, 72, 80, 162, 166, 280n33; Humphreys and, 193; Lee and, 7, 49, 162, 164; at Monmouth Court House, 173–175, 178–179; at New York, 102; Parker and, 8; Prescott and, 171; Rhode Island and, 105, 109; Robertson and, 65, 236n77, 236n78; strategy of, 17; Washington and, 66, 173
Closen, Ludwig von, 63
Coffin, Paul, 110, 123
Common Fence Point, 118, 119, 123
Compton, James, 42, 62–63
conditions, in jail, 241n47
Connecticut Gazette, 131
Continental Congress: Allen and, 87; on American prospects, 24–25; Barton and, 143, 192–193; on British perception of war, 83; Lee and, 8, 91–92, 93, 100, 180, 182–183; orders to Washington from, 18; prisoner exchange and, 165, 167; selection of leaders by, 5
Conway Cabal, 171
Cooke, Nicholas, 106, 111, 126, 140, 141–142, 148, 151, 211
Coore, Thomas, 120
Cornell, Ezekiel, 157–158
Cornwallis, Charles, 11, 14, 17, 34–35, 39, 40, 50, 63, 74, 75, 174
Cory, Samuel, 127, 148, 263n2, 266n24, 267n25, 301n33
Cox, Caroline, 83
Crafts, Samuel C., 201–202, 298n95
Crary, Archibald, 127
Creswell, Nicholas, 76
Crewe, Richard, 58–59
Culloden, Battle of, 113
Cummings, April, 264n11

Dalrymple, Hugh, 158
Dana, Francis, 96
Davies, Thomas, 11
Deane, Silas, 24
Deans, Robert, 146
Dechow, Friedrich Ludwig von, 251n61
Dennis, Joseph, 214, 271n50
Derby, Richard, 231n45
desertion, 211–212
Diamond, 66, 122, 131, 132, 139, 157, 269n36
Disney, Daniel, 162
Donop, Carl von, 24
Drake, J. W., 235n70
Drayton, William Henry, 181, 285n127
Duane, James, 285n127
Duncan, Henry, 234n68
Dunham, Asher, 40, 61, 241n47
Dunn, Elizabeth, 184
Durfee, Thomas, 114

Edwards, Evan, 285n132
Ellery, William, 64
Elliot, Robert, 127, 129, 139, 157
Ellsworth, Oliver, 285n127
Estaing, Comte d,' 185, 186
Eustace, Charles, 40, 43
Eustace, John, 29, 91, 255n115
Evans, Evan, 50

Experiment, 68, 109

Fielding, Charles, 66
54th Regiment, 120, 123
1st Rhode Island Regiment of Continentals, 213, 215, 217, 218, 219
1st Rhode Island State Regiment, 110, 118, 126, 127
Fisher, E., 73
Fitch, Jabez G., 199
Fitch, Samuel, 199, 201
Fleming, Thomas, 168, 224n91, 284n120
Fletcher, Isaac, 206
Flint, Royal, 196, 200
Folger, Timothy, 275–276n53
Ford, Jacob, Jr., 24, 34
Fort Duquesne, 220n8
Fort Lee, 2, 9, 11–12, 17, 38, 64
Fort Niagara, 3
Fort Pitt, 3
Fort Ticonderoga, 3, 84, 86, 153
Fort Washington, 1–2, 9, 10, 11, 32, 64, 81
Fortress Louisbourg, 3
43rd Regiment, 119, 144
44th Regiment, 3
Foster, Thomas, 258n32
Fowler, Orin, 219, 268n27
Fox, Charles, 83
Franklin, Benjamin, 141
Franklin, Henry, 82
Franklin, William, 91
Freeman, Douglas, 225n104
French and Indian War, 3–4

Gaine, Hugh, 68
Galloway, Joseph, 50, 68
Gaspée, 85–86
Gaston, James Clinton, 276–277n69
Gates, Horatio: Arnold and, 256n4; Barton and, 191; Burgoyne and, 161; Lee and, 5, 32–33, 53, 54–55; Sullivan and, 73; troop movements and, 18, 22, 227n2; Washington and, 25, 77; Wilkinson and, 11, 30–31
Gazetteer and New Daily Advertiser (London), 155
Geary, Francis, 40, 50, 209–210
General Evening Post (London), 49, 152
George III, 4–5, 71–72, 73, 89, 98, 102, 106, 153, 156, 162, 170, 187

Germain, George: Harcourt and, 72, 187; Howe and, 70, 71, 80, 102–103, 107, 151, 155, 160, 161, 162, 170; Lee and, 91, 98; portrait of, 155; Prescott's capture and, 152; prisoner treatment and, 89–90; Wallace and, 68–69
Gerry, Elbridge, 58
Goodwin, John, 259–260n55
Goodwin, Prince, 128, 134, 213–214
Gordon, William, 78, 226n114
Graham, Walter, 133, 134, 136, 146, 210–212
Grant, Ebenezer, 150, 161
Grant, James, 34, 81
Graves, Samuel, 258n33
Green Mountain Boys, 84, 170
Greene, Christopher, 56, 291–292n24
Greene, Nathanael, 1, 9, 10, 17, 22, 24, 56, 57, 111–112, 166, 172–173, 292n24
Greyhound, 122, 132, 269n36

Hagist, Don N., 210, 272n62, 275n45, 289n161
Hall, David P., 263n2
Hall, Moses, 203
Hamilton, Alexander, 168, 172, 178, 196
Hamilton, William, 47
Hancock, John, 21, 22, 56, 88, 91, 96, 141, 222n49, 250n33
Handright, Barney, 277n82
Hanson, John, 184
Hanstein, Ludwig von, 251n61
Harcourt, Simon, 35, 38–39, 66
Harcourt, William: on American prospects, 186–187; background of, 35–37; Barton compared to, 142; on course of war, 76; Dunham and, 61; Geary and, 209; later career of, 187–188; on Lee, 97; Lee's capture and, 45–50, 52, 59–60, 62, 63–64, 65, 66–67, 68, 69–70, 79; in New Jersey, 40; plan of, 42–44; praise for, 71–72; reward for, 186; route taken by, 41
Harlem Heights, Battle of, 1
Harris, Thomas, 67–68, 236n78
Hartford Times, 206
Haslet, John, 11
Hawkins, J., 47
Hazard, Ebenezer, 30, 239n20

Hazelwood, John, 292n24
Heath, William, 15, 16, 18, 22, 25, 54, 73, 96–97, 222n49, 222n58, 226–227n2
Heeringen, Heinrich von, 258n32
Hessian officers, 92, 93, 101, 103, 152, 161, 163, 165, 168–169
Hodgkins, Joseph, 19, 240n38, 246n117
Honeyman, James, 124
Honeyman, Quako, 124, 217–218
Hoops, Robert, 21–22, 23, 24, 27
Hopkins, Stephen, 148–149
Hotham, William, 255n115
Houlding, John, 288n161
How, David, 52
Howe, Richard, 8, 102, 106, 146
Howe, William: advance of, 20; boats and, 21, 24; Boisbertrand and, 99; Campbell and, 94, 96, 97; Cornwallis and, 17–18; Gates on, 77; Grant and, 33–34; H. Lee and, 58; Harcourt and, 38, 45, 71, 72, 187, 233n62; Lee and, 12–13, 63, 79–81, 90–91, 92–93, 98–99, 101–102, 160, 164–166; on Lee as deserter, 70–71; Lee's capture and, 62, 67, 69; New Jersey loyalists and, 19; in New York, 8; Philadelphia and, 22; portrait of, 81; Prescott and, 86–87, 146, 147, 152, 155–156, 170; prisoner exchange and, 163, 164, 168; prisoner treatment and, 90; replacement of, 172; Rhode Island and, 107–108; strategy of, 72–73; Washington and, 1–2, 74, 142, 151–152, 161–162; at White Plains, 9
Howland, John, 52, 54, 57, 77, 147–148, 200, 217, 263n2, 298n95
Hughes, Hugh, 60
Humphreys, David, 193–194
Humpton, Richard, 21, 22, 27
Hunt, John, 219, 266n21, 267n25
Hunter, Martin, 65
Huntington, Jedidiah, 276n57
Huntington, Samuel, 182
Hutchinson, Thomas, 277n82

Independent Chronicle, 114

Jarlier, Pierre, 292n25
Jefferson, Thomas, 60, 87, 207
Jenkins, Katherine Bilby, 175–176, 178

Jervis, Elizabeth, 29
Jones, Daniel, 170
Jones, John Paul, 198
Jones, Thomas, 4, 91, 96
Juno, 157–158, 269n36

Kemble, Stephen, 67
Kennedy, Primrose, 69–70
Kenrick, William, 277n69
Keppel, George, 36
Kingfisher, 157
Knerr, Henry, 287n147
Knowles, John, 137
Knox, Henry, 75, 194, 221n40

Lady Gage, 152
Lafayette, Marquis de, 171, 172, 173, 205–207
Landgrave Regiment, 119
Langworthy, Edward, 183, 287n148
Lark, 122, 128, 131, 138, 143, 157, 269n36
Laurens, Henry, 160, 167–168, 169–170, 191, 285n127
Laurens, John, 175, 180–181
Laurie, Walter Sloane, 113
Lauzun, Duc de, 184
Lee, Charles: after capture, 79–80, 81; alleged treason of, 100; on American prospects, 163–164; appointment of, 5–6; background of, 2–3; Barton and, 110, 130; behavior of, 67–68, 69, 151, 171–172; British on, 34–35; Burgoyne and, 36; call for independence from, 7; capture of, 45–46, 48, 49, 142; at Chatham, 21–22; classification of, 70–71; Continental Congress and, 24–25; Cornwallis and, 17; court-martial of, 177, 178, 179–180; death of, 183–185; description of, 2, 3; dismissal of, 182–183; dogs and, 6–7; on dragoons, 38; duels and, 181; exchange of, 141–142, 155, 156, 161, 163–164, 165, 167, 169; forged letter and, 69–70; Harcourt and, 42–45; Howe and, 164–166; illustration of, 47; impact of capture of, 72–76; indemnification agreement of, 221n23; military plans of, 167–168; military service of, 3–4, 7–8; at Monmouth Court House, 173–176, 179; at Morristown, 27–28; Moyney

and, 50; in New Jersey, 18–20; New
York campaign and, 8–9; at North
Castle, 9–10; parole of, 162; patriot
cause and, 5; portrait of, 7, 21;
Prescott and, 147, 152–153; reactions
to capture of, 54–58, 63–64, 66–70,
77–78; release of, 166–167; reputation
of, 1; returning to army, 171; in
Rhode Island, 111–112; route taken
by, 41; rumors of betrayal and, 59–62;
strategy of, 12–13, 23–24; Tarleton
and, 38; Tories and, 63; treatment of,
64–65, 90–93, 100–101, 102, 150,
160, 161; Washington and, 12–16, 18,
172–173, 176–178, 180–181; at
Widow White's Tavern, 29;
Wilkinson and, 31
Lee, Henry, 58–59
Lee, Isabella Bunbury, 3
Lee, John, 3
Lee, Richard Henry, 5, 7, 91, 180
Lee, Sydney, 2, 3
Liger, Claude-Raymond, 292–293n25
Liger, Pierre-Ambroise, 292–293n25
Lincoln, Benjamin, 184
Lippitt, Christopher, 15, 28
Livingston, Robert R., 86, 250n36
Livingston, William, 68
Lockhart, Mary, 187
London Chronicle, 37, 154
London Evening Post, 72, 153, 155
Loring, Joshua, 165
Lossberg, Friedrich Wilhelm von,
256n19
Lossing, Benson J., 217, 267n25,
269n39, 271n50, 272n57
Louis XVI, 195, 206, 294n47
Lovell, James, 285n127

Mackenzie, Frederick: on Brooklyn, 83;
on Fort Barton, 297–298n95; on
Graham, 146; on July 4, 1777, 128;
map of raid by, 145; on *Niger*,
259n49; on Overing house, 265n15,
270n47, 270n49; on Prescott,
143–144, 154, 155, 251n46, 270n45;
on raids, 158; on Smith house,
261n72
Macklewraith, Mr., 234n66, 235n70
Madison, James, 295n61
Malik, Aaron, 238n2
Malmedy, Francois Lellorquis de,
111–112

Marsh, James, 144, 261n71
Massachusetts Council, 10, 13, 94–95
Massey, Gregory D., 285n132
Mathaus, Johann Justus, 251n61
Mathew, Edward, 75
Matlock, William, 203
Mawhood, Charles, 50, 61, 74
Maxwell, William, 174
McCullough, David, 258n32
McDougall, Alexander, 227n2
McHenry, James, 175, 176
McKean, Thomas, 24–25
Meigs, Jonathan, 291n24, 292n25
Minghini, Giuseppe, 100, 161, 183,
184
Monmouth Court House, Battle of,
173–176, 178–179, 218
Monroe, James, 202
Montgomery, Richard, 84, 85, 86, 112,
257n27
Moore, William, 286n147
*Morning Chronicle and London
Advertiser*, 69
Morning Chronicle (London), 153–154
Morning Post and Daily Advertiser, 70,
155
Morris, Gouverneur, 180, 184, 285n127
Morris, Jacob, 29, 184
Morris, Robert, 7, 24, 56, 76, 101, 178,
183, 184, 193
Morton, Eliza, 48, 50–51
Moultrie, William, 7–8
Mowatt, Henry, 113
Moylan, Stephen, 23, 53, 60, 76, 220n7
Moyney, Major, 50
Muenchhausen, Friedrich von, 34,
43–44, 48, 62, 66, 67, 80, 98, 146,
165, 234n67, 235n73
Mundy, Catherine, 238n2
Munroe, Nathan, 127

Narragansett Bay, 106, 108, 109, 111,
114, 120–122
Nash, Thomas, 40, 42, 49
National Gazette, 208
Nelson, Paul David, 285n122
New England Chronicle, 56–57
New Jersey Gazette, 178
New York Gazette and Weekly Mercury,
68
New York Journal, 193
Newport Gazette, 158
Nichols, Jonathan, 125

Nichols, Samuel, 287n147
Niger, 147
North Castle, 9–10
Norwich Courier, 205
Nourse, Joseph, 29, 31

Old Jail in Concord, 97
Olney, Stephen, 53, 205
103rd Regiment, 4
Orpheus, 131, 269n36
Oswald, Eleazer, 288n154
Otway, William, 157
Overing, Henrietta, 125, 126, 134, 137, 154
Overing, Henry John, 110, 117, 122, 125–126, 134
Overing, Henry John, Jr., 125, 126
Overing, Mary (neé Whitehorne), 134, 137, 154
Overing house, 124–126, 127, 146
Owen, Daniel, 198

Page, Daniel, 128, 219
Parker, Nathan, 94
Parker, Peter, 7, 8, 106, 114, 132, 133, 138, 146
parole, 80–81, 83–84, 92, 94, 149–150, 162
Parsons, Samuel, 287n147
Paterson, James, 250n42
Paul, Edward J., 267n25
Peck, William, 150, 276n57
Peebles, John, 67
Penn, John, 177
Pennsylvania Evening Post, 142
Percy, General, 105, 108, 114, 122, 137, 144, 146, 154
Peterson, Edward, 263n2, 301n38
Peterson, Harold L., 292n25
Philadelphia Associators, 21
Phillips, Samuel, 119, 126
Pickens, Andrew, 292n24
Pierce, John, 300n22
Pierce, William, 292n24
Pigot, Robert, 147, 185, 190, 211
Pomp, 125
Poniatowski, Stanislaus, 4
Port Folio, 197, 202
Potter, Abel, 137, 212, 218–219, 266n21, 271n53
Potter, James, 126, 266n21
Prescott, James, 95

Prescott, Richard: Allen and, 84, 85, 86, 87; background of, 112; Barton on, 195, 197, 202; behavior of, 151; capture of, 86–87, 134, 136–139, 213–218; court-martial of, 170–171; in East Windsor, 150–151; exchange of, 89, 155, 156, 165; hatred of, 112, 116–117; later career of, 185–186; parole of, 149–150, 162, 185; plan to capture, 124; portrait of, 84–85; reactions to capture of, 140–142, 143–144, 146–147, 152–154; release of, 170; in Rhode Island, 105, 108, 110, 132; strategy of, 119–120, 122; treatment of, 87–89, 147–148, 155, 160, 161, 275–276n53; treatment of prisoners by, 113–114, 115–116; value of, 168; vulnerability of, 122–123; Walker and, 84–85
Preston, Charles, 88
Princeton, 72, 74, 75, 76, 77, 187
prisoners: exchange of, 155, 165, 168, 185; rewards for taking, 107; treatment of, 81–90, 97, 98, 113–115, 131, 163, 169–170, 185, 189–190
Providence, 148–149
Providence Gazette, 109, 114–115, 116, 140, 142, 158, 213–214, 218
provisions, lack of, 54
Public Advertiser (London), 153

Quakers, 106, 115

Rall, Johann Gottlieb, 251n61
Ramsey, David, 57–58
Randall, Willard Sterne, 169
Redwood, William, 122–123, 145
Reed, Joseph, 10, 11, 12, 14, 74, 180
Renown, 122, 129, 269n36
Rhode Island: attack on, 105–106, 108; Constitution and, 195–196
Rhode Island, Battle of, 185, 191, 219
Rhode Island Campaign, 185
Rhode Island Council of War, 189–190, 211
Rhode Island General Assembly, 107, 109–110, 124, 143, 157, 189, 192, 193
Rhode Island State Artillery Regiment, 127, 129, 139, 157
Rhodes, Richard, 218
Rider, Sidney, 301n38
Rittenhouse, David, 294n39

Robbins, William, 40
Robertson, James, 65, 91, 146, 162, 164, 170, 236n77, 236n78, 244–245n100, 279n28
Robin, 125
Rodney, Thomas, 25, 57, 61–62, 74, 77, 237n98
Rogers, Robert, 14
Rotch, William, 275–276n53
Rush, Benjamin, 2, 8, 10, 165–166, 180
Rutledge, John, 7–8
Ryan, Michael D., 278n4

Sabin, Thomas, 139
Saratoga, 187
Sargent, Paul Dudley, 222–223n60
Savage, Henry, 116
Scammell, Alexander, 31–32, 177
Scheffer, Franziscus, 251n61
Schenk, John, 209
Schulz, Emily, 292n25
Schuyler, Philip, 86, 87
Scott, Charles, 174, 177
Scull, G. D., 233n58
2nd Rhode Island State Regiment, 127, 218
Senter, Isaac, 115
Serle, Abraham, 89
Serle, Ambrose, 147, 231n45
Seven Years' War, 3–4, 94, 112
7th Regiment of Foot, 84, 112, 122
17th Regiment of Foot, 50
17th Regiment of Light Dragoons, 36, 39–40, 58–59, 122, 146
71st Regiment, 40, 50
Shaw, Samuel, 10
Sheldon, Elisha, 31
Sherman, Peleg, 302n42
Sherman, Roger, 285n127
Shippen, William, 62
Shy, John, 179
Sign of the Conestoga Wagon, 183
Simon, George, 186
Sisson, Jack, 127–128, 134, 213, 217, 267n25
16th Regiment of Light Dragoons, 35, 36–37, 38–39, 42, 50, 73, 187, 210
Skinner, General, 61
Smith, Francis, 119–120, 122–123, 142, 145, 146, 148, 149, 155
Smith, John, 19–20, 28, 53, 54, 138
Smith, Richard, 90, 250n37

Smith, Samuel, 291n24
Smith, William, 163
Snowden, Benjamin, 141
Souther, Daniel, 231n45
Southern Military District, 7
Southwick, Solomon, 258n43
Sparks, Jared, 239n29
Spencer, Joseph: Arnold and, 107; on Common Fence Point raid, 261n74; Fort Barton and, 298n95; on lack of troops, 119; Prescott's capture and, 126, 139, 140–141, 144, 147–148, 149–150, 269n39; prisoner exchange and, 157; Washington and, 142, 159
Spitfire, 118
St. James's Chronicle, 67
Stamp Act, 4
Stanley, Thomas, 39–40, 243–244n95
Stanton, Andrew, 126
Stanton, Joseph, 110, 126, 140, 141
Stedman, Charles, 235n70
Stephen, Adam, 60
Steuben, Friedrich Wilhelm von, 171–172, 175, 181
Stewart, Walter, 18, 27
Stiles, Ezra, 59, 65, 68, 109, 111, 147, 265n16, 267n25
Stirling, William Alexander, 25, 73
Stockton, Richard Witham, 40, 60–61
Stone, Michael Jenifer, 294n39
Straub, Thierry, 292n25
Sullivan, John: Barrington and, 185; Barton and, 190; Bradford and, 66; exchange of, 89; Gates and, 73; Lee and, 27, 43, 48; Lee's capture and, 52–53; Prescott and, 105, 156, 257n27; at Rhode Island, 191; Scammell and, 31–32; troop movements and, 28, 29; on Virnejoux, 58
Sullivan's Island, 8
Swan, John, 294n39
Sweet, John Wood, 300n20, 301n34

Tarleton, B., 229n26
Tarleton, Banastre, 37–39, 40, 42–44, 45–46, 48, 49, 50, 58–59, 62, 68, 209
Thacher, James, 56, 62, 95, 141, 213, 214, 276n53
Thayer, Theodore, 179, 225n99
Théodat, Charles Henri, 185
38th Regiment, 162
Thompson, Benjamin, 286–287n147

Thompson, Edward, 277n69
Tilghman, Tench, 174–175, 221n34, 291n24
Tobey, 125
Topham, John, 118
Trenton, 72, 73–74, 76, 77, 187, 251n61
Trevelyan, George, 257n27
Tripp, William, 115–116
Trumbull, John, Jr., 54, 56, 65
Trumbull, Jonathan (Governor), 59, 141, 148, 149–150
Tupper, Dr., 275–276n53
22nd Regiment, 119–120, 123, 124, 133, 138, 144, 150, 190, 210, 211
Tyler, Isaac, 118

Vanhorn, Philip, 60
Varnum, James, 111, 118, 151
Vaughn, John, 170, 183
Vermont General Assembly, 198, 202
Viomesnil, Baron de, 184
Virnejoux, Jean-Louis de, 28, 32, 45, 48, 58
von Bunau Regiment, 120
von Ditfurth Regiment, 119
von Huyn Regiment, 117, 120

Waldeck, Philipp, 163
Walker, Thomas, 84–85, 89, 112
Wallace, James, 68, 109, 111
Wanton, Joseph, 111
Ward, Artemas, 5–6
Warren, James, 58
Warren, Joseph, 113
Warren, Mercy, 64, 78
Washington, George: appointment of, 5–6; Barton and, 189, 196, 204; Campbell and, 95–96, 97; on capture of Prescott, 140–141; Clinton and, 172; Cornwallis and, 39; Howe and, 102, 103, 151–152, 161–162; instructions to Lee from, 12–16, 18, 22–23, 25; on kidnapping attempts, 158–159; Lee and, 6, 21, 32–33, 98, 163, 166, 167–168, 169, 171, 176–178, 180–181; Lee's capture and, 54–56, 64–65; Lee's treatment and, 91–93; at Monmouth Court House, 174–175, 176, 178–179; movements of, 75–77; New York campaign and, 7, 8–9, 10–12; on Philadelphia, 20, 23; possible replacement of, 12–13; Prescott and, 86–87, 150, 151; prisoner exchange and, 142, 156, 163, 164, 165, 167; reputation of, 1, 10–12; retreat of, 17–18; Rhode Island and, 106–107; Spencer and, 149, 157; Sullivan and, 53; support for, 172–173; on Tories, 62, 63; at Trenton, 73–74, 78; troop movements and, 226–227n2
Washington, Lund, 55–56, 62
Washington, Martha, 166
Waterman, John, 298n95
Watson, Guy, 128, 134, 213, 215–217, 218
Wayne, Anthony, 171, 177, 181, 283n88
Webb, Lt. Col., 63
Webb, Samuel Blachley, 57
Welch, Thomas, 146
West, Benjamin, 73
Whipple, William, 57, 285n127
Whitaker, Jonathan, 29
Whitaker, Mary, 29–30
White, Ebenezer, 29
White Plains, Battle of, 1, 9, 38, 81
Whitehorne, Johathan G., 125
Whitehorne, Mary, 125
Whitier, John Greenleaf, 205
Widow White's Tavern, 26, 29–30, 42, 44, 63, 239n20
Wielcocks, John, 126
Wightman, George, 265n16
Wilkinson, James, 11, 30–31, 32, 44–45, 46, 52–53, 54, 58, 65, 228n13, 235n73
Willett, Marinus, 291n24, 292n25
William IV, 187–188
Williams, Catherine, 143, 148, 216–217, 263n2, 267n25, 268n27, 270n49, 302n44
Williams, Ezekiel, 276n57
Williams, Griffith, 165
Winthrop, Hannah, 78
Wyllys's Regiment, 15, 16

York, Joseph, 77
Young, Samuel, 82